Zimbabwe's Unfinished Business

Rethinking Land, State and Nation
in the Context of Crisis

Zimbabwe's Unfinished Business

Rethinking Land, State and Nation in the Context of Crisis

Edited by

Amanda Hammar

Brian Raftopoulos and Stig Jensen

WEAVER
—PRESS—

Weaver Press
PO Box A1922
Avondale, Harare
Zimbabwe

DT
2891
.Z56
2003

All rights reserved. No part of this book may be reproduced in any form, or by electronic or mechanical means, including information storage or retrieval systems, without permission in writing from the publishers, except by a reviewer who may quote brief passages in a review.

© This collection: Weaver Press, 2003
Individual chapters: The respective authors, 2003

Typeset by Frontline Electronic Publishing, Harare
Cover: Danes Design, Harare
Cover photographs by Calvin Dondo
Printed and bound in Zimbabwe by Modern Press

ISBN 1 77922 011 1

Contents

Acknowledgements		vii
Notes on contributors		ix
1	Zimbabwe's Unfinished Business: Rethinking Land, State and Nation *Amanda Hammar and Brian Raftopoulos*	1
2	The End of Modernity in Zimbabwe? Passages from Development to Sovereignty *Eric Worby*	49
3	'Squatters', Veterans and the State in Zimbabwe *Jocelyn Alexander*	83
4	The Making and Unma(s)king of Local Government in Zimbabwe *Amanda Hammar*	119
5	Farm Occupations and Occupiers in the New Politics of Land in Zimbabwe *Nelson Marongwe*	155
6	Belonging to the Farm(er): Farm Workers, Farmers, and the Shifting Politics of Citizenship *Blair Rutherford*	191
7	The State in Crisis: Authoritarian Nationalism, Selective Citizenship and Distortions of Democracy in Zimbabwe *Brian Raftopoulos*	217
8	Land, Growth and Governance: Tenure Reform and Visions of Progress in Zimbabwe *Mandivamba Rukuni and Stig Jensen*	243
9	The Zimbabwe Crisis in its Wider Context: The Politics of Land, Democracy and Development in Southern Africa *Ben Cousins*	263

Acknowledgements

This book emerged out of a research seminar and conference in Copenhagen in September 2001 hosted by the Centre for Development Research, CDR (now the Danish Institute for International Studies, DIIS), which would not have been possible without the generous financial support of the then CDR itself, Danida at the Danish Ministry of Foreign Affairs, the Danish Research Council, the Swedish International Development Agency, Sida, and the Danish non-governmental voluntary organisation, Mellemfolkeligt Samvirke.

The editors are especially grateful to the following people at CDR/DIIS for their various forms of critical support for both the seminar and conference and the production of this book: Poul Engberg-Pedersen, Ane Toubro, Anni Hammerlund, Peter Gibbon, Finn Stepputat, Jannik Boesen, Jesper Linnell, Helena Maria Kyed, Peter Schulz, Helle Emborg, Søren Holm Eriksen, and Gerda Christensen.

We also wish to acknowledge the dynamic contribution to the debates that underlie this book, of all the participants at the Copenhagen research seminar – 'Rethinking Land, State and Citizenship through the Zimbabwe Crisis' – not all of whom could be represented in this collection. At the time, in late 2001, the 'neutral' space of the seminar, far from the immediate turmoil in Zimbabwe, was a rare and productive opportunity especially for the Zimbabwean participants to engage in open, non-partisan exchange.

We would further like to thank our consistently supportive and patient publishers, Irene Staunton and Murray McCartney at Weaver Press in Harare, whose dedication to sustaining open debate in and about Zimbabwe, especially in these times, is exemplary.

Most especially, we wish to thank all the contributors to this collection for their rich and insightful work, and their persistent commitment both to this particular project and, more generally, to generating alternative visions for a future, post-crisis Zimbabwe.

Amanda Hammar, Brian Raftopoulos, Stig Jensen
Copenhagen and Harare
July 2003

Notes on contributors

Amanda Hammar is a Zimbabwean researcher based at the Danish Institute for International Studies (formerly the Centre for Development Research), Copenhagen. Her current research and writing addresses the interplay between territorial and resource conflicts, practices of belonging and exclusion, and processes of state formation in the rural margins of Zimbabwe. Previously she worked for over a decade in Zimbabwe's public sector, both within the state and as an independent development consultant, focusing mainly on rural development and local government reform. She was co-convenor with Stig Jensen of an international conference and research seminar held in Copenhagen in September 2001, focused on 'Rethinking Land, State and Citizenship through the Zimbabwe Crisis'. In 2002 she was a Ford Foundation Fellow in Cultural and Environmental Politics at the Institute of International Studies, University of California, Berkeley.

Brian Raftopoulos is Associate Professor at the Institute of Development Studies, University of Zimbabwe. He has written and published widely on labour history, urban history, historiography, democratisation, NGOs and civil society, poverty, and human resource development. He was Deputy Director of the University of Zimbabwe's Institute of Development Studies from 1990-97, the first Chairman of the Poverty Reduction Forum in Zimbabwe from 1996-97, was a member of the founding executive of the National Constitutional Assembly (NCA), and has worked closely with the labour movement for the last decade. He is current chairman of the Zimbabwe in Crisis Coalition. He was editor of the NCA journal *Agenda* from 1998-2001, and is on the editorial board of the *Journal of Southern African Studies*.

Stig Jensen is a researcher at the Danish Institute for International Studies (formerly the Centre for Development Research), Copenhagen, and co-convenor with Amanda Hammar of the international conference and research seminar on the Zimbabwe crisis held in Copenhagen in September 2001. He is Assistant Professor at Copenhagen University (Centre of African Studies) and is currently engaged with research on the local management of natural resources in the context of globalisation, based on fieldwork in eastern Zimbabwe. His broader interests include questions of governance and environmental management in developing countries, especially in Africa, about which he has both written articles and edited several Danish-language journals. He has also participated in several consultancies related to Danish development assistance.

Jocelyn Alexander is a Fellow of Linacre College, Oxford, and University Lecturer in Commonwealth Studies. She has researched and published extensively on land, ethnicity, religion and political authority in Zimbabwe for over ten years. Her work appears in numerous Africanist and other journals and edited collections on Zimbabwe. She has recently co-authored a book with JoAnn McGregor and Terence Ranger entitled *Violence and Memory: One Hundred Years in the 'Dark Forests' of Matabeleland* (James Currey, 2000).

Ben Cousins is currently Director of the Programme for Land and Agrarian Studies and Professor of Development Management at the School of Government, University of the Western Cape, South Africa. He has extensive practical, training and academic experience spanning the past three decades related to agriculture, agricultural extension and training, land tenure and natural resource management, primarily in southern Africa. From 1976 to 1990 he worked in agricultural training and extension projects in Swaziland and Zimbabwe, and conducted research on rural social dynamics, much of it related to Zimbabwe's communal areas. Since 1991 he has been involved in policy, research and public commentary on South Africa's land reform process. His publications include *Homestead Farming* (1991); *Issues and Options for Institutional Change for Rural and Agricultural Development and Land Reform* (1994); and *People, Land and Livestock* (ed.) (1989).

Nelson Marongwe is a rural and urban planning research fellow with ZERO, a Zimbabwe environmental organisation, where he has focused on land and natural resource conflicts. Trained in rural and urban planning and in environmental policy and planning, he previously worked for the Zimbabwe government. He is presently the Zimbabwe contact person for the International Agrarian Reform Network. He has conducted extensive field research on Zimbabwe's farm occupations since 1998, and has published several papers, including 'Conflict over Land and other Natural Resources in Zimbabwe' (ZERO, 2002).

Notes on contributors

Mandivamba Rukuni is currently Program Director for the W. K. Kellogg Foundation, based in Pretoria, South Africa. He was formerly Professor of Agricultural Economics at the University of Zimbabwe, and was the Chairman the Commission of Inquiry into Land Tenure Systems of Zimbabwe, 1993-1994. He has published extensively in the field of agricultural economics, including two co-edited volumes with Carl Eicher, *Zimbabwe's Agricultural Revolution* (1994) and *Food Security for Southern Africa* (1987). His more recent focus is on the relationship between tenure reform and processes of democratisation.

Blair Rutherford is currently an Associate Professor in the Department of Sociology and Anthropology at Carlton University, Ottawa, Canada. He has been doing field and archival research on issues concerning commercial farm workers in Zimbabwe since 1992. In addition to a number of authored and co-authored articles in Africanist and anthropological journals, he wrote *Working on the Margins: Black Workers, White Farmers in Postcolonial Zimbabwe* (Zed Books and Weaver Press, 2001).

Eric Worby is an Associate Professor of Anthropology at Yale University, where he also holds a joint appointment in the School of Forestry and Environmental Studies and has served as Acting Director of the Program in Agrarian Studies. His research and publications have been concerned with development, modernity, the state, ethnicity and agrarian labor – primarily in the Gokwe region of northwestern Zimbabwe, where he has conducted research since the mid-1980s. In 2001, he edited a special issue of the *Journal of Agrarian Change* entitled 'The New Agrarian Politics in Zimbabwe'. He is currently completing a book on changing perceptions of sovereignty, state power, and development in northwestern Zimbabwe.

Chapter 1

Zimbabwe's Unfinished Business: Rethinking Land, State and Nation

Amanda Hammar and Brian Raftopoulos[1]

The constitutional referendum held in Zimbabwe in February 2000 challenged the hegemonic and increasingly authoritarian rule of President Robert Mugabe and his ruling nationalist Zanu (PF) party. Despite a prior trend of opposition, this marked a particular watershed in Zimbabwe's post-independence political history, precipitating dramatic shifts in the country's political, economic, social, cultural and spatial landscapes; shifts whose ongoing dynamics and extensive effects have generically – though not without fierce contestation – come to be termed 'the Zimbabwe crisis'. So far-reaching and multi-layered is Zimbabwe's 'mutating' millennial crisis, that it has become the subject of much intense reflection and heated debate, nationally, regionally and internationally: whispered daringly and desperately beneath the scratchy music of Zimbabwe's township beer halls, around the meagre fires of the newly dispossessed, and in the endless, nation-wide queues for food, fuel and other basics; confronted more openly in the bold polemic of political leaders and civic activists, in increasingly tense and incredulous diplomatic circles, and in the searching urgency of academic scholarship.

This book joins such a chorus of voices. It was born out of a collective concern for Zimbabwe among various researchers, policy analysts, politicians, activists and development practitioners, both Zimbabwean and non-Zimbabwean. Our broad aim was to examine 'the crisis' in ways that would counter narrow representations of its origins, forms and outcomes, and by working with and through its complexities and contradictions, open more productive pathways

---

[1] For their generous and insightful inputs into this chapter, our deep appreciation to Jocelyn Alexander, Peter Gibbon, Blair Rutherford and Stig Jensen. All errors of fact and judgment, however, remain ours alone.

to dialogue and understanding. An international conference convened in Copenhagen in early September 2001, just days before the attacks on the World Trade Centre and Pentagon in the USA on September 11, was one modest contribution to such a process.[2]

The conference intentionally brought together different political, theoretical and disciplinary perspectives in an attempt to reflect and generate a multiplicity of views on what constitutes 'the crisis'.[3] However, this did not mean an open-ended agenda. At the centre of the three-part conference was a research seminar (from which most of the chapters for this volume are drawn) that was shaped by a very specific question: 'How is "the land question" in Zimbabwe being reconstituted by the current political and economic crisis, and what does this mean for rethinking the state and redefining the contours of [nation and] citizenship in postcolonial Zimbabwe?' In turn, questions were asked about what might analyses of the state and ruling party's intensified assertions of sovereignty, increasingly violent modes of rule, deepening forms of authoritarian nationalism, and narrowing of spaces of citizenship, reveal about the changing politics of land in Zimbabwe.

Clearly the intention then, as now, was neither to reproduce the narrowly nationalist rhetoric of Zanu (PF) that identified the crisis as just 'a land crisis', nor to adopt the liberalist counter-position that asserted it was purely 'a governance crisis'. The basic starting point of this volume remains that the crisis is not about a single issue, neither is it rooted in a one-off event or single historical trajectory, nor is it the predictable outcome of an assumed pattern of 'failed states' in postcolonial Africa. While Zimbabwe may share with other African postcolonies – but no less with other colonised or globally marginalised states – the experience of certain broad historical, political and economic conditions and processes, there

---

[2] The conference consisted of three parts: a public debate on land, politics and aid in the context of crisis, based on the perspectives of various Zimbabwean and Danish politicians and scholars; a research seminar, 'Rethinking Land, State and Citizenship through the Zimbabwe Crisis'; and a workshop addressing specifically the governance crisis and challenges for civil society participation. The combined events were co-sponsored by the former Centre for Development Research in Copenhagen (now Danish Institute for International Studies), the Danish Ministry of Foreign Affairs, the Swedish International Development Agency, the Danish Development Research Council, and Mellemfolkeligt Samvirke (MS), a Danish NGO.

[3] Participants included senior Zimbabwean politicians both from the ruling and opposition parties, Danish politicians and policy makers, Zimbabwean scholars, a range of other Zimbabweanist scholars from Southern Africa, Europe, and North America, and representatives of both Zimbabwean and Danish non-governmental organizations. (This provided a rare 'neutral' space within which Zimbabweans in particular could dialogue freely. Nonetheless, certain polarities remained deep and persistent.)

can be no easy retrospective claim to the 'inevitability' of its tragic collapse. Zimbabwe's current crisis is specific in its location, timing, form and effects, while necessarily complex and dynamic. It is a crisis generated by and generating particular ensembles of politics and practice related to at least three interweaving analytical themes and empirical arenas: *the politics of land and resource distribution; reconstructions of nation and citizenship;* and *the remaking of state and modes of rule.*

These themes have provided a conceptual framing device for this book. But while terms such as 'land', 'nation', 'citizenship' and 'state' might occupy analytically discrete terrains, engendering their own vast bodies of literature, in practice they constantly converge. As such, most of the contributions in this book address different dimensions of the *relationship* between them within the present context of crisis in Zimbabwe. Collectively, they begin to reveal a pattern of projects – operating over different lifetimes and at different levels and scales – that are critical to our understanding of the complexity and persistence of Zimbabwe's ongoing crisis. These simultaneous, incomplete and competing projects of transformation, legitimation and resistance, constitute the 'unfinished business' of the book's title. The present chapter begins by chronicling the evolution and major consequences of the crisis. It traces the key, intersecting elements and polarities which have precipitated and now perpetuate the crisis in its continuously shifting forms. The subsequent section returns to some of these issues in more depth, focusing on them in terms of our three main thematic pillars: land, nation and citizenship, and state. The following section summarises the individual chapters, while the concluding one maps the broader terrain of Zimbabwe's unfinished business.

A chronicle of crisis

By any measure, Zimbabwe is *in* crisis, facing an 'interruption in the reproduction of economic, cultural, social and/or political life' (Johnston et al, 2000:123). However, there is much debate and disagreement on what constitutes and has caused the crisis, what its consequences are, and for whom. Below, we trace the multiple origins and emerging trajectories of crisis in Zimbabwe, and reflect on the critical political and conceptual polarities that contribute to its persistence.

Multiple origins of crisis

Zimbabwe's deepening economic and political crisis was well underway long before the dramatic events triggered by the constitutional referendum in February 2000.[4] Yet in the initial post-independence period of the early 1980s, the signs for Zimbabwe's growth and stability looked encouraging. The new nationalist government, under the statesmanship of a younger Mugabe, focused on reconstruction, reconciliation and redistribution under an apparently socialist banner carefully tempered by pragmatism. Zimbabwe became the latest favoured addition to the international community and donor assistance flowed in, giving rise to yet another postcolonial developmentalist state, albeit one decisively shaped by the particular modernising agenda and practices of its Rhodesian predecessor. A political priority for the new government, driving years of armed struggle, was to reverse seven decades of racially biased inequalities in land and asset distribution, and to bestow fundamental civic and human rights on all its citizens.[5] However, the Lancaster House constitution that dictated the terms of initial transition to independence, demanded uneasy ideological compromises for some of the nationalist leaders. Most significant was the entrenchment and protection of private property rights, permitting land acquisition for the first decade only through a 'willing-seller, willing-buyer' approach, with payments to be made in the currency of the seller's choice. Such conditions imposed substantial constraints on the legal means, financial scope and political pace of land reform.[6] Despite this, there were some early successes with the government's land resettlement programme (Kinsey, 1999).[7]

The 1980s were marked by the successful expansion of public services and basic infrastructure such as health and sanitation, water supplies, education and roads mainly to formerly neglected

---

[4] For different interpretations see, for example, contributions in Raftopoulos and Sachikonye (2001), Moore (2001), Zeilig (2002), as well as many chapters in this volume.

[5] Edison Zvobgo, veteran nationalist, in his presentation at the Conference underpinning this book, confirmed that civic rights were always a critical part of the struggle for national liberation.

[6] This constitutes one of Mugabe's key legitimations for the present 'land revolution', portrayed as 'a return to the unfinished land agenda of the liberation struggle' (Raftopoulos, 2002) whose adequate conclusion Britain is accused of sabotaging in a revised neo-colonialist form.

[7] Cliffe (2000) confirms this, but provides an additional interesting analysis of why such progress was not sustained. See also Sachikonye (2002a).

rural populations (Auret, 1990).⁸ Expansion of credit, marketing and extension services to small-scale farmers resulted in significant increases in their national share of sales of crops such as maize and cotton (Mumbengegwi, 1986). In addition, there were progressive changes in the legal status of women (Batezat and Mwalo, 1989), and the introduction of various local government reforms intended at least in part to broaden democratic participation.⁹ However, resources and 'progress' were unevenly distributed. Notably in the Matabeleland provinces and to a lesser extent in Midlands, where the main opposition party of the time, PF-Zapu, had its main support base, the then Zanu-PF government's strategy became one of terror and intimidation rather than development.¹⁰ This led ultimately to the crushing of Zapu by the army's specially-trained Fifth Brigade, forcing a unity agreement in late 1987 that established a *de facto* one-party state led by a seemingly reconfigured Zanu (PF). A period of relative calm and stability followed, but initially at the expense of democratic political space.¹¹

However, macro-economic and fiscal constraints in the late 1980s began to reverse what development gains had been made. By 1990, facing economic decline and under pressure from a new global neo-liberal hegemony after the collapse of Soviet socialism, the government designed a World Bank-style economic structural adjustment programme (ESAP). Officially cast as a 'home grown' reform, ESAP had initially been more about expansion than contraction. However, the devastating drought in 1991-92 seriously

---

⁸ This had mixed effects, improving services on the one hand if somewhat unevenly, but increasing the disciplinary reach of the state on the other. In addition, the rapid growth of the public sector created a black bureaucratic middle-class that progressively strained the fiscus, while laying the foundations for a future alliance with the political elite, so entrenching a process of 'accumulation from above' (Moore, 2001).

⁹ Makumbe (1998) argues that decentralisation was primarily aimed at establishing a one-party state. Hammar (this volume) argues for a somewhat broader perspective. See also Alexander (2001a) regarding especially the traditionalist dimension to shifting local authority debates and forms since 1980.

¹⁰ An estimated 20,000 people of mainly Ndebele ethnic identity were massacred during this period and many more were brutally tortured. (See *'Breaking the Silence – Building True Peace'*, Catholic Commission for Justice and Peace in Zimbabwe and the Legal Resources Foundation, Harare, 1997.) This campaign was built upon a growing 'Shona' nationalism generated through a rhetorical association made by Zanu-PF between 'Ndebele'/Zapu and 'dissident', that was used to legitimise state violence in defence of the nation. A different and more complex form of exclusive nationalism would subsequently be played out with familiar echoes of violence in the post-2000 period, as discussed later in this chapter.

¹¹ When 'Breaking the Silence' was finally published in 1997, the Preface noted optimistically that publication was only possible because 'Zimbabwe is currently enjoying a period of stability and national unity which did not exist ten years ago'. It also stated that 'Zimbabwe's current human rights record, while still not perfect, is better than it has ever been since Independence in 1980'. Within less than five years, these assertions had become redundant.

affected Zimbabwe's ability to fulfil its goals, leading to greater control of the reform process by the International Monetary Fund and hence the introduction of more orthodox stabilisation measures after 1993, including a stronger focus on public sector reforms. (It also constrained official promotion of a one-party state.) Bond (2001) describes the 1990s as the 'lost decade of development' for Zimbabwe, attributing it primarily to this neo-liberal turn, although he claims the signs were there much earlier.[12]

The negative effects of ESAP were both immediate and sustained. They included unprecedented increases in interest rates and inflation, a 65 per cent fall in the stock market, deindustrialisation precipitating a 40 per cent decline in manufacturing causing company closures and massive job cuts, and a substantial decline in real wages and overall standards of living (Bond, 2001; Raftopoulos, 2001). Increased levels of poverty followed, exacerbating the effects of an already rapid growth in HIV/AIDS.[13] A government Poverty Assessment Survey conducted in the mid-1990s noted the extensive prevalence of poverty in Zimbabwe, concluding that 'about 61 per cent of the population [lived] in households with income per person below a level sufficient to provide basic needs', with 45 per cent living below the Food Poverty Line (FPL). The majority of these were concentrated in the communal areas and among female-headed households.[14]

Not surprisingly, the 1990s was also a decade of growing public protests, labour strikes and a flourishing of civil society organisations and activities. By mid-decade, the labour movement – formerly 'a pliant wing of the ruling party' – had begun to assert its autonomy, consolidate its support base, strengthen its organisational capacity, and broaden and intensify its mobilisation strategies (Raftopoulos, 2001). A series of corruption scandals, brushed aside by President Mugabe, further tarnished the credibility of the ruling party and the state. Alliances began to form between the Zimbabwe Congress of Trade Unions (ZCTU), the student movement, women's

---

[12] Bond (2001) links the shift to earlier trends in the 1980s in the realignment of the petty bourgeois political leadership with foreign and local capital – abandoning its original peasant and worker alliances – as reflected in a rise in corruption, policy choices in line with international lending institutions, and widescale allocation of available land for redistribution to the political elite.

[13] Zimbabwe's HIV prevalence rate in adults was estimated in 2001 at 25 per cent, ranking second highest in the world next to Botswana (*Africa Notes*, No. 2, August 2001). More recent figures compiled from UNAIDS statistics on global HIV/AIDS prevalence, have placed the rate for Zimbabwe at 33.7 per cent of adults. See 'AIDS and hunger. Southern Africa's twin killers', *Oxfam Canada*, 2 December 2002.

[14] *Poverty Assessment Survey*, Ministry of Labour, Manpower Planning and Social Welfare, Harare, 1997, quoted in Tandon (2001:221).

organisations, frustrated public servants, and various civil society organisations, whose collective political voice and effective strike actions became increasingly threatening to the regime. The party-state's response was to become increasingly authoritarian and coercive.[15]

By contrast, when sustained lobbying of government by the Zimbabwe National Liberation War Veterans Association (ZNWLVA) for greater financial compensation, political recognition, and progress on land redistribution reached a dramatic crescendo in late 1997, President Mugabe gave in to their demands. Aware of the veterans' political capital in relation to their primacy in Zimbabwe's national liberation history, and reluctant to face losing their support or the prospect of an even more violent challenge from them as threatened, he yielded to their demands. He awarded all war veterans a one-off cash payment and an ongoing monthly pension, as well as a significant percentage of all newly acquired land for resettlement. These commitments placed an unsustainable burden on the economy, while giving clear signals as to the regime's strategic political preferences.[16] Further economic and political strains accompanied the President's subsequent extra-parliamentary decision in August 1998 to take Zimbabwe into the war in the Democratic Republic of Congo (DRC), where at one point at least 11,000 Zimbabwean troops were estimated to be stationed.[17]

Following on the heels of increased war veteran militancy and the successful mass anti-government strikes in urban areas, 1998 witnessed a series of mostly spontaneous land invasions onto commercial farms and other properties in various parts of the country.[18] These reflected limited but growing discontent with the pace and priorities of the government's land resettlement programme. The state's response to these invasions was primarily

---

[15] For further details see Raftopoulos (2001, and this volume) and Saunders (2000). Ironically, some of these strict measures could be legitimised within the growing donor-supported rubric of 'good governance'.

[16] Government's subsequent failure to respond to clear evidence of corruption in the distribution of the compensation fund to disabled war veterans, further reinforced this sense of political expediency.

[17] By late 2002, in line with a peace accord, it was claimed all Zimbabwean troops had been withdrawn. Up to 3 million people are estimated to have died in the war since 1998. Mugabe represented his intervention as an act of solidarity in defence of sovereignty and as concern for regional security, about which there is some scepticism. A UN Security Council report released in October 2002 implicated a number of senior army generals and politicians from Zimbabwe and the region in 'shady dealings' related to the plunder of diamonds and other key natural resources in the DRC.

[18] Both Marongwe and Alexander (this volume) distinguish these occupations from those after February 2000. See discussion later in this chapter.

to evict or arrest land activists, many of whom continued to return defiantly to the sites of occupation. At the same time, political mileage was made by Zanu (PF) of some of the most visible of the invasions, most notably those undertaken by villagers from Svosve communal lands, close to Harare.[19] In September 1998, a widely attended and highly significant donors 'land conference' was convened in Harare to discuss and raise international financial support for the government's new Land Reform and Resettlement Programme.[20] Conference participants were taken on tour to Svosve to demonstrate to donors the seriousness of demands being made by the land hungry.[21]

Despite valid scepticism about Zanu (PF)'s recurring political manipulation of 'the land question' since independence, the persistence of racialised patterns of inequitable land distribution and use in Zimbabwe prior to 2000, made the ruling party's assertions of the need for radical land reform difficult to dispute. At independence, over 6,000 white large-scale commercial farmers owned 15.5 million hectares (39 per cent) of land, with 8,500 African small-scale commercial farmers on 1.4 million hectares (4 per cent), and an estimated 700,000 indigenous communal area households subsisting on 16.4 million hectares (42 per cent), 75 per cent of which was in the driest and least fertile agro-ecological zones (Sachikonye, 2002a). According to government statistics, by 1998 4,000 mainly white large-scale commercial farmers retained 28 per cent (11.2 million hectares) of land, over one million communal area households occupied 42 per cent (16.3 million hectares) and 70,000 households had been resettled on 9 per cent (2 million hectares). The revised distribution pattern envisaged by the 1998 Land Reform and Resettlement Programme, projected a shift in

---

[19] In September 2002 up to 96 families among the Svosve occupiers were in fact forcibly 'relocated', 'to pave the way for Air Marshall Perence Shiri' (*The Daily News*, 18 September 2002).

[20] Besides some funding in the 1980s for resettlement, primarily from the British, and despite the significant potential contribution of land reform both to poverty reduction and economic efficiency, there had been remarkably 'little material and moral support given to land reform by most of Zimbabwe's influential bilateral and multilateral donors' (Moyo, 1999:4).

[21] In 2001, nationalist and political scientist, Masipula Sithole, turned Svosve symbolically on its head. Acknowledging the importance of land – alongside other issues such as jobs, health, education, and housing – he nonetheless suggested that prior to the February 2000 referendum, 'there was no land crisis qua crisis as such...The land issue became a crisis when the government itself became Svosve – invading, occupying or condoning the seizure of farms – and began resettling people hurriedly ("fast-track") as if running away from something' (*The Financial Gazette*, 20 September 2001). His point is well taken with regard to Zanu (PF)'s political *tactics*. However, the depth, persistence and complexity of struggles over land and natural resources are grounded in far more than this and cannot be under-estimated.

landholdings and land use to 13 per cent for large-scale commercial farming, 3 per cent small-scale commercial farming, 42 per cent communal area, and 21 per cent resettlement, besides an increase from 1 to 6 per cent in state farms, and a sustained 15 per cent for national parks and urban areas.[22]

However, the initially promising joint initiatives mapped out between the government, the mainly white large-scale commercial farmers, representatives of small-scale farmers, various other stakeholders, and donors at the conference, were stalled due to a combination of apparent bureaucratic incapacities and unmet donor conditionalities on the Zimbabwe government side, and perceived hesitations and inconsistencies on the donor side. Insistence by donors on transparency, accountability and the rule of law in the new land reform process was combined with what were considered by the government to be especially intrusive demands related to the issue of national sovereignty (such as pressure to withdraw Zimbabwean troops from the DRC). Sovereignty would subsequently form the centrepiece of the anti-colonial, anti-imperialist rhetoric used by Mugabe and Zanu (PF) to counter critics of their revived land revolution and new brand of authoritarian nationalism (Worby, this volume).

Triggering the expansion of crisis

1998 was also a watershed in terms of independent initiatives to develop a more democratically-based constitution for Zimbabwe. A popular campaign for a new constitution was spearheaded by the broad-based National Constitutional Assembly (NCA), a popular and powerful alliance of some 96 civil society organisations including church groups, trades unions, human rights organisations, and student and intellectual groups (Moore, 2001; Saunders, 2000). The strength of this campaign forced the government to establish an alternative Constitutional Commission. Although ruling party dominated and deeply mistrusted by the NCA, the Commission was initially quite well received by a public which at the time was able to openly voice concerns without fear of retribution. However, unilateral changes made to the final draft by Mugabe and the Zanu (PF) inner circle reinforced the view that they were not interested in people's

---

[22] All figures taken from Takavarasha (1998), quoted in Stoneman (2002). Slight variations appear in different sources. However, such aggregations necessarily obscure 'the differential interests, inputs, rights and obligations relating to land in rural Zimbabwe' (Gaidzanwa 1995:2), which have quite specific gender, class, ethnic and age dimensions generated by and through complex cultural and spatial politics.

opinions or the democratic process. By this point, the white commercial farming and business sectors had allied with the NCA and an emerging opposition movement (see below) in campaigning for a 'no' vote in the referendum. In February 2000, the draft constitution was rejected by a majority of voters. This outcome represented the first formal 'electoral' challenge to Zanu (PF) hegemony in twenty years of rule, and was to precipitate the first wave of war veteran-led land invasions and much else to follow.

Prior to this, in late 1999 – less than a year before the 2000 parliamentary elections – the NCA, together with the ZCTU, played a central role in the formation of a new opposition party, the Movement for Democratic Change (MDC) (Raftopoulos, 2002). This, too, was a critical turning point in Zimbabwe's political history and, alongside the country's (and continent's) inherited and deepening structural problems, is central to the present crisis. Reflecting historical rivalries between Zimbabwe's nationalist political parties and the labour movement, mirrored elsewhere in the region (Zambia, South Africa), the combined emergence of the labour-based MDC and a broad alliance of articulate and well-organised civil society organisations posed a significant threat to a delegitimised, nationalist-driven Zanu (PF) leadership.[23] With a parliamentary election in June 2000, just months after the 'no' vote, Zanu (PF) had to act decisively to reclaim its lost political ground.

A return to 'the land question' was a predictable strategy, as had been the case during most previous elections since 1985. Talk of a state-led 'land revolution' had been expressed publicly by the president and senior ruling party politicians since the late 1990s. In a speech made in 1997, Mugabe had proposed ignoring the constitution in order to redistribute land.[24] Yet in 2000, the tactics employed and the intended outcome went beyond mere political rhetoric. To begin with, a nation-wide campaign of land invasions

---

[23] For a comprehensive outline of post-independence civil society development and its contribution to the formation of Zimbabwe's first serious opposition party, the MDC, see Saunders (2000). This challenges Berman's (1998:339) over-generalised claim that 'the development of 'civil society' in African states [does not] serve as a force for social and political renewal in contemporary Africa'. On the other hand, its threat to existing regimes can and often does elicit a violent backlash that may consequently, if temporarily, limit its effectiveness, as also witnessed in Zimbabwe (Raftopoulos, 2002).

[24] Moyo (2001) argues in support of the legitimacy of a state-led revolution aimed at reversing historically-based inequalities and radically redistributing resources. Indeed such a project might have received much wider support had it been implemented according to such claims. But there is evidence from a multitude of sources to suggest this has not been the case, including an alleged internal Zanu (PF) national audit on the current land reform process, which has itself pointed to many anomalies and problems. See for example *Africa Confidential*, 21 February 2003; *The Sunday Mirror* (Zimbabwe), 16 March 2003.

onto mainly white-owned commercial farms was initiated, using unprecedented extremes of violence and intimidation against both white farmers and black farm workers. This was fronted at first by militant war veterans,[25] but subsequently expanded to include ruling party-trained youth militia and eventually, explicitly, co-opted state security forces. The aim at first seemed to be to 'destroy the world of the white farm'.[26] This acted firstly as a central (nationalist) strategy to reclaim 'the lost lands' and finally reverse the colonial legacy of racialised land and economic inequalities, and secondly, as a means of punishing and/or eliminating a constituency of white commercial farmers and 'their' farm workers widely viewed to have voted 'no' in the referendum, and, by implication, to support the opposition more generally (Reeler, 2003).

However, from early on in Zanu (PF)'s campaign, the violence rapidly spread well beyond the borders of 'the farm' to include widespread attacks on actual or suspected members of the opposition MDC, and has continued unabated since then. Such violence – including arson, threats, false arrests and incarceration, beatings, torture, rape, deliberate starvation, disappearances, and in some cases murder – has intensified around various elections, whether parliamentary (June 2000), presidential (March 2002), Rural District Council (September 2002), or urban and rural by-elections. Besides this, any public criticism of the regime, no matter how peaceful or non-partisan – curtailed as it is already by anti-democratic legislation such as the Public Order and Security Act (POSA) – has been met with increased brutality. The MDC and any who are assumed to support it, have been labelled by Zanu (PF) as 'sell outs' to 'the white enemy' at home and to Zimbabwe's former colonial masters abroad (Britain) or the West in general (Worby, this volume), and accused of sabotaging the final phase of the nationalist, anti-colonial revolution, the so-called *Third Chimurenga*.[27] Such 'traitors' are being systematically denied the right to citizenship, freedom of expression, protection under the law, access to land, or even in

---

[25] War veterans are not a seamless, homogenous category (Hammar, this volume). The proportion involved in the occupations and violence is thought to be small relative to the total number of veterans in the country, many of whom are members of the MDC or civil society organisations, including alternatives to the ZNWLVA, and have spoken out openly against the violence (Alexander and McGregor, 2001).

[26] See 'Land reform a cover for Zanu war on opposition', *Business Day* (SA), 23 August 2002.

[27] The *First Chimurenga* refers to the first anti-colonial struggle in 1896-7, brutally crushed by the colonial authorities, and the *Second Chimurenga* to the national liberation struggle of the 1960s and 70s, successfully culminating in Zimbabwe's independence in 1980.

some cases access to food.[28] In rural areas, teachers have been especially targeted (Hammar, this volume). In addition, a campaign of disruption and/or occupation of local government institutions perceived to be supporting the opposition has been carried out by party militants with backing from senior ministers and party officials as well as various central state agents (McGregor, 2002; Hammar, this volume).[29] A number of private businesses have also been attacked, occupied or closed down since early 2000, as have been several non-governmental organisations and independent media companies.

Although there were already threats and violence against independent journalists in 1999 (for example, for reporting unfavourably on the war in the DRC), since 2000 various instruments of intimidation have been used to undermine the independent media. On the one hand, there have been physical attacks such as the still 'unsolved' bombing of the printing press of the independent *Daily News*. On the other hand, the introduction of legislation such as POSA and the Access to Information and Protection of Privacy Act (AIPPA) is aimed directly at silencing critical reporting. New procedures for registering journalists places full control in the hands of the Minister of Information, while a new Broadcasting Services Act claiming to liberalise the airwaves threatens independent broadcasting through rules that prohibit foreign investment in or technical assistance to the media. Many of these laws are being constitutionally challenged in court, but they continue to narrow the space for independent reporting about Zimbabwe. The exclusion since late 2002 of foreign journalists from the country further limits international coverage, increasing the vulnerability of local journalists and citizens in general.[30]

Much of the regime's impunity and the uneven application of the law along partisan lines has been facilitated through undermining the independence of the judiciary. Using threats, harassment, the

---

[28] See for example 'War vets evict 40 families', *The Daily News*, 19 December 2002; 'Mayhem as war vets open 'torture office'', *The Financial Gazette*, 9 January 2003; 'Citizenship choice in Zimbabwe', *BBC News* online, 28 February 2003; 'Zimbabwe running on empty', *The Toronto Star*, 9 March 2003.

[29] MDC strongholds have been hardest hit, with repeated attacks on RDC staff, councillors and property in places such as Binga, while in urban councils such as Harare and Bulawayo there has been persistent interference by the Minister of Local Government and a threat in early 2003 to install politically-appointed governors in a move intended to undermine the authority and effectiveness of elected MDC mayors and councillors. See 'Mugabe loyalists to run opposition strongholds', *The Guardian* (UK), 7 January 2003.

[30] This discussion draws in part on a verbal presentation by Sarah Chiumbu, Director of MISA (Media Institute of Southern Africa), at a Globalisation Conference in Oslo, 29 November 2002.

Rethinking Land, State and Nation

rhetoric of race, and even arrests of judges, most long-standing senior judges, many of them white, have been forced to resign while important positions have been filled by those seen to be loyal to the ruling party. Court rulings felt to interfere with the party's land reform agenda or other interests, have met with moves to introduce new legislation through parliament to counter such rulings.[31] In some local areas, magistrates perceived to sympathise with the opposition have been physically attacked. This has been reinforced by the blatant partiality of many police officers, to some extent because of fears of punishment themselves.[32] While opposition supporters have been overtly persecuted, many known ruling party perpetrators of extreme political violence have gone unpunished. Such conditions have created profound insecurity, and together with deepening hunger and poverty, have precipitated extensive internal displacement, refugees in neighbouring states, and a mass exodus of trained professionals.[33]

All of the above is compounded by and has further deepened Zimbabwe's catastrophic economic decline, which might be characterised broadly in terms of the following: the disintegration of commercial farming, tourism and mining, with major losses in foreign currency earnings, a fall in GDP of 24 per cent, and a significant rise in arrears on Zimbabwe's foreign debt of US$3.4 billion from 2 to 30 per cent of GDP;[34] the withdrawal of most Western aid and substantial loss of foreign investment (prompting a turn to alternative sources such as Libya);[35] widespread business failure and massive job losses in most sectors, calculated modestly at over 300,000 out of a formal workforce of 1.3 million, not

---

[31] See 'Government gazettes new Bill to invalidate evictions', *The Daily News*, 16 September 2002.
[32] Such partiality reached absurd proportions when the *victims* of a Zanu (PF) shooting were arrested when reporting the incident. See 'Victim of Zanu PF shooting arrested', *The Daily News*, 17 October 2002.
[33] Between one and two million Zimbabweans are thought to be living (mostly illegally) in South Africa, 600,000 in Britain, and many more working or studying in Africa, Asia, Europe, the USA, Canada and Australia. See 'Zimbabwe's missing millions', *The Mail and Guardian* (SA), 4 December 2002; 'Zimbabwe in crisis as Aids kills 300 a day', *The Times* (UK), 5 December 2002. In March 2003, the South African Minister for Home Affairs commented on the growing threats this is posing to the region, breaking ranks with South Africa's otherwise official position of 'quiet diplomacy'. See 'Buthulezi breaks his silence on Zimbabwe', *The Mail and Guardian* (SA), 13 March 2003.
[34] See 'Zimbabwe's agony as Mugabe avoids crunch', *The Times* (UK), 28 October 2002. The International Crisis Group (ICG) put Zimbabwe's foreign debt at US$5.3 billion in its March 2002 report, 'Zimbabwe at the Crossroads: Transition or Conflict?'.
[35] Foreign direct investment was calculated to have dropped from US$436 million in 1998 to US$4.5 million in 2001. In March 2002, the World Economic Forum rated Zimbabwe the least competitive economy out of 75 countries surveyed. Cited in International Crisis Group, *Africa Report* No. 47, 'Zimbabwe: What Next?', June 2002.

accounting for informal sector losses and pre-existing unemployment; soaring inflation, officially recorded as 145 per cent by the end of 2002 and rising to 269 per cent by April 2003, but with some sources forecasting a rise to 500 per cent within a year;[36] crippling fuel shortages (due to foreign currency shortages), affecting all aspects of the economy; a drastic fall in the value of the Zimbabwe dollar, eroding real incomes significantly;[37] the collapse of key public services, among other things worsening the HIV/AIDS crisis; and finally, a severe national food crisis threatening to become a famine affecting over half of Zimbabwe's estimated 13 million population.

Impending famine is attributed by the regime to drought and foreign and local sabotage. While the former argument has at least some credibility, the latter hints at either paranoia or further political deflection. Either way, countless observers and analysts including the Commonwealth Secretariat and UN agencies such as the World Food Programme (WFP) and the Food and Agricultural Organisation (FAO), have blamed the food crisis on a combination of man-made and politically motivated factors.[38] These include the near-collapse of commercial agriculture following land invasions as well as insufficient support to newly resettled farmers under the 'fast-track' resettlement programme;[39] negligent government food security strategies despite numerous early warnings; lack of foreign currency to import food or the fuel to deliver food aid to the most vulnerable; erratic and badly managed price controls that have often deepened rather than eased food shortages;[40] and widespread evidence of the politicisation of food, including deliberate strategies of starvation of whole communities of alleged opposition supporters.[41] However,

---

[36] 'The Zimbabwean Model', *The Economist* (UK), 28 November 2002

[37] Where the opportunity exists, many Zimbabweans now rely on remittances from abroad. An estimated £20 million is thought to be transferred monthly from exiles in Britain via the black market, the significance of which was acknowledged by the Minister of Finance in late 2002. See Peta Thornycroft, "Send cash' plea from Zimbabwe to expats', *The Daily Telegraph* (UK), 15 November 2002.

[38] See for example 'Report adds to Mugabe isolation', *The Guardian* (UK), 10 April 2003.

[39] 'Famine looms as commercial farms reduced to zero activity', *The Daily News*, 2 December 2002. International food monitoring agencies estimated agricultural output had dropped to approximately 25% of normal production between 2000 and 2003.

[40] See 'Concern over new price controls', *IRIN* (UN), 18 November 2002.

[41] See for example *The Daily News*, 11 October 2002, *The Guardian* (UK), 18 October 2002, *ZWNEWS* 23 October 2002. The use of food as a political weapon by the Zanu (PF) government has been widely reported and criticised both within Zimbabwe and internationally. Despite all the evidence stacked against it, the regime has denied the allegations and instead accused the opposition of using food as a political weapon, using this argument to ban the delivery of food aid by independent charity organisations, claiming them to be 'hatcheries of political opposition' (*IOL* (SA), 12 October 2002). By April 2003, the UN had begun an unprecedented initiative of distributing food aid in urban areas. See 'UN brings food aid to cities as Zimbabwe's plight worsens', *The Independent on Sunday* (UK), 6 April 2003.

Rethinking Land, State and Nation

in addition to these widely-supported claims, it should be noted that the large-scale commercial farming sector had in the past decade shifted focus away from domestic food production (except beef) towards a more specialised export market and wildlife tourism (Moyo, 2000a). Together with the reduction in public sector support to small-scale production in the communal areas as part of structural reforms in the 1990s, this implies an already-existing slowdown of domestic food production prior to 2000.[42]

Paradoxically, in the face of such a severe and multi-layered crisis, there has been both an expansion and heightening of political awareness amongst all Zimbabweans. This built on the developments in civil society organising in the 1990s, and deepened with the initial successes of both the National Constitutional Assembly and Movement for Democratic Change in 2000. However, developments leading up to and since the 'stolen' presidential elections in March 2002 began to undermine severely these democratic gains, and to shrink the political space for all forms of democratic expression and oppositional challenge (Raftopoulos, 2002). The persistent introduction of repressive legislation since then has further entrenched political intimidation and tightened the hold of the ruling party over state mechanisms of arrest, incarceration, violence, and control of populations and resources. This has succeeded in driving underground or into exile or in other ways silencing many individual opposition activists and supporters.

While formal opposition organisations have managed to continue operating, they do so in substantially reduced ways in both urban and rural settings. In late 2002, one MDC activist interviewed in Matabeleland noted that the party's rural structures, 'once so jubilant and strong in these areas, are being decimated. The MDC can't protect people, can't provide food, and so can't muster open allegiance'.[43] And yet as conditions worsen on all levels, calls for 'mass action' by the MDC in March 2003 saw the biggest anti-government urban protest action in years with most supporters appearing to heed the two-day call to stay away from work or in other ways demonstrate their discontent with the regime, and most shops and businesses closed in all major towns.[44] The police called the protest a 'total

---

[42] In this case, the collapse of the commercial farming sector after 2000 would have contributed more directly to the balance of payments crisis (with its multiple spin-off effects, including those related to food production and distribution), but equally to large-scale unemployment and dispossession, hence increasing social vulnerability and household food insecurity overall. Thanks to Peter Gibbon for pointing this out.

[43] Reported by Jocelyn Alexander, personal communication, September 2002.

[44] See 'Zimbabwe protest fuelled by hunger and desperation,' *The Times* (UK), 19 March 2003.

failure' yet deployed thousands of officers around the country to try and keep it under control.[45] The extent of the subsequent political backlash ironically underscored the protest's success, with reports of over 500 opposition officials and supporters arrested, more than 1,000 driven from their homes, 250 admitted to hospital and scores beaten and tortured in police custody.[46] Yet within weeks, and despite continued intimidation by the army, police and Zanu (PF) militia, two of the MDC's parliamentary candidates won crucial by-elections in Harare at the end of March 2003. A subsequent call for mass stayaways in June 2003 was largely successful. However, mass *demonstrations* against the government were brutally contained through the deployment of state security and party militia, especially in the high-density areas and on the University of Zimbabwe campus.

Polarities in the politics of crisis

One of the main problems defining and sustaining the crisis has been a deepening pattern of partisan dichotomies, producing crude polarisations that entrench certain types of antagonisms and foreclose productive political dialogue.[47] Political and conceptual polarities are most easily generated through and reinforce static and essentialised representations of difference. While boundaries are frequently blurred, porous or shifting in practice, creating absolute distinctions holds real danger for those encased by such definitions (Dean, 2001). Rutherford (this volume) provides a compelling example of this through his analysis of the punishing effects on farm workers of both the limited and limiting views held about them by opposing ends of the political spectrum (namely radical Zanu (PF) nationalists and liberal democrats in the opposition), in particular their automatic conceptual pairing with 'farmer' and 'farm'.

---

[45] See 'Dozens of activists jailed in Zimbabwe', *The Mail and Guardian* (SA), 19 March 2003.

[46] See 'Mugabe seizes the chance to attack his rivals', *The Times* (UK), 27 March 2003.

[47] This critique does not propose a blurring of all ideological differences and political frontiers. As Mouffe (1995:263) notes, 'the presence of dissent and institutions through which such divisions can be manifested' is part of 'the very condition of possibility' of a democratic politics. Such a politics is not directed towards 'a rational consensus reached without exclusion' as many liberals and rationalists would promote, but rather acknowledges and embraces difference. Yet it 'presupposes that the 'other' is no longer seen as an enemy to be destroyed, but as an 'adversary'. Somebody with whose ideas we are going to struggle, but whose right to defend those ideas we will not put into question. We could say that the aim of democratic politics is to transform an 'antagonism' into an 'agonism'.'

Rethinking Land, State and Nation

As the crisis continues, polarities are multiplying and shifting, yet one can trace a number of consistently core discursive divides that continue to mark the present politics of crisis. These may be characterised, somewhat simplistically for now, in terms of the following kinds of political dichotomies: a historicised and racialised assertion of land restitution and justice, versus an ahistorical, technocratic insistence on liberal notions of private property, 'development' and 'good governance'; a new form of 'indigenous', authoritarian nationalism (based around claims of loyalty and national sovereignty), versus a non-ethnicised, 'civic' nationalism (grounded in liberal democratic notions of rights and the rule of law); a radical, Pan-Africanist anti-colonial, anti-imperialist critique of 'the West', versus a 'universalist' embrace of certain aspects of neo-liberalism and globalisation; and a monopoly claim over the commitment to radical redistribution, versus a monopoly claim over the defence of human rights.[48] In large part, these polarities and their persistence are founded on competing narratives of Zimbabwe's national liberation history which are critical both to the ruling party's ongoing attempts to sustain its hegemony, and to the counter-hegemonic moves of various opposition actors.

Part of what this book aims to do is to expose and interrupt such rigid polarities and the essentialisms that underpin them. Our collective intent is to work against the 'misplaced concreteness' of various commonsense categories and hierarchised binaries that naturalise boundaries and fix distinctions between an inside and an outside (Alonso, 1994). We wish to open out the space in which the crisis can be told or read so as to facilitate greater transparency and nurture critical intellectual and political debate. We are especially concerned to disrupt what Raftopoulos (this volume) calls 'the devastating rupture' that has been created between the notion of democratic rights on the one hand, and radical land and economic redistribution on the other.[49] Clearly, these are equally important and not mutually exclusive, despite how they have been portrayed.

---

[48] For some analysts, these distinctions might be subsumed under an over-arching polarity, defined largely in terms of 'modernity' versus its retreat. See for example Rukuni and Jensen (this volume). See Worby (this volume) for an interesting challenge to this perspective. For a further, incisive treatment of the notion of multiple modernities, see Moore (2003). The trope of modernity and its seemingly singular, 'traditional' other, is often interwoven with other kinds of dichotomies such as urban versus rural. See Andersson (2001) for a critique of this particular polarity in Zimbabwe's current discourse on land.

[49] For versions of this 'split', see Baregu (2001) and Moyo (2001). On combining land rights and human rights, see Hellum and Derman (2001). For an alternative perspective on democratic property rights, see Cousins (this volume).

However, a distinction needs to be made between the historically-embedded inequalities in land, and other dimensions of inequality, exclusion, oppression and resistance that are currently being played out *through* the politics of land.

Themes, schemes and dilemmas

Three inter-weaving themes have helped guide the individual and collective analyses pursued in this book. They are discussed in this section, respectively, as: Questions of Land and Resources: Revisiting 'the Land Question'; Reconstructing the Contours of Nation and Citizenship; and New Modes of Rule and Reinventions of the State.

Questions of land and resources: Revisiting 'the land question'

Perhaps more than any other phrase associated with Zimbabwe's colonial and postcolonial history, 'the land question' triggers a Pavlovian response of knowing head nods, as though there is a common agreement on what the phrase describes empirically and implies politically and otherwise. Yet the 'the' remains remarkably unspecified in some contexts while dangerously narrow in others. In its widest sense, 'the land question' potentially encompasses a broad range of critical issues that need to be addressed. These include: unequal, racialised and class, gender and age-based patterns of land distribution; dualistic forms of land tenure and distorted types and sizes of landholding; competing land uses and changing land markets; uneven degrees of land security and differential land and resource rights; and institutional distortions and inefficiencies in land allocation, access, control and management. On the other hand, 'the land question' – especially in the present crisis – has been narrowly reduced to *either* a parody of nationalism and sovereignty that excludes both alternative versions of liberation history and those subject-citizens deemed outside the (new) nation (Raftopoulos, Rutherford, Hammar, this volume), *or* an issue of human rights, within which there has been an over-valuation of liberal notions of private property (Cousins, this volume).

The colonial heritage of often violent land appropriations and dispossessions, and resistance to them, has engraved itself deeply into Zimbabwe's inter-related physical, political and psychic landscapes.[50] Not surprisingly, 'land' as an historical trope and

---

[50] See for example Palmer (1977), Worby (1994), Ranger (1999), Alexander et al (2000).

a metaphor of colonial subjugation and conflict, has lent itself easily to a particular nationalist narrative, serving especially the ruling party's need to assert its hegemonic claim to historical 'truth' and sustained legitimacy.[51] Land's seeming primacy as a signifier of just possession, indigenous location and national belonging has been woven as a central thread into the cloth of the dominant liberation message. Thus the seeming 'naturalness' of a certain version of 'the land question' is presented as the basis for its singular status, as the sole, authentic signifier of national identity. The complexity and multiplicity of colonial and postcolonial social, political and economic struggles in varied locations and among differentiated groups are obscured through their distillation into a 'timeless' and unchanged struggle over land; hence the simplistic sequential notion of Chimurenga I, II, and III. In Gramscian terms, Mugabe has tried to pose all political questions around the issue of land, attempting to unite economic and political questions around this one problematic so as to construct an historical, cultural, moral and political unity through the idea of its reclamation. In terms of mobilising regional and international support in particular, he has posed this not at the corporate level of a class in crisis, but on a 'universal plane' as a national and Pan-African problem.[52]

The portrayal of the 2000 land invasions or occupations as direct evidence of this teleology has been an important part of the regime's self-legitimation. The work of scholars such as Marongwe and Alexander (this volume), critically challenges this seamless nationalist story, for example by drawing a qualitative distinction between the 2000 invasions and the occupations occurring in 1998 or in previous periods since independence. Similarly, Sachikonye (2002:6) has argued that 'until 1998, there was little organized pressure from peasants and the landless.'[53] Moyo (2001) on the other hand sees the 2000 occupations as part of the longer continuum of an ongoing and clearly identifiable 'land occupation movement'. This contradicts an earlier position of Moyo's whereby he noted the

---

[51] See Ranger (2002) for an incisive analysis of Zanu (PF)'s use of a particular version of liberation history in its 2002 presidential campaign and beyond, and his general call for 'a complex, plural history' instead.

[52] See for example 'Zanu PF campaign to export land policies', *The Zimbabwe Independent*, 13 December 2002.

[53] Nor, argues Marongwe (1999:28), has any civil society organisation 'volunteered to be a leader in matters of land reform', at least not on any broad-based national scale. However, women's land rights have begun to be voiced formally through the Women's Land Lobby Group (WLLG), and it could be argued that war veterans had been lobbying for land reform for some time through their various organisations.

absence of 'a nation-wide political movement and/or peasant rebellion, over demands for land reform' (Moyo, 1999:5). He argued instead that 'the major sources of formal or officially exposed and negotiated demands for land are those of elite black farmers, aspiring black investors and agricultural graduates.' (ibid.)

As remarkable as it is (and in need of further research and debate) that in Zimbabwe's post-independence history there has been no organised, nationwide political movement of 'peasants and the landless' formally and collectively demanding land, this does not mean that land has not been centrally important in a wide range of localised livelihood and political struggles.[54] Numerous studies attest to the persistence and intensification of complex struggles over land and natural resources in a variety of contexts (as discussed below), yet ironically these trends have been largely ignored or at best marginalised in official debates on 'the land question' to date. For both the ruling party and its allies, and those analysts deploying a political economy framework, the problem of land has been conceived in terms of a particular framework of nationalist redress. Within this perspective, Mugabe's intensified nationalism and anti-imperialism are automatically assumed to be progressive because of his position on radical land redistribution.[55] In the process, serious analysis of the actual politics and practices of the regime has been side-stepped, and state-sponsored political violence and other perversions of democratic practice have been dismissed as epiphenomenal or secondary to the more fundamental issue of radically restructuring the economy.[56]

---

[54] The national Poverty Assessment Survey (1997) 'findings' that a negligible percentage of impoverished rural dwellers prioritise 'land' in their poverty alleviation strategies, has led to misinterpretations that mask the extent to which land constitutes a critical part of the diverse economic strategies of poor rural households in Zimbabwe and in migrant labour economies in general. Thanks to Jocelyn Alexander for emphasising this point. See for example Ellis (2000).

[55] Yet as Zeilig (2002:88) notes, Mugabe's government had earlier embraced IMF and World Bank-led reforms. But as popular local opposition to such reforms grew in the 1990s, and as populist anti-globalisation sentiments represented a new sphere of political support after 2000, a retreat from such an agenda and a fervent anti-imperialist rhetoric became central to Zanu (PF)'s legitimation strategy.

[56] Moyo (2001), for example, acknowledging the regime's shift from a 'development' to a 'restitution and justice' paradigm, largely underplays the violent wave of dispossession and displacement since 2000 of hundreds of thousands of farm workers and ordinary rural residents accused of supporting the opposition. In general this relates to a long-standing problem within anti-imperialist critiques, of neglecting democratic political concerns in favour of more structuralist analyses (see Hall, 1980).

Yet in over two decades of independence, as Alexander (this volume) discusses, there have been a variety of important and often contradictory shifts 'in official and popular discourses over land, in the nature of social movements seeking to claim land, and in the consequences for and role of the state'. Various other analysts have also identified several distinct phases in the discourses and practices around land since 1980, most of whom note a definite decline – after initial populist efforts and despite notable successes in the early resettlement programme – in government's commitment to radical land reform (Sachikonye, 2002a; Moyo, 1999). Clearly little has remained static in the agrarian landscape during this period (Worby, 2001) quite besides the intensive wave of land occupations begun in 2000. Land values and land uses changed, not least after the introduction of a structural adjustment programme in the 1990s (Moyo, 2000a; Suzuki, 2001). New and deepening land and resource conflicts emerged (Marongwe, 2002; Matondi, 2001). There was a revival, albeit somewhat ambivalently, of the land-related (and patriarchal) authority of traditional leaders (Alexander, 2001a). Groups of land-hungry peasants migrated into formerly marginal (mainly communal) areas, while various categories of land users were redefined as 'squatters' and often displaced, although not without a struggle (Chimhowu, 2002; Hammar, 2001; Nyambara, 2001; Moore, 2000; Alexander and McGregor, 1997, 2000). And both the urban poor and elites generated pressure on urban and rural land (Mbiba, 2001). In addition, the devastating effects of HIV/AIDS continued to alter demographic and social relations relative to land and resources everywhere.

What all this implies, among other things, is that there are increasingly complex layers of differentiation and combinations of social classes with competing interests in 'land' per se, as well as in specific pieces of land or territory.[57] Such a dense and dynamic social fabric and the multiplicity of land and natural resource conflicts which it generates, can hardly be explained only in terms of the legacy of colonial conquest and land appropriation, no matter how profound their imprints on agrarian structures and relations. Neither can land inequalities and conflicts be explained simplistically in relation to more contemporary manifestations of imperialism such as neo-liberal forms of globalisation. Nor can their resolution

---

[57] This includes at the very least: traditional leaders; war veterans; ordinary landless people from both rural and urban areas differentiated by class, gender, age and ethnicity, including farm workers and unemployed and unpropertied urban workers; agricultural graduates; emerging black entrepreneurs; various categories of white commercial farmers; the political and bureaucratic elites; and foreign companies and individuals.

be negotiated purely via the narrow nationalist discourse and authoritarian modes of rule and exclusion through which the ruling party has reappropriated and monopolised 'the land question'.[58]

Certainly, colonial history and aspects of present-day globalisation are key to any analysis of distortions in the distribution of land and assets in Zimbabwe. Yet it is precisely the need to address these issues *simultaneously* with other critical questions that marks this 'land revolution' as so full of contradictions and ambiguities (Raftopoulos, this volume; Worby, 2001). The core dilemmas revolve around several issues. On the one hand, since the start of the land invasions in 2000 and implementation of the 'fast-track' land reform programme, there has been an irreversible shift in the *de facto* distribution of land in Zimbabwe.[59] Such a profound alteration in the colonially-based racial patterns of land ownership, and an 'indigenisation' of the economy more generally, has been claimed by Zanu (PF) and its supporters as evidence of 'a land revolution of no small proportion; [which has] largely resolved and democratised the land in Zimbabwe, enhancing the economic (and agricultural) security of the country, far beyond the control of a white minority which hitherto accounted for 85 per cent of the overall economy. These profound changes are already evident in Zimbabwe, with most sectors of the economy now with a sizeable black presence'.[60] Far less of a claim can be made in relation to gender (Mgugu, 2001). At the same time, there has been a significant though far from consistent challenge to liberal notions of private property which, as modern

---

[58] In the 2002 presidential campaign, Zanu (PF) 'argued that it had now solved 'the land question' once and for all after acquiring more than 8 million hectares for redistribution' (Sachikonye 2002b:18). Continued forced acquisition of commercial farms well into 2003, despite official reassurances to the contrary, undermined such claims, while state versions of the 'fast-track' land reform programme – problematic in terms of its often opaque aims, violent and partisan methods and multiple and uneven effects – mask the simultaneous patterns of partisan dispossession being played out in the new politics of redistribution.

[59] By April 2003, over 11 million hectares of previously white-owned land had been seized, and only around 600 of the former 4,000-plus white commercial farmers were reported to still be on their farms. (See 'White farmers 'lawless': report', *News24* (SA), 6 April 2003). Official estimates claim 330,000 households have been settled on A1 (peasant) schemes, and around 55,000 households approved for A2 commercial farming schemes. (See 'Govt denies the existence of land audit report', *The Sunday Mirror*, 2 March 2003.) Yet other reports, official and independent, pointed to extremely low uptake of plots by the start of the 2002/3 rainy season, in some cases less than 50% even in some of the best agro-ecological regions. (See 'Half of confiscated land in Zimbabwe lies fallow', *The Mail and Guardian* (SA), 22 October 2002.)

[60] Excerpted from piece in Zimbabwe's *The Mirror*, 22 September 2002 – entitled 'The Zimbabwean Crisis: Myths and Realities' – by 'The Scrutator' (Ibbo Mandaza). Interestingly, neither A1 nor A2 resettled farmers have been given title deeds or leases to formalise their new occupancy or ownership, making the state the effective landlord of most of the 11 million hectares acquired since 2000. (See 'Perence Shiri denied bid to export', *The Zimbabwe Independent*, 11 April 2003.)

history amply demonstrates, is replete with 'constitutive exclusions'.[61] This has generated a partial revaluing of land, including prime agricultural land, on grounds other than principally economic.

On the other hand, a number of inter-related practices and effects of the 'fast-track' process raise serious doubts concerning the accuracy or validity of the above claims. Firstly, regarding 'resolving and democratising' land issues, one might consider the following developments since 2000: dispossession and impoverishment of hundreds of thousands of farm workers resulting from land invasions and forced evictions; explicit allocation of plots along partisan lines, largely excluding opposition supporters at all levels; sustained uncertainty about the legal status of tenure or title of the new occupiers and 'owners'; extensive and multiple land grabbing of prime farms by political, bureaucratic and business elites affiliated to the ruling party; and the construction of new regimes of 'private' land ownership and inequality along class, gender, ethnic and generational lines. While many landless households have accessed land, such trends point to a parallel, competing process of 'accumulation from above' through which a narrow class of politically-entrenched accumulators are positioning themselves for the future.

Secondly, with respect to claims of 'enhancing Zimbabwe's economic and agricultural security', the following needs to be considered: there has been a near-collapse of large-scale commercial agriculture, precipitating major losses in export earnings and widespread unemployment in both rural and urban sectors and contributing to a dire national food security situation;[62] the anticipated stimulation of successful small- and medium-scale capitalist farming has not materialised due to government's failure to deliver critical farm inputs, technical services, infrastructure and security to new settlers; environmental destruction has been widespread, threatening biodiversity in all tenure areas including national parks, undermining a once thriving eco-tourist industry; and all this, exacerbated by drought and ongoing conditions of political violence and instability, has contributed to a dramatic fall

---

[61] This refers broadly to social processes that naturalise the privileged entitlements of a dominant social category while excluding externalised 'Others'. See Moore (2003), and also footnote 69.

[62] This outcome contrasts sharply with the minimal losses in crop production predicted by Moyo (2000b) to result from the 1,471 farms (amounting to close to 4 million hectares) identified for compulsory acquisition by government in 1997 based on criteria enshrined in the Land Acquisition Act of 1992.

in GDP and rise in foreign debt, soaring inflation and collapsing currency, shortages of fuel, food and foreign currency, diminishing public sector capacity, rising rates of HIV/AIDS, and increased scales of poverty.[63]

Acknowledging such dilemmas and challenges demands moving beyond either vague or static notions of 'the land question' that seem to have dominated debates and practices around the politics of land in Zimbabwe for some time, towards a more transparent and plural set of inter-related *questions of land*.[64] This necessarily dislodges previous intellectual and political certainties about what constitutes the 'central' land issue, yet it does not imply political avoidance or paralysis. Rather it forces us to reconsider in dynamic and contingent ways the order of priority of land questions demanding attention in a given historical moment. To do so effectively requires empirical and analytical engagement with the specificity, diversity and complexity of such ongoing, inter-related questions of land as are being articulated in this volume and by emerging scholarship in and on Zimbabwe more generally.

Reconstructing the contours of nation and citizenship

Although Zimbabwe came into being largely through an armed nationalist struggle against a settler-colonial authority, what characterised its official brand of nationalism during its first years of independent existence was 'national development'.[65] This was a project, alongside the policy of reconciliation, geared towards unifying the newly independent but potentially fragmented nation.[66] It was also aimed at convincing a sceptical international community – given Mugabe's explicit Marxist predilections – of the sufficiently

---

[63] In the face of extensive reporting and analysis of these conditions (some previously cited), there have been frantic denials in the state-controlled media and intensive efforts by the regime to silence independent observers and mask or shift the blame for deteriorating circumstances. Sources are too numerous to cite here, however the chapters in this volume provide ample specific references in addition to constituting sources in their own right.

[64] Moyo's (1995) *The Land Question in Zimbabwe*, comprehensively covered the changing nature of the politics of land, and stressed the need for research on and across multiple empirical scales, moving analysis beyond the limitations of macro-level theoretical perspectives on land to include more local-level studies. Yet the very diversity that such a decentred approach was intended to highlight, and which a growing scholarship has subsequently begun to unfold, appears to have had little impact on the increasingly narrow, partisan terms under which 'the land question' – or 'the land revolution' – continues to be defined.

[65] At the same time, memorialising the nation in terms of the liberation struggle was never far from centre-stage (Werbner, 1998).

[66] In fact, much cruder methods of establishing 'unity' in the face of dissent were employed by the new government in Matabeleland and Midlands during the 1980s, through political and ethnic cleansing.

liberal-democratic (or at least modernising) credentials of the new government, in order to generate much-needed financial support. For Alexander (this volume), at this early stage nationalism 'was not to be about the popularly controlled restitution of the lost lands, but about modernisation and productivity, delivered through a highly centralised bureaucracy for the benefit of a disciplined citizenry.' Indeed such practices were remarkably consistent with the previous Rhodesian state's strategies of technical development and autocratic governance.[67]

At least on the surface, the post-independence national project corresponds with what Ignatieff (1994) defines as 'civic nationalism'. This is a form of broadly *inclusive* nationalism which 'maintains that the nation should be composed of all those – regardless of race, colour, creed, gender, language or ethnicity – who subscribe to the nation's political creed. This nationalism is called civic because it envisages the nation as a community of equal, rights-bearing citizens, united in patriotic attachment to a shared set of political practices and values. [It] is necessarily democratic since it vests sovereignty in all of the people.' (Ignatieff, 1994:3-4)[68] However, by the late 1990s Zimbabwe began to witness a shift away from this brand of nationalism. As previously noted, cracks in the façade of unity began to appear mid-decade with challenges from an increasingly autonomous and then left-leaning labour movement and a broadening civil society. As the regime systematically lost credibility and opposition to it multiplied and solidified (especially intensifying after 2000), and as the drive towards accumulation from above deepened, a new nationalism began to be articulated by the ruling party and its allies. This was a form of *exclusive* nationalism in which new, essentialised categories of authenticity, attachment, loyalty and entitlement began to be defined, producing what Ignatieff (1994) would characterize as 'ethnic nationalism'.[69]

This does not refer to any naturally based ethnicity but rather to a fictive one, whereby populations are 'ethnicised' (or essentialised) in particular ways in the processes and politics of nation-building,

---

[67] See Alexander (2000b) for a condensed summary of the continuities with these historical trends.
[68] However, even such inclusiveness is never total. As Ignatieff and others note (Dean, 2001; Worby, this volume), there are always exceptions; always those excluded from citizenship, varying across place and time. Yet the 'constitutive outside' is implicitly productive for the nation. As Alonso (1994:390) notes, '[t]he self-identity of nations has been secured partly through the construction of internal Others, whose markedness assures the existence of a national identity that, remaining invisible or unmarked, is successfully inscribed as the norm.'
[69] See Hammar, Rutherford, Raftopoulos, Worby (this volume) on the expanding modes of exclusion of selected categories of subjects from national belonging.

with specific institutional effects (Balibar, 1991). In relation to Zimbabwe's present crisis, this points to the construction of other more complex if narrower categories of identity defined in terms of political loyalty and war liberation credentials, rather than referring to the more familiar ethnic distinctions of, say, 'Shona' and 'Ndebele'.[70] Yet to sustain the fiction of such 'ethnic' difference on the one hand and of national unity on the other requires an unflinchingly authoritarian regime. Such a regime necessarily relies on and reproduces a powerful discursive link between the sentimentality of nationalism and the legitimation of violence: what Ignatieff refers to as 'blood and belonging' and Balibar as the 'bond of sacrifice'. Here, the equation combines the *political* belief in national sovereignty and each nation's 'right of self-determination'; the *cultural* principle that while all subjects have multiple identities, the nation 'provides them with their primary form of belonging'; and the *moral* ideal that 'nationalism is an ethic of heroic sacrifice, justifying the use of violence in the defence of one's nation against enemies, internal or external' (Ignatieff, 1994:3). In Zimbabwe, in recent years, these mutually reinforcing doctrines and ideals have invoked a language of nationalism that 'we' Zimbabweans cannot speak in any consensual way. Instead it has become a language that tends to 'speak us' through a range of coercive, discursive protocols, connotations, condensations and limits (Hall, 1988).

Claims to be defending national sovereignty have been especially central to Zanu (PF)'s discursive defence and masking of its exclusionary and violent partisan projects. Internationally, in a brilliantly-staged series of diplomatic 'victories' against Zimbabwe's 'imperialist enemies', Mugabe has personally deployed the notion of sovereignty in a populist rejection of 'Western' principles of democratic governance and neo-liberal economics, arguing instead for finding authentic 'African' solutions to African problems. Many outside the ruling party would and do welcome a challenge to the assumed universalism of liberal democracy, and support a critique of neo-liberal economics. And yet there is much to suggest that in the present context such tactics are geared less towards an incisive analysis of the pillars of Western hegemony than towards using such a critique both for its populist value and as a smokescreen for the regime's impunity with regard to democratic practices and international standards of justice and human rights.

---

[70] The fact that Zanu (PF)'s narrowing of nationalism did not or could not work through these former ethnic categories as it did in the mid-1980s, is in itself a fascinating shift, and at the same time testifies to the consciously and productively *non*-ethnic politics of the opposition.

At the same time, these very issues may well become the Achilles' heel of the MDC. At the point of its formation, the MDC talked of participatory democracy, a commitment to meeting basic needs, the equitable distribution of land, skills, capital and technology, gender equality, reducing dependence on foreign capital and reviving sovereignty, and an orientation towards working-class interests and the poor (Bond, 2001:33-35). Yet it appears to have shifted some way from this initial, broadly left orientation.[71] From various public policy statements made on its behalf, it would appear that the MDC supports a free-market approach, including reduced levels of taxation and 'fast-track privatisation', while at the same time mixing this with a strong social programme for free education, primary health care provision, higher minimum wage, a low-cost housing programme, and so on. There have also been some indications that the MDC plans to 'give tenure, freehold tenure, to everybody who holds tribal trust land leases, immediately we come to power.'[72] There are undoubtedly more varied perspectives than this within the MDC – as within Zanu (PF) – on tenure questions and on approaches to land reform more generally. However, given the political centrality of 'the land question', the MDC has some way to go in articulating policies on redistribution that will provide a convincing alternative to Zanu (PF)'s nationalist rhetoric on the 'land revolution'.

In the domestic arena, sovereignty has been turned inward and used to construct internal enemies accused of allying with neo-colonial and imperialist interests and hence being a threat to the final phase in the nationalist land revolution. In this 'war', the party leadership, loyalist war veterans and party youth militia (disparagingly called the 'Green Bombers' due to the clearly identifiable green uniforms they wear), are the legitimate promoters and defenders of liberation and hence are 'super-citizens'.[73] This

---

[71] According to Bond (2001:41), the MDC's appointment of Eddie Cross, a leading official of the Confederation of Zimbabwe Industries, as its economic secretary 'was the decisive signal that the core MDC leadership aimed to ally with big business.'

[72] Eddie Cross quoted in Bond (2001).

[73] In August 2002, state broadcasting began repeatedly playing a jingle, "Chave Chimurenga" (war has begun) as part of a wider Zanu (PF) mass advertising campaign called "Hondo ye Minda" (war in the fields). The Zimbabwe Union of Journalists criticised the portrayal of whites and other 'foreigners' as responsible for the problems and shortages in the country, cautioning that this was 'sowing the seeds of genocide'. (See 'Hearts, minds and a dancing skeleton', ZWNEWS, 8 December 2002.) The jingle was finally withdrawn in March 2003 and replaced with a new form of propaganda explaining the country's woes in terms of 'the fiction that Zimbabwe has been under seven years of "sanctions" ... stirred up by the British'. (See 'Propaganda shift', ZWNEWS, 13 March 2003.)

has been used to justify introducing draconian security legislation and the increased militarisation of state and parastatal institutions and everyday life. In a climate of deepening impunity this has generated a bizarre hierarchy of citizenship and security that elevates those directing the forces of brutality to the highest status beyond the reaches of the law, and those conducting acts of violence to the status of 'war heroes' (Hammar, this volume). By contrast, anyone seen as opposing the regime becomes a non-citizen, an enemy, subject to violent attack and beyond any protection by the state.[74] The notion of 'foreignness', and of constructing literal enemies out of so-called strangers and intruders, has been critical to the regime's strategic narrowing of national identity and belonging.[75]

What all this rests on in turn is the regime's iron grip on the 'origin story' of the nation; its monopolisation of history. Typically, this entails 'a certain version of the inevitable unfolding of critical events' sustained through a myth 'in which the imaginary singularity of national formations is constructed daily, by moving back from the present to the past.' (Balibar, 1991:86-7) For Raftopoulos (this volume), Zanu (PF)'s narrow narrative of the liberation struggle, its 'historical orthodoxy', has been aimed at 'closing down other perspectives on the struggle and other ways of imagining collectivities.' This has been attempted most overtly through efforts to control or destroy the independent media and to silence all alternative versions of history and the present, whether expressed in schools, in churches, on sports fields, in food and fuel queues, at trade union or rate payers' meetings, in opposition party offices or at foreign embassies. More ominously, the regime has established the so-called National Youth Service to produce a new generation of patriots – the infamous youth militia – whose education in a certain

---

[74] The secretary general of the MDC, Welshman Ncube, sees things as having become even more arbitrary: 'It doesn't matter who you are or where you are in this country, you can be beaten, gang raped and tortured any time, anywhere. All you have to do, the only crime you have to commit, is to come across members of Mugabe's militia.' See 'Zim officials would compromise task team', *The Cape Times* (SA), 11 April 2003.

[75] A new Citizenship Act, timed to pre-empt the presidential elections in March 2002, defined a range of new criteria for citizenship. Besides having broader implications for nationality, residence rights and basic security for hundreds of thousands of Zimbabweans, turning them overnight into 'foreigners', this deprived countless voters of their voting rights in those elections. In a move designed to revive and expand its waning support base, Zanu (PF) introduced a bill in February 2003 to amend the act, which if passed, would re-confer citizenship selectively on farm workers, miners and domestic workers born of parents from – or who migrated for such work to – SADC countries, but on no others currently affected by the new act.

version of nationalist history is critically linked to their training to torture and kill for the nation.[76]

Increasingly, this form of nationalism is being reinforced through a violent masculinity consistent with Mugabe's revived war idiom; through the promotion of a male warriorhood (despite the presence of a number of willing women 'warriors' among loyalist war veterans and the political elite) with precedents in Zimbabwe's anti-colonial struggle (Musengezi and McCartney, 2000). There is mounting evidence of the extensive use of rape and sexual abuse of women in youth militia 'training centres' around the country, as well as against individual women in both urban and rural areas accused of supporting the opposition.[77] There have also been growing reports of the rape of teenage boys in these camps and of adult male opposition activists more generally, as part of a campaign to brutally crush dissent[78] and to somehow feminise the MDC, not least through repeatedly associating it with the British government's so-called 'gay mafia'. Such violent links between gender, sexuality and nation have a long and disturbing history internationally (Mayer, 2000). At the same time there is an attempt by the regime to promote a particular type of black Pan-African femininity, such as through the Miss Malaika Contest, while simultaneously drawing on the Zanu (PF) Women's League to sustain its particular nationalist version of womanly virtue.

Despite the regime's best efforts to try and control the production of history (and the nation this defines) and to suffocate alternative knowledges and discourses, contested histories and versions of the nation *are* consistently being produced: by the MDC, students, women's groups, the media, independent war veterans' organisations, trade unionists, civic activists, intellectuals, artists and others.[79] Yet as Trouillot (1995:8) observes, '[n]owhere is history infinitely susceptible to invention'. 'What happened leaves traces, some of which are concrete – buildings, dead bodies, monuments, diaries,

---

[76] See 'I was ordered to kill my father', *The Sunday Independent* (SA), 9 March 2003. Although force and intimidation have been used widely in their 'recruitment', economic desperation compels others to join. In addition, the broad exclusion of youth from both domestic and public spheres of decision-making and accumulation – including access to land – would likely play a part in this process. See Ranger's (2002) discussion of the current youth mobilisation process and responses by parents and church groups to the 'twisting and breaking' of their children.

[77] See 'Mugabe's youth militias 'raping women held captive in camps'', *The Guardian* (UK), 18 March 2003; 'Rape as a political weapon', *The Mail and Guardian* (SA), 9 April 2003.

[78] See 'Savage beatings for Mugabe opponents', *The Sunday Times* (UK), 30 March 2003.

[79] See Ranger (2002) for especially rich examples of overt contestation around the presidential elections.

political boundaries – that limit the range and significance of any historical narrative. This is one of the many reasons that not any fiction can pass for history.' (ibid:29)

New modes of rule and reinventions of the state

Just as land and agrarian relations on the one hand, and the boundaries of nation and citizenship on the other, are being redefined and contested in the context of Zimbabwe's crisis, the contours of the state and formal and informal modes of rule are being reinvented on multiple levels. Such processes are crucial to the ruling party and its allies in asserting their hegemony, fulfilling their political aims, and reinforcing a new regime of accumulation. While equally significant for those opposing them with various counter-hegemonic strategies, the focus here is primarily on why, how, and with what effects Zanu (PF) has so intensively worked to remake the state and rule in recent years.[80]

As discussed earlier, challenges to Zanu (PF)'s hegemony increased exponentially towards the late 1990s. However, losing the constitutional vote just months before the parliamentary elections in June 2000 represented a threat too overwhelming to ignore: a threat not only to its authority and its persistent one-party state project, but to its control over the very terms and mechanisms of governance that could revive it and its fortunes. The challengers – including the National Constitutional Assembly and newly-formed MDC, both with their strong support initially in urban areas among a combination of workers, big business, civic organisations, students and intellectuals, and in rural areas among commercial farmers, farm workers, better-off small-scale farmers and public servants – would have to be stopped in their tracks. Loyalist war veterans would provide the vanguard for this new 'war',[81] soon to be bolstered by party youth militia and the national security services. It would take place literally and symbolically on the terrain of 'the lost lands'. But eventually the frontiers of the battle for political relegitimation and,

---

[80] Neither 'the state' nor Zanu (PF) are monolithic, seamless entities. Furthermore, in a Gramscian sense, processes of state formation are always incomplete and ongoing, and always include multiple and competing actors, institutions, discourses and material-symbolic practices. See Sylvester (1991, 1995) regarding the multiple 'regimes of truth' constituting Zimbabwe's earlier 'kaleidoscopic' state project.

[81] Such loyalty, however, is not permanently guaranteed (Hammar, this volume). Since 2000, numerous frustrations and demands have surfaced among war veterans that are unlikely to simply disappear. Tensions have erupted, sometimes violently, between veterans and state/party officials. See for example 'No pay for war vets', *Zimbabwe Standard*, 7 July 2002.

Rethinking Land, State and Nation

in a sense, recolonisation of the nation, would be expanded to include the full range of sites, institutions and practices of rule through which history could be remade, authority reasserted, assets controlled and redistributed, and subjects disciplined, including, perhaps most ominously, the sphere of everyday life.[82]

Alexander (this volume) speaks of the 'unravelling' by Zanu (PF) of the state, while simultaneously operating outside it through often fairly autonomous forces at district and provincial levels. Hammar (this volume) views the present 'context of chaotic, multi-layered transformation [including] the attacks on the rural local government system [as] contributing to the radical reconfiguration of who governs in which spaces, who is being governed, to what extent, and by what methods.' In summary, since 2000 there has been evidence of at least the following shifts in state practice and in various modes of rule: an effective merging of party and state; politicisation and cooptation of the army, police and intelligence agencies and to a lesser extent of traditional leaders, for partisan ends; de-professionalisation of the public service in general; undermining of the independence of the judiciary; normalisation of violence and the social production of terror against those considered outside of or dangerous to the new nation, while reinforcing a culture of impunity;[83] rejection of accountability to both domestic and international standards of justice and human rights;[84] severe constraints placed on the independent media and on civil society more generally through both legal and extra-legal means;[85] denial of democratic rights to the majority in terms of freedom of information, association and expression, the holding of free and fair elections, and equal protection under the law;[86] denial of

---

[82] Desperation among Zimbabwe's masses – one may now legitimately talk of 'starving' masses – has given the party-state a new form of control over everyday social life.

[83] In 2000 alone, over 18,000 incidents of violence and human rights violations associated with the June 2000 elections were recorded, 91 per cent of which were carried out by Zanu (PF) activists. See 'Amnesty clearly tailored for ZANU (PF) and its supporters', *The Daily News*, 17 October 2000. See also Amnesty International (2002), '*Zimbabwe: The Toll of Impunity*'. By March 2003, the Crisis in Zimbabwe Coalition had recorded "590 000 cases of serious human-rights violation...from arson to assault". See 'Zimbabwe running on empty', *The Toronto Star* (Canada), 9 March 2003. See also Reeler (2003).

[84] See 'Crimes against humanity and the transition', *The Zimbabwe Independent*, 28 March 2003.

[85] In addition there is almost total party control of the state media, while Zanu (PF) has attempted to occupy the space of civil society through, for example, establishing an alternative trade union federation as well as setting up other 'patriotic' cultural and social organizations.

[86] During almost half a century of anti-colonial struggle, 'democracy' was often used to justify claims to national sovereignty. As Bush and Szeftel (2002:5) suggest: 'If independence meant anything it meant the right of Africans to choose their own governments as free citizens'.

economic and social rights to many through the withholding of public and even private resources – including land and food – on partisan grounds; and support for or failure to intervene in attacks and disruptions by war veterans and youth militia of existing structures and processes of local governance.[87]

Rukuni and Jensen (this volume) mourn the loss of 'trust' in government, and the interruption of the liberal, modernisation project of previous decades. They see the 'fast-track' land reform programme as constituting a breakdown in 'rational' land tenure and use, and view institutional reform as critical to retrieving some sense of 'rational' governance.[88] Many in Zimbabwe and abroad feel similarly that while radical land reform is necessary, the methods used in the 'fast-track' programme have been erratic, inconsistent, and destructive to the economy and the well-being of millions of citizens. Others, however, remind us to pay attention to both historical and contemporary evidence, in a variety of contexts, of liberalism's 'illiberal' other sides (Dean, 2001).[89] In Zimbabwe's colonial and postcolonial past, self-declared liberal forms of rule and rational modernising programmes reinforced highly undemocratic practices and produced some extremely brutal forms of exclusion and dispossession. This was epitomised by the colonial Native Land Husbandry Act of 1951, and after independence by certain forms of resettlement and villagisation, as well as by violent state evictions of 'squatters', some of it done in the name of 'modern' forms of conservation, not least eco-tourism.[90]

In the meantime, the present crisis in Zimbabwe has reinforced an authoritarian and increasingly repressive rather than democratic mode of rule, much in keeping with Scott's (1998:7) pessimistic conclusion about 'the state' as 'the vexed institution that is the ground of both our freedoms and our unfreedoms.' He argues that 'certain kinds of states, driven by utopian plans and an authoritarian disregard for the values, desires, and objections of their subjects, are indeed a mortal threat to human well-being.' Yet despite the

---

[87] The significance for Zanu (PF) of regaining control over the mechanisms of governance in its rural constituencies was keenly demonstrated by the intensity of the battle over rural local government in the September 2002 council elections (Hammar, this volume). See, for example, 'MDC barred', *The Zimbabwe Standard*, 8 September 2002; 'Tongogara's brother held hostage in Shurugwi', *The Daily News*, 12 September 2002; 'Mugabe 'thugs' kidnap election candidates', *The Times* (UK), 13 September 2002.

[88] See Mouffe's (1995) critique of rational-liberal notions of politics as 'the calculus of interests' of rational actors whereby complex differences and antagonisms can be neutralised through consensus. She argues for the overt recognition of plurality and difference as critical to the democratic process. See also footnote 47.

[89] See footnote 69.

[90] See for example Alexander and McGregor (2000) and Hammar (2001).

Rethinking Land, State and Nation

systematic reduction of political space for opposition in Zimbabwe, the 'constitutive outside' of the current regime has remained diverse, well organised and active, which bodes well for Zimbabwe's longer-term democratic prospects. Officially, opposition has been resolutely non-violent, with the MDC strategically sustaining a clear distinction between itself and Zanu (PF) precisely on these grounds. The evidence confirms that the vast majority of violent acts and human rights abuses have been perpetrated by Zanu (PF) and its supporters (Reeler, 2003). On the other hand, there are also localised examples of both spontaneous and organised forms of violence from the opposition,[91] although only to the extent of making absurd Mugabe's accusations of the MDC spreading 'violence and terror' in the country.[92] Nonetheless there are concerns as to the degree to which violence from all sides might intensify before it subsides.[93] The increased role of state security forces in much of the violence so far compounds the problem in the present, while equally raising critical questions for any post-crisis government in the future.

The chapters

In his chapter, **Eric Worby** focuses on the apparent displacement of the previous decades' declared project of modernity and national development by the current focus on sovereignty and security. He notes that the increasingly unpredictable, unaccountable and often violent exercise of power now characterising statecraft in Zimbabwe has provoked a deeply anxious postcolonial question as to whether this represents a society in retreat from modernity. Worby observes that President Mugabe and his supporters constantly employ both the rituals and rhetoric of 'being modern' (not necessarily in its liberal, 'white' or Western version), while at other times invoking notions of tradition and indigenous authenticity to legitimise the project of finally resolving the question of national sovereignty. This is a sovereignty which Mugabe claims is threatened by a racially-grounded imperialism in the guise of Western, neo-liberal orthodoxy, and which he has been successful in exporting to both a continental and diasporic Pan-Africanist constituency. Yet as Worby argues, this 'sovereignty is revealed to be less about who is included in the

---

[91] See for example 'Backlash against Zanu PF youth militia', *IRIN* (UN), 18 December 2002. Also, Alexander and McGregor (2001).
[92] See 'Zimbabwe's Mugabe accuses west of funding violence, terrorism', *AFP*, 21 March 2003.
[93] Morrison et al, 'Time for Concerted International Action on Zimbabwe', *Africa Notes*, No. 2, August 2001.

protections of citizenship, and more about *who decides* who is included, and who excluded, from the protective (or violent) embrace of the law.' It is these strategies of exception and exclusion, he suggests, that constitute rather than undermine the rule of law, and that assert rather than abandon the project of political modernity.

Through an historical review of post-independence 'squatting' and resettlement in Zimbabwe, **Jocelyn Alexander** examines the changing relationships between contested control over land and land use, processes of state-making, definitions of nationalism, and constructions of citizenship. She contrasts earlier precedents in land occupation set immediately after independence and continuing through the 1980s and 1990s, with the current violent phase of land occupation begun in early 2000. The state's oscillating discourse on and response to occupations and occupiers over the past two decades have accompanied changing trends in official policy towards land reform and resettlement more generally. This moved from an initial pragmatic socialism immediately after independence, to a technocratic, modernising project of development during the 1980s, followed by a liberal period in the 1990s associated with structural adjustment but also responding to a growing black indigenisation lobby, and finally towards authoritarian nationalism accompanied by anti-colonial rhetoric since 2000. While both the earlier and current phases of land occupation implied a radical reconstruction of the state and a redefinition of nationalism, they have notably differed, denoting critical shifts in the stakes, terms and alliances marking Zimbabwe's unfolding politics of land.

Amanda Hammar explores the processes and politics of the recent violent disruptions of rural local government by a combination of war veterans, youth militia, ruling party politicians and party-allied central government bureaucrats. Noting that there have long been contradictions, conflicts and contestations within the sphere of local government, she questions the liberal-democratic assumptions that cast the period 'before the crisis' as some kind of mythical time of 'normal government'. However, Hammar notes that the scale, terms and intensity of the present disruptions denote an era of 'altering politics and practices of government and rule' requiring close attention. Yet she also argues that the sphere of local government isn't merely a frontier of national processes of state making, within which war veterans are playing a critical vanguard role. Rural local government has its own web of localised and translocal political, economic and social dynamics that, in combination with war veterans' own individual and collective projects, play out in historically and spatially specific ways. This equally needs to be considered when analysing how state and rule are being reshaped and citizens remade in the present conjuncture.

Nelson Marongwe notes at the outset that conflicts over land and natural resources in Zimbabwe are widely spread across all tenure regimes including state lands, communal and resettlement areas, and large-scale commercial farms. However, he specifically focuses on the results of unique empirical research – conducted under very difficult circumstances – on the post-February 2000 land occupations on mainly white-owned commercial farms. He compares these occupations and occupiers with an earlier series of land invasions in 1998, in terms of their respective historical, social, political and economic contexts. His work highlights important dimensions to the occupations, including the motives of occupiers themselves and the influence of outside interests, forms of mobilisation, selection of farms for occupation, and types and scale of occupation. He concludes that whereas in 1998 they were largely community-led actions borne out of frustration with the slow pace of government land reform, the occupations of 2000/1 were primarily led and organised by militant war veterans and had an explicitly party-political dimension linked initially to Zanu (PF)'s 2000 election campaign strategy. In addition, the chapter raises key questions that demystify simplistic representations of the latest land invasions as merely generated by the ruling party or through the force of war veterans. Marongwe's evidence points to a range of additional local factors and actors that imply a more complex and grounded interpretation of these occupations.

Blair Rutherford focuses on the discursive distortions traditionally associated with farm workers, challenging us to move beyond the limited 'prototypical discourses' of both radical nationalists and liberal democrats. Until very recently, both 'sides' have imagined farm workers in terms of their 'belonging to the farm(er)', in so doing confining their spatial and political mobility and restricting their options for pragmatic action. Historically, farm workers have been defined almost entirely through their place of work rather than by the nature of their work or their multiple subjectivities and agency. Having been co-opted into the national and individual projects of European farmers over time, Rutherford argues, farm workers did not easily fit into the postcolonial nation and as such were largely excluded from the national 'scale-making' project of development and its associated institutional arrangements. This has had devastating consequences for farm workers in the context of the present crisis, during which they have been, in large numbers and often violently, displaced by and excluded from the land resettlement process. Rutherford argues for a different kind of analysis of farm workers that acknowledges and responds to their own multiple life projects through inclusive practices of citizenship, access to both jobs and land, and appropriate institutional support.

In his chapter, **Brian Raftopoulos** focuses on the ways in which the crisis in Zimbabwe has been articulated by the ruling party on the terrain of 'the land question', based on a selective rendition of the legacy of the problem and of the history of the liberation struggle more broadly. This has shut down the space for other perspectives on the struggle or 'other ways of imagining collectivities' – not least the nation itself – and has been used to constitute an increasingly authoritarian nationalism. This has been played out domestically through an alliance between Zanu (PF) and a section of the war veterans movement, and both nationally and abroad through an ever-expanding politics of anti-colonial struggle. A central part of this process and politics has been a growing exclusivity around the concept of citizenship, reformulated not only around essentialised categories of race but also through the ruling party's increasing attacks on foreign residents, mainly farm workers. This strategy has been carried out using violence against a wide array of groups considered to be outside the national project. It rests, Raftopoulos argues, on a false yet 'devastating rupture' within contemporary political discourse, between political rights on the one hand and economic redistribution on the other.

The chapter by **Mandivamba Rukuni** and **Stig Jensen** is founded on a question about the long-term effects of the land occupations and 'fast-track' resettlement programme, which they view as disrupting the project of agricultural modernisation in Zimbabwe and profoundly altering the agrarian structure. In response to this trend, they focus on a predominantly rational-liberal vision of a post-crisis future, paying particular attention to the links between land tenure security and the promotion and protection of democracy and good governance. They argue that any successful land reform programme is dependent on establishing political stability, a sound economic base, relations of trust, and sufficient institutional capacity to undertake the reforms. Yet the present political, economic, social and institutional landscape in Zimbabwe has become increasingly complex and 'messy', with an expanding diversity of struggles over land between a variety of actors at different levels. All these changes, they suggest, will require a rethinking of former certainties; a re-examination of previous 'neat' categories, boundaries and relationships, not least those defining citizens and subjects.

In the final chapter, **Ben Cousins** examines the significance and effects of Zimbabwe's crisis in relation to a problem confronting Southern Africa more generally, namely the failure of post-liberation 'development democracies' to address the structural, social and political legacies of colonial and apartheid rule. Questions of land are deeply implicated in such failures. This makes 'land' a powerful symbol of incomplete transformation in broader social terms, and a critical and deeply contested political resource for a range of actors engaged in competing and often partisan projects, as in Zimbabwe. Drawing on experiences of both land reform and democratisation in the region – and with a special focus on South Africa – Cousins identifies two kinds of responses to this broad crisis that are underscored by opposing notions of property rights: on the one hand, a reassertion of Western, liberal-democratic values that emphasise the protection of private property under the rubric of 'good governance' and effective neo-liberal economic management; and on the other, the invocation of identity politics, authoritarian nationalism and a return to 'African traditional governance' accompanying calls for radical land redistribution, but which sometimes mask corrupt and exclusionary practices. Neither of these polarized positions nor their various hybrid versions, argues Cousins, respond adequately to the crisis of developmental democracy in the region. Instead, alternatives are sought that will help deepen democracy, reduce poverty, and undermine the foundations of structural inequality. Acknowledging the need for radical, redistributive land reform, alongside comprehensive agrarian reform that would include a rethinking of the role of both state and non-state agencies, he nonetheless insists on an equal recognition of the 'unfinished emancipatory process' of democratisation, and the need for open debate on the critical relationship between these simultaneous processes.

Mapping the terrain of unfinished business

As argued at the start of this chapter, investigating the evolving pattern of 'simultaneous, incomplete and competing projects of transformation, legitimation and resistance' currently underway in Zimbabwe – many of which are explicitly represented as 'unfinished business' by their protagonists – is critical to our understanding of the complexity and persistence of the ongoing crisis. Such projects are necessarily dynamic, constantly articulating with one another in an extremely volatile environment, and yet they are not infinitely open-ended. It is possible to trace, at least for a given period, certain 'nodal points' around which particular hegemonic or counter-hegemonic strategies are deployed (Jones III and Moss, 1995). While much of the foregoing discussion and the various chapters in this book are concerned with such strategies or projects, this final section briefly summarises the most significant of these, most though not all of which unavoidably relate to Zanu (PF).

The 'land revolution' and redistribution

In the postcolonial period, the unresolved (yet circumscribed) 'land question' has remained a persistent reminder of 'unfinished business' and been easily mobilised by Zanu (PF) as a political resource. The present project of 'land revolution', as articulated by the regime, aims at 'finally' reversing colonial land appropriations and inequalities, and redistributing land and other assets to their rightful, indigenous owners. However, this historically-embedded project has been discursively monopolised and over-simplified by the ruling party, serving as a disciplinary and exclusionary device in at least the following ways: as a constant reminder of which parties and individuals carry the mantle of liberation legitimacy; as an expression of anti-imperialist protest and global de-linking; as a means of marginalising opposition groups while masking its own failures and inconsistencies; in demarcating those with a 'legitimate' claim to land according to race, ancestral origin and political authenticity; and in the persistent location of the 'urban' as the space of the 'unrooted' and 'totemless' with lesser claims to the liberation legacy and to the revered nationalist appellation '*mwana wevhu*'.[94] On the other hand, the opposition has been slow to find its footing within the discourse of *radical* land redistribution, remaining largely within a liberal if not neo-liberal framework of private property and market-driven reform.

The new nation, sovereignty and modernity

Linked to the above is the ongoing project of completing the creation of the nation; of 'finally resolving the question of national sovereignty' on terms that explicitly reflect a process of 'writing back' against colonialism (Achebe, 2001), despite over twenty years of independence. The shift from national development to a revived

---

[94] In the terms set out by Mamdani (1996), even though the postcolonial structures have been deracialised, the question of citizenship remains contentious.

nationalist revolution, manifested and managed through an ever-deepening authoritarianism, has involved a radical reconfiguration of the terms of national belonging and access to land, security and citizenship. (This has been based primarily on an essentialised narrowing of the principles of inclusion, reversing the earlier rhetoric of reconciliation.) In parallel, there have been new challenges and tensions around competing projects of modernity. Moving away from its 1990s (neo)liberal inclinations, Zanu (PF) has reinvented itself in terms of a Pan-Africanist agenda, making a claim to an alternative political modernity that counters the West's civilising mission and its imposition of 'civilised governance'. Within this project, race is used by Mugabe to dislodge 'whites' as the symbol and vanguard of a colonially imposed modernity – whereby 'white' is automatically conflated with 'colonial' – creating space for an indigenous modernity to be asserted at any cost (Worby, this volume). By contrast, the opposition has taken on board the unfinished project of 'development'. Here, human rights discourses rub shoulders, not always comfortably, with the language of modernisation and the broader liberal-democratic project that holds the protection of private property as sacrosanct.

Hegemony, the state, and the terms of rule

The process of state making is an ongoing, always-unfinished project. The sometimes explicit, sometimes implicit one-party state project has been a constant feature of this process, underpinned by recurring discourses of national sovereignty and sustaining the nationalist revolution. At independence there were efforts to transform the inherited colonial state through key institutional, policy and legislative changes that secured the ruling party's hegemony for at least the first decade. Subsequently, in the face of waning legitimacy, there has been a deepening of authoritarian practices and a reterritorialisation of the country through violence. Critically, the 'no' vote in the February 2000 referendum represented a challenge to Zanu (PF) specifically in *constitutional* terms, with profound implications for the nature of the state and the framework and practices of rule. The regime's efforts since then have been directed intensively at redefining and reoccupying the structures of governance at all levels, using a mix of liberal and illiberal moves.

A new regime of accumulation

Alongside if not directly underpinning the projects of land redistribution, nation building and state formation, is a project aimed at putting in place a new regime of accumulation in Zimbabwe. The central location of this project is the land, but its ambitions extend into other areas of the economy such as mining, finance, telecommunications, and other sections of industry. The tensions that have begun to emerge in Zanu (PF) around the issue of Mugabe's succession revolve around the problem of putting in place a more 'acceptable' regime of accumulation driven by the new accumulators. Among other things this will imply a re-engagement with the international community around a new property rights regime. For some reformist intellectuals close to Zanu (PF), the current crisis in Zimbabwe is viewed as a kind of clearing operation making way for a renewed modernisation project around an emerging 'anchor class'.[95] However, it is clear that the economic strategies adopted so far have reached a cul-de-sac. It is around a way out of this that the battles within Zanu (PF) are likely to rage for the foreseeable future.

Resistance and radical democracy

Within all of the above broad projects and processes, there are various smaller supporting projects, as well as many counter-hegemonic projects that have not been mentioned. These include ongoing efforts towards constitutional change, challenging and strengthening democratic electoral processes, introducing a gendered perspective into the land reform process, formulating alternative strategies for economic recovery, and intensifying the search for nonviolent means of resolving the political crisis. At the heart of these multiple projects of resistance and revisioning must surely be a project of radical democracy in which 'multiplicity and otherness' are recognized and accepted, and 'diversity and dissensus' valorised, 'recognizing in them the very condition of possibility of a striving democratic life' (Mouffe, 1995:265).

Conclusion

The chapters in this book take up and expand upon various aspects of the inter-linking projects and polarities characterising Zimbabwe's current crisis, drawing on different empirical contexts and theoretical frameworks. At the same time, there are several common strands

---

[95] There is an interesting similarity between this position and that taken by the radical dependency theorists in the Kenya Debate of the 80s. As Gavin Kitching (1985) noted at the time, 'such groups are perfectly willing to make use of anti-imperialist slogans provided that they co-exist with a realisation (explicit or implicit) that no total alternative to the existing system is possible, that is, provided that anti-imperialism is understood as winning more space for local capitalists in national and international markets...'

that emerge out of their combined analyses. Firstly, there is a clear consensus that while land rights and redistribution are fundamental to the lives of most Zimbabweans, the Zimbabwe crisis is by no means simply a land crisis.[96] Clearly, it involves a complex set of historically specific, inter-related and mutually reinforcing crises that need to be unpacked and analysed in relation to one another. In this sense, the book argues for the analytic *inseparability* of questions of land, state, nation and citizenship. Secondly, in Zimbabwe's current politics of crisis, new configurations of alliance and animosity are emerging that simultaneously disrupt old essentialisms and construct new ones. The book argues that it is critical to deconstruct and examine these new relations and their dynamics of exclusion and inclusion in order to understand changing forms of rule and practices of government within the postcolonial state, and the shifting contours of nation and citizenship produced by such states. Such 'ways of seeing' become even more critical as Zimbabwe moves towards the complex challenges and uncertainties of a post-Mugabe era.

---

[96] This view was echoed by South African Archbishop Ndungane on a mediation mission to Zimbabwe in early 2003 (with the blessing of both countries' presidents). He asserted in his press statement on 13 March 2003 that 'the Zimbabwe crisis involves more than a land crisis' and that its resolution equally requires 'the restoration of political normality, a culture of human rights, hunger relief and political legitimacy.'

References

Achebe, Chinua, 2003 (2001). 'The Empire Fights Back'. In Achebe, Chinua, *Home and Exile*. Edinburgh: Canongate, pp. 37-72.

Alexander, Jocelyn, 2001a. 'Chiefs and the State in Independent Zimbabwe'. Paper presented to Conference on Chieftancy in Africa, St Anthony's College, Oxford, 9 June 2001.

Alexander, Jocelyn, 2001b. 'The Enduring Appeal of 'Technical Development' in Zimbabwe's Agrarian Reform'. In T.A.S. Bowyer-Bower and Colin Stoneman (eds), *Land Reform in Zimbabwe: Constraints and Prospects*. Aldershot: Ashgate, pp. 133-143.

Alexander, Jocelyn, and JoAnn McGregor, 2001. 'Elections, Land and the Politics of Opposition in Matabeleland'. *Journal of Agrarian Change*, Vol. 1, No. 4, pp. 510-533.

Alexander, Jocelyn, and JoAnn McGregor, 2000. 'Wildlife and Politics: CAMPFIRE in Zimbabwe'. *Development and Change*, 31 (3), 605-627.

Alexander, Jocelyn, and Joanne McGregor, 1997. 'Modernity and Ethnicity in a Frontier Society: Understanding Difference in Northwestern Zimbabwe'. *Journal of Southern African Studies*, Vol. 23, No. 2, pp.187-201.

Alexander, Jocelyn, JoAnn McGregor and Terence Ranger, 2000. *Violence and Memory: One Hundred Years in the 'Dark Forests' of Matabeleland*. Oxford: James Currey.

Alonso, Ana Maria, 1994. 'The Politics of Space, Time, Substance: State Formation, Nationalism, and Ethnicity'. *Annual Review of Anthropology*, Vol. 23, pp. 379-405.

Andersson, Jens A., 2001. 'Re-interpreting the Discourse on the Land: Urban Migrants, Rural Livelihoods and the Value of Land'. Paper presented at Conference on 'Rethinking Land, State and Citizenship through the Zimbabwe Crisis', Centre for Development Research, Copenhagen, 4-5 September 2001.

Auret, Diana, 1990. *A Decade of Development. Zimbabwe 1980-1990*. Gweru: Mambo Press, with The Catholic Commission for Justice and Peace in Zimbabwe.

Balibar, Etienne, 1991. 'The Nation Form: History and Ideology'. In Etienne Balibar and Immanuel Wallerstein, *Race, Nation and Class. Ambiguous Identities*. London and New York: Verso, pp. 86-106

Baregu, M., 2001. 'The Third Chimurenga: Human and Social Rights Confront Individual and Property Rights in Zimbabwe'.

Paper presented at Conference on 'Rethinking Land, State and Citizenship through the Zimbabwe Crisis', Centre for Development Research, Copenhagen, 4-5 September 2001.

Batezat, Eleanor, and Margaret Mwalo, 1989. *Women in Zimbabwe*. Harare: SAPES.

Berman, Bruce J., 1998. 'Ethnicity, Patronage and the African State: The Politics of Uncivil Nationalism'. *African Affairs*, Vol. 97, pp. 305-341.

Bernstein, Henry, and Philip Woodhouse, 2001. 'Telling environmental change like it is: Reflections on a study in Sub-Saharan Africa'. *Journal of Agrarian Change*, Vol. 1, No. 2, pp. 283-324

Bush, Ray, and Morris Szeftel, 2002. 'Sovereignty, Democracy and Zimbabwe's Tragedy'. *Review of African Political Economy*, No. 19, pp. 5-12.

Chimhowu, Admos Osmund, 2002. 'Extending the Grain Basket to the Margins: Spontaneous Land Resettlement and Changing Livelihoods in the Hurungwe District, Zimbabwe'. *Journal of Southern African Studies*, Vol. 28, No. 3, pp. 551-573.

Cliffe, Lionel, 2000. 'The Politics of Land Reform in Zimbabwe'. In T.A.S. Bowyer-Bower and Colin Stoneman (eds), *Land Reform in Zimbabwe: Constraints and Prospects*. Aldershot: Ashgate, pp. 35-46.

Dean, Mitchell, 2001. '"Demonic Societies": Liberalism, Biopolitics, and Sovereignty'. In Hansen and Stepputat (eds), *States of Imagination. Ethnographic Explorations of the Postcolonial State*. Durham and London: Duke University Press. pp. 45-64.

Ellis, F., 2000. *Rural Livelihoods and Diversity in Developing Countries*. Oxford: Oxford University Press.

Gaidzanwa, Rudo, 1995. 'Land and the Economic Empowerment of Women: A Gendered Perspective'. *Southern African Feminist Review (SAFERE)*, Vol. 1, No. 1, pp. 1-12.

Hall, Stuart, 1980. 'Race, Articulation and Societies Structured in Dominance.' In UNESCO, *Sociological Theories: Race and Colonialism*. Paris: UNESCO.

Hall, Stuart, 1988. 'The Toad in the Garden: Thatcherism among the theorists.' In Cary Nelson and Lawrence Grossberg (eds), *Marxism and the Interpretation of Culture*. Basingstoke: Macmillan.

Hammar, Amanda, 2001. '"The Day of Burning": Eviction and Reinvention in the Margins of Northwest Zimbabwe'. *Journal of Agrarian Change*, Vol. 1, No. 4, pp. 550-574.

Hellum, Anne, and Bill Derman, 2001. 'Land Reform and Human Rights in Contemporary Zimbabwe: Balancing Individual Social Justice through an Integrated Human Rights Framework'. Paper presented at Conference on 'Rethinking Land, State and Citizenship through the Zimbabwe Crisis', Centre for Development Research, Copenhagen, 4-5 September 2001.

Ignatieff, Michael, 1994. *Blood and Belonging. Journeys into the New Nationalism.* London: Vintage.

Johnston, R.J., Derek Gregory, Geraldine Pratt and Michael Watts (eds), 2000. *The Dictionary of Human Geography.* Fourth Edition. Oxford: Blackwell.

Jones III, John Paul, and Pamela Moss, 1995. 'Guest Editorial: Democracy, Identity, Space'. *Environment and Planning D: Society and Space*, Vol. 13, No. 3, pp. 253-257.

Kinsey, Bill, 1999. 'Land Reform, Growth and Equity: Emerging Evidence from Zimbabwe's Resettlement Programme'. *Journal of Southern African Studies*, Vol. 25, No. 2, pp.173-196.

Kitching, Gavin, 1985. 'Politics, Method and Evidence in the 'Kenya Debate''. In Henry Bernstein and Bonnie Cambell (eds), *Contradictions of Accumulation in Africa: Studies in Economy and State.* London: Sage Publications.

Makumbe, John Mw., 1998. *Democracy and Development in Zimbabwe: Constraints of Decentralisation.* Harare: SAPES.

Mamdani, Mahmood, 1996. *Citizen and Subject: Contemporary Africa and the Legacy of Late Colonialism.* New Jersey: Princeton University Press.

Marongwe, Nelson, 1999. *Civil Society's Perspective on Land Reforms in Zimbabwe. Some key suggestions from a survey.* Harare: ZERO.

Marongwe, Nelson, 2002. *Conflicts Over Land and other Natural Resources in Zimbabwe.* Harare: ZERO.

Matondi, Prosper Bvumiranayi, 2001. 'The Struggle for Access to Land and Water Resources in Zimbabwe. The Case of Shamva'. Unpublished doctoral thesis. Swedish University of Agricultural Sciences, Uppsala 2001.

Mayer, Tamar, 2000. 'Gender Ironies of Nationalism. Setting the Stage'. In Tamar Mayer (ed.), *Gender Ironies of Nationalism. Sexing the Nation.* London and New York: Routledge, pp. 1-22.

Mbiba, Beacon, 2001. 'Contemporary Land Invasions and the Urban Land Question in Southern Africa: With Special Reference to

Zimbabwe'. Paper presented at Conference on 'Rethinking Land, State and Citizenship through the Zimbabwe Crisis', Centre for Development Research, Copenhagen, 4-5 September 2001.

McGregor, JoAnn, 2002. 'The Politics of Disruption: War Veterans and the Local State in Zimbabwe'. *African Affairs* (2002), Vol. 101, pp. 9-37.

Mgugu, Abby Taka, 2001. 'Women, the Voiceless and the Landless. Where To?' Paper presented at Conference on 'Rethinking Land, State and Citizenship through the Zimbabwe Crisis', Centre for Development Research, Copenhagen, 4-5 September 2001.

Moore, David, 2001. 'Is the Land the Economy and the Economy the Land? Primitive Accumulation in Zimbabwe'. *Journal of Contemporary African Studies*, Vol. 19, No. 2, pp. 253-266.

Moore, Donald S., 2000. 'The crucible of cultural politics: reworking "development" in Zimbabwe's eastern highlands'. *American Ethnologist*, Vol. 26, No. 3, pp. 654-689.

Moore, Donald S., 2003. 'Beyond Blackmail: Multivalent Modernities and the Cultural Politics of Development in India'. Forthcoming in K. Sivaramakrishnan and Arun Agrawal (eds), *Regional Modernities in South Asia*. Delhi: Oxford University Press and Stanford, CA: Stanford University Press.

Mouffe, Chantal, 1995. 'Post-Marxism: democracy and identity'. *Environment and Planning D: Society and Space*, Vol. 13, pp. 259-265.

Moyo, Sam, 1995. *The Land Question in Zimbabwe*. Harare: SAPES.

Moyo, Sam, 1999. *Land and Democracy in Zimbabwe*. SAPES Trust Monograph Series No. 7. Harare: SAPES.

Moyo, Sam, 2000a. *Land Reform Under Structural Adjustment in Zimbabwe. Land Use Changes in the Mashonaland Provinces*. Uppsala: Nordiska Afrikainstitutet.

Moyo, Sam, 2000b. 'The Political Economy of Land Acquisition and Redistribution in Zimbabwe, 1990-1999'. *Journal of Southern African Studies*, Vol. 26, No. 1, pp. 5-28.

Moyo, Sam, 2001. 'The Land Occupation Movement and Democratisation in Zimbabwe: Contradictions of Neoliberalism'. *Millenium: Journal of International Studies*. Vol. 30, No. 2, pp. 311-330.

Mumbengegwi, Clever, 1987. 'Continuity and Change in Agricultural Policy'. In Ibbo Mandaza (ed.), *Zimbabwe: The Political Economy of Transition 1980-1986*. Dakar: CODESRIA.

Musengezi, Chiedza and Irene McCartney (eds), 2000. *Women of Resilience. The Voices of Women Ex-Combatants*. Harare: Zimbabwe Women Writers.

Nyambara, Pius, 2001. 'The Closing Frontier: Agrarian Change, Immigrants and the 'Squatter Menace' in Gokwe, 1980-1990s'. *Journal of Agrarian Change*, Vol. 1, No. 4, pp. 534-549.

Palmer, Robin, 1977. *Land and Racial Domination in Rhodesia*. London: Heinemann.

Raftopoulos, Brian, 2001. 'The Labour Movement and the Emergence of Opposition Politics in Zimbabwe'. In Brian Raftopoulos and Lloyd Sachikonye (eds), *Striking Back: The Labour Movement and the Post-Colonial State in Zimbabwe 1980-2000*. Harare: Weaver Press, pp. 1-24.

Raftopolulos, Brian, 2002. 'Briefing: Zimbabwe's 2002 Presidential Elections'. *African Affairs*, Vol. 101, pp. 413-426.

Raftopoulos, Brian, and Lloyd Sachikonye (eds), 2001. *Striking Back. The Labour Movement and the Post-Colonial State in Zimbabwe 1980-2000*. Harare: Weaver Press.

Ranger, Terence, 1999. *Voices from the Rocks. Nature, Culture and History in the Matopos Hills of Zimbabwe*. Oxford: James Currey, Harare: Baobab, Bloomington and Indianapolis: Indiana University Press

Ranger, Terence, 2002. 'The Zimbabwe Elections: A Personal Experience'. Paper presented at the Oxford Centre for Mission Studies, 19 March 2002.

Reeler, Anthony P., 2003. 'Who should be sanctioned?' Paper prepared for The International Rehabilitation Council for Torture Victims.

Sachikonye, Lloyd M., 2002a. 'From "Growth With Equity" to "Fast Track" Land Reform: The Discourse on Zimbabwe's Land Question'. Paper presented at Leeds University Conference on 'Peasants, Liberation and Socialism', Leeds, May 2002.

Sachikonye, Lloyd M., 2002b. 'Whither Zimbabwe? Crisis and Democratisation'. *Review of African Political Economy*, No. 91, pp. 13-20.

Saunders, Richard, 2000. *Never the Same Again. Zimbabwe's Growth Towards Democracy 1980-2000*. Harare: Open Society Institute of Southern Africa (OSISA)

Scott, James C., 1998. *Seeing Like a State. How Certain Schemes to Improve the Human Condition have Failed*. New Haven and London: Yale University Press.

Stoneman, Colin, 2002. 'Zimbabwe Land Policy and the Land Reform Programme'. In T.A.S. Bowyer-Bower and Colin Stoneman (eds), *Land Reform in Zimbabwe: Constraints and Prospects*. Aldershot: Ashgate.

Suzuki, Yuka, 2001. 'Drifting Rhinos and Fluid Properties: The Turn to Wildlife Production in Western Zimbabwe'. *Journal of Agrarian Change*, Vol. 1, No. 4, pp. 600-625.

Sylvester, Christine, 1995. '"Women" in Rural Producer Groups and the Diverse Politics of Truth in Zimbabwe'. In Marianne H. Marchand and Jane L. Parpart (eds), *Feminism/Postmodernism/Development*. London and New York: Routledge, pp. 179-203.

Sylvester, Christine, 1991. *Zimbabwe. The Terrain of Contradictory Development*. Boulder, San Francisco and Oxford: Westview Press.

Takavarasha, T., 1998. 'Land Policy and the Land Reform Programme'. Paper presented at conference on 'Land Reform in Zimbabwe: The Way Forward'. SOAS, London, March 1998.

Tandon, Yash, 2001. 'Trade Unions and Labour in the Agricultural Sector in Zimbabwe'. In Brian Raftopoulos and Lloyd Sachikonye (eds), *Striking Back: The Labour Movement and the Post-Colonial State in Zimbabwe 1980-2000*. Harare: Weaver Press.

Trouillot, Michel-Rolph, 1995. *Silencing the Past. Power and the Production of History*. Boston: Beacon Press.

Worby, Eric, 1994. 'Maps, Names and Ethnic Games: The Epistemology and Iconography of Colonial Power in Northwestern Zimbabwe'. *Journal of Southern African Studies*, Vol. 20, No. 3, pp. 371-392.

Worby, Eric, 2001. 'A Redivided Land? New Agrarian Conflicts and Questions in Zimbabwe'. *Journal of Southern African Studies*, Vol. 23, No. 2, pp. 475-509.

Zeilig, Leo, 2002. 'Crisis in Zimbabwe'. *International Socialism*, Spring 2002, pp. 75-96.

Chapter 2

The End of Modernity in Zimbabwe?

Passages from Development to Sovereignty[1]

Eric Worby

The sovereign is the surplus of power that serves to resolve or defer the crisis of modernity. (Hardt and Negri, 2000: 325)

The sovereign is the point of indistinction between violence and law; the threshold over which violence passes into law, and law passes over into violence (Agamben, 1998: 32).

We agree to kill anyone who votes for MDC...I am the Minister of Defense. For all who vote for MDC, there will be war. There will be a machine that will detect who you voted for.[2] (Moven Mahachi, 4 June, 2000)

Prologue: **The sovereign and the banned**

On 23 July 2002, the ceremonial procession of President Robert Mugabe filed into central Harare, where he was to inspect a Guard of Honour before opening the third session of Zimbabwe's fifth

---

[1] An earlier version of this chapter was presented at the conference on Rethinking Land, State, and Citizenship through the Zimbabwe Crisis, held in Copenhagen in September, 2001. I am enormously indebted to Steffen Jensen, my generous commentator on that occasion, for suggesting how Agamben's work might be useful in thinking through the relationship between sovereignty and development, as well as that between law and violence. I was lucky to receive a second round of very insightful commentary at a workshop organised by Christian Lund and Kristine Juul at Bornholm, Denmark in September, 2002. Special thanks are due to Jeremy Gould, Simon Turner, Tania Li, Carola Lentz, and Peter Geschiere. My deep appreciation extends as well to the editors of this volume, and most especially to Amanda Hammar, not only for their very useful suggestions, but also for their patience beyond reason. Finally, Harry West, who 'knows a little something' about writing and other things less visible, suggested a way for me to save the entire enterprise by bringing to light the form hidden within. If I have failed to do so, the fault is mine alone.

[2] This quotation from a speech made in Makoni West by Moven Mahachi, the late Zimbabwean Minister of Defense, comes from testimony given to the Amani Trust, on 19 March, 2001. See http://www.mdczimbabwe.com/archivemat/elections/pres2000/amani010319btxt.htm

49

parliament. The President's vintage Rolls Royce was accompanied by soldiers on horseback, according to a tradition established during colonial rule. Yet relatively few people were on hand to witness this ritual of state: streets leading to the city centre were blockaded, cars searched, and demonstrators and suspected supporters of the opposition, banned.

Once inside the House of Parliament, the President addressed an audience of loyal ruling party MPs, the opposition members having staged a walk-out to signal their refusal to recognise Mugabe's victory in the March presidential elections. He lost little time in turning to the food crisis besetting the country, and the role of foreign governments and organisations in providing and distributing food aid. While admitting the great challenge presented by food shortages – he was to avoid using the word 'famine' which had figured prominently in recent press coverage – he warned that the government would not surrender control to 'sinister interests which seek surreptitiously to advance themselves under cover of humanitarian involvement':

> While Zimbabwe accepts drought-related assistance from the international community, we remain quite wary of countries and organisations which seek to take advantage of our hour of need to attenuate our sovereignty or even reverse those vital policies we have adopted as a sovereign people.[3]

He heralded the two-year-old Fast-Track Resettlement Programme – under which the last of over 5,000 white-owned commercial farms would soon be commandeered for redistribution by the state – an 'unqualified success'. Nevertheless, he added,

> We need to put all this land to productive agricultural use... This indeed is the best insurance against drought-related food pressures, while it is also our way of ensuring that no one takes advantage of our stomachs to get to the soul of our sovereignty.[4]

Outside, riot police fought running battles with some two thousand angry youths who had breached the security perimeter. Bystanders who got in the way were beaten, detained, and charged with 'obstructing the presidential motorcade.'[5]

---

[3] 'Mugabe warns against interference under pretext of aid.' IRIN (United Nations), 23 July 2002

[4] 'Devaluation is Dead (Editorial)' *The Herald*, 24 July 2002.

[5] The leader of the National Constitutional Assembly had been arrested the previous evening in an effort to pre-empt protests organised by that broadly based civic organisation. See 'Heavily armed police quash planned NCA demonstration', *Daily News*, 24 July 2002.

The End of Modernity in Zimbabwe?

After the speech to Parliament, Mugabe attended the traditional lunch hosted by the Ministry of Local Government, Public Works and National Housing. In the course of a wide-ranging discussion with cabinet ministers, chiefs, and civic leaders, he scoffed at the travel ban and other 'smart sanctions' imposed on himself, his cabinet, and the party politburo by British Prime Minister Tony Blair, to whom he referred as 'that young man at 10 Downing Street':

> *He thinks by ganging together countries of Europe, pressure can be brought to bear on us sufficient enough to make us desist from the [land acquisition and resettlement] programme. But he has also learnt that here in Zimbabwe we have the people and leadership committed to principles, especially principles that have to do with the sovereignty of the people of Zimbabwe. We are Zimbabweans, the soil we tread is ours, the land belongs to us, we fought for it, we died for it, we shall continue to fight for it and die for it. But somehow this young fellow thinks no, if he piles up sanctions on us we will surrender. Nobody has taught him that we don't know the word surrender in relation to our rights. That word we can't spell, it's not in our dictionary either. (Ibid.)*

He parodied those black Zimbabweans who had been drawn into what he referred to as a 'dependency syndrome' – those who believe, as he put it, that 'If we do not get a job from the white man, we will die of hunger, especially so when Mr Mugabe is taking farms from the whites. Are there still any blacks out there who still think like this in their own country?'[6]

****

On the afternoon of that same chilly day in late July, 2002, Caleb Chikwamba and two hundred other workers on Leopardvlei Farm in Central Mashonaland were ordered out of their compound by the new owner, a man named Reward Marufu, the brother of Grace Mugabe, the President's wife. Marufu had forcibly taken possession of the property in March after receiving it under the 'A2' scheme in the Fast-Track Resettlement Programme – a part of the Programme intended to give land to emergent black 'commercial' farmers. A

---

6   'Devaluation is Dead' *op.cit.* I have cited the translation given in the *The Herald*. The original ChiShona reads as follows: *Kana tisina kupiwa basa nevarungu taparara. Ivo vaMugabe zvavarikutora mapurazi evarungu. Evarungu? munhu mutema achiri kutaura kudaro vakomana munyika yedu? Tichazogona kurima iyesu tichafa nenzara.*

51

reporter for the independent *Daily News* interviewed Chikwamba about what happened next:

> "Marufu first told us that everyone was fired," Chikwamba said. "We thought it was a joke. He came back later with several of his guards and known Zanu PF youths and set ablaze our huts."
>
> Chikwamba said Marufu made it clear he was the new farm owner and no longer needed their services.
>
> He said property worth thousands of dollars was destroyed during the inferno that engulfed the compound, razing most of the huts to the ground... [and that] elderly women and children were indiscriminately assaulted and tortured.
>
> He said after their huts were burnt down, the youths and guards ordered everyone on the farm to immediately seek alternative accommodation or risk intensive beatings and torture.[7]

Despite President Mugabe's barbed reassurances to the contrary, Chikwamba and his fellow workers may well die of hunger. Abandoned by the law, their huts in flames, they are among the millions of Zimbabweans who have been effectively banished from 'their own country'.

A paradoxical politics

Two decades after achieving independence, Zimbabwe's rulers present an apparent paradox for any theory of postcolonial politics. How can one explain a government's relentless effort to elevate the principle of national sovereignty over the survival of the very people – such as Chikwamba – who would seem to constitute its mass public? Is such an effort to be understood as an aberration of postcolonial modernity, or merely its logical, if grotesque, consummation? How, in short, can the exclusion and killing of

---

[7] See '200 farm workers stranded as Mugabe's brother-in-law allegedly torches their homes.' *Daily News*, 26 July 2002. Background on Marufu's seizure of the farm, including some Z$200 million in assets and standing crops, may be found in 'Reward Marufu Grabs Farm,' *Daily News*, 27 April 2002. Marufu was charged, but ultimately not prosecuted, for defrauding the War Victims Compensation Fund of over Z$800,000 in 1997. Assigned a diplomatic post in Canada through the President's office in that year, he was recalled two years later while being investigated for assaulting his 16-year-old daughter.

citizens by their own government be defended as a *modern* act – an act of *progress*, the consummation of national *development* – in short, as an act of *reason*?[8]

These are the central questions that I will be posing in the somewhat unorthodox tour through theory, personal memory, and transnational public culture that follows. They are questions that entail others of a more general character. What, for example, is the relationship between claims to *sovereignty* and the politics of life and death in Zimbabwe? How and why is this relationship, in turn, taken to be elemental to the question of Zimbabwe's *modernity*, the question around which so much political discourse turns? And finally, how has the invocation of race (or the redemption of racial inequality) returned *both* as a key diacritic of sovereignty, *and* as a measure of modernity in Zimbabwe? I do not pretend that I have answers to these large, and admittedly abstract questions. My modest intention is to indicate how we might usefully think about them, and why it might be important to do so. My method is correspondingly exploratory, tacking back and forth between theoretical exposition and idiosyncratic illustrations drawn equally from the press, casual conversation, and more formal fieldwork. To put it another way, the mode of exposition that I have deliberately chosen is 'cubist', rather than linear in its organisation; that is, I approach a complex reality from several vantage points, the sequence of which is less relevant than the totality of perspectives presented.[9]

Suicidal governance or contested sovereignty?

No nation-state is an island, and Zimbabwe – even as its leaders assert a pugnacious inclination toward autarky – is no exception to this rule. Suspended from the Commonwealth, and cut off from IMF and World Bank assistance as well as from most forms of European and North American bilateral aid, the Zimbabwean government is nevertheless preoccupied with the procurement of

---

[8] The joining of what Scott (1998) calls 'high modernist' ideology to a politics of exclusion and death is hardly unique to Zimbabwe, of course. After Nazi Germany and Stalin's Soviet Union, in the last quarter of the twentieth century one thinks of Pol Pot's Cambodia, of Saddam Hussein's Iraq and Kim Il Sung's North Korea, not to mention Argentina, Columbia, and Guatemala. The regime of George W. Bush in the United States, insofar as it has advocated the running of treason trials by secret military courts, and suspending the constitutional rights of citizens more generally in the aftermath of the September 11 attacks. Israel's efforts to eliminate 'terrorism' through a combination of occupation and exclusion of Palestinians makes the point equally well.

[9] My thanks to Keith Hart for this metaphor.

emergency grain supplies from those same countries through the World Food Program of the United Nations, and several well-known western charities and non-governmental organisations (such as Save the Children and World Vision). Mugabe has made a concerted effort of late to nurture relations with regimes that are themselves cast as 'rogues' by the international financial institutions and the political entente that they underwrite. Libya's Quaddafi has thrown Mugabe the most critical lifeline – a third of a billion dollars in emergency oil credits annually – but at the likely cost of mortgaging some of the very assets that Zanu (PF) has been seizing from white farmers and businessmen.[10]

This paradoxical position of isolation and dependence, of simultaneous exclusion and inclusion from the dominant regime of international governance, is not immediately or easily apparent in the swirl of discourse and debate about the causes of, and solutions to, the Zimbabwean situation. The accelerating crisis besetting the country is often described or indexed through the presentation of statistics that are said to characterise the national economy and the national population, as if these two things, together, made up a kind of autonomous – if very unhealthy – organism or body. Thus, in 2002, the inflation rate was said to approach 140 per cent, the formal unemployment rate to run at an estimated 70 per cent, and as many as one out of three adults were estimated to be infected with the virus that causes AIDS. And yet it is not the descent of Zimbabweans into conditions of extreme poverty and disease under Mugabe's stewardship that has drawn the ire of northern governments and multilateral institutions. It is, rather, the uses to which the power of the state has been put, and specifically, what is understood to be the deployment of the law as an instrument of violence against many of the very citizens (farm workers, white commercial farm owners, opposition politicians and supporters) whom the law is presumably intended to protect.[11] Emblematic of

---

[10] Even this resource may be drying up, as Libya is reported to be demanding hard cash up front for further fuel allocations. 'SA Cuts Off Fuel', *Zimbabwe Standard*, 3 November 2002.

[11] The relevant new laws include the Citizenship Act, which places the onus on all Zimbabweans with a possible claim to dual citizenship to actively renounce the non-Zimbabwean claim or else be stripped of Zimbabwean citizenship; the Public Order and Security Act (which criminalises statements that 'incite or promote public disorder or public violence'); and the Access to Information and Protection of Privacy Act, which provides for the restrictive licensing of journalists and media organisations, while criminalising 'false' reporting.

this apparently perverse moral sensibility has been the willingness of the ruling party to use food aid as an explicit weapon of political coercion.[12]

But what his critics call an offence to the very precepts of liberalism and modern governance, Mugabe justifies in terms of a demand both to redeem the legacy of colonial dispossession and to complete the unfinished history of national liberation. All evidence suggests that he is committed to staying the course, in spite of the apparent priority such a course gives to the preservation of sovereignty over the right that citizens have to life. Insofar as such a philosophy seems unlikely to secure either the legitimacy of the Mugabe regime, or the life of the country's inhabitants, the entire enterprise might equally be described as a project of suicidal governance. But how to explain such a project?

Modernity lost, or not yet found?

Zimbabwe's slide toward catastrophe has, predictably, precipitated a flurry of moralising commentary about *how* power is being deployed and to what end – whether by the state, Zanu (PF), or most especially by Mugabe himself.[13] Should the practices of governance now afoot be characterised as fascist and tyrannical, or merely as a calculated manoeuvre to shunt land and assets into the greedy hands of the party elite? Do they betray the cunning of cynical reason or a descent into irrationality and reactive paranoia? Often unspoken, but always implicit, is a question saturated with post-colonial anxiety: does the capricious and unaccountable exercise of power in Zimbabwe indicate a government, and perhaps even an entire national society, in retreat from modernity?

This last question seems to be of such central importance to commentators of every political inclination and allegiance, that it cries out for closer scrutiny. Why should the question of Zimbabwe's *modernity* so insistently demand an answer at this juncture (as if the term 'modernity' itself carried a single signification, or the question a single answer)? What would an answer to this question

---

[12] As a rule, a Zanu (PF) party membership card must be shown to obtain grain from the Grain Marketing Board, which retains a legal monopoly on grain distribution in the country. As widely reported, known supporters of the opposition, or the areas in which they live, have been denied access to emergency food rations altogether. For a recent account, see 'Maize meal only sold to ZANU (PF) card holders', *Daily News*, 19 November 2002.

[13] In relation to the role being played specifically by war veterans in this process, see McGregor, 2002, and Hammar, this volume.

possibly resolve, or make it possible to understand? Robert Rotberg's (2002:135-7) recent remarks in the American policy journal, *Foreign Affairs*, provide us with as good an example of this discourse as any:

> *Zimbabwe, once unquestionably secure, economically strong, socially advanced, and successfully modern, has plummeted rapidly toward failure...No one in the West or in Africa effectively warned Mugabe that attacking one's own people, destroying a state, and stealing an election were impermissible.*

But the health of the state and its relation to social advancement and 'modernity' are a matter of dispute.[14] Mugabe clearly does not seek 'permission' to govern according to principles whose logic appears opaque to the West, as Rotberg and others would have him do. Indeed, he evidently regards the current conjuncture as a final resolution of the question of national sovereignty, a sovereignty that he claims is threatened by a racially-grounded imperialism in the guise of neo-liberal orthodoxy. He repeatedly represents the extraordinary rise and momentum of the opposition Movement for Democratic Change (MDC) – a movement that has united trade unionists, civic and religious groups, business leaders, as well as students, teachers, and urban youth – as the culmination of a plot orchestrated by Zimbabwean whites and their British allies to subvert the nation's autonomy and reassert control over its assets, not least its land. Attributing his electoral victory to the people's 'resolute anti-imperialist stand', he put the matter this way in his presidential inaugural address:

---

[14] Indeed, the state has remained remarkably vigorous throughout the period of precipitous decline in the formal economy. Consider its capacity to marshal the armed forces domestically and abroad. Zimbabwe maintains a standing army of roughly 35,000 professional soldiers. Fully one-third of these were deployed for at least four years (1998-2002) in a non-contiguous country – the Democratic Republic of Congo – ostensibly to shore up the government of Kabila against secessionist movements, but with a thinly disguised mission to secure timber and mining investments granted as concessions to Zimbabwean generals and ruling party officials. (See West (2001) for a detailed consideration of the role played by the defense establishment in both facilitating and engaging in business activity in the DRC). The remaining forces were instrumental in ferrying illegal 'farm invaders' – some voluntarily and others forcibly conscripted – onto nearly two thousand commercial farms and wildlife conservancies, beginning in March 2000. In the cities, troops have been periodically called upon to quell food riots and anti-government demonstrations by students and opposition activists. Training camps were set up by the ruling party with the explicit purpose of training youth as an armed auxiliary militia – the so-called 'Green Bombers' – in the run-up to presidential elections in March 2002. On the other hand, other provinces of conventional state responsibility – health care, education, local government, and basic infrastructure – suffer from serious, if not entirely deliberate, neglect (Hammar, this volume).

In 1980, as we celebrated the advent of our independence...we least expected that twenty years down the line we would, once again, have to wage another struggle for the defence of that sovereign independence against our former colonial power seeking in a determined way to diminish it so as to regulate our policies and our lives, including the choice of our rulers.[15]

In other words, liberation is *not yet* an accomplished fact: *a luta continua*.

These sound like platitudes, long ago emptied of rhetorical force. Yet it must be remembered that national sovereignty and self-determination are at the heart of twentieth century political discourse. They are still respectable goals (if barely so after September 11) that sit comfortably on the horizon of modernity alongside the ideals of citizenship, human rights, and democracy. But what kind of political society is actually sought or anticipated to lie on that horizon? How does that anticipation structure the terms of political discourse and practice?

Here, the political debate within and about Zimbabwe becomes ensnared in a contradiction that besets the larger world of which it is a part. Zimbabwe was born (albeit belatedly, in 1980) of the global reordering that made nation-states the institutional shells through which the flow of labor and capital was managed globally after the Second World War. Within that system, a fictional equality (established through the United Nations) was established between ex-colonial powers and the 'national' entities that arose to seek and be granted the right to self-determination in the wake of decolonisation.[16] Self-determination – the realisation of political autonomy and membership in the community of sovereign nations – became the *sine qua non* of political modernity; to settle for anything less was tantamount to frustrating the *telos* of national self-realisation. In the case of Zimbabwe, the continued presence of protected white seats in Parliament for seven years after independence, and the continued white occupation of the lion's share of prime commercial farmland served as visible reminders of a sovereignty promised but not yet fully realised. For Mugabe, it has been precisely that *lack* of realisation that has proved central to his continuing legitimacy.

---

[15] *The Herald*, 18 March 2002.
[16] Both Hardt and Negri (2000) and Kelly and Kaplan (2001) have made important reassessments of this moment in the construction of modernity and the political order of nation-states.

Sovereignty and development: The see-saw of modernity

If the transnational debate over Zimbabwe's modernity cannot therefore be easily disentangled from Mugabe's persistent preoccupation with the question of sovereignty, neither can it be separated from the question of how the management of life (what Foucault (1990[1979]) called 'biopolitics', and Agamben (1998) calls 'bare life') becomes central to projects of governance. In late colonial and postcolonial contexts such projects have typically been gathered under the rubric of *development*.[17] The imperative to engage in 'development' that normatively guides public policy in postcolonies such as Zimbabwe, is constructed around the effort to optimise the life of the population over time (its birth rate, labor productivity, relation to the environment, and so on). Development embodies a paradox: it draws metaphorically upon a figure of immanent, *autonomous*, organic growth; yet it is historically grounded in a colonial ethic of trusteeship – by the imperative, in other words, to buffer or protect those whose livelihoods are destroyed by an expanding industrial capitalism in the metropolitan centres, and by the expropriation of natural resources and ruthless exploitation of labor in the tropics (Cowen and Shenton, 1997). As an heir to this complex ideology, the nation-states of the post-war period are expected to 'develop' autonomously, to follow a teleological trajectory that parallels that of all others; and yet, such a trajectory can neither be pursued, nor ever achieved, except in relation to something outside of itself (most obviously in the imperative to receive aid and foreign investment as well as to engage in external trade).[18] Nor can the development of the nation-state's constituent communities, sub-populations, and individual citizens take place without their being simultaneously free of the state (or its surrogates) for tutelage and care, even as they remain dependent upon it to constitute, through law, the conditions of such freedom.

---

[17] It is important not to forget, however, that 'development' in Africa (as indeed elsewhere) often becomes entangled with other strategies and discourses of what might also be called 'biopower': for example, witchcraft, satanism, and charismatic healing. (I am indebted to Peter Geschiere for suggesting that 'biopower' might usefully be stretched to encompass these kinds of knowledges and techniques devoted to the management of life.)

[18] In this sense, as James Ferguson (1997:136) has written, 'none of the impoverished nations of the world are truly "sovereign" or "independent"; and nowhere do we find a true "national economy."'

They must be taught and told how to become modern, autonomous, and free.[19]

The modern theory of sovereignty embodies a paradox of its own. The concept proposes a single uncontested centre of authority from which both the law, and the use of force may legitimately emanate (see, e.g., Hoffman, 1999). The sovereignty of states is implicitly accepted as absolute in international law; yet the question of the limits and legitimacy of sovereign authority are constantly called into question. Indeed, sovereignty as a problem or preoccupation only comes clearly into view at the threshold of its realisation, and most especially when it is challenged to make its efficacy known (a state of war or the threat of terrorism, for example). In this sense, sovereignty is most easily identified under a state of exception or emergency, when the law, and the rights it theoretically protects, are suspended. It is precisely at these moments, as Mugabe has made clear time and again, that sovereignty is revealed to be less about who is included in the protections afforded by citizenship, and more about *who decides* who is included, and who excluded, from the protective (or violent) embrace of the law. Sovereignty is about *who decides* who lives and who dies.

Let me conclude this abbreviated theoretical discussion by proposing that we think of the figure of political modernity as the fulcrum of a see-saw, one that has 'sovereignty' seated at one end, and 'development' at the other. I will return a bit later to the crucial place of race in the balance of this equation – a matter that in Zimbabwe, as in so many other postcolonial formations, remains central to any discussion of modernity. For now, suffice it to say that the race problem is a quintessentially *modern* problem: it is precisely the point at which 'biopolitics' – the calculation of the life-chances of theoretically discrete populations – becomes linked to the question of sovereignty, by determining who qualifies for inclusion in the legal protections of citizenship, and who is excluded or banned from the law's purview of application.[20]

---

[19] As Louis Menon (2001:409) observes, 'Coercion is natural; freedom is artificial. Freedoms are socially engineered spaces where parties engaged in specified pursuits enjoy protection from parties who would otherwise naturally seek to interfere in those pursuits. One person's freedom is therefore another person's restriction: we would not have even the concept of freedom if the reality of coercion were not already present. We think of a freedom as a right and therefore the opposite of a rule, but a right *is* a rule. It is a prohibition against sanctions on certain types of behavior.'

[20] These ideas derive from Agamben (1998) and Dean (2001). Mamdani's (1996) argument about the distinction between citizen and subject – mapped as a rule onto distinctions in race throughout colonial Africa – is of obvious relevance.

A coming of age?

It should not surprise us that 'development' is often imagined through the metaphor of maturation. The morning after the 2002 presidential polls closed, Tim Chigodo, a political analyst from the government-owned newspaper (*The Herald*), felt compelled to proclaim Zimbabwe's political 'coming of age'. Predicting a landslide victory for President Robert Mugabe, Chigodo put the following gloss on an electoral process that, over a period of two years, had been marked by widespread political murder, rape, torture, and the detention of hundreds (and perhaps thousands) of opposition party activists, sympathisers, and innocent bystanders: 'The tranquility that prevailed during the period of polling did not only shame the country's detractors but showed that Zimbabweans have come of age democratically,' Chigodo wrote. 'The country's prophets of doom had expected the elections to be marred by violence. Although there were some rowdy elements who wanted to cause mayhem during the elections, Zimbabweans remained calm and exuberant during the period. They proved beyond doubt that they can hold their elections peacefully without involvement of foreigners.'[21]

Given the well-documented brutality of the Mugabe regime, it would be easy to write off this sort of journalism as little more than vaporous cant. But I would argue that it is worthy of more serious attention. What does it mean, after all, to say that a people have "come of age democratically"? Why the need to assert that voters are not merely "calm", but also "exuberant," in the face of provocations to engage in violence? Why, and for whom, is it important that such a people demonstrate that they can hold elections not only peacefully, but also "without involvement of foreigners"?

Chigodo's claim that Zimbabweans *are* able to discipline themselves in matters of politics – to vote without resorting to violence, and to do so without the tutelary care of foreign powers – has an unambiguously defensive tone. But against what kinds of accusations does he feel such a defence must be mounted? He does not say. And yet it seems obvious that his comments are intended to counter an implicit judgment that Zimbabweans are *not yet* ready for democracy, and that the Zimbabwean nation-state is *not yet* a

---

[21] *Herald*, 13 March 2002.

The End of Modernity in Zimbabwe?

fully modern political formation.[22] His remarks serve as a riposte to the so-called 'smart' sanctions that had recently been applied by the United States and the European Union, just as they anticipated the deliberations of the Commonwealth that resulted in the suspension of Zimbabwe from membership in that organisation. In this sense, he was making a claim for *inclusion* based on evidence that Zimbabweans have met some kind of standard that has been established somewhere else at some prior period of time – a standard that might well be summarised as that of 'political modernity'.

Such an argument for political modernity is not necessarily a liberal vision. Chigodo is quite happy to extend his argument about Zimbabwe's democratic coming of age with an assertion of its capacity to bring police power to bear on the threat of disorder:

> *Under the Public Order and Security Act, police have adequate power to deal with perpetrators of political violence and public disorder, including terrorism. The Zimbabwe Republic Police was able to defend all citizens and ensure that they were able to vote in a free and fair environment.*[23]

In other words, police violence – insofar as it is undertaken in the name of a demand to uphold democratic freedoms, the rule of law, and the defence of citizens against disorder – can serve as further evidence of the condition of modernity into which the Zimbabwean state is said to have matured. Here, the relation between law and the defence of citizens against disorder are taken to constitute another kind of claim to modernity: the actions of the state are asserted *not* to be arbitrary, but to be authorised *by law*; the citizens are said to be *protected* from political violence waged by 'terrorists' (a term I interrogate below).

---

[22] As Dipesh Chakrabarty (2000:8) has argued, postcolonial nationalism has always been predicated upon a refutation of the historicist proposition that the colonised subject is 'not yet' at a fully mature stage of political development, a stage that the European citizen has, by definition, already achieved: 'Historicism has not disappeared from the world, but its "not yet" exists today in tension with this global insistence on the "now" that marks all popular movements toward democracy.' Of course, such an insistence must still work through and against a developmental view of time. One of the conclusions of this chapter will be that Zanu (PF) has begun to withdraw from such a dialogue within the historicist frame. Displaced by the Movement for Democratic Change (MDC) as the standard-bearer for popular democracy in Zimbabwe, Mugabe's party has increasingly sought legitimacy in terms of the discourse of sovereignty and security. Even so, commentators such as Chigodo feel constrained to make the party's practice conform to a narrative of historical arrival and maturity.

[23] Chigodo, *op.cit.*

Sovereignty and its terrorists

I cite these discussions for two reasons. The first is to illustrate what kinds of evidence are taken to be symptomatic of the modernity of the Zimbabwean state and its citizenry. I would argue that the presence or absence of such evidence constitutes a kind of pivot around which the legitimacy and sovereignty of the state are not merely debated, but constituted. And they are constituted through a dialogue that engages transnational interlocutors (both specific and imaginary) as much as it engages those who think of themselves as Zimbabweans. Secondly, this discourse gives expression to the paradoxical way in which the law authorises violence in the name of preventing it. Indeed, I would argue that it is only through a process of exteriorising violence *through* violence that the sovereignty of law is produced and its legitimacy claimed.

This exteriorisation of violence – attributing it to a dangerous, invisible other that lies, like a demon, within – is realised through the figure of the 'terrorist'.[24] 'Terror' and 'sovereignty' in this sense reciprocally constitute one another; indeed, each provides the condition by which the other category can be thought. If we think of terrorism as a politics whose means is violence and whose end is to delegitimate the claim made by the state to 'secure' citizens under the monopoly of its territorial and legal protection, then we may understand terror precisely to be what generates, as a requirement, the production of a discourse on sovereignty. Sovereignty is required to master terror; indeed, terror (alongside related figures such as 'chaos' and 'lawlessness') may be understood as sovereignty's constitutive outside – the exterior that defines it. 'Terrorists' are not merely those who rival the state as authors of violence, or who live as amoral citizens within a sovereign territory (these are merely marked as 'criminal elements'); rather, they are, by definition, those who challenge the sovereign's unique and exclusive capacity to secure *or suspend* the rule of law and the conditions of peace. That they are *invisible* to detection through state strategies of technical and social surveillance, is an inherent feature of the faceless, 'monstrous' threat that they are felt to represent. The terrorists are said to be everywhere among us; the key question is, how will we separate *ourselves* from *them*?

---

[24] There is a close and significant parallel here with the figure of the witch in Zimbabwe – often imagined to be close relative, 'one of us', who does secret, destructive work in the invisibility of night. See Lan (1986: 37).

The End of Modernity in Zimbabwe?

Viewing the couplet 'sovereignty/terror' as mutually constitutive in this way, helps us to understand why Mugabe was delighted to mirror George W. Bush's eagerness to suspend the rule of law (and specifically, the Bill of Rights) when it came to the pursuit of 'terrorists' (a label that Mugabe wasted no time in applying to Morgan Tsvangirai and other members of the opposition party, as well as to members of the local and foreign press).[25] This mirroring shades into parody, especially when one remembers that Mugabe and his fellow liberation fighters were themselves labeled terrorists by the renegade Rhodesian regime of Ian Smith.[26] To reverse positions – to transpose the position of the white accusers and the black accused – yields an undeniable redemptive pleasure, not least because racial distinctions were the pre-eminent criteria by which some people internal to African settler colonial polities were positioned on the threshold of inclusion under the law. This heritage of racialised inclusion/exclusion figures prominently in the transnational discourse on postcolonial modernity and sovereignty, perhaps more so with reference to Zimbabwe than anywhere else in the postcolonial world. And it is to the strange work of this discourse, as it circulates and undergoes partial translation in diverse contexts of transnational encounter, that I turn next.

Race and inclusion in transnational conversation

Two decades ago, on my first visit to newly independent Zimbabwe, I was choosing vegetables from one of the hawkers in a shopping centre parking lot in one of Harare's low-density suburbs. An elderly woman in a faded housedress was picking through packets of tomatoes and okra being offered for sale by several vendors alongside me. She was white. Hearing my accent, and noting my skin colour (also white), she squinted at me through wing-tipped bi-focals. 'And where are you from, young man?' she asked.

'Canada,' I said, which was more or less true at the time.

'And how do you find our country?' she probed.

'I love it,' I replied. 'Lovely scenery, such friendly people.' It seemed like the sort of polite, if insipid, reply that was called for, but it was not unreflective of my feelings.

---

[25] See 'Mugabe says UK backs opposition "terrorists"'. *The Independent* (UK), 19 November 2001.

[26] For Smith's regime the key question became how to differentiate a 'terr' from a docile black political subject. See White (2001) for a discussion of the crack counter-insurgency unit known as the Selous Scouts in this process, and of the strange strategies of cross-racial identification that this sometimes entailed.

"'Tis, isn't it,' she replied, catching her breath before purposefully adopting a more wistful tone: 'Ah, but you should've seen the *old* Rhodesia.' She pronounced it, 'the *ow-wald Rhodeezee-a*', thereby providing me with a cherished illustration of imperialist nostalgia that I was to parody as an amusement for leftist intellectual friends for years to come back in North America. But at the time, I was so acutely embarrassed by the implication that I would 'naturally' take a sympathetic view of her 'lost' Rhodesia that I reddened and ran, feeling like a stranger in a very strange land.

This was only the first among many such uneasy conversations that I was to have either in or about Zimbabwe, conversations that were often doomed to failure by the premise, by one party or another, that assumed affinities of race implied a shared vision of the politics of modernity. In March, 2000, shortly after the land invasions in Zimbabwe began, a member of the Zimbabwean High Court paid a visit to New Haven to address a conference on the Yale campus where I teach. We dined together at a downtown Malaysian restaurant, along with a distinguished Professor Emeritus and long-time chair of Yale's African Studies Council, and a young West African political scientist, who was, like myself, a junior member of the Yale faculty. We asked the Justice about the deteriorating security situation in her country, about the recent disregard for rulings of the very court upon which she sat, about the self-evident irregularities in the compilation of the voter rolls as the probable date for parliamentary elections drew near, and about the widespread invasions of white-owned commercial farms, only recently underway. As might be expected among people whose political positions, sympathies, and intentions she could only guess at, the Justice expressed her sentiments in cautious generalities. 'It's truly terrible,' she said, looking down and shaking her head. 'And we just don't know what is going to happen.'

Midway through the meal, an African-American man sporting dreadlocks and a black, green, yellow, and red T-shirt approached us from a table across the room; about a dozen people had apparently gathered to commemorate the 30th anniversary of the Black Panther trial in New Haven. Someone at the table must have heard the Justice speak earlier that afternoon and told the man now sauntering towards us who she was. He introduced himself to the Justice and addressed her exclusively, he standing to one side, she seated with her fork poised over a tepid plate of coconut curried chicken, rotating her torso so as to politely receive his display of homage and solidarity: 'We stood by you in the struggle against Smith,' he said in a voice

The End of Modernity in Zimbabwe?

rather too loud for an upscale restaurant with an open seating plan. 'And now you and Comrade Mugabe and Zanu (PF) are showing all *black* people the road to freedom from colonial oppression, taking back the *land*. I want to congratulate you, Comrade.' He went on in this vein for five or ten minutes without pause. Meanwhile, we three academics remained silent, shifting awkwardly in our seats, watching the food growing cold, as afraid to interrupt him as we were to eat. It was not clear when the tribute would end, nor how. At last the man clenched a fist in what he imagined would be a transparent signification of solidarity, shook her hand, and strode back across the room to his table. Her Honour shook her head in complete bewilderment.

I tried strenuously to provide a context that would account for the man's presumptive claim to be her natural ally. I struggled to assemble an explanatory narrative about how pan-Africanism had transmuted in the United States into Afrocentrism, with the global race-based histories and solidarities that it took for granted. I thought aloud about the mythological time-frame in which Mugabe's 1980 triumph against British imperialism and white settler colonialism could be seen by many Americans (and not only aging Black Panthers) as having occurred just yesterday and not a generation ago. But the discomfort lay like a sticky residue over what remained of the food and the evening. What common ground could be *assumed* among four people ostensibly divided by the culturally marked attributes of race, gender, and geographical origin when it came to discussing the exploding political violence – much of it marked in the media as being *essentially* 'racially motivated' – that made a judge's presumed neutrality almost a liability?

Zimbabwe is making for uncomfortable dinner table conversation well beyond its borders, and not only in American university towns like New Haven. Why? The conversations are uncomfortable because the rhizomic chains of discourse on 'race' and 'racism' can be used to establish promiscuous links and profound meanings among social histories, processes, and memories that are widely disparate in time and space.[27] They are uncomfortable because what is happening in Zimbabwe can evidently *only* be rendered and evaluated in ways that appear to weigh the grave injustices of the past against those of the present in a macabre equation of injury and retribution that has no interest in the future. And finally, they are uncomfortable because they must inevitably expose and wrestle with a kind of default

---

[27] As exemplified by the UN conference on racism and discrimination held in Durban in September, 2001.

pairing of 'white' identity and consciousness (absurd as such a postulated homogeneity may sound) with political and cultural *modernity* both within and outside of Zimbabwe.

In making reference to 'modernity', I am not, of course, talking about some objective state of social advancement, but rather of a social construction that has become a compelling trope. If, at that dinner table on that night in New Haven, the four of us could presume to share any common ground of understanding at all, it was with respect to the implicit proposition that, all things being equal, all Zimbabweans *ought* to be able to live under a recognisably *modern* regime of governance. If pressed, we might have agreed that such a regime would be characterised, minimally, by a uniformity in access to the rights and responsibilities of citizenship, by the accountability of elected officials and public servants, and by the safety of citizens from the abuse of power by those entrusted with ensuring the public peace. But there are other possible modernities than this implicit consensus, as a chorus of scholars now contend (see Eisenstadt, 2000; Arce and Long, 2000), all of them enabling social agents to make a claim to living in the present albeit on terms that confound self-identified Western observers with their apparent impurity, hybridity, or mimesis of established modalities of the modern (Bhabha, 1984; Clifford, 1988).

Of course the meaning of the word 'modern' only comes clear when it is understood semiotically, and thus in a relational context where its implicit contrast is with modes of thought or being that are presumed to exist in an altogether other kind of time – the 'savage', the 'barbaric', the 'traditional', the 'enchanted'.[28] But modernity's 'other' – that which it is supposed to overcome – can also be construed as a past-time of slavery, colonial racism, apartheid, or colonised consciousness.[29] This was, of course, the double message of the Black Panther who addressed the High Court judge on that evening in New Haven: there is, he suggested, a 'white' modernity that belongs to our common enslaved or colonised past as black people, and it is time to get past it by whatever means necessary.[30] The insistent

---

[28] See, inter alia, Fabian (1983), Torgovnick (1990), Trouillot (1992), Schneider (1994).

[29] That race-based slavery and colonialism were as central to post-Enlightenment modernity as was capitalism, is an argument that has been vigorously made by a number of scholars in the past decade. See especially Gilroy (1993), Stoler (1995), and Kelly and Kaplan (2001).

[30] The notion that there is a distinctively *black* project for modernity, one that must expunge the traces of the colonial past, clearly underpins Mugabe's symbolic legitimacy in remarkably diverse contexts. For an illustrative interpretation of the presidential elections from within a U.S.-based Pan-Africanist perspective, see Elombe Brath, 'Western Imperialism Loses in Zimbabwe' 18 March 2002 (Posted on: http://www.mumia.org/afrikan.net/html/article.php?sid=433&mode=thread&order=0&thold=0

question of whether or not a decisive break has been made with the colonial condition (and whether that break, to the extent that it has been made, is a good thing) animates public political rhetoric and private conversation to a striking degree within Zimbabwe as much as without. Take the commentary recorded at the Youth Conference of the National Constitutional Assembly (NCA) in March, 2001: 'Sometime during the war of liberation, Josiah Tongogara said while in Tanzania: "We are not fighting against Ian Smith or the colour of the skin, but against a system"...Can we therefore say that the struggle is over when the system has not changed? As far as we are concerned, the fight is still on until the system is changed.' And another delegate opined, according to the attending journalist, that 'apart from a few minor differences, Mugabe and his government were now behaving in the same manner as Smith and his colonial regime did in the 1970s when they ruled the country, then a British colony of Rhodesia.'[31] Of course these 'youths' – children at best during the Smith regime – would have little direct experience from which to draw. So the debate for them becomes the rather abstract one of locating the nation in relation to the promise of modernity that has been betrayed.

Mugabe's 'savage' supper

Western journalists, bereft of explanation, are beginning to see things rather more simply and ahistorically. For most of them, Zimbabwe is plunging into darkness – an anti-civilisational state, a perverse and amoral condition. The farm invasions, the electoral violence, the blatant disregard for the authority of the judiciary and the rule of law, Mugabe's stubborn refusal to come to terms with the international donors even in the face of imminent famine, all amount to one thing above all others: a retreat from that implicitly universal goal to which all human beings on the planet are assumed to aspire, the goal of becoming modern people who belong to a modern, 'developing' nation-state. Note that it is the aspiration to achieve this goal that counts, not its realisation. Yet Zimbabwe's rulers have evidently renounced even the aspiration to conform to anyone's 'expectations of modernity' (to borrow James Ferguson's (1999) phrase) – or at least those versions of it that are granted recognition outside its borders.

Since the inter-war period, 'development' in Zimbabwe has been closely associated with discipline and the way it entrains a subject

---

[31] 'Youths back move for a new constitution', *Financial Gazette*, 7 March, 2001.

willingly into a set of novel practices (see Worby, 2000). Structural Adjustment made it clear that states are susceptible to regimes of discipline in the name of development just as much as individual citizens. But 'development' is also about an exchange – about giving something up in return for something else. And the successful exchange is one that culminates in an identification that occurs between parties of unequal power. To the extent that this identification through exchange is taken to compromise the integrity of the national body, it is felt as a threat to sovereignty. Mugabe's apparent disregard for the 'laws of economics' – that a national economy bled dry of fuel, food, and foreign currency cannot afford to vilify and alienate its patrons in aid and trade – makes clear that the nation itself is undergoing redefinition, and that a fantasy of perfect sovereignty has at least begun to displace that of development. To recall my earlier metaphor, the see-saw of political modernity has tipped to one side – the side of sovereignty.[32]

There is much talk of self-destruction – of the head of the body politic hell-bent on eating his own flesh by authorising the burning or abandonment of standing crops. But there is little beyond the attribution of madness to Mugabe and a certain gullibility to his followers by way of explanation.[33] For these pundits, there are measures of civilised governance that need not be made explicit but which are better exemplified by contrast. What else are we intended to make of the report in the British Sunday Times (*Paranoid Mugabe Dines with a Ghost; Mugabe Eats Supper with Dead Rival*, 12

---

[32] None of this squares, of course, with the solicitation of the abundant gift of oil from Quaddafi, nor with the exchange of the services of the national army for mineral and lumber concessions in the forests of the Democratic Republic of Congo. But it is consistent with the genocidal war in Matabeleland of the early 1980s.

[33] Chabal and Daloz (1999) are among those who offer a rational, means-ends explanation for these kinds of uses of power through the notion of what they call the 'instrumentalization of disorder'; by this they mean that within a characteristic set of cultural norms and practices, it is entirely rational for politicians and their supporters in Africa to eschew the institutionalisation of a rule-bound political and economic system in favour of one in which all relations are essentially negotiable, and where politics is fundamentally about the distribution of resources in exchange for the power to command future wealth and loyalty. Agamben, it seems to me, avoids the tautological claims that characterise all arguments that claim either the rationality or the madness of political strategies in Africa or anywhere else. Following Carl Schmitt, he argues that 'since "there is no rule that is applicable to chaos," chaos must first be included in the juridical order through the creation of a zone of indistinction between outside and inside, chaos and the normal situation – the state of exception (1998:19).' In other words, the apparently permanent state of exception that allows the ruler, for example, to issue a pardon (as Mugabe did for all of those in Zanu (PF) charged with politically-motivated crimes leading up to the 2000 parliamentary elections), or to declare a permanent state of emergency (that allows for the suspension of the rule of law and constitutionally protected rights), affirms the capacity of the sovereign to decide when the law applies.

The End of Modernity in Zimbabwe?

August 2001) that Mugabe is haunted by an angry ghost of his old rival, the very same Josiah Tongogara whose name was invoked at the youth conference mentioned above?[34] The report, citing testimony from the Presidential guard, describes an increasingly restless and paranoid Mugabe, his face inflated by steroids, his dinner table set with an empty place for the *ngozi* of Tongogara, the aggrieved spirit whom he desires to appease. He was said to be fearful of the imminent solar eclipse, a portent of evil that followed closely on the deaths of three of his most ardent commandants within the space of a month. Thus portrayed, this curious hybrid who dines with ghosts in his Saville Row suits – this monstrous persona – seems to confuse, rather than to synthesise, two modes of thought: the civilised and the savage. Never mind that a century of social anthropology has worried itself about the validity of the distinction.[35] It has proven to be a convenient way of constructing the divide between Mugabe's men and those in opposition: on the one side, people apparently hell-bent on a 'return' to Hobbesian violence – tropical, hot-headed, blood-thirsty; on the other, a restrained, civilised, and rational coalition centred upon Morgan Tsvangirai, coded temperate, cool, northern, and often enough, a proxy for 'white' ambitions. This rhetorical contrast has been so often enunciated, and so overdetermined by the strands of finance and transracial alliance that provide the MDC with support, that it has become a liability for Tsvangirai and the opposition more generally.

This example well illustrates a rather dramatic shift in international media attention that has accelerated since the beginning of the land invasions in February 2000, a shift from the backward white subject during the era of Ian Smith's Unilateral Declaration of Independence (an embarrassment to white Britain) to the bad black subject today – exemplified by the war veterans – who is said to prefer anarchy to the discipline required for nation-building and economic development.

For a long time, it was easy to assume an uncomplicated and uniform intransigence and smugness among white farmers in Zimbabwe, an immunity to the tide of history which promised liberation in the most humanistic, enlightened sense of the term. Whites were often portrayed as clinging to a culture and identity

---

[34] Tongogara, according to this account, was the then Zanu (PF) guerilla leader who was widely expected to be named to the Zimbabwean Presidency (at the time, a largely ceremonial post) at Independence. He died in a car crash just after the April, 1980 elections – an event that was suspicious for its timely elimination of a charismatic and potentially threatening rival to Mugabe.

[35] See Rutherford (1999) for a critical review grounded in Zimbabwean ethnography.

grounded in a historical stage now identified with the pre-modern past of colonial racism. (What else did the 'Rhodie' slur denote if not this – an anachronistic attachment by whites to 'the old Rhodesia'?) Certainly foreign researchers did not care to find out much more about white Zimbabweans, although the leaders of the white farming and business communities struggled mightily in public forums to present their constituents as patriots, whose acumen in matters of farm and business management, it was claimed, made them indispensable to the national development project, whatever its guiding ideology might be. But now the white farmers are the poster-children of the BBC, and it seems nearly acceptable, even respectable, for the media to talk once again about the Dark Continent.

Mugabe as modern sovereign?

If not through the figure of 'primitive' government, then how indeed should anyone interpret Mugabe's insouciant disregard for the moral requirements of modernity? How indeed should we account for the apparent desire on the part of Zanu (PF) to divest the Zimbabwean state of the guise of liberal governance entirely? For clearly we are no longer talking about an ephemeral political tactic; nor even about a selfish desire on the part of a handful of callous leaders to retain power for its own sake and at any cost. Some scholars see through the fog of contradictions and brutality the sincere pursuit of an alternate path to agrarian justice and national economic development. Moyo (2001), for example, has argued that the Zanu (PF) government, itself deeply divided, has been trying to anticipate and contain a groundswell of popular demand for land, a demand that has been registered in occupation movements that date back to the liberation war. On this view, the government's 'legal activism' is merely catching up with a more radically democratic politics emerging from social movements in the countryside, movements that unite farm workers and peasants in a practical critique of private property.

One could imagine the early land invasions prior to the elections as being orchestrated by a few fraudulent war veterans – the now deceased leader Chenjerai 'Hitler' Hunzvi pre-eminent among them – with the backing of the Central Intelligence Organisation, perhaps the army, and Zanu (PF) or other willing youth-for-hire. Yet this scenario has been overtaken by events. There are too many participants, too many agents fully in charge of their intentions now

The End of Modernity in Zimbabwe?

to write off the entire affair as an entailment of anarchic elements with nothing at stake and nothing to lose who have run amok.[36]

Still, we might well ask: What are they thinking, those who consent or are coerced to 'invade', to loot, to pillage, rape, and burn? What do they imagine they are doing and why? Of course the answer will be plural and diverse. Just as we have discovered that 'nationalism' is not one story in Zimbabwe, but rather many, each shaped by a kaleidoscope of social and historical locations (Raftopoulos, 1999) and that 'development' must be understood in relation to its sequential instantiations across geographical and social space (Worby, 2000), so we will one day understand the invasions to be a complex playing out of local histories in conjuncture with rapidly evolving strategies that emanate both from central government and from provincial party structures, as well as other dynamics of local and translocal politics.[37] As the invasions expand in scale and duration, it seems, on the face of it, to be increasingly unlikely that anything will be resolved by elections and the restoration of an inclusive national development project, as if somehow a country now so tainted and riven by violence could be redeemed in this way.

And yet there is another way of understanding the relationship between this kind of violence, the political rhetoric that supports it, and the language of sovereignty that provides its discursive frame. For the violence accompanying the invasions and the elections has neither been 'anarchic' nor uninformed by a political rationality and a specific justification *in terms of* the rule of law. It is, as Mugabe puts it, about the reassertion of 'national sovereignty' through the application of the law. How can we explain the apparent paradox in this formulation, when the very judiciary charged with upholding the law has been threatened into resigning (or been filled with apparent Zanu (PF) loyalists)?

---

[36] Researchers such as Blair Rutherford have even begun to document a process of highly localised negotiation on the occupied farms, where Mugabe's suspension of the rule of law has spurred the innovation of evolving and contingent property arrangements. In some cases, Rutherford writes, 'white farmers and workers continue to work alongside new settlers, who in turn benefit from the expertise and infrastructure found on the still-operating commercial farm,' adding, however, that 'these arrangements are often made under duress and may be a tenuous foundation.' See 'Not All Black and White' *Globe and Mail* (Toronto), 20 August 2002.

[37] For a long time, the war veterans, or those who were acting in their name, remained something of a black box. A number of scholars have now done a good deal of the historical groundwork that, at the least, documents their complex relationship to violence and society during the liberation war and after. See the collection edited by Bhebe and Ranger (1995) and recent work by Alexander, McGregor, and Ranger (2000), as well as Kriger (2003). Recent research by Marongwe (this volume) finds that although veterans are, almost always, the initiators and on-site administrators of invaded lands in 2000-2001, the people invading have diverse motives and independent agendas.

The threshold of modernity

Michel Foucault famously argued that political theory continues to depend upon conceptions of power appropriate to monarchical rule – conceptions based on the figure of the sovereign as the source and arbiter of law and right. Such theory is wholly inadequate to the actual mechanisms, tactics, and objects of power that have organised the disposition of social action in Europe since the end of the eighteenth century:[38]

> *At bottom, despite the differences in epochs and objectives, the representation of power has remained under the spell of monarchy. In political thought and analysis, we still have not cut off the head of the king. Hence the importance that the theory of power gives to the problem of right and violence, law and illegality, freedom and will, and especially the state and sovereignty (even if the latter is questioned insofar as it is personified in a collective being and no longer a sovereign individual.) (Foucault 1990: 88-9).*

For Foucault, what is characteristic of modern societies is the emergence on the one hand, of institutions devoted to the inculcation of self-discipline: schools, armies, medical clinics and mental hospitals; and on the other, the attempt to measure and modify the features of population in relation to economic wealth and resources. In contrast to sovereignty, with its foundation in the application of law and the claiming of rights, he calls these techniques and strategies of investigation and intervention 'biopower', a term he uses 'to designate what brought life and its mechanisms into the realm of explicit calculations and made knowledge-power an agent of transformation of human life.' The exclusive power of the sovereign, under the law, to cause death is replaced by the investment of power in the control over life.

> *Power would no longer be dealing simply with legal subjects over whom the ultimate dominion was death, but with living beings, and the mastery it would be able to exercise over them would have to be applied at the level of life itself; it was the taking charge of life, more than the threat of death, that gave power to its access even to the body.*

---

[38] Indeed, political theory in this respect becomes complicit with modern power's deceptions and disguises. As Foucault puts it, 'power is tolerable only on condition that it mask a substantial part of itself. Its success is proportional to its ability to hide its own mechanisms.' (1990:86)

The End of Modernity in Zimbabwe?

Foucault finds in this shift the 'threshold of modernity':

> But what might be called a society's "threshold of modernity" has been reached when the life of the species is wagered on its own political strategies. For millennia, man remained what he was for Aristotle: a living animal with the additional capacity for a political existence; modern man is an animal whose politics places his existence as a living being in question.

This formulation seems strikingly appropriate to the times that Zimbabweans have been living in. One need only peruse the shelves of studies devoted to the calculation of optimal land use and tenure patterns in terms of food production and income generation, and the presentation of such data *as though* it had nothing to do with politics. But now it would seem that the power over death and the exercise of the power of the sovereign through laws that he himself continues to create have taken the upper hand. Is this not a retreat from the 'threshold of modernity'?

The Italian philosopher Giorgio Agamben, whose thought has already provided much of the tacit underpinning for this essay, has suggested otherwise.[39] In his work *Homo Sacer: Sovereign Power and Bare Life*, Agamben concurs with Foucault that the decisive event that demarcates the modern is the bringing of what he calls 'bare life' (from the Greek *zoe*) under the purview of politics. And yet unlike Foucault, he does not think that this marks the end of the principle of sovereignty in political life, and the inauguration of something entirely new:

> The inclusion of bare life in the political realm constitutes the original – if concealed – nucleus of sovereign power. It can even be said that the production of a biopolitical body is the original activity of sovereign power (1998: 6).

Drawing upon the work of Carl Schmitt, Agamben suggests that sovereignty is established not under the law but rather by claiming a state of exception in relation to it: 'The sovereign, having the legal power to suspend the validity of the law, legally places himself outside the law (1998:15).' It is this, the "sovereign exception," that establishes the very possibility of any legal order. Moreover, Agamben argues, it

---

[39] I am grateful to Steffen Jensen for suggesting this path of analysis in his comments on the first draft of this paper, just one week before the attacks on the World Trade Center. It is remarkable how many scholars have since found Agamben useful in thinking about the Bush administration's efforts to suspend the rule of law in the United States, under a declared state of emergency, in what he calls the 'war on terrorism'. See, for example, Zizek (2002).

is in the power of the sovereign to *decide* to whom the legal order applies, and who stands outside of it (i.e. who is "banned" from subjection to the law) that the very authority of the law is established. And finally, it is in the figure of *homo sacer*, the person who stands on the threshold of society as one who can be killed without the killer being punished ("he who may be killed, but not sacrificed"), that the convergence of sovereignty and biopolitical governance is most clearly represented. As the Zimbabwean situation makes strikingly clear – no less than the American situation after the World Trade Center attack – far from being a contradiction of political modernity, such a convergence may well define it.[40]

Here one may cite any number of strategies of rule pursued by Mugabe. There is, of course, his capacity to both make law virtually by decree – most recently the Citizenship Act, the Public Order and Security Act, the Land Acquisition Act, and the Access to Information and Protection of Privacy Act – and to suspend its applicability to certain persons under certain circumstances virtually at will.[41] But it is in the modes of exclusion of Zimbabwean citizens from the right to obtain the means of life through access to food and protection from violence, that the convergence of sovereign with biopolitical power comes most sharply into view.[42]

'Selling out': The politics of suspicion

In the tortured economy of national inclusion and exclusion, there is much talk about striking 'bargains' – about 'buying in' (a metaphor for gullibility) and about 'selling-out'. Here are Vice-President Msika and Speaker of Parliament Mnangagwa haranguing youth in Bindura, as reported in *The Herald* (25 September 2000). Joseph Msika claims:

> *Whites do not like us: do not be fooled by their smiles. These people are the same everywhere. They are going behind our back and yet every farmer, both white and black, has agreed that we have to share land equally...You think whites create jobs. It is because you are brainwashed. You have a sell-out mentality, you are sell-outs.*

---

[40] For Agamben, it is the refugee camp and the concentration camp that best exemplify this modern convergence.

[41] Thus, the capacity of the youth militia to maim and commit arson with impunity when the targets are suspected members of the opposition. Thus, the detention without trial of over one hundred protestors on 16 June 2002, and the denial of medical care to those among them who were beaten ferociously by police. Thus, also, the violent eviction and arrest in August 2002 of hundreds of white farmers, many without eviction orders and in violation of earlier Supreme Court rulings.

[42] The Citizenship Act can be read as a strategy of both racial and national purification, converting citizens into refugees on their own soil as well as forcing many into exile.

Referring to the parliamentary seats lost to the MDC in the Midlands, Emmerson Mnangagwa announces:

> We discovered that money was the uppermost thing during the campaign period. Takazvambaradzwa vekuzvambaradwa zviya izvi *(we were thoroughly beaten)*. This is why we failed dismally to garner all seats as before. What consoles us is that even in Munhumutapa's era, there were sell-outs.

As we know well enough, those named sell-outs – both during the liberation war, and during *gukurahundi* – were usually humiliated, sometimes tortured, and often shot. The bitter metaphorical language of the market thus finds its way into the politics of exclusion. But what exactly does a sell-out sell? Sometimes it is their own identity, and sometimes it is someone else's, someone who held them in their trust. In this latter sense there is a close kinship with witchcraft, and witch-finding blurs with the identification of 'sell-outs' repeatedly in narratives of the liberation war (see especially Alexander et al., 2000:172-79). The motivation for these acts is most often explained retrospectively in terms of personal animosity or jealousy, but the homology between the figure of the witch and that of the sell-out is grounded in the notion that both dissimulate their identities in order to betray their victims. Appearing to be one of us, they in fact are preparing to eat us alive.

At a time such as this, to be identified, or still worse *named* as belonging outside of the nation, can instill the most profound kind of fear, erasing in an instant the horizon of belonging in future time to the nation-space. For some, this presents a dilemma and a temptation to compromise, to 'sell-out.' When farm workers were being driven off occupied farms in Hwedza and Doma by the thousands in August, 2000, Brian Latham, in the trade journal *The Farmer*, warned white commercial farmers not to be duped by offers emanating from Zanu (PF) officials to make individual deals in return for cooperating with the invasions:

> [T]here are still those out there promising salvation through appeasement, making promises that have no substance and reassuring troubled farmers that the solution lies in capitulation. Well it doesn't...Too many people are turning to people with perceived connections to solve their problems. That makes no sense when you consider that these alleged connections are...the very people who are orchestrating the violence. And did these people, with all their infamous connections, stop Doma's destruction? Did they prevent the

> *torrent of farm workers made homeless in Hwedza when so-called war veterans drove them out like cattle? No, they did not. In fact they have not prevented a single act of destruction since Zimbabwe's madness started.* [43]

Then, in a remarkable formulation, he calls upon them to keep an open mind about the Joint Resettlement Initiative, an undertaking by commercial farmers and ministry representatives to arrive at a mutually acceptable resettlement and land sharing solution:

> *...when things come right for Zimbabwean farmers, and they will, life will be very different to the old status quo that has existed for the last 20 years. Farmers do not live in liberated zones surrounded by enemy territory and future governments are going to insist on a great deal more integration than previously existed. In that regard, the MDC's message is clear: "Be Zimbabwean or be off." Fortunately they won't use the same heinous tactics employed by the present rogue regime, but that aside, they will still want to see an end to a white enclave, whether real or perceived.*

He casts a final barb at the large, multinational operators who are apparently willing to condone the nationalisation of all white-owned commercial land in exchange for the right to retain their own – to 'sell the soul of agriculture', as Latham puts it. 'The appeasers and dealers, the quislings and deceivers will lose because they always do. And as for the future, understand that Zimbabwe is about to grow up, to come of age. Racism will be derided from black and white – and by black and white.' Here is a dream of rational enlightenment in the midst of despair, of a modernist apotheosis ('salvation') that can restore to the national body the 'soul' that it stands to lose should some strike a Faustian bargain with a seductive state. Race, and the interior borders it articulates, will vanish, and Zimbabwe will 'come of age,' although perhaps it will be measured somewhat differently than it is by Tim Chigodo (the government-allied journalist whom I quoted earlier.)

---

[43] This, and subsequent quotations are from Latham's article, 'Losing Agriculture's Soul', *The Farmer*, 20 August 2001. (I am grateful to Bill Derman for bringing this piece to my attention.) Latham is now Deputy Editor of *The Standard*, a newspaper whose journalists have been persecuted for their criticism of the Mugabe regime.

Conclusion: A burning fear

Let me return to the events of late July, 2002, with which I began this chapter. There is a curious circularity underlying the politics of that day – a circularity of exclusion, of banishment. Mugabe bans the (critical) public from recognising the performative act that establishes him as head of state in parliament. Through his brother-in-law Marufu, he effectively bans the farm workers from the entitlement to land and to jobs.[44] He in turn is 'banned' by the opposition, who refuse to recognise his claim to office as being within the rule of law. And he (along with his ministers, senior army officers, and senior civil servants) have had their assets frozen, and have been banned from travel by the U.S., the European Union, and other western governments.

These last may sound like the relatively innocuous or merely ineffectual gestures of international diplomacy. But some forms of banishment that follow from contests of sovereignty have, as their objective or consequence, the reduction of their victims to the status of *homo sacer* or bare life. That status is confirmed, indeed constituted, through the ascription of the name 'terrorist'. It has often been observed – especially in the aftermath of the World Trade Center attacks – that in any violent contest over sovereignty, one side's 'terrorists' are the other side's 'freedom fighters'. Victory for those challenging sovereign power can produce a quick reversal of these attributions. Indeed, such has been the case with those who were once labeled 'terrs' by the Rhodesian state, and who were subsequently recast after the liberation struggle as 'war veterans' (and rather more selectively as 'heroes'). After 1980, the spectre of terrorism was displaced, first onto those called 'dissidents' who were pursued by the Fifth Brigade in 1983-84, and much more recently onto the opposition MDC.

Yet along the shifting semiotic boundary that divides 'terrorists' from 'patriots' in Zimbabwe, lies a kind of no-man's land – a ground in which loyalties and identities are negotiated under the pressure of extreme brutality. Here, the agents of violence are given a status at the boundary of institutionalised power and what lies beyond it. In the past, they have been called 'auxiliaries', 'militias', or 'special forces' – names that suggest a certain freedom of manoeuvre at 'the threshold on which violence passes over into law and law passes over into violence' (Agamben, 1998:32).

---

[44] Only two per cent of the beneficiaries of the Fast Track Resettlement Programme have been farm workers. An estimated 70,000 workers have been driven off the farms where they formerly worked and resided.

In the no-man's-land that separates the horror of the Zimbabwean present from the dreamtime of a non-racial, 'fully mature' nation-state, the government announced in December 2001 that it would henceforth require all youth to perform six months of 'national' service. The first ten thousand who were so conscripted and trained at camps across the country were rapidly dubbed the Green Bombers, after a particularly aggressive breed of flies. Now they are known as the Black Boots. In the months leading up to and following the Presidential and then Rural District Councils elections, they torched the huts and businesses of thousands of opposition sympathisers, beating and often sexually assaulting or torturing their occupants.[45] We are reminded that to set a hut alight in Zimbabwe has long been the performative act that sentences one to banishment and ostracism, whether for an infringement on the moral order (Worby 1997), for 'selling-out' (Alexander et al., 2000:109) or for defying the local authority of the state (Hammar, 2001). Zimbabweans have altogether too much experience with this kind of terror, as both victims and perpetrators (Werbner, 1991; Worby, 1998; Alexander et al., 2000). But this is no more evidence of anarchy than it is of irrationality. It is, rather, evidence of both a continuation and a rearticulation of the relation between sovereignty and the power over life through strategies of exception and exclusion; it is the strategy of the ban that, ironically, constitutes the rule of law. The utopian narratives that envision a nation on the threshold of modernity in Zimbabwe do not preclude the practices of exclusionary violence that have been so well rehearsed in the past. At the moment, it is by no means clear how many Zimbabweans will survive to decide whether and how that threshold has been crossed.

---

[45] For graphic documentation, see Christina Lamb, 'Dora, 12, gang-raped by Mugabe's men for four hours'. *Sunday Telegraph* (UK) 25 August 2002. An interview Lamb conducted with a young man who had fled one of the training camps is indicative of how women are being situated as 'bare life', beyond the threshold of morality and the rule of law: 'There were about 200 of us in the camp and we called ourselves 'the taliban'. Our doctrine was to be against the white man, he was our worst enemy, and our hero was bin Laden because of the way he stood up against the West. We were trained to be vigilant, always looking for opposition supporters, and were told if we saw anyone with an MDC T-shirt we must assault them with whips, catapults, steel bars. The idea was to instill fear in people so they would be frightened to vote and to take revenge against those who had. Then a couple of months ago they said it is the women who are behind this campaign to bring back white rule. They told us to take them to the bush, that they are daughters of dogs and coconuts, and to bring young ones back to the camp to service us. When I said we can't do this, that these are our sisters, they accused me of being a 'sell-out' and beat me.'

References

Agamben, Giorgio, 1998. *Homo Sacer: Sovereign Power and Bare Life*. Stanford: Stanford University Press.

Alexander, Jocelyn, JoAnn McGregor and Terence Ranger, 2000. *Violence and Memory: One Hundred Years in the 'Dark Forests' of Matabeleland*. London: James Currey.

Arce, Alberto, and Norman Long, 1999. 'Reconfiguring Modernity and Development from an Anthropological Perspective.' In A. Arce and N. Long (eds), *Anthropology, Development and Modernities: Exploring Discourses, Countertendencies and Violence*. London: Routledge, pp.1-31.

Bhabha, Homi, 1984. 'Of Mimicry and Men: The Ambivalence of Colonial Discourse.' *October*. 28:125-133.

Chakrabarty, Dipesh 2000. *Provincializing Europe: Postcolonial Thought and Historical Difference*. Princeton, NJ: Princeton University Press.

Clifford, James, 1988. *The Predicament of Culture*. Cambridge: Harvard University Press.

Chabal, Patrick, and Jean-Pascal Daloz, 1999. *Africa Works: Disorder as a Political Instrument*. Oxford: James Currey.

Cowen, M, P., and R.W. Shenton, 1996. *Doctrines of Development*. London: Routledge.

Dean, Mitchell, 2001. 'Demonic Societies: Liberalism, Biopolitics and Sovereignty.' In T.B. Hansen and F. Stepputat, *States of Imagination: Ethnographic Explorations of the Postcolonial State*. Durham: Duke University Press. pp. 41-64.

Eisenstadt, S.N. (ed.), 2000 'Multiple Modernities.' *Daedalus*. Winter, pp. 1-29.

Fabian, Johnannes, 1983. *Time and the Other: How Anthropology Makes its Object*. New York: Columbia University Press.

Ferguson, James, 1997. 'Paradoxes of Sovereignty and Independence: "Real" and "Pseudo" Nation-States and the Depoliticization of Poverty.' In Karen Fog Olwig and Kirsten Hastrup (eds), *Siting Culture: The Shifting Anthropological Object*. London and New York: Routledge. pp. 123-141.

Foucault, Michel, 1990 (1978). *The History of Sexuality. Volume 1: An Introduction*. New York: Vintage.

Gilroy, Paul, 1993. *The Black Atlantic: Modernity and Double Consciousness*. London: Verso; Cambridge, MA: Harvard University Press.

Hammar, Amanda, 2001. "The Day of Burning': Eviction and Reinvention in the Margins of Northwest Zimbabwe'. *Journal of Agrarian Change.* 1(4), pp. 550-574.

Hardt, Michael, and Antonio Negri, 2000. *Empire.* Cambridge, MA: Harvard University Press.

Hoffman, John, 1999. *Sovereignty.* Minneapolis: University of Minnesota Press.

Kelly, John D. and Martha Kaplan, 2001. *Represented Communities: Fiji and World Decolonization.* Chicago: University of Chicago Press.

Kriger, Norma, 2003. *Guerrilla Veterans in Post-war Zimbabwe: Symbolic and Violent Politics, 1980-1987.* Cambridge: Cambridge University Press.

Lan, David, 1986. *Guns and Rain: Guerillas and Spirit Mediums in Zimbabwe.* London: James Currey.

Mamdani, Mahmood, 1996. *Citizen and Subject: Contemporary Africa and the Legacy of Late Colonialism.* Princeton, NJ: Princeton University Press.

McGregor, JoAnn, 2002. 'The Politics of Disruption: War Veterans and the Local State in Zimbabwe'. *African Affairs,* 101, pp. 9-37.

Menon, Louis, 2001. *The Metaphysical Club.* New York: Farrar, Strauss, and Giroux.

Mitchell, Timothy, 1999. Introduction. In T. Mitchell (ed.), *The Question of Modernity.* Minneapolis: University of Minnesota Press. pp. xi-xxvii.

Moyo, Sam, 2001. 'The Land Occupation Movement and Democratisation in Zimbabwe: Contradictions of Neoliberalism'. *Millenium: Journal of International Studies,* 2001, Vol. 30, No. 2, pp. 311-330.

Raftopoulos, Brian, 1999. 'Problematising Nationalism in Zimbabwe: A Historiographical Review.' *Zambezia.* XXVI (ii), pp. 115-134.

Rotberg, Robert I., 2002. 'Failed States in a World of Terror'. *Foreign Affairs.* 81 (4), pp. 127-140.

Rutherford, Blair, 1999. 'To Find an African Witch: Anthropology, Modernity, and Witch-Finding in North-West Zimbabwe.' *Critique of Anthropology.* 19(1), pp. 89-101.

Schneider, Mark, 1993. *Culture and Enchantment.* Chicago: University of Chicago Press.

Stoler, Ann Laura, 1995. *Race and the Education of Desire*. Durham: Duke University Press.

Torgovnick, Marianna, 1991. *Gone Primitive: Savage Intellects, Modern Lives*. Chicago: University of Chicago Press.

Trouillot, Michel Rolph, 1991. 'Anthropology and the Savage Slot'. In R. Fox (ed.), *Reinventing Anthropology*. Santa Fe: American Research Press.

Werbner, Richard, 1991. *Tears of the Dead. The Social Biography of an African Family*. Washington, DC: Smithsonian Institution Press.

Worby, Eric, 1997. 'Eleven Guilty Men From Goredema: Parallel Justice and the Moralities of Local Administration in Northwestern Zimbabwe'. *Anthropologica*. 39,1-2, pp. 71-77.

Worby, Eric, 1998. 'Tyranny, Parody, and Ethnic Polarity: Ritual Engagements with the State in Northwestern Zimbabwe'. *Journal of Southern African Studies*. 24, 3, pp. 337-54.

Worby, Eric, 2000. "Discipline without Oppression': Sequence, Timing and Marginality in Southern Rhodesia's Post-War Development Regime'. *Journal of African History*. 41, 1 (2000), pp. 101-125.

White, Luise, 2001. 'Race, Regiment, and Counter-insurgency: An Exploration in Military History and Ideas about Nationality in Rhodesia'. Paper presented to the Agrarian Studies Colloquium, Yale University, 12 October 2001.

Zizek, Slavoj, 2002. 'Homo Sacer in Afghanistan'. *Lacanian Ink*. No. 20, pp. 100-113.

Chapter 3

'Squatters', Veterans and the State in Zimbabwe[1]

Jocelyn Alexander

It is something of a truism to state that the process of controlling and contesting access to land powerfully shaped the Rhodesian state, and both white and black politics in the colonial period. It has no less obviously played a central role in independent Zimbabwe. Since 1980, land has served as a source of political patronage; its control and distribution has played a key role in shaping the post-independence state, and the state's relationship to its citizens; and it has been central to political mobilisation and the legitimating ideology of Zimbabwe's rulers.[2] At the same time, however – and this has gone less widely noted – there have been profound shifts in official and popular discourses over land, in the nature of social movements seeking to claim land, and in the consequences for and role of the state. In this chapter, I trace some of these shifts in order to place the land occupations that started in February 2000 in perspective. I argue that the unstable alliances that currently dominate debates over land stand starkly at odds with official practice and popular initiative for most of the independence period. Current developments suggest that nationalism, social movements engaged in the struggle for land, and state authority are being radically reconstructed, in ways likely to have a profound impact on both claims to land and the political future of Zimbabwe.

Claiming land in the 1980s

Occupations of 'white' land after independence were a key force behind the pace of early land redistribution. If we were to look for

---

[1] Thanks are owed for insightful comments to the participants in the 'Rethinking Land, State and Citizenship through the Zimbabwe Crisis' Conference, Copenhagen, 3-5 September 2001, and to Amanda Hammer, Stig Jensen, Brian Raftopoulos, and Sam Moyo for additional detailed comments.
[2] The post-independence history of land is most fully treated by Moyo (1995, 2000c).

precedents for the boom in occupations in 2000, this would appear an obvious place to start. However, while both phases marked a radical reconstruction of the state and redefinition of nationalism, the nature of these processes was very different, and in some ways they constituted mirror images of each other.

From radical redistribution to 'rationality'

Zimbabwe's liberation movements had promised a radical redistribution of land as well as an accountable, responsive state (see e.g. Alexander et al., 2000; Ranger, 1985). The transition to independence in 1980 was, however, hedged in by the constraints of a negotiated independence, and the related choice of the new Zanu (PF) government to emphasise 'moderation and reconciliation'. In stark contrast to today's rhetoric, the government defended the central role of whites in the economy. Rather than targets of attack, white farmers rapidly became 'something of a protected species' (Palmer, 1990:167). Moderation and reconciliation also left much of the Rhodesian state's bureaucratic and security structures in place. This was a highly centralised and powerful state, ill-suited to accommodating popular demands. Post-independence efforts at decentralisation were notably ineffective. Newly elected representative institutions at district level were imbued with neither decision-making authority nor substantial control over resources (Alexander, 1994:326-31). Instead, Zanu (PF) used the powerful state it had inherited to reinforce its control over popular movements as well as over political opposition, most dramatically in a violent campaign against Zapu (see Alexander et al., 2000).

Zanu (PF)'s political programme and the centralised nature of the state had significant implications for agrarian policy reform. The failure to decentralise power within ministries or to local authorities reinforced the influence which Rhodesian ideas and practices exerted over agrarian reform. Crucially, the responsible ministries did not challenge the beliefs and practices which had informed Rhodesian 'technical development', the set of modernising policies which had long shaped interventions in African farming, and which reached their height in the Native Land Husbandry Act (NHLA) of 1951. The colonial myth of African farmers as traditional, subsistence-oriented and inefficient, in contrast to the 'commercial' white farmers, was left largely intact in the early 1980s (Alexander, 1994:330-32; Drinkwater, 1991). Land redistribution was rapidly construed as a technical exercise, and one in which the goal of productivity came to hold a central place. The success of resettlement would lie in its ability to produce marketed surpluses. To achieve this, officials stressed the need for bureaucratic control over settler selection and careful land-use planning. In this vision, there was little room for popular participation or the historically informed claims to restitution that had animated the liberation war. By far the most dominant resettlement model followed the pattern of the NLHA, and within resettlement schemes (at least theoretically) settlers were dependent on state-issued permits, and had no elected representation (Kinsey, 1983; Alexander, 1994:333-35).

The technical and economic analysis of resettlement within the key ministries thus paved the way for a shift away from the liberation war rhetoric of reclaiming the lost lands, to a discourse cast as rational and scientific. It was a shift that depended on centralised, bureaucratic decision-making, not local democracy. This was of course not a shift that went uncontested. The first few years of independence were a period of transition in which land redistribution was a key demand of the government's most populous constituency. At least initially, local Zanu (PF) leaders, chiefs and others had access to powerful patrons and the space to act beyond the reach of state institutions. The 1980s were nonetheless to see a profound re-making of the relationship between the state, the ruling party and citizens, and a redefinition of nationalism. In stark contrast to recent developments, this period was primarily about asserting the prerogatives of a modernising state, and of limiting and controlling demands made on the basis of liberation war promises. It was top-down development, not bottom-up restitution that would legitimate the new government.

'Squatting' in Chimanimani District

Chimanimani District in Manicaland Province dramatically illustrates the messy process through which control over land redistribution and the ideological content of nationalism was centralised. Early 1980s' Chimanimani enjoyed a propitious combination of factors as far as resettlement was concerned – large swathes of abandoned land, loyalty to the ruling party, powerful patrons within Zanu (PF). Many other areas faced more difficult circumstances: in some provinces the number of abandoned farms was tiny; in areas dominated by Zapu, political patronage rapidly evaporated; in lower rainfall areas, the occupation of land was less desired than additional grazing land, and 'poach grazing' proved a far less secure means of staking a claim to land than occupation (Alexander, 1991). Nonetheless, even in districts such as

Chimanimani, deep fissures rapidly opened between official and popular notions of land redistribution, as well as over a host of governance issues, from tax collection to the establishment and functioning of courts and councils (Alexander, 1996).

Immediately after independence, expectations of a rapid and popularly controlled redistribution of land ran high, fed by guerrilla promises and nationalist claims to the 'lost lands'. Guerrillas launched attacks on some white farmers in the first year of independence, but they were rapidly removed from the picture as demobilisation and army integration proceeded (Kriger, 1996:77-80). They had little impact in post-independence Chimanimani, due to its distance from guerrilla Assembly Points. Instead, people turned to the local party to demand specific pieces of land from which communities, often defined in terms of chieftaincies, had earlier been evicted. These demands stood at odds with the official view that equity, conservation and productivity could only be ensured through state control over settler selection and careful technical planning. Initially, however, government ministries were ill-prepared for the enormous and complex task of planning and administering resettlement.

In Chimanimani, these contradictions caused a great deal of consternation among local Zanu (PF) leaders. Zanu (PF) committees were initially the most important representative institutions, and were loyal to the ruling party. They were not, however, effectively subordinated to a national hierarchy: Zanu (PF) existed as a thin veneer at the national level and a multitude of autonomous and often independent-minded committees at levels below the district. District steering committees were formed in 1980, but these remained poorly incorporated into the national structure of the party, and pursued an agenda based on the expectations raised in the war years, not on the policies formulated since the war (Alexander 1996:180-84). Unsurprisingly, they expected a sympathetic hearing from higher levels. In 1980, for example, Chimanimani's Zanu (PF) steering committee repeatedly pressed for faster land redistribution through government channels, requesting information about resettlement and reporting demands for land from its communal area constituency again and again.[3] The (still white) district commissioner merely counselled patience. Distrust rapidly marked both sides of the equation: local appeals were based on a nationalism that was rapidly losing favour.

---

[3] Minutes of the Second Meeting for the Formation of a District Council in Melsetter, 25-26 June 1980.

In early 1981, Deputy Minister of Lands Moven Mahachi visited Chimanimani's newly established district council. The council's elected members were drawn entirely from the ranks of somewhat suspicious local Zanu (PF) leaders who feared the new council was all too similar to its toothless and much attacked colonial predecessor. Mahachi did not assuage their fears; he informed them that 49 of Chimanimani's farms were to be acquired, but would not tell councillors which ones. He also emphasised that claims to land based on colonial evictions or chieftaincies were 'not practical', a view that clearly diverged from councillors' understanding of legitimate claims. Mahachi's views also diverged from those of politicians, chiefs and some district officials, leading to land occupations that were sometimes led by chiefs themselves and condoned by politicians.[4]

Unofficial occupations were common because resettlement criteria had not been fully explained at the outset and because the criteria were considered unacceptable even when they were explained.[5] As a result, a rift opened between people and their elected representatives in the district, and between both of these and the national government. When resettlement forms finally arrived in Chimanimani, few were filled out;[6] rumours spread that those resettled would have their crops taken or their permits revoked.[7] As the 1981 rainy season approached, people's objections to official resettlement led to a large-scale movement onto the vast areas of commercial land lying vacant in the district, a movement that was paralleled in much of Manicaland. In late 1981, councillors again sought government approval for popular land occupations, stressing in a letter to the Ministry of Lands the approach of the rains, and the 'landless plight' in the communal areas.[8] The Ministry did not respond – in fact the first formal resettlement would not get underway

---

[4] Minutes of a Meeting at the District Commissioner's Conference Hall, Melsetter, 27 February 1981. In 1981, for example, Chimanimani's MP pressed for recognition of the abolished Saurombe chieftaincy, and for recognition of the Saurombe people's collective claims to land from which they had been evicted in the colonial period. Officials, chiefs and Zanu (PF) leaders in the district backed the Saurombe claim; members of the chieftaincy began returning from Mutare and elsewhere, expecting a return of alienated land. The Saurombe chieftaincy and its claim to land did not receive official sanction. Nonetheless, and with the backing of politicians, 'Chief' Saurombe proceeded to authorise the occupation of neighbouring farms.

[5] Minutes of the Mabvazuwa District Council, Melsetter, 27 May 1981.

[6] This was not a unique reaction: in the province as a whole only just over ten per cent of resettlement forms were returned. Minutes of the Provincial Meeting with the Deputy Minister of Lands, Resettlement and Rural Development at the Office of the Undersecretary (Development), Mutare, 1 October 1981.

[7] Interview, Local Government Promotion Officer, Chimanimani, 31 October 1988.

[8] Minutes of the Mabvazuwa District Council, Chimanimani, 29 October 1981.

until 1983. Nonetheless, people continued to occupy land purchased for resettlement, often under the aegis of local party branches and chiefs, and often with the perceived or actual encouragement of officials and politicians.

Though official concern over the occupations – or 'squatting' as it was called – grew in 1981 and early 1982, policies remained largely sympathetic in this part of the country. 'Squatters' had regular access to ministers and politicians; police were instructed not to arrest them until resettlement was underway; and land redistribution was speeded up through the 'accelerated' resettlement programme, distinguished by its lack of planning and infrastructure (Kinsey, 1983:176-77). Those who had occupied land in the early 1980s were in fact largely accepted as settlers, leading councillors and others in Chimanimani to query whether filling out forms was indeed the best way to gain access to land.[9] However, the attitude towards new occupations, and particularly towards those occupying private land, quickly hardened. This shift was justified largely in terms of protecting the foreign currency earning capacity of commercial estates and farms. Evictions focused on clearing private, largely white-owned, land. Minister of Lands Mahachi described 'squatters' as 'undisciplined and criminal elements' who 'intended to frustrate the agricultural industry and resettlement process'. He stressed the importance of evicting squatters in terms of their effect on 'foreign exchange earners'.[10]

The heyday of large-scale occupations was coming to a close. Their effectiveness in Chimanimani declined as vacant land became scarce, resettlement schemes fuller, politicians less sympathetic and government bureaucracies stronger. Enforcing evictions, sometimes with brutal force, became more acceptable and more common with time. The first half of the 1980s can thus be seen as a period in which the demands for control over land redistribution from autonomous and outspoken local party leaders, chiefs and others were rejected in favour of centralised state control and planning. This process required the marginalisation of the political institutions that had emerged from the war, and a rejection of their attempts to create a new relationship between people and government. Nationalism was not to be about the popularly controlled restitution of the lost lands, but about modernisation and productivity, delivered through a highly centralised bureaucracy for the benefit of a disciplined citizenry.

---

[9] Minutes of the Mabvazuwa District Council, Chimanimani, 13 April 1983; interview, resettlement officer, Shinja, 26 October 1988.
[10] *The Herald*, 23 December 1983.

Consolidating control: Squatter Control Committees

The slowdown in resettlement after the early 1980s boom was marked by a sustained, if contentious, economic critique of land redistribution, a growing tendency for members of government to enter the ranks of commercial farmers, and the rising influence of technical bureaucracies in the making of agrarian policy (Moyo, 1995). The primary focus of 'resettlement' shifted to the deeply unpopular policy of communal area reorganisation, i.e. land-use planning within the former reserves, a policy that bore a striking resemblance once again to the modernising NLHA (Alexander, 1994:338-43). Reflecting these changes, a new discourse emerged around 'squatting', emphasising its destructive and criminal nature, and the threat that it posed to orderly government, the environment and the economy. This was an ideologically ambivalent critique, and it was often contradicted by praise for the resourcefulness, productivity and tenacity of 'squatters', as well as sympathy for their status as nationalists and land-starved peasants. Mashonaland West's Provincial Administrator, for example, defended 'squatters' on moral grounds, but concluded that, 'morality breeds a soft approach to dealing with squatters and this invites more and more squatters who probably will run away from those areas where seemingly tougher action is taken'.[11] Under pressure from tens of thousands of 'squatters', the moral argument gave way to administrative coercion in the second half of the 1980s.[12]

The hardened official critique of 'squatting' was accompanied by the introduction of new control measures. In 1985, the Ministry of Local Government took responsibility for 'squatters' and rapidly instituted a number of changes. 'Squatters' were denied the automatic access to ministers and politicians they had previously enjoyed, and powerful Squatter Control Committees were established.[13] Squatter Control Committees were designed to co-ordinate the actions of all government departments involved in evictions and resettlement. In 1986, Minister of Local Government Enos Chikowore stressed that 'land grabbers' would be 'ruthlessly removed and dealt with in accordance with the existing legal machinery.... [N]o squatter ... will be selected for resettlement.'[14] Developments in the mid to late 1980s were thus singularly inauspicious for those desiring land: land redistribution no longer held pride of place in official agrarian

---

[11] MWPDC (n.d. [1987]). Also see Yeros (1999: 20-21); MPDC 1985.
[12] Mashonaland West hosted some 36,000 'squatters' in 1987 (MWPDC n.d. [1987]), while Manicaland hosted an estimated 50,000 in 1985 (MPDC 1985).
[13] Ministry of Local Government, 1985, Circular No. 10, Addendum A.
[14] Ministry of Local Government Policy Statement, 7 May 1986.

reform strategy, a formidable ministerial machinery was devoted to squatter control, and a hostile – if morally ambivalent – critique of squatter activities pervaded government.

In this process, the burden of disciplining squatters – but not the capacity to do so – was passed down to district levels. In the context of land shortage, growing unemployment, and huge 'squatter' populations, District Administrators (DAs) found themselves, as chairmen of the Squatter Control Committees, with the unenviable task of controlling occupations and enforcing evictions, but with very little resettlement land, and little control over decisions regarding resettlement. Few issues divided both the state and the government as occupations did. DAs criticised their lack of control over land acquisition, and the criteria applied by technical planners; they complained of the pressure they came under from politicians; and they bemoaned the intransigence of squatters and the unpopularity that followed from eviction (e.g. CDDC, 1986). In practice, District Squatter Control Committees simply compiled lists of people illegally occupying land and lists of farms which might be available for resettlement and then sought to match the two in such a way as to quickly clear private land and forestall further squatting. Committee debates largely excluded consideration of those who had filled out resettlement forms, while councillors were kept in the dark regarding land purchases on the grounds that they would use this knowledge to encourage further occupations; as a result, people who remained in communal areas had little chance of resettlement. One district official admitted, 'Squatters take advantage of the DA who wants to resolve the conflicts so he settles the squatters and the communal area people don't have a chance.'[15] This logic was clear to chiefs who 'complained that all farms bought are geared towards the resettlement programme at the expense of the people in communal areas'.[16]

The pressure to remove people from private land meant that, ironically, 'squatters' continued to dominate resettlement, while those who had played by the book were largely excluded from consideration. The exclusion of communal area representatives from decisions regarding resettlement bred deep resentment. To councillors, resettlement land, which was less heavily populated and stocked than communal areas, looked underused, and so the exclusion of communal area farmers seemed unjustified. Moreover, the unequal distribution of land between commercial and communal

---

[15] Interview, District Agritex Extension Officer, Chimanimani, 4 November 1988.
[16] Minutes of the Manicaland Provincial Council of Chiefs, Mutare, 5 January 1989.

areas was still all too visible and keenly felt.[17] Chiefs, drawing on the promises of the guerrilla war, argued, 'they need the land that their children liberated from the hands of the white commercial settlers'.[18] The privileging of the technical and economic over the moral and the historical left the promises of the liberation war ringing hollow in their ears, and undermined both chiefs and councillors in the eyes of their own constituencies.

Altering relations between state, government and people

Land thus played a complex role in state formation, nationalism and political mobilisation in the first decade of Zimbabwean independence. The land occupations of the early 1980s relied on a unique set of circumstances, and were a powerful expression of popular nationalism defined in terms of the reclamation of the lost lands, as a process of restitution. These occupations expressed a desire to right historical and moral wrongs. They just as importantly expressed a desire to reject the long-established colonial practice of exerting central state control over how and where people lived and farmed. That is, they expressed a desire for a new relationship between state and people. Local party committees, themselves only weakly linked to provincial or national party leaders, at first assumed that their demands would be heard. They appealed again and again to Ministers and officials and politicians, seeking to establish the legitimacy of their claims, and their right to make demands upon the state. But while some politicians remained sympathetic, the development bureaucracies did not. Zimbabwe's new rulers considered the political need to redistribute land paramount in the early 1980s, but they rejected popular control over the process. This choice was central to the process of state making, and to the redefinition of nationalism from the top down in terms of a modernising and increasingly neo-liberal project. The rapidly instilled lack of state accountability in this realm undid popular attempts to build a new relationship between government and people. Instead suspicion, distrust and a host of informal means of claiming land flourished.

The contradictions between post-independence policy and the popular nationalism of the liberation war produced deep divisions within the state and the party, as well as between them. The beleaguered district-level state institutions were left to deal with the

---

[17] Interviews with councillors, Chimanimani, 1988.
[18] Minutes of the Manicaland Provincial Council of Chiefs, Mutare, 5 January 1989.

consequences of limited land redistribution, and did so in ways which prejudiced the access to land of those who had remained in communal areas, while protecting private property and foreign exchange earnings. The legitimacy of local representative institutions was badly tarnished in the process.

Land in the 1990s

Though resettlement had proceeded on a vast scale in the first decade of independence, and though it was judged a success by donors, it did not effectively redress the historical grievances or economic woes of communities living in the former reserves. In this sense, resettlement was symbolically and politically weak. It is no surprise that as the Zanu (PF) government began to come under threat from political opposition, and as a result of anger over declining living standards and corruption, it reached for the land question once again.

Recasting redistribution and race

The renewed focus on land was clear in the run-up to the 1990 elections (Alexander, 1991:604-5), and in the promulgation of the New National Land Policy of 1990 which seemed to mark a real shift in commitment to redistribution. The policy promised an additional five million hectares for 110,000 families, while the constitutional changes of 1990 and 1993 and the 1992 Land Acquisition Act made it possible to compulsorily acquire land, signalling a new phase in land acquisition strategies in the post-Lancaster House era. Through the whole of the 1990s, Mugabe repeatedly made strong pronouncements on land, and stressed the moral duty of Britain as the previous colonial power to pay for the land. At the Zanu (PF) national people's conference in 1995, Mugabe called for the establishment of provincial committees which would identify land to be acquired, and attacked white farmers: 'The whites grabbed that land from us. However, we chose to buy it after independence. But do we have the money? No. Whether the money is available or not it is time we had the land to distribute to many landless people.... We risk losing our credibility as a Government.'[19]

---

[19] *The Chronicle*, 16 December 1995.

The concern for credibility proved well founded. As Sam Moyo has demonstrated, there were other priorities in the 1990s than that of giving the land to the landless.[20] It was programmes to benefit what was called the 'indigenous' elite that dominated. The most actively pursued policy was the 'promotion of black farmer entry into large scale farming' (Moyo, 1998:10). Moyo has called this 'economic nationalism', and seen its emergence as linked to the rise of the market ideology of structural adjustment, and a growing concern with racial inequality in the economic sphere (Moyo, 1994; 1995:7; 2000a:12). Race had not played a major role in the rhetoric of the 1980s – it had been explicitly subsumed under arguments regarding the economic importance of whites and the need for reconciliation – but in the second decade of independence, in a context of economic decline and state contraction, the very visible continued economic clout of whites became a target, and one that was all too easy to hit (Moyo, 2000a:23, 33).

State involvement in black elite accumulation of land in fact preceded the 1990 Land Policy. The leasing of state land to prominent figures seems to have started during the period of military and political repression in Matabeleland. In this region, state land purchased for resettlement was leased to Zanu (PF) elites, or people with Zanu (PF) connections, or taken over by the state farm parastatal. After the end of the conflict in December 1987, this process was scrutinised in the press, but it did not end. Instead, a newly absorbed elite – Zapu leaders – also benefited from access to state land in Matabeleland (Alexander, 1991:594-96). The practice subsequently spread: Mugabe's 1995 populist pronouncements on land were accompanied by the announcement that 56 commercial farms had been allocated to 'indigenous farmers'.[21] According to Moyo, some 400 black farmers leased state land under various programmes in the 1990s; approximately 350 others had acquired commercial farms.[22]

Despite the radical promises, resettlement in the 1990s seemed to focus on the highly visible – if not very significant in terms of its overall impact on the commercial farm sector – accumulation of land by the black elite.[23] It was not so much the existence of this

---

[20] Ministries charged with smallholder resettlement were not afforded the resources to proceed any faster than the rate of roughly 2,000 families per year (Alexander 1991; Moyo 1998).

[21] *The Chronicle*, 16 December 1995.

[22] Moyo (2000b:7). In a later paper, Moyo (2001:7) cites the figure of 800 black commercial farmers by 1997.

[23] Moyo (2001:7) estimates only some ten per cent of commercial land was black-owned in the late 1990s.

goal that caused disillusionment as the way in which it appeared to sideline other claims to land, and to buttress an image of Zanu (PF) as corrupt and out of touch. Land redistribution still seemed to be occurring 'at the expense' of the communal areas, though now for very different reasons.

Local land claiming processes

It is important to note that the slow pace of land redistribution did not mark a diminution in land occupations in the 1990s, despite the relative invisibility of such processes, and the lack of 'civil society' advocacy for land claims (Moyo, 2001). The implementation of a structural adjustment package in 1991, and the ensuing decline in public investment in services and land redistribution, as well as economic decline and drought, placed a premium on gaining access to land and other resources. As Paris Yeros (1999) and Sam Moyo (2000c) have documented, land occupation and resource 'poaching' in the rural areas were essential to people's survival in a context of rising unemployment and spiralling costs of living. 'Squatting' took on new characteristics, however. It more often surfaced within communal areas and state lands, or took the form of illegal gold panning or grass cutting or poach grazing. Commercial farm lands were less centrally targeted due to their more effective – and at times brutal – protection, and the added weight placed upon them under structural adjustment as foreign exchange earning assets.

These sorts of 'squatting' nonetheless had important consequences for the state and its relationship with its constituencies. In communal areas, lines of patronage and conflict developed among councillors, party committees and chiefs, and between central and local government, as they competed for control over the processes through which people gained access to land. Land markets spread in the communal areas (though they had long existed). Membership in communities was defined in increasingly exclusive, and at times violent, ways as scarce grazing land was settled by people from other communal areas or those retrenched from urban, mine or farm employment. The local state's capacity to control these processes was severely undermined, leading to a drop in legitimacy in the eyes of both those demanding land, and those seeking to keep people off land they regarded as theirs. Yeros notes, 'a deepening break-down of rural institutions, increased ambiguity of authority in land administration, and the flourishing of "illegal", and costly, arrangements in pursuit of security of tenure – none of which bodes well for citizenship' (Yeros, 1999:13; Moyo, 1998:8-11).

Encroachments on resettlement schemes and state land were also significant and had similar effects. The terrible insecurity and narrowing of citizenship rights that accompanied these processes had high costs for those deemed to be 'squatters', whatever the land tenure regime.

Political strategies and alliances

In the latter half of the 1990s it was clear that, politically, resettlement was still not delivering while the demand for land remained extreme, and posed a threat to both the state's capacity and the ruling party's legitimacy. And this was of course far from the only threat: in the second half of the 1990s, Zanu (PF)'s brand of nationalism came under attack as never before. In 1996, civil servants went on strike, signalling an alliance with the increasingly confrontational Zimbabwe Congress of Trade Unions (ZCTU). The rise of the trade union movement in particular directly challenged Zanu (PF)'s control of the nationalist mantle, as did the protests of intellectuals, students, the urban middle classes and war veterans (Raftopoulos, 2001; Yeros, 2000). Veterans demonstrated violently in 1997, threatening the Zanu (PF) leadership (Kriger, 2001; Alexander et al., 2000; Moyo, 2001). Amidst all this, Mugabe faced challenges to his leadership from within Zanu (PF) (Moyo, 1998:5). He responded by allying with the veterans, acceding to their demands for compensation in late 1997, and at a stroke bringing economic chaos and a new political alignment.

It was in this heated context that the government designated 1,471 farms for compulsory acquisition. Land was one of the few goods it could still promise: in the straitened circumstances of the late 1990s, delivering employment, education and health care was a distant dream of the now politically suspect modernising state. The designation was accompanied by an uncompromising – though not unprecedented – rhetoric, aimed at whites and Britain. Mugabe maintained, 'We are going to take the land and we are not going to pay for the soil. That is our set policy. Our land was never bought [by the colonialists] and there is no way we could buy the land back' – Britain would have to do that.[24] However, the hasty and politically charged way in which the listing of farms took place, largely through the Zanu (PF)-dominated provincial land committees mooted in 1995, meant that 625 farms were simply 'de-listed' as they did not meet the government's own criteria. As Moyo (1998:5, 35) writes,

---

[24] *The Guardian*, 15 October 1997.

the designations 'tended to be marred by the increasingly provincialised political pressures which can be characterised as parochial and elitist': 'Fear of discrimination and exclusive tendencies in the land redistribution and wider indigenisation process cast heavy doubts on the decision makers in charge of land reform.' Many of the acquisition orders for the remaining farms were successfully challenged in court, to the great frustration of government (Moyo, 2000a:25-7). The government responded with efforts to mobilise donor support, producing a new land policy in June 1998 which reiterated the goals of acquiring five million hectares for smallholders as well as land for commercial settlement, and culminating in the high profile Donor's Conference of September 1998.

Land occupations in the late 1990s

The listing of farms raised expectations as well as suspicions among the land hungry, and was followed by a spate of occupations. These took a new form, evocative of the early 1980s in the sense that they received a great deal of media coverage and the attention of prominent politicians. Sam Moyo (2001:12) reports some 30 occupations in 1997, starting in September, mostly on farms listed for compulsory acquisition. From June to August 1998, occupations spread in central, southern and northern Zimbabwe. In Marondera in Mashonaland East, people from Svosve occupied four farms in a particularly high-profile case.[25] The occupiers were visited repeatedly by high-ranking party and government members, including Vice President Simon Muzenda from whom promises of resettlement were extracted. Further occupations followed in Guruve, Makonde, Macheke, Hurungwe and Odzi, involving thousands of people. People in Dende Communal Area north-east of Harare occupied Munenga Farm, on which they said their ancestors were buried, when they heard that it had been 'de-listed' and sold. Their MP, Minister Herbert Murerwa, assured them they would be settled on the farm. They said they would not leave until they had received a written undertaking from government.[26] In Matabeleland North, 500 people settled themselves on four farms in Umguza District apparently with the encouragement of senior politicians, and proceeded to defy the efforts of Joseph Msika, Zanu (PF) national chairman and chair of

---

[25] On Svosve, see Yeros (1999: 13-16), who bases his account on field work by Rachael Knight (1998).
[26] *The Chronicle*, 11 August 1998.

the National Land Acquisition Committee, to remove them.[27] In Matabeleland South, people from Irisvale resettlement scheme who had occupied neighbouring Mbalabala Ranch received the attentions of Provincial Governor Stephen Nkomo and Zanu (PF) leaders.[28] These occupations were dominated by people from communal areas and resettlement schemes, but also included unemployed workers and war veterans. Most of the land occupied was white-owned commercial land, but state, church and black-owned farms were also targeted. Occupiers generally justified their actions in terms of their exclusion from resettlement, and their historical claims to land, i.e. in terms of restitution and broken nationalist promises (see Marongwe, this volume).

The official reaction to the occupations was mixed. In June 1998, Mugabe defended them, stressing that force should not be used to evict the land hungry, but reversed his position in August, warning of stern government action. In some places police moved in and burnt camps, or made shows of force in removing occupiers. Mugabe was nonetheless happy to use the Svosve occupiers as evidence of land hunger during the September land conference: donors were taken in minivans to speak to them themselves (Yeros, 1999:14-15).

The origins of these occupations remain subject to debate: there have been accusations that the government, through veterans and the party, organised them so as to pressure donors. The occupations certainly involved new actors, and evoked a new, if uneven, response from government. That people made alliances with the party or veterans, that they responded to official encouragement, does not however mean that there was not also a popular desire for land. Occupiers knew that they risked becoming targets of state violence, as some of them did. Sheltering under the umbrella of Zanu (PF) was a sensible strategy, though occupiers were also willing to angrily challenge MPs and Ministers, and showed an increasing sophistication in the targeting of particular farms. Rather than trying to label these occupations as *either* managed *or* popular, it is more useful to see them as both, as the result of the interaction between the needs of politicians for a constituency, of people for land, and of the government for a means to pressure donors.

The scale of ongoing occupations in 1999 is unclear. Moyo notes that there were reasons for waiting: the government seemed to be

---

[27] *The Mirror*, 31 July - 6 August 1998.
[28] *The Chronicle*, 11 August 1998.

showing clear signs of negotiating seriously for land at the Donors' Conference, and of taking action through the Inception Phase Framework Plan of early 1999, under which various resettlement models were to be tried out on one million hectares (Moyo, 2001; Moyo and Matondi, 2001). But there were continued and carefully targeted occupations nonetheless. As the rainy season dawned, at least four farms were occupied in Matabeleland North, including a state farm in Bubi, and a farm leased by Deputy Minister Obert Mpofu. Those on the state farm told Joseph Msika that he should act or they would peg the land themselves. In Matabeleland South, war veterans threatened to occupy the 47 farms comprising Marula Estates, already leased to a collection of people, including some prominent politicians, under the Commercial Farm Settlement Scheme.[29] People demanded that farms leased by the late Joshua Nkomo and other prominent Zapu officials after the Unity Accord be turned over for resettlement. Msika promised that three farms in Matobo would be resettled and that others (some already occupied) had been acquired.[30]

In 1999, expectations clearly ran high: tens of thousands of people reportedly registered for resettlement in Matabeleland North alone.[31] This expression of confidence in the government's resettlement plans stood in stark contrast to the suspicion of resettlement forms countrywide in the early 1980s. The renewed momentum of occupations was soon to be drastically accelerated, however, and to take on a very different form.

2000 and after: the new politics of land

The constitutional referendum of February 2000 marked a watershed in Zimbabwean politics. It developed into a battle between Zanu (PF) and the gathering forces of opposition. In a last-minute bid for votes, and very much under pressure from war veterans, Zanu (PF) had tacked onto its draft constitution a clause obliging Britain to pay for land confiscated by the state (Marongwe, this volume). Nonetheless, the 'No' vote won. Land was not the only issue for the majority of voters – wider economic questions, governance issues and the curbing of presidential powers were also key areas of concern (Rich Dorman, 2001:218-223).

---

[29] *Financial Gazette*, 9 November 1999; *Mirror*, 19 November 1999.
[30] *Financial Gazette*, 25 November 1999; 30 December 1999. See Ranger (1999: 279-82) on the longstanding struggles for land in this region.
[31] *Financial Gazette*, 21 October 1999.

The referendum defeat marked the moment when it became clear that the ruling party faced a major electoral challenge in the shape of the Movement for Democratic Change (MDC), and it forced a dramatic shift in the strategies of Zanu (PF). In this context, that war veterans should be so publicly invoked, and that they should be so prominently linked to the land issue was a political theatrics of great effectiveness. The populist rhetoric of land no longer convinced – action had to be taken. And who better to lead the charge than the newly on-side war veterans? In the new nationalist vision, veterans were the legitimate liberators of the land from whites seen as too slow to change and a former colonial power now cast more vehemently than ever as the major obstacle to 'real' decolonisation. The modernising agenda slipped entirely from view while parallels to the war years abounded: Mugabe donned combat fatigues and spoke of enemies and war, veterans occupied farms and held *pungwes*; white farmers reverted to their agric-alert security systems and were killed for the first time since the conflict in Matabeleland in the mid-1980s.

All this seemed to herald a return to the politics of the early 1980s when land occupations flourished with the patronage of politicians. Sam Moyo (2001:11, 3-4) has argued that though 'the character of the occupations has changed slightly' over the independence period 'their essence has remained the same'. He argues that the Zanu (PF) elite 'engineered' the land occupations up to 1984, then demobilised the movement only to remobilise it in the late 1990s through war veterans: the occupations that started in 2000 were the 'climax of a longer, less public, dispersed struggle over land'. It is certainly the case that land demands and their expression through occupations remained a constant, though the extent to which they were 'engineered' in the early 1980s by the ruling elite is questionable. There were other significant differences between the occupations of the early 1980s and those that started in 2000 in two linked respects: the ideology behind them, and their implications for the state and its citizenry. Grass-roots nationalism in the early 1980s had encompassed a desire both for the return of the land, and for an accountable, responsive state. Zanu (PF) in 2000 promised the land, but at the price of an extreme and violent political intolerance that severely undermined the long-standing popular aspirations for a 'good' state, and labelled as enemies a range of social groups that had once been included in the nationalist constituency. It was not a revived pre-independence nationalism that lay behind the wave of occupations in 2000, but a far narrower one.

Land occupations from the referendum to the parliamentary elections

The land occupations began in earnest shortly after the referendum defeat and spread rapidly in the run up to the parliamentary elections in June 2000. The spread of occupations introduced a range of new dynamics. War veteran leaders initiated the occupations, though certainly not all veterans participated in them, and some in fact emerged as strong critics (Alexander and McGregor, 2001; Kriger, 2001). Nonetheless, the hierarchy of national to district level veterans' committees, much strengthened through its mobilisation over the claims for and then distribution of compensation, was key in organisational terms, and in publicly defending the occupations. Despite variations based on local agendas, alliances, and histories of land (Moyo, 2001), there were patterns in the strategies of veterans in this period. Veterans tended to move into farms and establish bases and base committees responsible for mobilising and keeping registers of occupiers, for fund-raising, and for organising food and security. Veterans played the central leadership roles, despite the fact that almost everywhere they made up only a tiny minority of occupiers, the bulk being drawn from communal and urban areas as well as party youth.[32]

Veteran leaders were also consistent in their justification of the occupations. From the outset, veteran spokesmen explained their decision to lead occupations as a response to the rejection of the new constitution, and specifically its clause on land. They explicitly blamed white farmers for the 'No' vote, and portrayed the vote as primarily about blocking land redistribution.[33] They used their high profile position to maintain pressure on their patron, Robert Mugabe, to harangue ministers who developed cold feet, and to argue that anyone who opposed Zanu (PF) was by definition opposed to land redistribution.[34] Veteran leaders were important in popularising a political discourse that legitimated the abrogation of the law. Unfavourable judicial decisions were met with threats of 'going to war'; whites and the MDC were cast as 'enemies', and hence as legitimate targets of violence, who would undo the revolution in the making.[35]

---

[32] Marongwe (this volume). The CFU estimated that fifteen to twenty per cent of the occupiers were veterans in March 2000. *Financial Gazette*, 16 March 2000.

[33] See war veteran leader Chenjerai Hunzvi's statements in *The Herald*, 1 March 2000; also see Media Monitoring, 28 February-5 March 2000.

[34] *Financial Gazette*, 13 April 2000; *The Herald*, 14 April 2000; BBC Online, 8 May 2000; *New York Times*, 8 May 2000; *Daily News*, 30 May 2000; *Zimbabwe Independent*, 2 June 2000.

[35] BBC Online, 16 March 2000, 8 April 2000; *The Herald*, 16 March 2000, 20 March 2000; *Mail and Guardian*, 7, 10 April 2000; *Financial Gazette*, 6 April 2000.

Regional variations were nonetheless significant. The first occupations focused on Masvingo where the provincial veterans' committee led the way.[36] Occupations spread to Mashonaland and Manicaland in the first few weeks, and involved not just veterans but people from communal areas, chiefs and urban residents in a difficult to control process.[37] Mashonaland rapidly came to the fore, spurred on by Provincial Governor Border Gezi, and thereafter this region dominated in terms of numbers of occupations and violence.[38] Gezi dubbed the occupations the 'third liberation'. They were also dubbed the 'third chimurenga', placing them in a long line of violent struggle against white rule.[39] Matabeleland only later entered the fray, and then only half-heartedly. Leading politicians from the region such as Joseph Msika and Dumiso Dabengwa did not share Gezi's enthusiasm for occupations, and many veterans in Matabeleland were unwilling to engage in violence in this period (Alexander and McGregor, 2001:514-20).

There were other new actors involved in the occupations as well. In early March 2000, reports in the independent press first asserted that the Central Intelligence Organisation (CIO) and Zanu (PF) Headquarters were involved in directing veterans to specific farms, notably those where farmers had contested designations.[40] It was certainly the case that veterans were given lists of farms to occupy (Alexander and McGregor, 2001), and that the veteran organisation as a whole was provided with funds to 'campaign' for Zanu (PF).[41] As the occupations accelerated in March and increasingly focused on political mobilisation, there appears to have been added official support. The involvement of the army and CIO in 'negotiations' with the CFU, alongside veteran leaders, at times in meetings held at State House, underlined the range of powerful actors in play.[42] In the following months, reports of ZNA and CIO involvement

---

[36] *The Herald*, 24 February 2000.
[37] See Moyo (2001); *The Herald*, 29 February 2000.
[38] Three weeks after the start of the occupations, the CFU reported that over 250 of 300 occupied farms were in Mashonaland. *Financial Gazette*, 9 March 2000.
[39] *The Herald*, 1 March 2000; 24 February 2000.
[40] *Zimbabwe Independent*, 26 May 2000. Also see Marongwe, this volume.
[41] Veteran leader Hunzvi stated that the veteran organisation was given Z$20 million in early 2000 for campaigning. See *Financial Gazette*, 16 March 2000; *Zimbabwe Independent*, 9 June 2000.
[42] See *Financial Gazette*, 16 March 2000; interview with David Hasluck, Director CFU, Harare, July 2000. The CFU was warned in no uncertain terms to eschew any involvement in politics - if it did not, the situation would 'explode' and occupations escalate. *Zimbabwe Standard*, 2 April 2000.

multiplied. The independent press alleged that they had provided trucks, food and logistical support, as well as direction regarding farms to be occupied.[43] Members of the army and air force were reportedly involved in the occupations under the direction of Air Force Commander Perence Shiri, who also participated in government meetings with the CFU leadership as a 'veteran'.[44] The alliance between security agencies, politicians and veterans marked a sharp departure form earlier patterns of occupation, and placed an increasingly divided state in a new relationship with occupiers as well as commercial farmers.

The timing of the occupations underlined the necessity of outside support in this period, and the unusual – in terms of previous occupations – nature of the boom. From the point of view of someone interested in farming, this was the worst time of year to occupy land. It was harvest season and no productive use of the land could be made for months to come. Many of the land hungry were, in the period between the referendum and election, limited in their capacity to sustain occupations without support. Those with jobs or crops to harvest could not easily remain on the farms for months. Those without jobs could not remain on the farms without support in the form of at least food. The difficulties of sustaining occupations partly explained the rise and fall in numbers of occupied farms and numbers of occupiers.[45] It was in fact very difficult to judge how many occupations were sustained, as opposed to temporary, and how many farms were occupied overall.[46] In a sense, calling the occupations 'demonstrations', as the government did, was not overly misleading in some cases. The fact that several government Ministers, notably Msika and Dabengwa, called for the occupations to end as the various pieces of enabling legislation regarding land acquisition were passed in this period demonstrated that some senior members of government genuinely conceived of the occupations as no more than temporary, symbolic 'demonstrations' in favour of land

---

[43] *Zimbabwe Independent*, 20 April 2000, 28 April 2000; *New York Times*, 23 April 2000.

[44] *Zimbabwe Independent*, 5 May 2000, 21 May 2000; *Financial Gazette*, 4 May 2000.

[45] Funds raised locally or from government sources were often insufficient. See *Zimbabwe Independent*, 5 May 2000; *The Mirror*, 19 May 2000; *Mail and Guardian*, 19 May 2000.

[46] See Marongwe (this volume); Moyo (2001). In mid-April 2000, the CFU, in a bid to convince the courts that it was not unreasonable for the government to remove occupiers, reduced its estimate of the numbers of farms occupied and the number of occupiers to 6-7,000 occupiers on 500 farms, a far cry from the Attorney General's claim of 60,000 people on 1,000 farms. The figure of 1,000 farms was repeated consistently in press reports. See Moyo (2001:12-13); BBC Online, 10 April 2000; *Financial Gazette*, 13 April 2000; *New York Times*, 13 April 2000.

redistribution – but their views were hotly contested from within Zanu (PF) and by veterans.[47]

Linking occupations and party politics

'Demonstrating' a desire for land was, however, not the only purpose of occupations: they also came to play a central role in the election campaign. They were intended to appeal to Zanu (PF)'s most numerous constituency, communal area farmers, by demonstrating a tangible commitment to land redistribution, but they were also intended to punish constituencies seen as illegitimately engaged in opposition politics, specifically the white farmers and their workers. The levels of violence directed at farmers and farm workers, the political mobilisation of farm workers, the direct warnings against supporting the MDC, the searches for MDC materials, all indicated the importance of the electoral agenda. Zanu (PF) and veteran suspicions of farmers were constantly reiterated in the press, and fanned by the CFU's appeals to the courts. The response to CFU legal interventions was vitriolic, and accompanied by escalations in violence and occupations. Mugabe told farmers that 'very, very, very severe' consequences would follow if they took action against occupiers.[48] He described white farmers as 'our enemies, not just political enemies, but definite enemies in wanting to reverse our revolution and our independence'.[49] The fact that war veterans, in alliance with Zanu (PF) and the CIO, were also central in directing violence against the MDC in communal areas and towns underlined the goal of electoral victory and the multitude of roles veterans had come to play.[50]

---

[47] In early March, following the gazetting of the rejected constitutional clause on land, Minister of Home Affairs Dabengwa stated that veterans no longer needed to demonstrate, and thus should be evicted. He was promptly contradicted by Mugabe and denounced by veteran leaders. See *The Mirror*, 3 March 2000; *Mail and Guardian*, 3 March 2000, *The Herald*, 3 March 2000. In mid-April, Msika declared that the occupations should stop as the constitutional amendment had been passed, and hence there was no bar to government's plans for land reform. As in Dabengwa's case, the veteran leadership responded angrily, and received Mugabe's backing. See *Mail and Guardian*, 13 April 2000, *Zimbabwe Independent*, 14 April 2000; *The Herald*, 14 April 2000; *Financial Gazette*, 13 April 2000. Also see Msika's later remarks, in *Zimbabwe Independent*, 20 April 2000; *Financial Gazette*, 20 April 2000. Dabengwa once again told veterans to prepare to move off farms after the passage of the Presidential Powers Temporary Measures (Land Acquisition) Regulations had been passed, but received the same treatment. *Daily News*, 30 May 2000; *Zimbabwe Independent*, 2 June 2000. Also see Moyo (2001:12).

[48] *Financial Gazette*, 23 February 2000, 30 March 2000.

[49] *New York Times*, 18 April 2000.

[50] On political violence, see Human Rights NGO Report (2001); ICG (2000); Feltoe (2001).

The charge that Zanu (PF) was 'using' land or 'politicising' the land question in the run-up to the 2000 elections was frequently made. Certainly, Zanu (PF) tried to make land the central issue of the election, and to convince the electorate that only Zanu (PF) could deliver land by casting the MDC, white farmers and the British in an unholy alliance of re-colonisers. Writers such as Moyo (2001:5-6; 13-14) have countered that land has always been a political issue in Zimbabwe, and that it would be unreasonable to expect a campaign to be run without reference to land. He has also stressed the extent to which popular demands for land drove the occupations as time passed, dividing and radicalising veteran and Zanu (PF) leaders who struggled to maintain control of the process. Others, myself included, have felt ambivalent about criticising the occupations, and thereby seeming to belittle the real desire and need for land that motivated popular participation in them. Mugabe's political genius was to place the clearly unjust and unresolved question of land redistribution at the heart of his campaign. However, to focus narrowly on the occupations alone misses the point that what they marked was not just an unprecedented assault on the unequal distribution of land but also an extraordinary transformation of the state and political sphere. Land was far from the only political issue at stake in this period, and it cannot be considered in isolation.

The combination of Zanu (PF)'s violent electioneering and the land occupations required an extreme attack on the institutions of the state, in very sharp contrast to the government's response to occupations in the 1980s when it had sought to strengthen and insulate a modernising bureaucracy. In 2000, the judiciary was severely undermined as ruling after ruling was ignored. The police force was increasingly politicised, purged of critics, and prevented from carrying out its duties. The army was drawn into roles that did not befit its professional status. Civil servants came under tremendous pressure to support Zanu (PF), and came under violent attack where they did not.[51] The ministries charged with agrarian policy were meanwhile marginalised from control over land policy, in favour of an alliance led by Zanu (PF) and veterans. The powerful donor community was removed from the negotiation process as Mugabe swore to 'go it alone'. The Zanu (PF) leadership had set in motion processes that redefined its nationalist mantle, transformed the state, and irrevocably altered the politics of land.

---

[51] See McGregor (2002); Feltoe (2001); IBA (2001).

Land redistribution after the 2000 elections

Following the parliamentary elections of June 2000 there was no return to order, and no renewal of relations with donors and international financial institutions. Instead, the tactics developed in the period after the referendum defeat were intensified. Whites and Britain continued to be attacked and blamed for both the MDC's successes and blocking land redistribution. The army was deployed against MDC supporters in the urban areas; the police and army attacked protesting students; threats were issued against any attempt at mass action; by-elections were a focus of extreme political violence. War veterans continued to play a central role in political violence, in attacking journalists and civil servants believed to be sympathetic to the opposition or who participated in strikes, and in intervening in labour disputes as a means of challenging the ZCTU directly. Veterans received funding to help campaign for the presidential elections of March 2002 and, of course, they continued to play a central role on the white-owned farms and in volubly leading demands for land.[52] The continuation of pre-election strategies heralded new developments as well, notably in the vast expansion of permanent land occupations, at times outside the control of any centralised authority, over two rainy seasons, and the far-reaching implications of escalating attacks on state institutions and the political opposition.

'Fast Track' resettlement

Shortly after the June 2000 elections, veteran leaders increased the pressure for action, attacking both the Zanu (PF) leadership and civil servants. Veterans and their allies began to force farmers off their land, largely in Mashonaland. National veteran leader Hunzvi loudly denounced the slow pace of settlement while other veteran leaders complained that they had as yet received nothing for their campaigning on behalf of Zanu (PF).[53] Hunzvi held a meeting in mid-July with veterans at which he demanded that all targeted farms be redistributed within two weeks, attacked white farmers for holding up the process in the courts, and accused civil servants of 'conniving with whites' to slow resettlement. He described them as 'evil', and called for them to be sacked.[54]

---

[52] See Feltoe (2001).
[53] See *Daily News*, 7 July 2000; *Zimbabwe Independent*, 7 July 2000, 14 July 2000.
[54] *New York Times*, 15 July 2000.

In this context, the government launched its Accelerated Land Reform and Resettlement Implementation Plan, or 'Fast Track' resettlement. The defining feature of this programme, as with the accelerated resettlement of the early 1980s, was its minimal attention to infrastructure and support for those settled. The programme was designed to settle a total of five million hectares. To begin with, 30,000 families were to be settled 'as soon as possible' on one million hectares (GoZ, 2000). It was clear, however, that the ministries involved had nothing like the necessary budgets, equipment or personnel to achieve even this goal. Even if the plan were fully funded, there were no budgets for supporting new settlers with inputs, or social or agricultural services.[55]

These problems were severely exacerbated as the scale of Fast Track resettlement expanded. The new targets emerged in response to political pressure from veterans and Zanu (PF), and popular demands for land from an ever expanding and only loosely controlled set of constituencies led by chiefs, local veterans, local party leaders, and other community leaders with variable goals and grievances (Moyo, 2001:14-15; Marongwe, this volume). Escalating targets were also a response to court cases launched by the CFU. In late July 2000, the CFU filed a law suit owing to what it described as a 'major resurgence' in occupations over the previous two weeks, notably in Mashonaland.[56] Mugabe was angered by the court case; he was also incensed by the CFU's support for strike action by the ZCTU. His response was to announce that he would acquire a much increased total of 3,000 farms.[57] The CFU's return to the courts in September 2000 met another angry response. Mugabe broke off negotiations and threatened to prosecute whites for crimes committed in the liberation war.[58] Zanu (PF) placed a two-page newspaper advertisement which accused 'unrepentant and unapologetic Rhodesians' of using the courts to deprive people of their heritage: 'This land is your land, Don't let them use the courts and the constitution against the masses'.[59] Subsequent court defeats for the government made no dent in the momentum of the programme. Mugabe simply warned farmers that they would be kicked off the land if they persisted with their legal challenges.[60]

---

[55] *Zimbabwe Independent*, 21 July 2000.
[56] There were many reports of new occupations, violence and pegging. See *The Herald*, 25-7 July 2000, *The Daily News*, 24, 26-8 July 2000.
[57] See *The New York Times*, 30 July 2000; *The Daily News*, 31 July 2000
[58] See *Financial Gazette*, 12 October 2000; *Daily News*, 1 November 2000.
[59] *Daily News*, 6 November 2000; BBC Online, 21 November 2000.
[60] BBC Online, 3 December 2000.

The failure of the courts to have any impact on the occupations led to divisions within the CFU as it struggled to find a new strategy. Its legal challenges were at any rate much undermined by the passage of new legislation in 2001.[61] The CFU's attempts to adopt a more conciliatory approach through the Zimbabwe Joint Resettlement Initiative, which offered land and support for resettlement, was met with a cold shoulder by Minister of Lands Made. The government seemed in no mood for compromise. Instead, it gazetted thousands of additional farms for acquisition from mid-June 2001: 2,030 farms were reportedly listed in two batches on 15 and 22 June.[62] The listings were chaotic. The CFU held that after eliminating duplications, and the de-listing of some farms, a total of 4,797 farms – the vast majority of commercial land – had been listed under the Fast Track programme.[63] By November 2001, 4,874 farms had been listed, totalling 9.23 million hectares, or nearly double the original Fast Track goal of five million hectares (UNDP 2002:12).

The new politics of land authority and allocation

The escalation of farm listings and of settlement under the Fast Track programme meant that the already massively over-burdened ministries charged with implementing the programme were entirely overwhelmed. In response to the promised escalation of listings in July 2000, Minister Chombo stated that the ZNA would be used to provide logistical support to the programme.[64] At the start of the rainy season, however, Chombo appeared to give up entirely: he urged settlers to simply settle themselves as the government did not have the capacity to demarcate plots.[65] The pressure to identify farms rapidly gave the district and provincial land committees new scope, as did the pressure to identify settlers. These committees had been established to aid in the first rounds of farm listings in 1997, but took on a more prominent and less supervised role in this round. Committees were theoretically headed by DAs at district level and Provincial Governors and Administrators at provincial

---

[61] The Rural Land Occupiers (Protection from Eviction) Bill protected those occupying land for a specified time from eviction; the Land Acquisition Act was further amended to extend the time during which confirmation of acquisitions in the Administrative Court could be granted. See *The Herald*, 26 April 2001, 23 May 2001.

[62] *Mail and Guardian*, 30 June 2001; *Financial Gazette*, 5, 19 July 2001; *Daily News*, 18 July 2001.

[63] See *Zimbabwe Independent*, 3 August 2001; *Zimbabwe Standard*, 10 August 2001.

[64] Soldiers reportedly visited farms in Mashonaland in August 2000 on an intelligence gathering mission in which farmers were roused from bed by armed soldiers and forced to fill in questionnaires. *Mail and Guardian*, 4 August 2000; *Zimbabwe Independent*, 4 August 2000.

[65] *Daily News*, 1 November 2000.

level. Members included veterans, Zanu (PF), chiefs and others. Mugabe made it clear to whom these committees were allied. As he put it, 'Zanu (PF)'s land acquisition committees' would identify the thousands of farms needed.[66] These measures were in part an effort to bolster Zanu (PF)'s control over the expansion of land occupations, but also acted to further undermine and de-professionalise the developmental state.

The Provincial Governors emerged as the key figures in pressing forward with Fast Track listings and settlement. To varying extents, they pressed a partisan agenda, in keeping with their position as political appointees. At district levels, it was Zanu (PF) and veteran leaders, at times in alliance with others such as chiefs, who dominated decision-making. Unsurprisingly, the Fast Track programme in Mashonaland was immediately controversial, with charges from farm workers that they were cast as 'traitors' while all the land was allocated to veterans and occupiers.[67] In Mutoko, veteran leaders of an unofficial 'land committee' threatened to evict occupiers they accused of voting MDC.[68] In Masvingo, the provincial Zanu (PF) political commissar said MDC supporters 'should be bundled off the land'. They should go to the MDC if they wanted land.[69] Charges that only veterans, Zanu (PF) card holders and long-standing occupiers were given land raised complaints very widely – from the Zimbabwe Farmers' Union (representing smallholders), district administrations, farm workers, councils and communal area residents.[70]

The politicisation and autonomy of land committees was particularly stark in Matabeleland where Zanu (PF) had been resoundingly defeated in both urban and rural areas, winning just two seats in the region as a whole. In Matabeleland North, newly appointed Provincial Governor Obert Mpofu provoked a massive protest when he said that only Zanu (PF) and veterans qualified for Fast Track land.[71] In both Matabeleland provinces, veteran leaders and Zanu (PF) stalwarts distrusted virtually all institutions of the state. Civil servants and elected councillors were seen as suspiciously

---

[66] *Zimbabwe Independent*, 4 August 2000.
[67] Rutherford (2002 and this volume); *Mirror*, 10 August 2000. Moyo (2001: 15) states that there were some alliances between farm workers and veterans, and cites research indicating that '8% of settlers are farm workers'. Official figures indicate that only 1.7% of resettled households are headed by farm workers (UNDP, 2002: 34-7).
[68] *Daily News*, 10 October 2000.
[69] *Zimbabwe Independent*, 27 April 2001
[70] *Mirror*, 10 August 2000; *Zimbabwe Independent*, 11 August 2000; *Daily News*, 22 August 2000.
[71] *Daily News*, 8, 10 August 2000, 11 September 2000; *Zimbabwe Independent*, 27 October 2000.

sympathetic to the MDC, as were certain Zanu (PF) leaders. In Matabeleland South, veterans on the land committee lashed out at civil servants for derailing resettlement due to their MDC sympathies, eventually chasing Provincial Administrator Angelous Dube from her offices. Dube was transferred to Harare, and replaced by the Beitbridge DA, a veteran.[72] The Gwanda DA also came under attack, as did the provincial Zanu (PF) leadership. Veterans launched protests until they managed to take over key posts in the party and administrative hierarchies.[73] Land committees here were exceptionally narrowly based Zanu (PF) and veteran affairs, and they spent much of their time, as JoAnn McGregor has clearly shown, attacking institutions they considered suspect, eventually shutting down many of Matabeleland's councils as well as schools, thus striking another blow at an already much weakened local state.[74]

As the Fast Track programme progressed, conflicts that were not overtly related to party competition multiplied, indicating the force of older – and often competing – demands for land, and the sense of entitlement that the more recent occupations had produced. Such processes await further research, but it is clear that they encompassed a very wide range of agendas and alliances and often occurred outside central control.[75]

In some places, there were clashes between people who had filled in resettlement forms, and those who had earlier occupied land.[76] In Masvingo, villagers from Gutu and Bikita competed for access to particular farms, as did residents of Chivi and Mwenezi, with both sides claiming precedence based on their history of occupation, or chiefly and ancestral claims.[77] In Midlands province, villagers kicked off a farm by veterans appealed to Minister of Local Government Chombo, alleging that the provincial land committee had 'hijacked' the Fast Track programme such that it only benefited veterans, politicians and business people.[78] In Nkayi, settlers fought over access to property on the farms. One settler commented: 'we have realised that most of the prominent people like civil servants and top war vets have been allocated land that includes farmhouses'.[79]

---

[72] *Financial Gazette*, 3 August 2000; *Mirror*, 25 August 2000, 1 September 2000.
[73] *Daily News*, 16 April 2000; *Mirror*, 24 November 2000.
[74] See McGregor's excellent discussion of this neglected and highly significant process (2002).
[75] Moyo (2001) draws on some new research and is currently involved with a host of research projects documenting developments on the ground.
[76] *Daily News*, 6 September 2000.
[77] *Daily News*, 21 September 2000, 30 October 2000.
[78] *Daily News*, 5 December 2000.
[79] *Daily News*, 10 August 2001.

Even different groups of veterans clashed over particular pieces of land, such as in Chiredzi.[80] The splintering of authority over land and the kaleidoscope of alliances that shaped access proved to be diverse, unstable and difficult to control.

The decentralised and politicised nature of control over the Fast Track programme at times led to direct conflict with central government. Shortly after the high profile launch of the programme, the newly appointed Minister of Home Affairs, John Nkomo, stated that government would start moving occupiers off unlisted farms, and enforce law and order. The great difficulty of enforcing evictions in this context became clear when he sought to back up his words on the occupied farms surrounding Harare. These were peri-urban occupations, driven by the massive housing shortages and poverty of the city, and had rapidly expanded after the June 2000 elections (Moyo, 2001:14). Self-styled commander of farm invasions Joseph Chinotimba had run into opposition from the Ministry of Local Government and city officials with his 'official' allocation of residential plots around the city in late July 2000.[81] In early August, national veteran leader Hunzvi himself backed the calls to end occupations around Harare, and towards the end of the month police moved in to burn structures on stands allocated by veterans, apparently to the cheers of some urban residents.[82] Veterans subsequently protested in Harare, and denounced John Nkomo. Nkomo was called in to explain his actions to the Politburo, and Mugabe declared that the police were in the wrong.[83] People moved back onto the demolished sites thereafter and began to rebuild, insisting that they should receive compensation for their losses.[84]

The autonomy of occupiers sometimes brought them into conflict with individual politicians where they occupied their farms, such as in the case of Dumiso Dabengwa's farm in Matobo.[85] It at times caused violent clashes and evictions where the land in question was state land, such as in the case of the Matopos Research Station, which underwent a series of occupations by the Inqama Settlers' Association in defiance of the land committee headed by Provincial Governor Stephen Nkomo.[86] The occupation by veterans and villagers of the massive Nuanetsi Ranch, owned by the Development

---

[80] *Daily News*, 7 February 2001.
[81] *Daily News*, 28 July 2000; *The Herald*, 28 July 2000.
[82] *Daily News*, 18, 22-4 August 2000,
[83] *Daily News*, 24, 29 August 2000; *Zimbabwe Independent*, 25 August 2000.
[84] *Daily News*, 29 August 2000, 5, 19 September 2000, 14 November 2000.
[85] *Daily News*, 18 October 2000.
[86] *Mirror*, 13 October 2000; *Daily News*, 5 April 2001.

Trust of Zimbabwe, formerly headed by the late Joshua Nkomo, produced another running battle.[87] There were also instances where central ministries clashed with Provincial Governors who acted in alliance with veterans and other occupiers, such as in the case of the Minister of the Environment and Tourism's long-running battle over the Save Conservancy.[88] All this indicated that boundaries between political, administrative and technocratic agendas had been blurred on a massive scale, that popular and populist agendas and agents were to the fore.

Critics of Fast Track resettlement

As the Fast Track programme proceeded there were signs of unease. The MDC and CFU were naturally prominent critics, but so were the black commercial farmers' union (ICFU), the farm workers' union (GAPWUZ), the smallholders' union (ZFU), and women's groups. They directed their complaints to the central government and to the state bureaucracies, but it was clear that a radical devolution of power had occurred outside the state. The ICFU protested in August 2000 that its members' farms had not escaped the attention of land committees and occupiers.[89] The ICFU also proved suspicious of the A2 model of Fast Track resettlement, launched in January 2001. This was, according to Minister of Lands Made, commercial resettlement aimed at de-racialising large-scale agriculture. It was intended for farmers with resources, such as businessmen, professionals and technicians.[90] The farmers were to buy the land, and would be provided with title. By May 2001 there were reportedly some 100,000 applicants for A2 land, but the ICFU complained that all land appeared to be destined for small-holder settlement, while none was reserved for commercial farmers.[91]

GAPWUZ repeatedly highlighted the discrimination against farm workers under the Fast Track programme, and claimed that more than 40,000 farm workers in Mashonaland had been displaced to shacks around Chinhoyi, Rusape and Centenary by mid-2001.[92]

---

[87] *Daily News*, 11 April 2001; 4, 6, 11, 15, 19 June 2001.
[88] See *Daily News*, 11,18, 20 September 2000; 11, 17, 19, 25 October 2000; 19, 21 February 2001; *Zimbabwe Independent*, 15 September 2000
[89] *Daily News*, 15 August 2000.
[90] *The Herald*, 17 January 2001.
[91] *The Mirror*, 4 May 2001; *Daily News*, 23 May 2001. These concerns are beginning to be addressed: by late 2001, 51,000 applicants for A2 resettlement had been approved by the Ministry of Lands, Agriculture and Rural Resettlement, and the Ministry was reportedly in the midst of processing offer letters for some 10,620 farms (UNDP, 2002: 20).
[92] *Financial Gazette*, 31 May 2001; *Mail and Guardian*, 8 June 2001; *Zimbabwe Independent*, 8 June 2001. The UNDP mission of late 2001 estimated that there were some 30,000 displaced farm workers (UNDP 2002: 34-37).

Women's groups complained of gender bias in land allocation.[93] The ZFU had its own complaints, largely over the lack of support given to the farmers settled under the Fast Track programme and the biases in settler selection.[94] The ZFU's views were backed up by government departments overwhelmed by the scale of the task. Clearly there were serious problems in the 2000/1 season due to late settlement on the land, a lack of draft power and inputs, as well as the absence of infrastructure and services. Some settlers apparently left for communal areas due to the hardships, or at least left children behind so they could stay in school and nearer to health services.[95] In southern regions affected by drought, vast numbers of settlers were reportedly suffering food shortages.[96]

None of this led to a slowdown in Fast Track resettlement; instead the government sought to keep pace with – and some control over – the contested and diverse processes on the ground. Minister of Local Government Chombo announced in May 2001 the '40 days and 40 nights' Fast Track programme, designed to settle an additional 35,000 people in advance of the next rainy season. The process of allocation was to be speeded by the recruitment of 200 teams of experts, drawn from universities, polytechnics and government departments.[97] In late July, Minister of Lands Made added that school students would be deployed to demarcate land over their holidays, under the supervision of the Zimbabwe Defence Forces; the ZDF would – in a sinister turn of phrase – instil a 'psychology of obedience and law and order in the farming sector'.[98] The steps taken by late 2001 did not, however, impress a visiting UNDP mission. The mission found that the vast scale of the Fast Track programme posed a threat to national agricultural production and food security at least in the short term, and made the provision of 'essential public infrastructure' for settlers 'impossible' to achieve within a reasonable time period (UNDP, 2002:23, 37).

As the ministries concerned struggled to create order within the Fast Track programme, it was clear that a radical splintering of

---

[93] See Farm Community Trust et al. (2001) and UNDP (2002) for these and many other concerns.
[94] *Zimbabwe Independent*, 1 December 2000; *Zimbabwe Standard*, 3 December 2000; *Financial Gazette*, 12 July 2001.
[95] *Zimbabwe Independent*, 1 December 2000; *Zimbabwe Standard*, 3 December 2000; *Daily News*, 5 December 2000; *Mail and Guardian* 17 January 2001; *Mirror*, 26 January 2001. Also see the highly critical assessment of service and infrastructure provision in the UNDP's report (2002: 21-24).
[96] *Financial Gazette*, 12 July 2001.
[97] *The Mirror*, 4 May 2001; *The Herald*, 1 June 2001.
[98] *The Herald*, 27 July 2001; *The Chronicle*, 15 August 2001.

'Squatters', Veterans and the State

power over land had occurred. It had brought with it a very wide range of profound social divisions, extreme divisions within the state and between political parties, and the irrevocable transfer of control over vast swathes of commercial land. A new phase in Zimbabwe's land politics was well underway.

Conclusion

The racial aspect of Zimbabwe's recent land reform dominated the headlines, as well as government rhetoric, from the beginning. Certainly, the use of race marked the recent occupations apart from their counterparts in the early 1980s, as did the sheer scale of the resulting resettlement programme.[99] But the contrasts reach well beyond these factors, to the nature of the interaction between the state, political ideology, and social movements seeking to claim land.

The heyday of 'squatting' in the early 1980s was a transitional one during which the new government effected a local level political demobilisation and instituted a powerful, centralised bureaucracy intended to control and plan the distribution of land along lines designed to ensure productivity. This was a period of ambitious state expansion, legitimised through the delivery of 'development'. The management of occupations required, and justified, the strengthening of the technocratic and administrative arms of the state, and their isolation from bottom up demands and the pressures of political patronage. 'Squatters' were (with moral misgivings) increasingly defined as beyond the pale of citizenship. In sharp contrast, the occupations of 2000 were spearheaded by war veterans and actively encouraged by the President in a process that directly undercut the developmental state. Technocrats found themselves utterly side-lined: they were left to lament that the painstaking plans produced by their 'serious scientific analysis of Zimbabwe's agricultural needs' were now 'dead'.[100]

By the year 2000, the state was much weakened, and was becoming increasingly politicised, not least as a result of unresolved struggles over land. The land occupations sped this process, undermining spectacularly the impartiality and capacity of the Zimbabwean state. The occupations produced a strange spectacle:

---

[99] Government Ministries held that 114,830 households had been resettled on 4.37 million hectares, and that 7.3 million hectares had been planned and pegged under the Fast Track programme by late 2001. See UNDP (2002: 11). As the UNDP report makes clear, it remains difficult to quantify accurately the number of people settled on commercial farms.

[100] *Zimbabwe Independent*, 16 May 2000.

a government effectively unravelling its own state with great vigour, and operating outside it through often fairly autonomous forces at district and provincial levels, led by veterans and Zanu (PF). The sustained political violence and attacks on the civil service and opposition in and after 2000 served to undermine radically the prospects for constituting an accountable state and a culture of political tolerance.

There were ideological differences as well. In the 1980s, nationalism was redefined from the top down as a modernising force, linked to a developmental state, and was used to exclude the claims of popular nationalism to righting the historical wrongs of colonial land alienation. In the occupations of 2000, Zanu (PF) leaders certainly invoked a liberation war rhetoric of reclaiming the land, but they did so alongside a dramatic narrowing of the nationalist constituency. This marked a significant shift in the context of intense political competition and economic decline: faced with the demands of strikers, food rioters, protesting students, a thwarted bourgeoisie, angry war veterans, and a powerful new opposition, the Zanu (PF) leadership had to rebuild its constituency. It used the vehicle of the veterans and the issue of land and by so doing redefined nationalism once again (see Raftopoulos, 2000a, 2000b, this volume). Nationalism was now about armed men liberating the land from white settlers; it was reconstituted as authoritarian anti-colonialism, not modernising developmentalism. Neither version encompassed the full range of goals of the nationalism of the 1970s, which had so centrally called for freedom, democracy, equality and an accountable state alongside a restoration of the land to the people.

There is, however, one constant through the whole period under consideration and that is the existence of popular demands for land from a wide set of social groups, driven not only by historical injustice but also increasingly by the pressures of a faltering economy. The actions of Zanu (PF) in alliance with war veterans offered these groups a new means of making claims to land, one that bore little resemblance to those of the early 1980s, but one that they have used, and no doubt will continue to use in the future. This new set of unstable and conflict-ridden alliances exists as part of a process that has served to re-make the Zimbabwean state and political sphere.

References

Alexander, Jocelyn, 1991. 'The Unsettled Land: The Politics of Land Distribution in Matabeleland, 1980-1990'. *Journal of Southern African Studies*, 17 (4), pp. 581-610.

Alexander, Jocelyn, 1994. 'State, peasantry and resettlement in Zimbabwe'. *Review of African Political Economy*, 61, pp. 325-345.

Alexander, Jocelyn, 1996. 'Things fall apart, the centre can hold: Processes of post-war political change in Zimbabwe's Rural Areas'. In N. Bhebe and T. Ranger (eds), *Society in Zimbabwe's Liberation War*. Oxford: James Currey.

Alexander, Jocelyn, and JoAnn McGregor, 2001. 'Elections, Land and the Politics of Opposition in Matabeleland', *Journal of Agrarian Change*, 1 (4), pp. 510-533.

Alexander, Jocelyn, JoAnn McGregor and Terence Ranger, 2000. *Violence and Memory: One Hundred Years in the 'Dark Forests' of Matabeleland*. Oxford: James Currey.

Chimanimani District Development Committee, n.d. [1986]. *Chimanimani District Five Year Development Plan*.

Drinkwater, Michael, 1988. *The State and Agrarian Change in Zimbabwe's Communal Areas*. Basingstoke: Macmillan.

Farm Community Trust Zimbabwe, Women and Land Lobby Group and Friedrich Naumann Foundation, 2001. *Summarised Report on the one-day Workshop to Review the Land Reform Programme in Zimbabwe*, Harare International Conference Centre, 10 May.

Feltoe, Geoff, 2001. 'The onslaught against democracy and rule of law in Zimbabwe.' Ms., Harare.

Government of Zimbabwe, 1998. *Land Reform and Resettlement Programme Phase II. A Policy Framework*. Harare, June.

Government of Zimbabwe, 2000. *Accelerated Land Reform and Resettlement Implementation Plan: 'Fast Track'*. Harare.

Herbst, Jeffrey, 1990. *State Politics in Zimbabwe*. Harare: University of Zimbabwe Press.

Human Rights NGO Forum, 2001. *Politically motivated violence in Zimbabwe, 2000-2001. A report on the campaign of political repression conducted by the Zimbabwean Government under the guise of carrying out land reform*. Harare: Human Rights NGO Forum, July.

International Bar Association [IBA], 2001. *Report of Zimbabwe Mission 2001*. London: IBA, April.

International Crisis Group, 2000. *Zimbabwe in Crisis: Finding a Way Forward*. Africa Report No 32, Harare/Brussels: ICG, 13 July.

Kinsey, Bill, 1983. 'Emerging Policy Issues in Zimbabwe's Land Resettlement Programmes'. *Development Policy Review*, 1, pp. 163-195.

Knight, Rachael, 1998. 'Zimbabwe's 1998 Land Invasions: An Investigation into the Grassroots Politics of Land Redistribution and Resettlement'. Ms.

Kriger, Norma, 1996. 'Zimbabwe's Guerrilla Integration: Entitlement Politics'. Ms.

Kriger, Norma, 2001. 'Les Veterans et le parti au pouvoir: Une cooperation conflictuelle dans la longue duree'. *Politique Africaine*, 81, March, pp. 80-100.

Manicaland Provincial Development Committee, 1985. *Manicaland Provincial Development Plan*, Vol. 1, draft study, September.

Mashonaland West Provincial Development Committee, Council and Squatter Control Committee, n.d. [1987]. *Mashonaland West Squatter Problem: Towards Effective Action*, compiled by F.H. Munyira, PA and Chairman, Provincial Squatter Control Committee.

McGregor, JoAnn, 2002. 'The politics of disruption: War veterans and the local state in Zimbabwe'. *African Affairs*, 101 (402), pp. 9-37.

Ministry of Economic Planning and Development, 1981. *Zimbabwe Conference on Reconstruction and Development (ZIMCORD): Record on Conference Proceedings*. Salisbury: Government Printer.

Moyo, Sam, 1994. *Economic Nationalism and Land Reform in Zimbabwe*. Occasional paper series no. 7, Harare: SAPES.

Moyo, Sam, 1995. *The Land Question in Zimbabwe*. Harare: SAPES.

Moyo, Sam, n.d [1998]. *The Land Acquisition Process in Zimbabwe (1997/8)*. Harare: UNDP.

Moyo, Sam, 2000a. 'The Political Economy of Land Acquisition and Redistribution in Zimbabwe, 1990-1999'. *Journal of Southern African Studies*, 26 (1), pp. 5-28.

Moyo, Sam, 2000b. 'The Interaction of Market and Compulsory Land Acquisition Processes with Social Action in Zimbabwe's Land Reform'. Paper presented to SARIPS Annual Colloquium on Regional Integration: Past, Present and Future, Harare, 24-27 September.

Moyo, Sam, 2000c. *Land Reform Under Structural Adjustment in Zimbabwe: Land Use Change in the Mashonaland Provinces.* Uppsala: Nordiska Afrikainstitutet.

Moyo, Sam, 2001. 'The land occupations movement and democratisation in Zimbabwe: Contradictions of neoliberalism'. *Millennium: Journal of International Studies*, 30 (2), pp. 311-330 [note that pagination in the text refers to a mimeograph of this article].

Moyo, Sam and Prosper Matondi, 2001. 'Conflict Dimensions of Zimbabwe's Land Reform Process'. Harare, May.

Palmer, Robin, 1990. 'Land Reform in Zimbabwe, 1980-1990'. *African Affairs*, 89 (355), pp. 163-81.

Raftopoulos, Brian, 2000a. 'Constitutionalism and Opposition in Zimbabwe'. Paper delivered to the African Studies Seminar, Oxford, June.

Raftopoulos, Brian, 2000b. 'The Labour Movement and the Emergence of Opposition Politics in Zimbabwe'. Ms.

Raftopoulos, Brian, 2001. 'De l'emancipation du mouvement syndical a l'affirmation du MDC'. *Politique Africaine*, 81, March, pp. 26-50.

Ranger, Terence, 1985. *Peasant Consciousness and Guerrilla War in Zimbabwe.* Harare: Zimbabwe Publishing House.

Ranger, Terence, 1999. *Voices from the Rocks: Nature, Culture and History in the Matopos Hills of Zimbabwe.* Oxford: James Currey.

Rich Dorman, Sara, 2001. 'Inclusion and Exclusion: NGOs and Politics in Zimbabwe'. Oxford: PhD thesis.

Rutherford, Blair, 2002. 'Zimbabwe: The politics of land and the political landscape'. *Green Left Weekly*, 487, April 10.

UNDP, 2002. *Zimbabwe. Land Reform and Resettlement: Assessment and Suggested Framework for the Future. Interim Mission Report.* UNDP.

Yeros, Paris, 1999. 'Peasant Struggles for Land and Security in Zimbabwe: A Global Moral Economy at the Close of the Twentieth Century.' Draft PhD chapter, LSE.

Yeros, Paris, 2000. 'Labour struggles for alternative economics in Zimbabwe: Trade union nationalism and internationalism in a global era.' Ms., London.

Chapter 4

The Making and Unma(s)king of Local Government in Zimbabwe[1]

Amanda Hammar

Our customary visible order is not the only one:
it coexists with other orders.
John Berger, 2001:5

In February 2002, an article in Zimbabwe's independent daily newspaper, *The Daily News*, summarised what it saw as the profound undermining of 'normal' practices of government by the actions of 'so-called war veterans', so giving voice to a fairly widespread public fear that Zimbabwe had entirely lost its bearings.

> *The grim reality...is that we haven't got a normal government in Zimbabwe. Whatever the so-called war veterans say is what goes. They can sack teachers, nurses, and district council officials, order the transfer of magistrates, district administrators and senior police officers, close down schools, clinics and rural district council offices. They can disrupt any court proceedings. And, with absolute impunity, they can harass, torture or order anybody's arrest [emphasis added].*[2]

Besides the occupation of commercial farms that heralded the start of 'the crisis' in February 2000, local government institutions – primarily but not only in rural areas – were also subject to intensive and often violent disruptions, occupations or closures by alleged

---

[1] I thank Donald Moore for critical provocations at the early stages of this chapter, and for generous and thoughtful comments on earlier drafts I thank Blair Rutherford in particular, and Jeremy Gould, Eric Worby, Stig Jensen and Brian Raftopulos. Responsibility for all errors in judgment remains mine alone.

[2] *The Daily News*, 2 February 2002. One might add to this already extensive list the denial of access to their homes and livelihoods of an expanding number of Zimbabweans, primarily farm workers and commercial farmers, and thousands of others forced to flee the communal areas, as documented by the Human Rights Forum in Zimbabwe. Also, widely reported denial of food and water to opposition 'enemies' of Zanu (PF) in the face of an impending famine.

war veterans and Zanu (PF)-trained 'youth militia'.[3] As early as June 2000, reports were made of several Rural District Councils (RDCs) being 'occupied' and turned into Zanu (PF) campaign bases, and sometimes even alleged torture bases, in advance of the parliamentary elections.[4] Since then, a vast array of attacks have been recorded against both rural and urban councils and associated institutions, as well as against targeted central government officials in district and provincial posts. This has worsened during the three elections conducted since mid-2000: parliamentary in June 2000, presidential in March 2002, and Rural District Council elections in September 2002. All this has radically altered the landscape of local government, and of government more generally, in Zimbabwe

The Daily News echoed a more general critique among various independent commentators, of the impunity of ruling party-provoked and state-sanctioned violence by war veterans and Zanu (PF)-trained youth militia, against farmers, farm workers and opposition supporters. However, the article went on to argue that the state-supported farm invasions that began in early 2000 were far from 'peaceful demonstrations against the government for its slow pace in land acquisition and redistribution' as officially claimed. Rather, they were 'the beginning of the anarchy which has now become a national curse: *the tragedy of government by war veterans*' [emphasis added].

The re-emergence of 'war veterans' as a significant political category in Zimbabwe, and the specific claim that Zimbabwe is being governed by war veterans, will be critically examined later in this chapter.[5] However, the wider claims provoke questions about different conceptions and changing practices of 'normal' government during very 'abnormal' times, and a consideration of how this is affecting the mode of rule in present-day Zimbabwe. In popular liberal-democratic parlance, these perceived changes are construed as Zimbabwe's 'governance crisis'. Yet this catch-all phrase too easily glosses over the ways in which normative notions of *normal* government are constructed and reproduced. In the present

---

[3] The significance of assaults by war veterans on 'the local state' is extensively discussed in recent work by JoAnn McGregor (2002), upon which I draw widely here, in addition to media sources and my own professional and research work with/in local government in Zimbabwe through much of the 80s and 90s.

[4] For example, *The Daily News*, 8 June 2000, 'Gokwe council offices turned base for attack on opposition'.

[5] The category of war veterans, colloquially dubbed 'war vets', is an increasingly loose umbrella term that now extends to cover a wide range of militant Zanu (PF) activists, many of whom cannot – merely by their ages – have been guerilas of the nationalist liberation struggle of the 1970s.

conjuncture, there are clearly competing ideas about what could or should constitute 'normal' government, linked in no small way to alternative ideological visions and political projects.[6] This chapter examines some of these notions and their effects, but limits itself to doing so through the specific lens of local government, tracing the altering politics and practices of government and rule being played out in this arena since 2000.

The chapter focuses principally on *rural* local government and its continued disruption, principally by war veterans, but often with the complicity or in some cases explicit participation of senior politicians and key bureaucratic arms of the state itself. Not only is rural local government currently the site of some of the most direct and brutal challenges to existing forms and practices of government; for many Zimbabweans, during both colonial and postcolonial periods, it has represented their most immediate and perhaps most intimate experience of official state authority. As such, rural local government has been critical to the construction and reproduction of Zimbabwe's changing modes of rule over time. Playing a key role in successive states' territorial and political strategies, rural local government institutions have been central in facilitating both state and ruling party attempts to order, control and 'develop' spaces, resources and populations. Collectively, local government policies and practices have provided a key mechanism for the shaping and disciplining of subject-citizens. At times, and in collaboration with other governmental and political authorities, they have altered the very criteria by which selected groups are included or excluded as citizens at all.[7]

However, neither the idea, nor the actually practicing rural institutions, of local government are simply a front for (or frontier of) *national* processes of state making and governmentality (Foucault, 1979). They have, simultaneously, their own *localised* and translocal sets of dynamics and demands specific to their situated histories and the ways in which these have articulated with broader conditions and relations of power, production and accumulation. One of the interesting tensions in Zimbabwe is precisely that generated through the competing yet interconnected projects of state-making (at the scale of 'the nation'), and place-making (concerned with the production and control of localities). Within these partially discrete,

---

[6] While on the surface these may appear to have petrified into a clear dichotomy between Zanu (PF) and the opposition Movement for Democratic Change (MDC), the reality is much messier and more diverse. See Raftopoulos (2001), and Bond (2001).

[7] See for example Mamdani (1996), Hammar (2001a), Hansen and Stepputat (2001).

partially overlapping spheres of spatial, social, economic, cultural and political production, performances of state sovereignty and rule, and everyday practices of government, necessarily get expressed in both universal and unique ways.[8] Together with the distinct projects and priorities of war veterans currently engaged in the disruption of local government institutions – which connect to both spheres – this accounts for the fairly extensive local variations in the forms and effects of disruption observed by McGregor (2002). Yet no matter how uneven the disruption of the landscape of local government, war veterans have played a crucial vanguard role in Zanu (PF)'s project of reconfiguring territory, power and production in the countryside, and in redefining the boundaries of entitlement and belonging to the nation. However, what remains unclear is what the growing strength and spread of war veterans will mean in the longer term, in ongoing processes of state- and place-making in the multiple sites of the 'new' nation.

In search of 'normal' government

Implicit in the critique of the collapse of standard practices of government expressed by *The Daily News* article, is a longing for the return of some kind of 'normality' to Zimbabwe. This has become a common refrain in everyday life. But what exactly is being longed for, and by whom? And what kinds of politics and practices are involved in constructing and naturalising the different ideas of 'normal' government in Zimbabwe?[9] In the absence of substantial empirical research, to which this chapter makes no claim, the extent to which it can address such existential dilemmas is limited, and the discussion is necessarily more reflective than assertive. However, what is evident is that the kind of 'normal' government envisioned within a broadly liberal or liberal democratic framework is not the 'normal' being claimed and created through President Mugabe's present political project – although there are certain overlaps and echoes between the two (see Worby, this volume) – nor is it necessarily the same 'normal' for the urban unemployed or landless peasants.

---

[8] See Peluso and Vandergeest (2001) – with reference to Southeast Asia – regarding the significant variations in how government institutions and practices get manifested in different localities, particularly through the differential application of territorial strategies. For specifically African examples, and with a greater emphasis on 'state-countryside' political dynamics, see Boone (1998).

[9] The varied politics and practices of normalising government and the state are explored in rich ethnographic and theoretical detail in the collection by Hansen and Stepputat (eds) (2001). See also Worby, this volume.

Within the liberal framework, 'normal' government assumes a democratically elected, transparent and accountable ruling body that upholds the constitution, upholds the rule of law, protects the independence of the judiciary, respects the independence of the media, sustains the professionalism of state agencies including the police and army, protects basic human rights, ensures all citizens equal security and protection under the law, and, most critically, protects private property. Somewhere amidst all this, the state is also expected to provide public goods and services and deliver or facilitate economic growth and 'development'. While some, appropriately, caution against the idealisation of liberalism (Dean, 2001), current expressions of longing for this particular ideal denote naïve nostalgia for a mythically stable situation prior to February 2000, even among many of those noticeably disadvantaged within it. Zimbabwe was not only already in economic and political crisis long before February 2000,[10] but the assumed rights and security inherent in this ideal were far from being evenly applied. For example, hundreds of thousands of farm workers in particular have long been on the receiving end of 'illiberal' practices (Rutherford, this volume). And the sacred cow of liberalism – private property – has itself been responsible for decades if not centuries of dispossession in both colonial and postcolonial states.

Certain ideals of liberalism formed the basis of the political compromises forged at the conference in Lancaster House in 1979 that ended Zimbabwe's liberation war. But while many were upheld as part of the assumed norm for much of the first two post-independence decades – this being necessary to sustain Zimbabwe's international credibility and ensure access to development aid and investment – their actual application was patchy and erratic. In practice, liberal principles had to coexist within the same ideological and political space as the self-consciously non-liberal vision of rule of the then incumbent Prime Minister, now President, Robert Mugabe.[11] Despite conceding to don the cloak of liberal democracy in the tense moments of transition from Rhodesia to Zimbabwe, Mugabe's Marxist-Leninist leanings were widely known. He expressed an explicit commitment to ending imperialist exploitation, reversing

---

[10] See for example Raftopoulos and Sachikonye (2001) and Hammar and Jensen (2002).
[11] Among the most violent manifestations of non-liberal or illiberal practice were the *Gukurahundi* state massacres in Matabeleland and Midlands in the early to mid 1980s, aimed at crushing opposition support for ZAPU. Other examples include the disenfranchisement of farm workers in local government elections until as recently as 1997. The origins and ongoing manifestations of this diminished civic status are extensively discussed by Rutherford (this volume and elsewhere).

decades of colonial racist bias in economic and civic life, ensuring redistribution of wealth through more equitable ownership of natural resources, especially land, and promoting participation more generally in ownership of the economy by the state and (indigenous) nationals (Tshuma, 1997:53).[12]

Mugabe's speeches and writings in the early years, while largely conciliatory and pragmatic, were nonetheless explicit about a nationalist, socialist vision for Zimbabwe, one he claims he was forced to abandon by Britain, the former colonial power, but which he has since resurrected with religious zeal. The uneasy weave of ideologies this produced was clearly evident in his foreword to the Transitional National Development Plan (TNDP) of 1982.

> The Plan [...] recognises the existing phenomenon of capitalism as an historical reality, which [...] has to be purposefully harnessed, regulated and transformed as a partner in the overall endeavour to achieve set national goals. Accordingly, while the main thrust of the Plan is socialist and calls for a greater role by the State through the instrumentality of State enterprises, worker participation, and socialist cooperation, ample room has been reserved for performance by private enterprise.'[13]

This gives some indication of the kinds of historically competing ideas of 'normal' government that inform the political actions of those currently engaged in either disrupting, reconstructing or re-imagining a quite different form of rule.

Establishing a one-party state was and has remained a key ambition and pillar of Mugabe's philosophy of rule and his vision for the transformation of government since well before independence. Although frequently challenged, this project has underpinned some of his most overtly political policy reforms, such as decentralisation (Makumbe, 1998), as well as his pattern of punishing political dissent. However, it suffered a blow in ideological credibility and political support after the collapse of Soviet communism at the end of the 1980s, which in turn unleashed a broad 'wave of democratisation' in Africa during the 1990s that was difficult to ignore (Geschiere and Gugler, 1998). Initially these new global conditions prompted various smokescreens in attempts to disguise

---

[12] These are principles that many among Mugabe's critics would themselves broadly support, while disagreeing strongly with his methods.
[13] *Transitional National Development Plan 1982/83 – 1984/85*, Government of Zimbabwe, Harare: Government Printers. Quoted in Tshuma (1997:53).

Zanu (PF)'s ongoing drive towards a *de facto* one-party state. But with the emergence in 1999 of a politically viable opposition party, the Movement for Democratic Change, a new set of rules defining politics and the practices of government had to be constructed.

For Mugabe and Zanu (PF) this has entailed a constant discursive reassembling of diverse 'regimes of truth' and 'selective traditions', be these in the guise of revolutionary nationalism, democracy, tradition, or various alternative visions of modernity.[14] Within this ever-changing kaleidoscope, one finds juxtaposed assertions by Mugabe and his agents, of holding free and fair elections and maintaining law and order (despite evidence to the contrary), while portraying liberal democracy as a tool of Western imperialism and anathema to Zimbabwe's historically legitimate land revolution. One can hear populist declarations that only the deeply rural, that is those who adhere to their 'traditional roots in the village' and who are still in possession of their totems, can be considered 'true' citizens of Zimbabwe. At the same time, both war veterans and the new Zanu (PF) youth militia have been required to abandon alliances with their own historical traditions, namely their links to chiefs, kinship or locality, in favour of loyalty to Zanu (PF),[15] the reward being their redefined status, along with a narrow political elite, as super-citizens.

Normalising violence and reconstituting war heroes

In this strange landscape of smoke and mirrors, what we seem to be witnessing is the *production of the norm of violence*; that is, the process by which violence – including the rapid spread of direct physical violence such as torture, rape, kidnapping, intimidation and sometimes murder, as well as a range of other forms of social, economic, emotional, cultural and sexual violence – has become obscenely normalised as an everyday mode of rule and technology of government. In the deliberate absence of official state intervention to protect its citizens from acts of violence, and in many cases the direct participation in such acts by state agents themselves, there

---

[14] See Sylvester (1990) concerning Zimbabwe's 'contradictory terrain of development'. See Worby (this volume) and Moore (forthcoming) for richly nuanced reflections on the notion of 'alternative modernities'.

[15] This is not uniformly the case. Alexander and McGregor (2001) have noted for Matabeleland, for example, that locally based war veterans and Zanu (PF) militants were constrained by their links to familiar local networks. On the other hand, they and others cite examples of Zanu (PF)'s strategy of importing outsiders to undertake acts of violence and terror.

has been a strategic move by the ruling party to decriminalise, and hence legitimise, violence against a specifically targeted yet abstract category of (non)citizens, namely opposition supporters.

According to a recent biography of Robert Mugabe, violence has been a consistent personal creed of Mugabe's. Meredith (2002:225) quotes a radio broadcast in 1976 from Mozambique, at the height of the liberation war, during which Mugabe summed up his view of electoral democracy as follows:

> *Our votes must go together with our guns. After all, any vote we shall have, shall have been the product of the gun. The gun which produces the vote should remain its security officer – its guarantor. The people's votes and the people's guns are always inseparable twins.*

As Meredith points out, Mugabe and his close supporters have consistently used extremes of violence to overcome many of the political challenges they have faced, not only during the liberation struggle but also since independence in 1980.[16] In the run-up to parliamentary elections in June 2000, Mugabe boasted of having 'a degree in violence', while a close political ally and minister in his cabinet, Nathan Shamuyarira, noted publicly: 'The area of violence is an area where Zanu (PF) has a very strong, long and successful history.' Violence and terror have certainly paid off for the party in the past.

These references to a 'successful' history of violence perform a double-act of memory work. On the one hand, the reference to the *Second Chimurenga* reaffirms the status of Zanu (PF) as the legitimate liberator of Zimbabwe from colonial rule, through 'the gun' (although in effect the enforced Lancaster House agreement in 1979 deprived Mugabe of an all-out military victory). At the same time, it is a coded reminder of the price of dissent to those who suffered brutally under Mugabe's Fifth Brigade in Matabeleland and Midlands during the 1980s. It is not by chance that the present state-sponsored land occupations, disruptions of local government institutions and of selected private businesses, and violent attacks on all forms of opposition including the independent media, have been defined, within the same metaphorical code, as the *Third Chimurenga*. Not only does this discursively locate the present moment along a narrowly-defined historical trajectory of (unfinished)

---

[16] Besides the *Gukurahundi* massacres of the 1980s, there are numerous examples of smaller-scale violence used by the state against its own citizens since independence (Alexander et al., 2000; Moore, 2000; Hammar, 2001a.) This includes previous electoral violence. All this occurred during a period when many positive development programmes and projects were initiated and supported by the state.

struggle against colonial injustice – the final phase of national liberation – but quite pointedly locates it along a continuum of violent struggle, even 'war'.

In December 2001, at the Zanu (PF) party congress, Mugabe extended the notion of war to include a national 'war on terror'. This capitalised on the post-September 11 discourse on terror, much as other authoritarian states have done since then, to defy growing international criticism and further legitimise his anti-democratic practices. Artfully deflecting the evidence stacked against his own party, he accused the MDC of deliberately hatching 'a campaign of violent intimidation' and of posing 'a real terrorist threat to the country which will not be allowed to go unchecked.'[17] Further reinforcing this rhetoric, the cabinet sworn in in August 2002 was described by Mugabe as 'a fully-fledged war council set up to fight the country's economic problems', and as 'a political war cabinet which will take into account actions being taken by Britain and its allies against Zimbabwe.'[18] Such language, and its (re)structuring effects on political, institutional and social practices, sets the scene for a parallel, deadly politics of identity and belonging now at play. This is a politics that attempts to redefine those entitled to belong: to the land, as legitimate sons and daughters of the soil; to the state, as valid and loyal citizens; and to the nation, as either racially, ethnically or politically 'pure' insiders, set against an ever-expanding category of dangerous Others now tainting the national body.[19] This seems consistent with what Geschiere and Gugler (1998:313) observed elsewhere in Africa: 'Now that elections have real meaning again, the fear of being outvoted by 'strangers' – whatever their origins or the precise definition of their otherness – has evoked an obsession with roots and origins.'

In the present times in Zimbabwe, there has been a replacement of the more classic autochthony trope by a different and even narrower version of authenticity and insiderhood, that of *liberation-war credentials*.[20] This has powerfully revalorised actual war

---

[17] Based on author's personal transcript of Mugabe's speech delivered at the Zanu (PF) party congress in Victoria Falls, 13 December 2002, broadcast live on Zimbabwe radio.
[18] *Financial Times* (UK), 26 August 2002.
[19] See Mamdani's (2001) chilling discussion of the 'colonial crime' of politicising indigeneity, and how this has been adapted by postcolonial regimes to construct historically grounded 'indigenous' and 'alien' (native/settler) political identities, then used to legitimise political violence, if not genocide.
[20] See Werbner (1998) for a powerful discussion of the official use of the trope of 'heroic nationhood' in postcolonial nation-building; and of the moral economy of the 'liberation smoke – the trace in memory of the political violence' of the liberation struggle, used to inscribe, or erase, 'national rank' in post-independence Zimbabwe.

veterans from the *Second Chimurenga*, whose growing disenchantment with the state and ruling party by the late 1990s was in urgent need of rechanneling into some kind of unifying 'nationalist' project.[21] This was especially so after Mugabe, in 1997, personally acceded to forceful demands for compensation and pensions by war veterans, who had mobilised themselves very effectively through the new and powerful Zimbabwe National Liberation War Veterans Association (ZNLWVA). At a time of waning support for the party, these concessions bought Mugabe and Zanu (PF) a degree of loyalty from an important symbolic constituency, which they have since harnessed to great effect in their simultaneous campaigns to 'destroy the world of the white farm',[22] crush the opposition, and reinvent the terms of rule and practices of government. But as McGregor (2001:10) importantly observes, veterans 'brought their own economic and political interests to the alliance, which have sometimes threatened central party control.'

War veterans are far from being a seamless category of homogenous social actors sharing a common past or present. Their multiple differences in terms of class, gender, ethnicity, spatial origin, ideological orientation, party and leadership affiliation, translated into different experiences of the liberation war itself, and also into differential levels of accumulation and marginalisation in the post-independence years. According to McGregor (2002:11), those in active alliance with Zanu (PF) 'have been drawn overwhelmingly from the ranks of the unemployed or poorly remunerated, who lack education and prospects.' Yet it is primarily those from these same ranks who have suffered the betrayal of the party, in many cases being neglected for months on the farms they dutifully invaded, but worse still, being evicted from these farms to make way for 'private' ownership by the party elite.[23] Not surprisingly, cracks have begun to appear in the political facade of the ZNWLVA.[24] Queried about

---

[21] However, war veterans who have become MDC supporters are no longer accorded this hero status. In the context of the *Third Chimurenga* they have been recast by Zanu (PF) as 'sell outs' and counter-revolutionary. Consequently they are being victimised by, among other things, being denied land in the new 'fast track' resettlement programme, while having their ex-combatants' pension benefits terminated. See *Zimbabwe Independent*, 18 October 2002.

[22] See R W Johnson, 'Land reform a cover for Zanu war on opposition'. Comment from *Business Day* (SA), 23 August 2002.

[23] See *The Daily News*, 18 September 2002, 'Government evicts resettled villagers to pave way for Shiri'.

[24] Members of an alleged war veterans' breakaway party calling itself the New People's Party (NPP) felt 'forgotten' by Zanu (PF), and that the reason for the armed struggle had been lost. As one spokesman noted, 'Look at how we are being harassed and left out of the land redistribution exercise'. *The Standard*, Sunday 14 July 2002: 'War vets split from Zanu PF party'.

alleged defections of some veterans from his organisation, the secretary-general, Andy Mhlanga, dismissed them, asserting that 'anyway, true war veterans remain loyal to Zanu PF and President Mugabe because we fought the liberation war together. It is a marriage for life.'[25]

Internal differences between war veterans manifested themselves in earlier organisational splits, for example with the setting up in May 2000 of an alternative to the ZNLWVA, the Zimbabwe Liberators Platform for Peace and Development. As noted by Alexander and McGregor (2001:514-15), those who formed this group explicitly distanced themselves from political violence and condemned the farm invasions. In addition, they 'spoke out angrily against what they saw as the exploitation of veterans by a weak and unpopular party.' Others are active members of the opposition MDC or smaller opposition parties. Such acts of 'treachery', in the logic of Zanu (PF), cancel out their war hero status and hence their political authenticity. Yet the loss by Zanu (PF) of a substantial proportion of its seemingly natural constituency has been effectively countered by a strategic expansion of the category of war veterans. By defining the present 'revolution' as the *Third Chimurenga*, the party has been able to reclassify the recently formed Zanu (PF) youth militia as legitimate 'war liberation' heroes. This was confirmed by President Mugabe in his speech to mark Heroes Day in August 2002, in yet another shrewd reworking of the terms of his critics, in this case rebuffing those critics who have queried the authenticity of 'so-called war veterans' spearheading 'the land revolution'. While paying tribute to the past heroes of the country's struggle for independence, the President noted that even those accused of being too young to have fought with the guerilla forces were entitled to be called war veterans. After all, he noted, 'they are the *new* war veterans...not impostors but genuine fighters for their land.'[26]

Tensions in the terms of rule

In this context of growing militarisation in almost all aspects of political, economic and social life, one might be tempted to conclude that Mugabe and Zanu (PF) have shifted away from using 'power' as

---

[25] *The Standard*, Sunday 14 July 2002: 'War vets split from Zanu PF party'.
[26] That the overwhelming majority of this militia are young, unemployed men, emasculated by economic and social marginalisation, accounts to some extent for the reported widespread use of rape and sexual torture, mainly against women, as a means of cowing the opposition.

the basis of rule, in the Foucauldian sense of governing by 'acting upon the actions of others' which requires the freedom of its governed subjects, and replaced it with 'domination', which requires force against subjects who refuse to be governed. Ironically, under the former Rhodesian regime, the present war veterans were the archetypal ungovernable subjects, overtly resisting settler-colonial domination. Now these same subjects have been reworked by the present post-colonial regime, albeit in an elastic version that incorporates the youth militia, to provoke and empower them to crush a new category of ungovernable subjects: 'aliens' or 'foreigners' in Mamdani's (2001) terms; those constituting a real or imagined political threat to the ruling party.

Yet there are very few conditions under which absolute domination is possible, or easily sustained. With reference to – but moving beyond – Foucault, Dean (2001:53) argues that 'the exercise of government in all modern states entails the articulation of a form of pastoral power with one of sovereign power.' Here, pastoral power, or biopolitics, describes a politics and practice of government concerned with the 'administration of life'. It works at the level of 'the population', through measurable phenomena such as health status, sanitation, birth-rate, mortality, environment, race, genetics, housing, levels of employment, patterns of migration, standard of living, and so on.[27] Sovereignty on the other hand 'is characterised by a power of life and death', and has as its main instruments 'laws, decrees, and regulations backed up by coercive sanctions ultimately grounded in the right of death exercised by the sovereign' (Dean, 2001:47-9). All modes of rule, argues Dean, be they liberal or authoritarian, are compelled to addess both biopolitics and sovereign power.[28] What distinguishes their rule is the distinctive way in which they assemble and apply this combination of elements. Some, for example, may be more concerned with the use of power to *foster* life, others to *deny* it.[29]

According to such an approach, Mugabe would ultimately be constrained in his attempts to construct a new 'normality' of rule

---

[27] As Li (1999:296) points out, 'in the postcolonial era, concern with welfare and improvement falls under the rubric of "development" and provides many governing regimes with a significant part of their claim to legitimacy.'

[28] Whereas Foucault's approach to sovereignty and biopolitics was applied to/under conditions of relative stability, and the Zimbabwe crisis is clearly far from 'business as usual', I would nonetheless argue that these concepts, as Dean has developed them, are relevant to the present analysis of rule in Zimbabwe.

[29] See Worby, this volume, for a rich discussion of the intricate workings of sovereignty and Agamben's notion of 'bare life'.

and government in Zimbabwe based purely on assertions of sovereignty. Rather he would have to conjure up an image of the *caring* sovereign, concerned as much, or enough, with the pastoral care of his subjects as with sustaining discipline and domination through force. Indeed, this is an intrinsic part of his rhetoric of restoring the lost lands through a 'land revolution'. By reinventing, and shrinking, the 'legitimate' forms and spaces of citizenship – by renaming (as internal 'enemies') those active subjects no longer entitled to pastoral care – he might go some way towards reducing such constraints on his expressions of sovereign power, but he can never entirely eliminate them. Alternatively, Kuehls (1996:41) argues: 'Sovereignty does not regulate everything that exists within its territory. There is a beyond, an outside, that exists within the geopolitical walls of the sovereign state.' Whether these potential constraints apply to loyalist war veterans, or whether veterans are inside or outside 'the walls of the state', is another matter. Unlike the sovereign or the state, in their present (partial) constitution as the vanguard of 'the revolution', militant war veterans are not bound by the demands of pastoral care, at least not in the short term. Their initial work has been that of disruption, disorder and domination. Specifically in relation to rural local government institutions such as Rural District Councils, schools and clinics, it has been the work of violently undermining the existing mechanisms and processes through which biopolitics – the 'politics of life' – have so far been constituted and practiced. But will this localised mode of rule by force persist, or will war veterans be confronted with local, national or even international pressures that alter the new terms of rule they appear to be setting?

This partly depends on what constitute the underlying projects and powers of the war veterans themselves. Are they mere pawns in a partisan project of anarchic destruction on behalf of Zanu (PF), aimed at eliminating the presence of the opposition in key nodes of governmental power? Does their involvement have certain 'revolutionary' qualities in terms of genuine attempts at transforming the direction, framework and practices of postcolonial rule? To what extent does their extensive disruption of the multiple spaces and practices of government, as identified by *The Daily News* article, constitute 'government by war veterans'? What defines the limits of their interventions, and what will be their longer-term effects on the sphere of local government, and on their own political status and future trajectory? It is with these kinds of questions in mind that this chapter considers the significance of local government and its present disruption by war veterans. Besides the other key targets of attack since February 2000 – primarily the commercial farms, but also businesses, the judiciary, non-governmental organisations, the independent media, and opposition party structures and individuals – why have local authorities and associated institutions been so violently attacked? What characterises the historical relationship between local government and the postcolonial state? What is fundamentally at stake in the current struggles over, and within, local government in Zimbabwe?

Colonial encounters and the formation of governable subjects

It had been clear to many nationalists during colonial rule that gaining control of and changing the institutions, policies and procedures of local government was an essential step in national liberation.[30] Not surprisingly, colonial local government offices were a key target of the nationalist guerillas during the liberation struggle. The personal experiences of one former Permanent Secretary for Local Government explain why this was so in general, and why he himself became politically active against the minority white settler regime during the 1970s, and subsequently trained in public administration (in Britain, no less), waiting to transform local government after independence. In an interview conducted in Harare in January 1999, he reflected on his early life growing up in a rural village in the south-east of the country during the 1950s and early 1960s, and the powerful impact his encounters with the colonial practices of local government had had on him:

> The point of contact was the District Commissioner's office. From my village in Buhera we would see landrovers passing by and we'd point and say it was the DC's vehicle. We saw the coming of a government. We saw the white administration spreading its tentacles into the rural areas, coming into communities that were closed, more traditional. We saw it as an invasion. Gradually I saw communities being subdued to this rule. I saw forced labour.[31]

---

[30] Confirmed by veteran nationalist politician, Edison Zvobgo, who stated that transforming racialised civic and legal frameworks was as much what underlay the liberation struggle as questions of land. (Zimbabwe Crisis Conference presentation, Copenhagen, September 2001.)

[31] This and subsequent transcripts are taken from an interview with the former Permanent Secretary for Local Government and National Housing, Mr. F. Munyira, Harare, 29 January 1999.

His image of 'spreading tentacles' captures vividly the territorialising strategies of the colonial state at a particular time in its career,[32] expanding its sovereignty, surveillance and control through both the symbolic authority and literal rule (often violently enforced) of the infamous District Commissioner.[33] As his further recollections indicated, the intrusions were not merely spatial, but began to define the limits and legitimations of everyday life and livelihood practices, as well as the ways in which racially subjected bodies moved through space:[34]

> One had to approach the DC's office to get certain things, certain services. We had to have our things, like our cattle and our fields, recorded or registered there. We got to see the DC's office as a place of legitimisation, otherwise you could get arrested. It was an office that was scary. My father used to take me to the DC's office to have a ticket to register cattle in my name [to circumvent destocking]. This had quite some impression on me. I remember, as we approached the DC's office, my father took off his hat well before we got to the building itself. Black messengers were doing things in the name of the DC. It was a terrifying experience. I grew up with a fear and hatred for the offices.[35]

Colonial local government in rural areas dates back to the Matabeleland Order in Council of 1894 which created the first reserves for Africans, in Shangani and Gwai, ushering in nine decades of rule marked by highly racialised spatial, economic, social and political divides between blacks and whites (and overlaid through time with class, gender and ethnic differences).[36] Orders, commissions and legislation in the subsequent three decades facilitated widespread expropriation of African lands for use by white

---

[32] See Munro (1998) for an account of the varying degrees to which consecutive governments – early colonial, late colonial and post-colonial – attempted either to 'extract' the state from or 'embed' it in rural society, as well as the different policy and political mechanisms used to do so.

[33] Although by this time there was an apparent form of African 'local self governance' in the 'reserves' or Tribal Trust Lands, this was nominal, being without either the resources or powers of government. In effect, local government during the late colonial period – much as in the first post-independence decade – took the form of delegation of central government authority to government-appointed public administrators.

[34] Underpinning the physical manifestations of colonial authority were the deeply intrusive – but also highly contested – legislative mechanisms aimed at altering and controlling land access, land tenure and land use patterns as well as social practices, most notoriously the Native Land Husbandry Act of 1951.

[35] The irony and tragedy of the present is that in some cases local government offices have once again become sites and sources of terror for selectively subjected citizens.

[36] See Mutizwa-Mangiza (1991) for a history of the various local government boards and councils established by the colonial state in 'native' or African areas.

settlers and the colonial state, culminating in the passing of the 1930 Land Apportionment Act. This further entrenched the distorted terms of racially-divided land through its creation of 'European Areas' (primarily white commercial farming areas), as distinct from the categories of Native Reserves (later renamed Tribal Trust Lands, and, after independence, Communal Lands) and African Purchase Areas (present-day Small Scale Commercial Farming Areas) for black Africans. This was mirrored by a racially, spatially, economically and politically divided system of rural local government, which the new Zimbabwe government inherited at independence. Relatively autonomous and well-funded Rural Councils, originally Roads Councils, existed in the white, large-scale commercial farming areas, while highly fragmented, poorly resourced African Councils, fully dependent on central government, served the black Tribal Trust Lands.[37]

The layout of urban settlements paralleled these same racial divides, creating the basis for effective colonial surveillance, domination and control of black Africans (Raftopoulos and Yoshikuni, 1999), especially control over their labour power (Makumbe, 1998). The intensified segregation policies and practices in both rural and urban areas following the Land Apportionment Act, became 'an effective means of stifling all African competition – political and economic' (Thornton, 1999:46).[38] Paradoxically, while colonial urban labour and housing policies for Africans reinforced urban-rural divides, they also played on the idea that the 'real' home of the urban worker was 'his' rural area, 'the site of traditional structures and control' (Raftopoulos and Yoshikuni, 1999:9).[39] In either case, there was little space for autonomous African local government until official government debates in the 1950s began to address this question more directly, as much in an attempt to curtail growing African nationalism as a concern with expanding rights and improving conditions and services for Africans. It wasn't before amendments were made to the Urban Councils Act in 1973 and further changes in 1980, that all black urban dwellers gained

---

[37] Historically in Zimbabwe there has been a consistently strong relationship between the reconstruction of 'administrative' boundaries of rule, ambiguous definitions of local authority, and the political economy and cultural politics of land.

[38] Despite the widespread negative effects of these measures, Parry (1999) and others in Raftopoulos and Yoshikuni (1999) point to the 'uneven structure of urban colonialism', the 'limits of colonial power', and various African 'oppositional' practices aimed at countering these measures. This could equally be argued for rural areas (see for example Ranger 1985, and Alexander et al, 2000).

[39] This has an eerie resonance with Mugabe's pseudo-traditionalist attacks on urbanites 'without totems'.

full entitlement to elect council representatives in their own constituencies.[40]

Postcolonial practices in the (re)making of local government

At independence, the newly elected government was faced with an immense task of reconstruction and reinvention on all levels. With regard to rural local government, there were two parallel yet related projects to address: firstly, the problem of 'development', especially in those areas (mainly Communal Areas) that had suffered most through many decades of colonial underdevelopment, followed by the years of the liberation war that left infrastructure devastated and rural development administration depleted or entirely destroyed in some areas (Brand, 1991); secondly, the problem of creating and legitimising a new order, through establishing new or reformed institutions and practices of local government. Both were inherently connected to the continuous projects of state-making and sustaining ruling party hegemony.[41]

A whole flurry of policies and programmes were introduced soon after independence to address the most pressing administrative and political challenges in the local government system, the more economic and social aspects constantly lagging behind.[42] The District Councils Act of 1980 primarily tackled the problem of fragmentation of 220 African Councils, facilitating their consolidation into 55 'more viable' District Councils, although these remained severely marginalised, under-resourced and dependent on central government. The Act was also instrumental in formally stripping chiefs and headmen of both their judicial and land allocation powers. This was a symbolic political act, which didn't translate evenly into altered local governance practices, but rather deepened the ambiguities in localised authority that have persisted for the past

---

[40] This contrasts markedly with the much longer delayed enfranchisement of farm workers in rural local council elections, which took a further 17 years. However, such *de jure* enfranchisement has been seriously undermined by electoral violence since 2000. In all elections since then, political violence and intimidation has deprived mainly opposition parties, especially the MDC, of their constitutional right to campaign, while voters have been denied the right to vote freely.

[41] These projects were not starting in a vacuum, but had to contend with the inherited colonial structures, personnel and practices. Given the experiences of these, in some areas, such as Hurungwe, inhabitants were strongly opposed to having a District Council at all. Thanks to Blair Rutherford for pointing this out.

[42] Ranger (1996:274) suggests that even as colonial and postcolonial governments enlarged the administrative and political spheres of governance for black Africans, there was 'a narrowing down [of] the African religious, social and economic world'.

two decades.[43] Subsequent directives, legislation and policies in the mid-80s focused more specifically on 'decentralisation'. In combination, these measures detailed the new local government hierarchy, including the composition and functions of councils and committees from village to ward to district to provincial level (Mutizwa-Mangiza, 1991:56-59).[44] In addition, they established a comprehensive range of local government cadres to operate the system: on the one hand, elected members of Village and Ward Development Committees, and ward councilors who constituted the District Council; on the other, central government-employed Village Community Workers (VCWs), Local Government Promotion Officers (LGPOs), District Administrators (DAs), and so on.

In principle, in terms of administrative (re)form and practice, these changes were geared towards altering the size and boundaries of villages and wards, introducing 'integrated and coordinated' rural development planning, and facilitating 'popular participation' (Mutizwa-Mangiza, 1991:57).[45] These were consistent with both the post-independence rhetoric of state-building on new terms, and the globally dominant developmentalist discourse of the 1980s. Within the bureaucracy itself, a strong public administration ethos and professionalism characterised many of those responsible for designing and implementing the relevant policies and procedures.[46] At the same time, one has to take seriously Makumbe's (1998:60) assertion that 'the decentralisation structure was primarily conceived for the purposes of creating the one-party state'. Brand (1991:92) suggests that there was 'deliberate (con)fusion of political and administrative structures at the district and local level', signaling 'an important step towards the one-party state'. In addition, he observed that the 'various administrative tiers of decentralisation were explicitly designed to parallel those of the party structures' (Brand, 1991:85). Village and Ward Development Committees, for example, bore a close resemblance to former village and ward level party structures.

---

[43] The question of traditional authority has been politically reworked several times since independence, depending on the vulnerability of the ruling party, most recently via the Traditional Leaders Act of 1998.

[44] A range of scholarship has addressed the numerous challenges, problems and opportunities these changes provoked, especially during the first decade of independence. See for example the collection by Helmsing et al., 1991.

[45] An assessment of the extent, effectiveness and effects of these changes would require a different kind of discussion, neither intended nor possible here.

[46] My experience working in or with the Zimbabwe state between 1983 and 1997, much of it concerned with local government, confirms an initial professionalism that was gradually undermined both by the changing conditions associated with structural reforms in the 1990s, and increasingly by overt politicisation.

The post of LGPO, a key frontline field worker, was filled with recently-demobilised political commissars from the liberation armies, bringing not only valuable political mobilisation experience from the war to the project of 'development', but enhancing the revolutionary credentials of the new government. These posts did not last the decade, giving way instead to the more technocratic sensibilities and recentralising tendencies within the bureaucracy. However, the initial shift from liberation struggle to regular public administration at independence posed some interesting and awkward challenges for local government. As the former Permanent Secretary for Local Government observed just a year before the land occupations and local government disruptions began:

> In 1980, when we started, we were administering with the emphasis on power. The rationale was that it was a government system that came about through a war situation, and so a military type of approach was in place. It derived from the Party. The threat to the newly-won independence through hostile forces, both external and internal, required government institutions that would demonstrate change.... If you're dealing with a power situation you have to use power to reverse it. We've developed since then. The manner in which I was running my office has changed. I'm looking now at a system conscious of people's rights. There were no people's rights before.[47]

Towards the late 1980s, the emphasis of decentralisation policies was primarily on creating a unified rural local government system, through amalgamating the existing Rural Councils serving mainly white Large Scale Commercial Farming Areas, and the still under-resourced District Councils serving mainly the Communal Areas. The ongoing split reflected the government's retention of two distinct property regimes – communal and freehold – which, as Munro (1998:226) argues, not only accepted the 'different concepts of rights that accrued to those regimes', but equally 'underwrote different conceptions of social being and citizenship' that had a direct bearing on the practices and politics of local government.[48] While the tenure regime was to remain in place, the Rural District Councils Act was passed in 1988 to facilitate institutional and political amalgamation

---

[47] Interview with the then Permanent Secretary for Local Government and National Housing, Mr. F. Munyira, Harare, 29 January 1999. Part of doctoral fieldwork research on a case of local government eviction of migrant farmers in northwest Zimbabwe.

[48] This split is mirrored in the ongoing administrative divide between rural and urban local government. See Mamdani's (1996) historicisation of related distinctions between 'ethnic' and 'civic' spaces.

of the councils. At the same time it was designed to enhance autonomy and further decentralise powers and resources from central government agencies to the new local authorities.

It took five years before the actual amalgamation was implemented, a period during which there was intense debate, experimentation and negotiation within government itself concerning the meanings and modes of decentralisation. Both the amalgamation process itself, and the deepening of decentralisation, raised fears and objections in many quarters. The resistance was not only from the mainly white and relatively well-to-do Rural Councils afraid of merging with black, under-resourced District Councils, but equally from various line ministries anticipating the loss of control over personnel and resources. In addition, there were tensions in the 'parent' ministry responsible for implementing the RDC Act, the then Ministry of Local Government, Rural and Urban Development, emanating not least from the uncertainties and 'demotion' faced by District Administrators (DAs) who had until then been *de facto* Chief Executive Officers of the District Councils.[49]

With a worsening economic crisis by the end of the 1980s, and the growing hegemony of neo-liberalism, in 1991 the government introduced standard economic structural reforms. Decentralisation had become an important component of associated public sector reforms being promoted by the World Bank and other donors, and the push towards implementing the RDC Act was thus intensified. Consequently there was fairly robust financial support during the early and mid-90s for a range of local government policy development and capacity building initiatives.[50] Eventually then, the new unified rural local government system came into being, and in 1993, the first Rural District Council elections were held. The process of amalgamation was inevitably messy and complicated, a fact acknowledged by all parties and accepted as the basis of a conscious 'learning by doing' approach to capacity building. It nonetheless signified a moment of great optimism, at least in official spaces, especially for more efficient and effective delivery of services. At the time, there was an unusually high level of political commitment to the process expressed in the upper echelons of government. Both a Cabinet Committee on Decentralisation and a special committee of

---

[49] DAs derived immense power from the central state and in many cases acted much as the District or Native Commissioners of the colonial past. This generated much tension in the former District Councils.

[50] Besides government-sponsored programmes, a number of NGOs were supporting decentralisation activities too, but usually from the more explicit ideological standpoint of wanting to strengthen participatory democracy.

Permanent Secretaries were formed in the mid-90s to 'guide' and give political weight to the decentralisation process.[51]

The unma(s)king of local government

Yet the reality for many of the new RDCs, especially those in the rural margins, was that they were assuming their authority at a moment of national economic decline, reduction in public sector spending, and growing popular discontent with government in general. The increasing pressure on RDCs to generate local revenue for their own administration and local development activities placed severe strains on them, and in some cases brought them into direct competition and often outright conflict with their constituencies; arguably a case of the tension between sovereignty and biopolitics. In one marginal district in northwest Zimbabwe in the late 1990s where I undertook doctoral fieldwork, these tensions played themselves out in persistent and increasingly violent ways (Hammar, 2001a). In a not unprecedented case in national or historical terms (Patel, 1998; Alexander, this volume), the RDC in question forcefully evicted a community of migrant farmers from land bordering a national park and safari area, in order to gain greater access itself to wildlife revenues, ostensibly to be 'shared' with communities under CAMPFIRE.[52] Redefining the settled area as a 'wildlife buffer zone' instead of communal farming land, and reconstructing the migrant settlers as 'squatters' rather than farmers, the council evoked the multiple tropes of environmental sustainability, development and security to justify its brutal and legally suspect actions.[53] This kind of practice was far from what had been envisaged within the ostensibly 'democratic' framework of decentralisation, or in relation to such instruments of 'development' as the national Rural District Council Capacity Building Programme.

In addition to the revenue dilemma facing RDCs, there was a growing unease around the question of authority itself. On the one hand, local political tensions mushroomed as the ruling party's hegemony waned and it feared losing its grip on local councils long

---

[51] In 1997, the latter committee drafted and agreed on 'Thirteen Principles of Decentralization', which provided important clarification and backing for those trying to implement the reforms. However, attempts at outlining a comprehensive 'vision of local government' were made several years later for consideration by the Cabinet Committee, but the outcome and effects of a draft document on this are not presently known.
[52] Communal Areas Management Programme for Indigenous Resources.
[53] This case study has formed the basis of my doctoral research.

dominated by Zanu (PF). Where Zanu (PF) local officials, including those elected as district councillors, exhibited questionable loyalty to the party, efforts were made to have them removed from their posts. But there were also direct challenges to the RDC and to the state from ordinary citizens. For example, recounting the tale of the above-mentioned eviction in a community gathering in 1999, and reaching a crescendo of exasperation at the violent betrayal exhibited by the RDC, one woman evictee demanded to know 'where does the council get its power.' This unambivalent questioning of rule – this refusal by 'active citizens' to be governed solely on the RDC's terms – represents a significant moment in the persistent yet paradoxical struggle between the making and unmaking of local government.[54] One of the key paradoxes of local government is its parallel role in both discipline and democracy. As Hansen (1999) has noted for India, while democracy was envisaged and promoted through greater decentralisation of local government, this process in fact facilitated a channel for greater control and discipline of populations. Alternatively, Scott (1998) suggests that while decentralisation enhances the legibility (and hence susceptibility) of populations, it equally expands the opportunities for people to pressurise the developmental state to actually deliver 'development'.[55] More than that, it is often a battleground for contestations over authority, and over the very definition of citizenship and the obligations, rights and resources associated with it (Hammar, 2001a).

Whatever democratic principles and visions of local government were espoused within the official framework of decentralisation during the 1980s and 90s, since 2000 they have been largely abandoned in favour of an overtly partisan project of domination and control of Rural District Councils by Zanu (PF). This has occurred not only through disruption and occupation by war veterans, but in collaboration with the party leadership and the bureaucracy itself. One might note for example, the clearly intimidatory remarks made by Zimbabwe's Vice President at the biennial conference of the Association of Rural District Councils (ARDC) in July 2001:

---

[54] A long history of challenges to state-centric, hegemonic representations and practices of local government predates the present crisis, as much in the rural margins as in large urban constituencies. More generally, one needs to consider the numerous ways in which local government (and the state) is made and remade through the intimacies, complicities and contestations of citizens themselves (Mbembe, 1992; Hansen and Stepputat, 2001).

[55] On development as disciplinary practice, see Ferguson, 1994; Li, 1999; Moore, 2000; Worby, 2000.

> Vice President Joseph Msika yesterday stunned officials attending a meeting of rural local authorities in Mutare when he ordered them to openly declare their support for President Mugabe by a show of hands. "Those of you who support him must raise your hands," Msika said to deafening silence from the hundreds of delegates attending the third biennial congress of the Association of Rural District Councils. He then challenged those who do not support the President to also identify themselves, saying Zimbabwe would never have another Mugabe. Almost immediately afterwards, the delegates raised their hands to pledge their support for Mugabe.[56]

The ARDC initially rejected this type of political interference, but such an explicitly critical stance was rapidly curtailed, and more general commentary by the ARDC on the extensive council disruptions has since been muted.[57] This is despite the fact that the very survival of RDCs has been substantially threatened in several ways: their human resource capacity; their revenue base, for example from unit taxes in commercial farming areas and from wildlife tourism in marginal agricultural areas; their ability to deliver services; or their hold over their legislated authority, including land allocation authority 'in consultation' with traditional leaders.

The response to war veterans' interference by councils themselves has varied. Those demonstrating direct support for the opposition MDC, or more specifically where MDC candidates have been voted in as councillors, have paid a severe price in terms of the extent and degree of violence involved in attacks.[58] However, as noted specifically for Matabeleland North by McGregor (2002), some RDCs tried to resist through council resolutions to reinstate officials and councillors, or by demoting the council chairman who was seen as being 'too close to the war veterans'. But given the high levels of support for the war veterans' actions by the party and bureaucracy, ultimately 'accommodations had to be made'. Both councils and District and Provincial Administrators (DAs and PAs) were forced to 'take the war veterans' demands seriously, even though the demands were illegal, circumvented existing channels for presenting complaints and ignored procedures for dismissing and recruiting

---

[56] *The Daily News* (Harare), 31 July 2001.
[57] The current President of the ARDC is high up in Zanu (PF)'s Mashonaland East provincial hierarchy.
[58] This became evident both prior to and after the September 2002 RDC elections. Binga RDC for example, experienced recurrent and severe 'punishment' for MDC success in the area, as did ordinary inhabitants who were terrorised and deliberately denied food aid by the ruling party and government. See for example *The Financial Gazette*, 24 October 2002.

public servants' (McGregor, 2002:34). In addition, the growing conflation of party and state roles played by DAs and PAs, especially in relation to the new 'land committees' and implementation of the 'fast track' resettlement programme, has produced even greater 'confusion of authority' at district and provincial levels.

It has been more difficult for Zanu (PF) and war veterans to sustain overt disruption of the now mainly MDC-dominated urban local authorities, although violent attacks have taken place there too. Nonetheless, verbal attacks and ministerial manouevres by the Minister of Local Government, Public Works and National Housing, Ignatius Chombo, have become legend. In one widely publicised case, Harare City Council's strenuous efforts to counter corruption and inefficiency were repeatedly threatened by the Minister's interference on partisan grounds.[59] This contrasts sharply with the complete lack of protection provided by the state to large numbers of government employees accused of supporting the MDC. These include staff in local government institutions throughout the country, as well as 'dissident' central government employees, and chiefs and headmen, who have been subjected to countless acts of intimidation, humiliation and violence, in some cases murder, allegedly at the hands of known Zanu (PF) militants.[60]

The attack on rural school teachers, viewed by Zanu (PF) as a key constituency of the MDC, has been particularly extensive and severe. Thousands of acts of violence and intimidation against teachers have been recorded since 2000. Abductions, torture, beatings, murder, intimidation, illegal dismissals and extortion for 'protection', have all been reported, with little if any response from the relevant ministries, the Public Service Commission, or the police. Thousands of teachers have been forced to flee their posts.[61] Much

---

[59] This involved the Minister instructing the council to 'amicably resolve' a dismissal dispute by paying out a proposed exit package of Z$31 million to one of its junior employees, a prominent war veteran leader active, allegedly during working hours, in illegal farm evictions, company invasions and other militant Zanu (PF) campaigns. See *The Daily News*, 14 August 2002.

[60] Interestingly, while sympathies for the MDC in rural areas appear to have been high among public servants and the wealthier, more educated and more mobile inhabitants in general, it was often the lowest paid and least conspicuous council workers who were the most committed activists and became MDC office bearers (Alexander and McGregor, 2001).

[61] In mid-2002, the Progressive Teachers Union of Zimbabwe (PTUZ) instituted legal proceedings against the Minister of Education, Sports and Culture, Aeneas Chigwedere, to sue for compensation for the political murder of one of its members, the forced retirement of another and defamation of the union. See *The Daily News*, 7 August 2002. The Minister has frequently been reported as publicly refusing to provide protection for teachers. In a national teachers' pay strike led by the PTUZ in October 2002, union leaders were arrested and beaten, while many striking teachers were suspended or fired. At the same time, in November 2002, The President and cabinet ministers were awarded substantial salary increases.

as elsewhere, teachers constitute perhaps the largest group of decentralised local government employees. As such, they are important 'bearers of the designs of the state' (Wilson, 2001:313), acting as frontline workers in the formation of subject-citizens. Despite their sometimes ambiguous position in rural communities – being at times highly respected for their knowledge and at others resented as arrogant outsiders – they nonetheless occupy a potentially influential position in relation to both current and future generations of voters, a fact not lost on any political party. In addition, the rural school itself is 'an emblem that demarcates the territory effectively governed by the state, an institution that relays ideas about state, nation, and citizen' (Wilson: 2001:313).[62] In rural Zimbabwe, with few brick-built structures, it also acts as a multi-purpose community centre. Occupation of these spaces by Zanu (PF) supporters further limits the capacity of the MDC to campaign, or for independent civic organisations to hold meetings. In addition, schools often act as important feeding centres in times of drought. In the context of an impending famine in late 2002, the removal of 'opposition' teachers allowed the ruling party even more control over the political distribution of food for millions of Zimbabweans.

With regard to Rural District Council elections at the end of September 2002, the intimidations and terror campaigns were persistent and widespread, and explicitly targeted at MDC candidates. With less than one month to go before the elections, in one province alone, Midlands South, at least 36 MDC candidates had reportedly withdrawn, 'fearing for their lives after being threatened with violence by Zanu PF supporters'.[63] In Chegutu District in Mashonaland West, eight out of eleven MDC candidates attempting to register their nominations were chased away by Zanu (PF) youths, while MDC officials assisting them were allegedly assaulted or detained, 'in the presence of the police'.[64] In Manicaland and Masvingo, the police are alleged to have actively assisted in both the intimidation and false arrest of MDC candidates to prevent them from standing in the elections.[65] Elsewhere, police in uniform are alleged to have directly participated in assaulting MDC candidates and supporters.

---

[62] Since the mid-90s, rural schools have been 'decentralised' to fall directly under the RDCs.
[63] *The Daily News*, 2 September 2002, '36 MDC candidates pull out of poll after threats'.
[64] *The Daily News*, 6 September 2002, 'Zanu PF supporters detain MP'.
[65] *Zimbabwe Independent*, 19 July 2002, 'Zanu PF militia impose 'curfew' in Buhera'; *The Daily News*, 7 August 2002, '17 MDC members arrested in Chipinge'.

Recapturing the frontiers of rule, in which rural local government is key, has been a central project of Zanu (PF) since independence, just as it was a key goal of the liberation forces fighting colonial rule. At first this was about the newly-independent government countering 'the spreading tentacles' of the former settler-colonial state with its own territorialising practices. This was, and continues to be, an attempt by the post-colonial state to mark itself in ways that deepen both its physical and its imagined presence, and that extend the authority of its varied and often ambiguous agents through their access to and control over natural resources and human populations. However, the present drive to reoccupy these frontiers is portrayed by Zanu (PF) as part of the new war against recolonisation by whites and the West through their so-called proxy agent, the MDC. For the ruling party, party militants in general and war veterans in particular, are not only critical to its broader hegemonic strategy, but equally to its attempts to recapture the space of local government.[66]

War veterans: New gatekeepers at the frontiers of government?

McGregor (2002) has provided rich empirical detail and historically grounded analysis of war veterans' systematic disruption of the institutions and independence of rural local authorities since 2001.[67] Together with anecdotal evidence sourced from media reports and personal testimonies from across the country, the emerging pattern includes at least the following: illegal dismissal or 'chasing away' of council employees, councillors, and even central government employees accused of supporting the MDC, and in some cases their replacement by war veterans; death threats and cases of alleged assault and even murder of suspected MDC supporters among council staff, teachers, and traditional leaders; physical closure, occupation and in some cases destruction of council offices and property; removal of council vehicles; disruption of council meetings and routine

---

[66] The distinction between 'state' and 'party' is always important, both analytically and politically. While presently in Zimbabwe the two appear to be operationally and discursively joined at the seams, well-suited to David Scott's (1995) nomenclature of 'state-party', in practice there are different if complicit and overlapping projects, processes and politics at play for each. This may provide some optimism for a less fractured, less obsessively partisan future.

[67] Although the interventions became more systematic in 2001, disruptions began at least as early as June 2000 with the occupation and use of some RDC offices as bases for 'terror campaigns' building up to the parliamentary elections.

operations; control over land distribution lists; and violent disruption of council elections. What becomes evident from McGregor's work in particular is that when the disruptions first began, there was already a context, albeit spatially and historically varied, of popular dissatisfaction with some councils and 'genuine grievances' which war veterans could draw on to legitimise their actions.

Despite years of investment in RDC capacity building and capital development initiatives, the tide of post-amalgamation pressures on RDCs had clearly been impossible to contain or counter. Policies and practices were adopted that seemed to exacerbate corruption and inefficiency in councils rather than curtail them, and this had already prompted interventions by the Ministry of Local Government (in its successive incarnations) that have consistently undercut the spirit if not the word of the RDC Act. Yet even if there were serious problems in the RDCs that needed addressing, it appears that the combined and cumulative disruptions by war veterans, the central state and the ruling party have by no means resolved these.[68] Instead, the overall effect of 'the politics of disorder' has been to exacerbate the councils' problems. In the short term, experienced personnel have been forcibly removed and replaced with unqualified party loyalists, many routine council procedures have been interrupted, clinics and schools have been closed, revenues have been lost from unit taxes, forestry, tourism ventures and former donor-funded development projects, and there is ongoing violence and a menacing 'atmosphere of fear'.

According to McGregor (2002:37), the long-term consequences are 'potentially devastating':

> *Corruption and cynicism have become pervasive, professionalism has been undermined, local authorities have been forced to respond to an authoritarian centre and its local agents, and public confidence in the local state may be difficult to win back. The goal of decentralized, accountable local state bodies seems further away than ever.*

There is no underestimating such effects. Nor can one underestimate the 'success' of Zanu (PF) in its determined efforts to reconquer and colonise Rural District Councils, at least for the moment. But there are several factors that will necessarily temper these moves in the

---

[68] The role of the state and party in disrupting both rural and urban local government has been as much through their formal absence, silence, or failure to intervene in the violence being perpetrated by war veterans and party militia, as by the kinds of political statements, policy directives and administrative interference that have revealed their assent to if not direct incitement of such practices.

long run. To begin with, local government, like 'the state', is in a continuous process of reconstruction and reinvention through its multiple articulations with different actors, processes and politics. In this sense, one cannot view RDCs as 'empty vessels' devoid of their own agency, merely open to external invasion or manipulation. There is a far more complex 'micropolitics of locality' that makes such external interventions contingent, and constrains 'the pace, scope, and direction of local-level political change' (Boone, 1998).[69] In fact the deeply and violently contested RDC elections in September 2002 are evidence of how seriously all political players take the question of control over local government.

Overlaying the politics of locality associated with the disruption of local government, is a *cultural politics of authority*, here with reference to the specificity of war veterans as the prime agents of disruption. As demonstrated, war veterans have clearly acted as the vanguard of Zanu (PF) in its move to recapture the 'edges of sovereignty', but neither Zanu (PF) nor the veterans themselves are entirely in control of this project. While loyalist war veterans have actively supported the ruling party, those involved in local government disruptions seem to be less 'willing clerks of the state-party' (Scott 1995:205) than unpredictable gatekeepers at the frontiers of government. They have their own agendas, both collectively through their identities as 'war veterans', and in terms of their own localised interests and power relations. Many war veterans, for example, had become increasingly economically impoverished since independence, dispossessed of the 'promised land' they fought for during the liberation war, and often excluded from positions within the state that would facilitate accumulation. Those that had not risen up the ladder to 'chefdom' during the nationalist struggle were also politically marginalised, further exacerbating class differences between an expanded yet still minority political elite and the rank and file of war veterans.

These exclusions fuelled both the formation of the ZNLWVA towards the end of the 1980s, and the intensive push for compensation for their members that finally succeeded in 1997. The war veterans' revived warrior status since 2000 has become a powerful political card for Mugabe to play in the context of the present politics of land. However, the subsequent remarginalisation and redispossession of some war veterans, in particular those being evicted from newly settled farms to make way for possession by

---

[69] For a rich evocation of the politics of locality in a Latin American context, see Raffles, 1999.

party bosses, points to the unevenness and fragility of some of these accommodations (see Alexander, this volume). Yet this precariousness could be as much a threat to the state-party as to war veterans themselves. As long as veterans are not fully integrated into or controlled by it, there is the potential danger of their constructing something of a 'parallel state' (Kuehls, 1996) especially through the medium of local government.

However, for now this isn't especially likely. For a start, their revived political authority – the basis for their current 'influence, status and importance' (Boone, 1998) – is derived quite pointedly from the state-party's present revalorisation of political heroism linked to the national liberation struggle. From experience, we know that such support can also be withdrawn. Besides this, war veterans must necessarily compete with traditional leaders and other 'local notables', whose authority is derived historically from a combination of situated cultural, religious, familial, economic and other factors, and whose own value and influence, while frequently deepened by translocal relations, is often highly localised and lies 'beyond the state' (Boone, 1998). In addition, RDCs and their constituencies are engaged in constant processes of contestation and renegotiation over the terms of rule and practice of government that, even if severely constrained at present, are unlikely to disappear entirely. Those war veterans presently occupying and 'running' RDCs will ultimately be faced with such challenges in trying to sustain their legitimacy as a local authority: the challenge of combining sovereignty and biopolitics. Given these various 'contingencies and constraints', one needs to be somewhat circumspect about the assertion made by *The Daily News* that Zimbabwe has reverted to 'government by war veterans'.

Reshaping government, remaking citizens

What have been naturalised for many years as the formal and 'normal' workings and institutions of local government in Zimbabwe, such as councils, schools, legislation, policies and procedures, can no longer be taken for granted. In recent years, new forms of irregular, unregulated, and ambiguous authority have emerged to disrupt not only the physical structures and routine practices of local authorities and associated institutions, but also the normative liberal notions of local government itself. The ongoing crisis and the (partial) production of disorder have undeniably altered the overall project and mode of rule, the broad terms of government practice, and the distribution and texture of political space. Within this context of chaotic, multi-layered transformation, the attacks on the rural local government system are contributing to the radical reconfiguration of who governs in which spaces, who is being governed, to what extent, and by what methods.

Describing the newly appointed Permanent Secretary for Local Government, Public Works and National Housing, Vincent Hungwe, as 'one of the regime's rising young stars', a media report in August 2002 quoted his view on the necessary changes to the previous form of government: 'We may have to take this whole system back to zero before we can start it up again and make it work in a new way.'[70] The report concluded by suggesting that many Zimbabweans 'already have a taste of what he means by zero'. Such cynicism may be well placed, nonetheless there are important questions to consider regarding what this 'new way' might incorporate. Hungwe's implied (though as yet unspecified) version of authentic, sovereign government, seems intent on defining itself on the basis of quite different notions of normality than those associated with anything 'colonial' or even 'Western'. This is consistent with Mugabe's ideological legacy and the sustained rhetoric of his vision of radical redistribution and genuine African government. There is much to recommend such a vision in itself. Indeed it is hardly the intellectual property of one man, or even one political party.[71] But this is part of the trick and tragedy of the present political moment in Zimbabwe, namely that the narrative of historical injustice and the critical project of correcting it – through radical land and economic redistribution – have been both simplified and monopolised by one man and one party. In the process, the vision has become fetishised and commodified, and the only valid currency of exchange is membership of Zanu (PF). All other people are violently excluded from the vision and its bounties, or from buying into them at all.

In fact, Zanu (PF)'s current vision of redistribution and authentic African government is radically partisan and partial, and rests on dramatically altered and narrowing boundaries of national citizenship and belonging. A senior Zanu (PF) official, Didymus Mutasa, quoted in the same news report as Hungwe, revealed this in unapologetically stark terms. Apparently responding to

---

[70] *The Sunday Times* (UK), 11 August 2002.
[71] As Bond (2001) notes, despite the MDC's increasing domination by a neo-liberal discourse, there are many within its ranks, as well as among the independent opposition to Zanu (PF), who are strongly supportive of these principles and who do not see them as contradicting a commitment to human rights.

widespread accusations that the government was trying to starve to death close to half its population of over 12 million in the face of impending famine – and primarily those perceived as opposition supporters – he was quoted as saying: 'We would be better off with only 6 [million] people, with *our own people* who support the liberation struggle' [emphasis added]. Referring especially to farm workers, who are viewed by the ruling party as both foreign and disloyal to 'the nation', he nonchalantly quipped: 'We don't want all these extra people.'[72]

The resonance of Mutasa's stated desire to discard surplus populations, with historical precedents such as National Socialism in Nazi Germany and its implied translation into routinised governmental practices of exclusion and annihilation, is too obvious and ominous to ignore. The political space granted to Zanu (PF) politicians to voice such inflammatory views, clearly reflects an intensification of authoritarian nationalism in Zimbabwe (see Raftopoulos, this volume). Nonetheless, Dean (2001) counsels us against a too-complacent distinction between authoritarian and liberal governmentality. Certainly, one should expect and value the conditions of a mode of rule in which the state acts as the guarantor of democratic rights, security, justice, access to livelihoods, health and education, for all its citizens. Yet we are advised to consider the growing spread of 'illiberal components of liberalism', and hence to reflect on 'the dangers of not calling into question the self-understanding of liberalism as a limited government acting through a knowledge of the processes of life, yet, at the same time, safeguarding the rights of the political and juridical subject' (Dean, 2001:60-61).[73] Furthermore, we need to remain attentive to both the historical precedents and future potential for violent exclusions and dispossession – whether inflected through race, class, gender, generation or ethnicity – associated with upholding core liberal principles, not least that of private property.[74]

This cautionary note is not intended to underplay or legitimise acts of violence and torture, forced displacement and dispossession, and the wide range of other unconstitutional practices being perpetrated in Zimbabwe in the name of a renewed war of national

---

[72] *The Sunday Times* (UK), 11 August 2002.
[73] Dean gives as one example of these 'illiberal components' the increased incarceration of illegal migrants in self-defined liberal democracies such as Western Europe, the United States and Australia.
[74] See Moore (forthcoming) for a critical discussion of the 'constitutive *exclusions* of liberal modes of rule', drawn in this instance from an Indian context but resonating across time and space.

liberation. Clearly, as Hansen and Stepputat (2001:9) assert, 'one can and should criticise specific forms of governance, undesirable institutions, and oppressive state practices'. However, the result of such critiques should not be 'visions of the absence of government or the state as such, but rather the possibility of other, more humane and democratic forms of governance'. This must surely be on the minds of all those trying to imagine and create a progressive post-crisis Zimbabwe; one that incorporates what Adrienne Rich (1993) envisions as 'a democracy without exceptions'.

References

Alexander, Jocelyn, and JoAnn McGregor, 2001. 'Elections, Land and the Politics of Opposition in Matabeleland'. *Journal of Agrarian Change*, Vol. 1, No. 4, pp. 510-533.

Alexander, Jocelyn, JoAnn McGregor and Terence Ranger, 2000. *Violence and Memory: One Hundred Years in the 'Dark Forests' of Matabeleland*. Oxford: James Currey.

Berger, John, 2001. *The Shape of a Pocket*. New York: Pantheon Books.

Bond, Patrick, 2001. 'Radical Rhetoric and the Working Class During Zimbabwean Nationalism's Dying Days'. In Brian Raftopoulos and Lloyd Sachikonye (eds), *Striking Back: The Labour Movement and the Post-Colonial State in Zimbabwe 1980-2000*. Harare: Weaver Press. pp. 25-52.

Boone, Catherine, 1998. 'State Building in the African Countryside: Structure and Politics at the Grassroots'. *Journal of Development Studies*, Vol. 34, No. 4, pp. 1-31.

Brand, Coenraad, 1991. 'Will Decentralization Enhance Local Participation?'. In Helmsing et al., *Limits to Decentralization in Zimbabwe. Essays on the Decentralization of Government and Planning in the 1980s*. The Hague: Institute of Social Studies. pp. 79-96.

Dean, Mitchell, 2001. '"Demonic Societies": Liberalism, Biopolitics, and Sovereignty'. In Hansen and Stepputat (eds), *States of Imagination. Ethnographic Explorations of the Postcolonial State*. Durham and London: Duke University Press. pp. 45-64.

Ferguson, James, 1994. *The Anti-Politics Machine: "Development", Depoliticization, and Bureaucratic Power in Lesotho*. Minneapolis: University of Minnesota Press.

Foucault, Michel, 1979. 'Governmentality'. *Ideology and Consciousness: Governing the Present*. Autumn 1979, No. 6, pp. 5-21.

Geschiere, Peter and Josef Gugler, 'Introduction. The Urban-Rural Connection: Changing Issues of Belonging and Identification'. *Africa*, Vol. 68, No. 3, pp. 309-319.

Gupta, Akhil, 1995. 'Blurred Boundaries: The Discourse of Corruption, the Culture of Politics, and the Imagined State'. *American Ethnologist*, Vol. 22, No. 2, pp. 375-402.

Hammar, Amanda, 2001a. "The Day of Burning': Eviction and Reinvention in the Margins of Northwest Zimbabwe'. *Journal of Agrarian Change*, Vol. 1, No. 4, pp. 550-574.

Hammar, Amanda, 2001b. 'Locating Zimbabwe's Rural District Councils in the Politics of Crisis and the Process of Democratization'. In Yuka Suzuki and Eric Worby (eds), *Zimbabwe: The Politics of Crisis and the Crisis of Politics*. Summary of Workshop Proceedings. New Haven: Yale Center for International Area Studies, African Studies Council Working Paper Series. pp. 45-52

Hammar, Amanda, and Stig Jensen, 2002. 'Zimbabwe in Crisis'. Issues paper in Aid Policy and Practice Series, Copenhagen: Centre for Development Research.

Hansen, Thomas Blom, 1999. *The Saffron Wave: Democracy and Hindu Nationalism in Modern India*. Princeton: Princeton University Press.

Hansen, Thomas Blom, and Finn Stepputat, 2001. 'Introduction: States of Imagination'. In Thomas Blom Hansen and Finn Stepputat (eds), 2001. *States of Imagination. Ethnographic Explorations of the Postcolonial State*. Durham and London: Duke University Press. pp. 1-38.

Hansen, Thomas Blom, and Finn Stepputat (eds), 2001. *States of Imagination. Ethnographic Explorations of the Postcolonial State*. Durham and London: Duke University Press.

Helmsing, A.H.J, N.D. Mutizwa-Mangiza, D.R. Gasper, C. Brand, K.H. Wekwete, 1991. *Limits to Decentralization in Zimbabwe. Essays on the Decentralization of Government and Planning in the 1980s*. The Hague: Institute of Social Studies.

Kuehls, Thom, 1996. *Beyond Sovereign Territory. The Space of Ecopolitics*. Minneapolis and London: University of Minnesota Press (Borderlines Series, Vol. 4).

Li, Tania Murray, 1999. 'Compromising Power: Development, Culture, and Rule in Indonesia'. *Cultural Anthropology*, Vol. 14, No. 3, pp. 295-322.

Mamdani, Mahmood, 1996. *Citizen and Subject. Contemporary Africa and the Legacy of Late Colonialism*. Princeton, NJ: Princeton University Press.

Mamdani, Mahmood, 2001. *When Victims Become Killers. Colonialism, Nativism, and the Genocide in Rwanda*. Princeton, NJ: Princeton University Press.

Mbembe, Achille, 1992. 'Provisional Notes on the Postcolony'. *Africa*, Vol. 62, No. 1, pp. 3-37.

McGregor, JoAnn, 2002, 'The Politics of Disruption: War Veterans and the Local State in Zimbabwe'. *African Affairs* (2002), 101, pp. 9-37.

Meredith, Martin, 2002. *Our Votes, Our Guns: Robert Mugabe and the Tragedy of Zimbabwe*. Oxford: PublicAffairs.

Moore, Donald S., forthcoming. 'Beyond Blackmail: Multivalent Modernities and the Cultural Politics of Development in India'. In K. Sivaramakrishnan and Arun Agrawal (eds), *Regional Modernities in South Asia*. Delhi: Oxford University Press, and Stanford, CA: Stanford University Press.

Moore, Donald S., 2000. 'The Crucible of Cultural Politics: Reworking "Development" in Zimbabwe's Eastern Highlands'. *American Ethnologist*, Vol. 26, No. 3, pp. 654-689.

Munro, William A., 1998. *The Moral Economy of the State. Conservation, Community Development and State Making in Zimbabwe*. Athens: Ohio University Center for International Studies. Monograph in International Studies, Africa Series No.68.

Mutizwa-Mangiza, Naison, 1991. 'Decentralization and Local Government Administration. An Analysis of Structural and Planning Problems at the Rural District Level'. In Helmsing et al., 1991, *Limits to Decentralization in Zimbabwe. Essays on the Decentralization of Government and Planning in the 1980s*.The Hague: Institute of Social Studies. pp. 51-78.

Parry, Richard, 1999. 'Culture, organisation and class: the African experience in Salisbury, 1892-1935'. In Brian Raftopoulos and Tsuneo Yoshikuni (eds), *Sites of Struggle: Essays in Zimbabwe's Urban History*. Harare: Weaver Press. pp. 53-94.

Patel, Heena, 1998. *Sustainable Utilization and African Wildlife Policy. The Case of Zimbabwe's Communal Areas Management Programme for Indigenous Resources (CAMPFIRE). Rhetoric or Reality?* Cambridge, MA: Indigenous Environmental Policy Center (IEPC).

Peluso, Nancy Lee and Peter Vandergeest, 2001. 'Genealogies of the Political Forest and Customary Rights in Indonesia, Malaysia and Thailand'. *The Journal of Asian Studies*, Vol. 60, No. 3, pp. 761-812.

Raffles, Hugh, 1999. '"Local Theory": Nature and the Making of an Amazonian Place'. *Cultural Anthropology*, Vol. 14, No. 3, pp. 323-360.

Raftopoulos, Brian, 2001. 'The Labour Movement and the Emergence of Opposition Politics in Zimbabwe'. In Brian Raftopoulos and Lloyd Sachikonye (eds), *Striking Back: The Labour Movement and the Post-Colonial State in Zimbabwe 1980-2000*. Harare: Weaver Press. pp. 1-24.

Raftopoulos, Brian, and Lloyd Sachikonye (eds), 2001. *Striking Back: The Labour Movement and the Post-Colonial State in Zimbabwe 1980-2000*. Harare: Weaver Press.

Raftopoulos, Brian and Tsuneo Yoshikuni, 1999. 'Introduction'. In Brian Raftopoulos and Tsuneo Yoshikuni (eds), *Sites of Struggle. Essays in Zimbabwe's Urban History*. Harare: Weaver Press. pp. 1-17.

Raftopoulos, Brian and Tsuneo Yoshikuni (eds), 1999. *Sites of Struggle. Essays in Zimbabwe's Urban History*. Harare: Weaver Press.

Ranger, Terence, 1985. *Peasant Consciousness and Guerilla War in Zimbabwe*. London: James Currey.

Ranger, Terence, 1996. 'Postscript: Colonial and Postcolonial Identities'. In Terence Ranger and Richard Werbner (eds), *Postcolonial Identities in Africa*. London: Zed Books. pp. 271-281.

Rich, Adrienne, 1993. *What Is Found There: Notebooks on Poetry and Politics*. New York and London: W.W. Norton and Co.

Scott, David, 1995. 'Colonial Governmentality'. *Social Text*, 43, pp. 191-220.

Scott, James, 1998. *Seeing Like a State. How Certain Schemes to Improve the Human Condition Have Failed*. New Haven: Yale University Press.

Sylvester, Christine, 1991. *Zimbabwe: The Terrain of Contradictory Development*. Boulder: Westview.

Thornton, Stephen, 1999. 'The struggle for profit and participation by an emerging petty-bourgeoisie in Bulawayo, 1893-1933'. In Brian Raftopoulos and Tsuneo Yoshikuni (eds), *Sites of Struggle: Essays in Zimbabwe's Urban History*. Harare: Weaver Press. pp. 19-52.

Tshuma, Lawrence, 1997. *A Matter of (In)Justice: Law, State and the Agrarian Question in Zimbabwe*. Harare: SAPES Books.

Werbner, Richard, 1998. 'Smoke from the Barrel of a Gun: Postwars of the Dead, Memory and Reinscription in Zimbabwe'. In Richard Werbner (ed.), *Memory and the Postcolony. African Anthropology and the Critique of Power*. London and New York: Zed Books. pp. 71-102.

Wilson, Fiona, 2001. 'In the Name of the State? Schools and Teachers in an Andean Province'. In Thomas Blom Hansen and Finn Stepputat (eds), 2001, *States of Imagination. Ethnographic Explorations of the Postcolonial State*. Durham and London: Duke University Press.

Worby, 2000. '"Discipline Without Oppression": Sequence, Timing and Marginality in Southern Rhodesia's Post-War Development regime'. *Journal of African History*, Vol. 41, pp. 101-25.

Worby, Eric, 2001. 'A Redivided Land? New Agrarian Conflicts and Questions in Zimbabwe'. *Journal of Agrarian Change*, Vol. 1, No. 4, pp. 475-509.

Chapter 5

Farm Occupations and Occupiers in the New Politics of Land in Zimbabwe

Nelson Marongwe

When people hear of land conflicts in Zimbabwe, they normally think of the colonial injustices that divided the country into fertile large-scale commercial farms for whites and semi-arid and infertile communal areas for blacks. More immediately, these days they think of the occupation of large-scale commercial farms by war veterans and communities in 2000. This is because of the extent, intensity, visibility and repercussions of the occupations. Yet the large-scale commercial farming sector is not the only locus of land conflict in Zimbabwe. There are many other struggles over land and other natural resources taking place elsewhere, with varying degrees of intensity, such as in state lands and in both communal and resettlement areas. While the larger study from which this chapter is drawn examines this broader spatial and historical landscape of conflicts over land and natural resources, the present discussion focuses on the two recent waves of farm occupations, occurring in 1998 and 2000, and more specifically on the latter.[1] It tests the hypothesis that war veterans were mere catalysts in the 2000 farm occupations. The root cause of Zimbabwe's land conflicts, including the 2000 farm occupations, was the frustration felt by communities over the non-restitution of their historical rights to land.

---

[1] Besides addressing the more general questions concerning the nature and forms of recent land and resource conflicts in Zimbabwe, and the roles of various actors in these conflicts, the broader study also aimed to: examine various types and capacities of conflict resolution and management mechanisms; explore whether the current farm occupations constitute a land reform model in the making; and make recommendations on 'ways forward'.

Conflicts over land and other natural resources in Zimbabwe are both a pre- and post-independence phenomenon. They had been evident in the country between individuals and among communities even before the arrival of British settlers in 1890. The colonial era, however, introduced new dimensions that exacerbated the conflicts. Conquest and a series of oppressive legislation effected a racially discriminatory settlement pattern. The key legal instrument was the Land Apportionment Act of 1931. It legalised the allocation of 198,539 square kilometres of mainly prime agricultural land to 50,000 whites, and 117,602 square kilometres to 1,080,000 Africans. The remaining 74,859 square kilometres was set aside for national parks, forestry and other forms of state land ownership.

Oppressive legislation by the colonial government only served to strengthen the resistance by the native black population. Grievances over the racially skewed distribution of land stood as one among the major mobilising factors in the struggle for the political independence. In fact, the peasantry supported the guerrilla war during the late 1960s and 70s because of their grievance over land (Ranger, 1985). The liberation struggle and subsequent political independence was expected to resolve Zimbabwe's land problems. That did not happen. The 1979 Lancaster House Constitution presented many constraints that hindered the speedy distribution of land in independent Zimbabwe, including an emphasis on the supremacy of market forces in the land acquisition process, a factor that has haunted the land reform programme since 1980.

It is a fact that Zimbabwe's land reform programme has not done well in acquiring high value land for redistribution in the agriculturally productive natural regions I-III. For instance, between 1980 and 1999 only 24.27 per cent of land in natural region I was acquired, while 12.63 per cent, 15.41 per cent, 7.42 per cent and 3.97 per cent was acquired in natural regions II, III, IV and V, respectively. Thus, the land reform programme has not yet satisfactorily addressed the mismatch in the distribution of both quantity and quality of land.

Land acquisition and land redistribution have generated controversies among the different stakeholder groups. For example, large-scale commercial farmers have been accused of frustrating equitable land redistribution and resorting to litigation to further their own interests. On the other hand, the government has been accused of supporting lawlessness by not compensating farmers for acquired land and not evicting war veterans and communities from occupied commercial farms. In addition, beneficiary selection and land allocation have created distrust towards government by local communities.

At the national level, the main cause of confrontation between the government and the large-scale commercial farmers has been land acquisition. Sam Moyo (2000b:6) observed that, '...the conflict over land acquisition includes: the lack of agreement on the means and the scale of acquiring land; the source of resources and forms of compensation for the land acquired, as well as the high profile confrontation that engulfs all sides, through inadequate media reports over the process.'

In the absence of speedy land reforms that might meet social expectations of Zimbabwe's black population, many experts had predicted that violence over land was bound to happen. In the view of these analysts, the land occupations of 1998 and 2000 came as no surprise. What could have been different was the trigger to such events. The core aim of this chapter is to place land occupations in their historical, social, political and economic context.

Land occupations did not start with the farm occupations of 1998 and 2000. They have been taking place since the 1980s. The intensity of farm occupations has, however, tended to vary, largely depending on the political environment. For example, Moyo (1998, 2000b) has shown that land occupations tended to increase during election periods. (For an alternative perspective, see Alexander, this volume.) The unresolved nature of the land question has meant that the situation can be exploited for political objectives. Many experts believe this was the case during the occupations in 2000.

This chapter argues that policy failure, particularly the non-recognition of indigenous people's historical land rights, has been a fundamental cause of clashes over land and other natural resources in Zimbabwe. The failure of land reform programmes and the planning system either to achieve consensus and clarity, or to provide appropriate practical options that enhance communities' access to natural resources, has contributed to the deepening of the land problem.

The chapter draws upon a detailed study of farm occupations undertaken in 2000. Of particular importance is an in-depth analysis of the mobilisation of peasants to participate in the farm occupations, the role of war veterans in the process, the scale of the farm occupations and the main reasons for occupying specific farms. Determining the identity of farm occupiers, examining the relations between farm occupiers and farm owners, and the analysis of livelihood strategies of the farm occupiers was also important to the study.

The research was conducted using both primary and secondary data sources. Informants included members of local communities, chiefs and village heads, government officials, civic organisations including the predominant war veterans association, and large-scale commercial farmers and their representative organisations. In addition, a case study approach was used on selected farms across the country, where interviews and focus group discussions were held. Entry into the occupied farms had to be negotiated with the war veterans' leaders at the district and local levels. The politically sensitive nature of land conflicts meant that primary data collection, particularly for the farm occupations, remained very random and no sampling was done. Ability to access an area largely dictated the choice of farms for field data collection. The idea was also to develop case studies that were of national relevance and, as such, most provinces were captured in the data collection process. Newspapers and other media reports were crucial in assisting in the development of profiles of case studies, particularly those on farm occupations. Court documents provided an important source of information on the dynamics of land conflicts that had been brought before the court for adjudication.

Key theoretical underpinnings in land and natural resource conflicts

Discourse on land conflicts in Zimbabwe has centred largely on the processes and politics of land acquisition and land redistribution (Moyo, 1995, 1998, 2000a). More recently Moyo (2000b) has elaborated on land-use changes as a critical factor. Studies on CAMPFIRE – which has long promoted land-use changes within many agriculturally marginal communal areas, directed especially towards wildlife management in place of assumed 'subsistence' farming – have increasingly pointed to the significance of conflicts between wildlife and human populations (Hawkes, 1991; Murombedzi, 1992; Sithole and Bradley, 1995) have more specifically analysed institutional conflicts in the management of natural resources in the communal areas, including, among others, conflicts between the state and non-governmental organisations as well as amongst local indigenous institutions. The commercialisation and commodification of communal land resources is clearly an emerging cause of conflict in the communal areas (Sithole and Bradley, 1995; Moyo et al., 1998). In a study on conflicts in the management of miombo woodlands in three case study areas across Zimbabwe, Mamimine et al. (2001) classified such conflicts into ethnic friction, contested boundaries, institutional conflicts, intergenerational conflicts and co-management problems.

In the section that follows, selected theoretical issues are discussed that help conceptualise natural resources conflicts more broadly, and point to ways of understanding the forms of resistance that such conflicts often generate.

Conceptualising conflict

Conflicts are a feature of all societies and societal conflicts have been a subject of research in the social sciences for a long time (Widstrand, 1980). Conflict is a form of social interaction, a struggle over claims to scarce resources, in terms of power and status, in which the aims of the opponents might be to neutralise, injure or eliminate rivals (Coser, 1956; Widstrand, 1980). Conflicts occur in various types and forms. For example, conflicts can be classified into violent or non-violent conflicts, direct or indirect conflicts, and so on.

Conventional wisdom has tended to focus on two major reasons to explain the occurrence of conflicts in society, namely the scarcity of resources induced by increasing human population numbers, and ethnicity. Hildyard (1999:3) terms these the 'blood and babies' explanation. People have for a long time used 'blood' (ethnicity) and 'babies' (population) to explain far-off conflicts in which they themselves are not involved. But '...scratch below the surface of the violence that is increasingly explained by labels such as population wars or inter-tribal conflict and the shallowness and deceptiveness of the "blood and babies" line is soon revealed' (Appadurai, quoted in Hildyard, 1999:3).

Following on from this, one can argue that hatred between ethnic groups is not a natural phenomenon but a product of different processes that cut across politics, economics, history and even psychology (Keane, 1996). In analysing conflicts, therefore, it is important not to rely on simplistic explanations such as that of population and ethnicity. What is often assumed to be population-induced scarcity turns out to be socially constructed scarcity, a completely different phenomenon. Three forms of scarcity are widely perceived to induce conflicts in society. These are supply-induced, demand-induced and structurally based scarcity. The limited supply of a resource can lead to the development of conflicts. This happens when renewable resources do not have sufficient time to recuperate, when excess demand is created, or when population growth leads to increased demand. Structurally based scarcity leads to skewed distribution of a resource, resulting from the failure of existing policies, institutions and programmes to distribute the resource in a more equitable and socially acceptable way.

On the other hand, the ethnicity-based explanations are often linked to the agenda of small but powerful, self-interested and highly partisan groups in society. Such groups often manipulate other people using the false 'blood'-based explanations to further their own interests, creating conflicts that in the long run become extremely difficult to handle:

> The shared values, histories, customs and identities that generate ethnicity are socially constructed, not biologically determined and ... at root, ethnic conflicts result not from blood hatred but from socially generated divisions which, more often than not, reflect deep-seated conflicts over power and resources between groups and within groups. (Hildyard, 1999:4)

Overlaying these kinds of socially constructed differences, and making power relations and their political manifestations even more complex, are other differences related to, for example, issues of race, class, gender, political ideology or traditional norms. In addition, more recently globalisation and the call for improved human rights have added new dimensions to struggles over power, especially those linked to structurally based scarcity.

Perhaps we may understand the links between structurally based scarcity and the production of conflict by considering Assefa's (1993:3) notion of structural violence, which is defined as 'social and personal violence arising from unjust, repressive and oppressive national or international political and social structures.' In this respect, 'a system that generates repression, abject poverty, malnutrition, and starvation for some members of society while others enjoy opulence and unbridled power inflicts covert violence, with the ability to destroy life as overt violence, except that it does it in more subtle ways.' In Zimbabwe, the legal and social structures, especially the division of the country into wealthy large-scale commercial farms and poor communal farms, have perpetuated injustice in society. Additionally, the government's land reforms have failed to reduce poverty for almost twenty years and this has brewed conflicts. Generally, farm occupations were associated with a lot of violence. Altercations often broke out between, on the one hand, farm owners and their workers, and on the other, the occupying communities and war veterans. Such violence resulted in the disruption of farm operations that led to losses of jobs and income, and a number of people lost their lives. However, it was not within the scope of this paper to investigate the specific forms and levels of violence associated with the farm occupations.

In conclusion, over-population and ethnicity are relevant factors that should be considered in the discourse on Zimbabwe's land conflicts, but they are not the only issues. There are other important factors that must be considered in the search for lasting solutions. The bulk of later sections of this chapter focus precisely on elaborating such factors.

Understanding resistance

Peasant mobilisation has taken place, with various degrees of intensity, in many parts of the world. Huizer (1999:5) observed that,

> ... a certain level of frustration incites peasants to risk building or joining a peasant organisation. Peasants who wanted to solve a specific problem or deal with a concrete grievance engineered the first steps towards peasant organisation. A real impulse was often achieved ...when those who were in a position to solve the problem ...were not willing to do so. This forced the peasants to become more aware of their frustration....The availability of charismatic or solidarity inspiring leadership among the peasants was highly important in getting an organisation to the point where it could confront the elite.

The 1998 land occupation by the Svosve people and the participation of various communities in the 2000 farm occupations can be analysed in the light of Huizer's observation. Frustration at the inability of the formal authorities to resolve land problems led communities to form social groupings ('peasant organisations' in Huizer's terms) that initiated (1998) or participated in (2000) land occupations.

Several writers, including Barraclough (1991), Huizer (1999) and Wolf (1969), have noted the proliferation over the past century of peasant movements meant to defend, conserve or recover their ancestral land and livelihood. However, such processes often slowed down as a consequence of the firm entrenchment of commercial land interests (Huizer, 1999). Various researchers have shown the strong linkages between social mobilisation and peasant-initiated land reforms. Shanin (1971) makes reference to three types of peasant mobilisation: independent class action, guided political action and fully spontaneous amorphous political action (as quoted in Huizer, 1999:5).

The land occupations that took place in Zimbabwe in 1998 and 2000 have been analysed in this study in consideration of Shanin's theoretical framework. This has entailed analysing the dynamics of land occupations by unravelling the different forces at play, the motivations, mobilisation and organisation of communities. Were the land occupations the result of independent class action by peasants? Were the occupations spontaneous or were they the result of politically guided action?

Overview of recent land occupations in Zimbabwe: 1998 and 2000

Historically, land conflicts in the Large Scale Commercial Farming (LSCF) areas have included illegal settlements – mainly by ex-farm workers who have no home in communal areas – poaching of resources by neighbouring Communal Lands communities, and illegal grazing of communal cattle. At the present moment, the most significant form of conflict affecting the sector is the land occupations that began in February 2000, which have thrown into disarray the concept of security of tenure in Zimbabwe. The occupations have also precipitated a wider range of confrontations at the local, regional and global levels.

Illegal land occupations have been a feature of Zimbabwe's political landscape since the attainment of independence in 1980, at which point around 200 farms were occupied. The figure, however, increased to a peak of about 800 farms during the mid-1980s. During this time, the government responded by adopting an accelerated land resettlement model. As Tshuma (1997:62) observed, 'In response to peasant occupation of vacant land in the early 1980s, the government modified the model A scheme and introduced an accelerated version.'

This section examines firstly the 1998 and then the 2000 farm occupations in Zimbabwe. Land occupations before this period have been analysed in many other studies (see Moyo, 1995, 1998 and 2001, and Alexander, this volume). However, the 2000 farm occupations were significantly different in terms of their character and the kind of state support they received. Further, the apparent 'immediate causes' of the 2000 farm occupations differ materially from the previous scenarios. The analysis of the 2000 occupations in this chapter builds on some of the work of Sam Moyo.

Land occupations in 1998-99

Whilst what Moyo refers to as self-motivated land-provisioning methods, have been ongoing in the country since independence, perhaps the most widespread and publicised initiatives were those experienced in 1998 and 2000. In 1998-99, community-led land occupations took place in various provinces of the country, such as Mashonaland East, West and Central, Masvingo and Matebeleland North and South. A combination of residents primarily from communal lands, but also from resettlement areas and elsewhere (and henceforth generically termed here 'communities'), together with farm workers, played an important role in these occupations. The major concerns of the communities were the delay by the government in resettling them and the fact that in general they were not informed about the land reform programmes. The proximity of the commercial farms to their homes, poor relations between farmers and neighbouring communities and historical land claims by the communities acted as major reasons for the occupation of the farms (ZERO field interviews 1998, 2000).

In Mashonaland East, residents of Svosve Communal Lands spearheaded the 1998 campaign when they occupied four commercial farms in Marondera District, whilst in Matebeleland, press reports indicated that 200 families occupied about four farms in the Nyamandhlovu area. The de-listing of 25 of the 26 farms that had been earmarked for compulsory acquisition by the government in Matebeleland also contributed to the communities' frustrations. The communities who participated in the farm occupations were from the surrounding sawmills, parts of Tsholotsho and Nyamandlovu, while others came from surrounding resettlement schemes, such as Irisvale and Zimdabule, which were established in the 1980s. About 200 families occupied three state lands in the mountainous Muzura area of the Nyakapupu small-scale commercial farming area in Guruve District, Mashonaland Central. The belt of state land stretches for about 10 kilometres and was presumably left vacant when the colonial government demarcated land in Nyakapupu in 1957. In Masvingo Province, some 36 war veterans occupied ARDA Mkwasine Estate in Chiredzi in 1999 (*The Herald*, 8 December 1999), while some 700 'squatters' occupied Longdale farm, 15 kilometres south of Masvingo town (*The Daily News*, 15 December 1999).

The government's reaction to the 1998 land occupations was generally antagonistic and unsupportive of this community-led land action. Although earlier government statements ruled out the use of force, in some cases force was used to remove communities from occupied farms. Provincial and district government institutions, particularly the Governor's and the District Administrator's offices, took the leading role in persuading occupiers to withdraw from the farms they had occupied as their actions were deemed illegal. As indicated explicitly at the time by the late Governor of Mashonaland Central, Border Gezi (who was later to spearhead the invasions in 2000): 'What you have done is unlawful and the Government will not let you do that. Be prepared for eviction anytime...' (*The Herald*, 29 June 1998).

This reflected the general response of the government to the 1998-99 farm occupations. In some cases, such as on two farms in Odzi, in Manicaland province, eviction orders were served and the occupiers' temporary structures were burnt down. In enforcing the evictions, there were violent skirmishes when communities fought running battles with the riot police. In extreme situations, occupiers were arrested, charged with public violence offences or under the Miscellaneous Offences Act, and brought before the courts where they were made to pay fines. Those who failed to pay fines faced jail sentences. Elsewhere, such as on a farm leased by a Harare City councillor, farm workers were involved in beating up occupiers and headmen.[2] Local politics also came into play, as in Chegutu district where political differences between two senior Zanu (PF) officials led one of them to incite communities to occupy the state land that was being leased by the other.

An analysis of the 1998-99 land occupations has shown them to have been triggered by two different processes. First, it was the non-recognition of historical land claims within the existing policy framework, which led the Svosve community to doubt the seriousness of the land-reform programme or the government's willingness to address their grievances. Second, the non-consultative nature of previous resettlement programmes raised more questions than answers for the Svosve community, as they saw what they considered to be 'foreigners' being allocated land on farms surrounding their localities at their expense. If they understood the objectives of the land reform programme and its principle that people can be resettled anywhere in the country, regardless of who is close to which acquired farm, then they did not agree with those objectives. The Svosve and, subsequently, the Mbalabala communities, saw spontaneous farm occupations as the only way of making their voices

---

[2] These and other cases were drawn from *The Herald* 4/11 September and 19/23/24/25/27 November 1998.

heard. In the case of Mbalabala Ranch, it was the failure of the resettlement policy to address the land needs of resettled farmers' offspring and the perpetual problem of overcrowding in the communal lands, that led to the occupations.

Generally, the land occupations were an indication that something was fundamentally wrong with the existing land reform and resettlement programme. There was increasing impatience among both communal and resettlement area residents over their land grievances and yet neither policy makers nor donors noticed the extent to which the situation was deteriorating. It can be argued that communities were ready to take any action that would give them good farming land, and such an opportunity emerged in the form of the war veteran-led farm occupations in 2000.

Overview of the farm occupations in 2000

These occupations differed from previous ones in two ways. First, it can be argued that the occupations were precipitated more by politically motivated intentions than by social, moral or economic considerations. The ruling Zanu (PF) party used farm occupations as their 'official campaigning strategy' for wooing voters in the June 2000 parliamentary elections. Second, and related to the above, was the issue of mobilising communities to participate in the farm occupations. Militant war veterans, with direct state support, took the lead in this regard. The 2000 farm occupations were, therefore, led and organised by war veterans rather than by peasants.

The land occupations started in February, soon after a referendum rejected the government's proposed Draft Constitution. The main opposition party, the Movement for Democratic Change (MDC), together with a host of civic organisations, had campaigned against the draft. Parliamentary elections, in which the young opposition party performed surprisingly well, were held in June. These two political events shaped the dynamics of the land occupations. It seems reasonable to argue that the land occupations, directed by war veterans who are predominantly Zanu (PF) members, were a crucial element in the party's election campaign strategy

On the other hand, although Zanu (PF) and its structures, down to the district level, played a pivotal role in initiating and sustaining the land occupations, this does not suggest that it had complete control of what was happening on the ground. For example, issues pertaining to, say, the type of land that was to be occupied, were decided on local factors that might have been independent of the party. This partially explains why certain categories of state land, e.g. forest estates, national parks and ARDA (state-owned) estates were also occupied.

The land occupations were shaped by a combination of political, economic and social factors and processes. Though some analysts have described them as 'an organised activity along political party lines' (ZERO interviews, 2000), they nevertheless had more varied origins and effects, the latter including important policy implications for Zimbabwe's development, and in particular for its land reform programme.

Focus on the occupations of 2000

In the following discussion, the land occupations will be considered in terms of three inter-related sets of questions. What were the overall dynamics and directions of the occupations in terms of their general form, the types of land targeted for occupation, and the ways in which they were or were not sustained? What were the major reasons for the occupation of specific farms? What were the patterns and practices of mobilisation for the occupation, and who were the occupiers?

The dynamics of land occupations

Targeting occupations

The fact that land occupations targeted white owned large-scale commercial farms is undisputed. However, there were many others 'owners' of land that were also affected. For example, farms belonging to some black indigenous commercial farmers were invaded, such as in Makoni District in Manicaland. Discussions with the affected farmers revealed that they believed their farms had been targeted on the grounds of suspicion that they were MDC supporters; however, this study could not verify such claims. NGO lands were also occupied, including the property of some organisations directly involved in land reform and resettlement activities. A case in point is DAPP, a Danish NGO long supportive of Zanu (PF), which had two of its farms occupied, one in Mutasa and the other in Shamva District. In some incidents, state forests and national parks such as Gonarezhou were occupied as a result of long-standing land claims by adjacent communities.

Statistics regarding the actual numbers of farms occupied varied according to source and time. Thus, the Zimbabwe National Liberation War Veterans Association (ZNLWVA), the Commercial Farmers' Union (CFU), the police and the press each gave different figures on the extent of occupations. The figures from the police, for example, only related to commercial farmers who had actually reported cases. Various experts have suggested that statistics could have deliberately manipulated to support particular agendas (Moyo, 2000b), and so figures for total farms occupied at any given time, or for levels of violence, cannot be divorced from organisational propaganda. In addition, the informal nature of the occupations meant that the data tended anyway to be rather crude.

Available data nonetheless seemed to confirm that the intensity of farm occupations varied across provinces and districts. Occupations by district and locality seemed to have been most intense in areas around Chegutu, Masvingo, Macheke and Mazowe. The percentage of farms occupied also varied. For example, in Mashonaland East province, Seke District had the highest number of farms that were occupied, at about 16.7 per cent of the total, whilst Chikomba had only 8 farms (6.6 per cent) occupied. In Mashonaland West province, the percentage varied from 0.35 per cent in Makonde District to 3.25 per cent in Zvimba District. According to Moyo (2000b), preliminary indications seemed to show that Matebeleland North and South, Manicaland and Midlands provinces experienced fewer occupations than the three Mashonaland provinces and Masvingo.

The size of the occupying communities varied from farm to farm, with some being described as merely 'symbolic'. Symbolic occupations were those where a few war veterans occupied certain farms as a way of demonstrating the urgent need for land redistribution. In other situations, large numbers of people were involved.

On most farms with high numbers of occupiers, 'bases' (in the occupiers' language) were established, which the occupiers had selected as their residential area and where they put up their temporary housing structures. Building materials, mainly in the form of poles, dagga and thatch grass, were sourced from the occupied farm. In many cases, this acted as the first cause of tension between the occupiers and the farm owner. The occupiers were quickly labelled as 'degraders' of the environment.

Settlement patterns were basically of two types: the village approach and the individual, isolated settlement. Under the former, occupiers were settled in villages where they only had 'residential plots', while arable plots were demarcated elsewhere, as, for example, at the Tongogara Base on Longfield Farm, Makoni District. Under the isolated settlement system, occupiers allocated themselves 'self-contained units', with individual grazing and arable plots. There seemed to be no clear guideline as to how occupiers decided the type of settlement. Interviews with occupiers revealed that the village pattern was used when the occupying communities wanted to come together for their own 'security'. This model was also selected as a way of maintaining 'community' cohesiveness, as well as boosting occupiers' morale.

As already observed, the number of farms occupied varied from time to time. Some were temporarily occupied and then abandoned while others were occupied for longer periods. As later sections will show, social relations and the reaction of the large-scale commercial farmers to the farm occupation process became important in defining the fate of a given farm.

Sustaining the occupations

Generally, occupiers relied on their own sources for food, built their own temporary housing structures and cared for their own health, making the occupation of farms closest to their original homes strategically preferable. In situations where the original homes were far away, a variety of strategies were used to ensure ongoing food reserves. In some instances, relatives were left at home to bring more food supplies on a weekly or fortnightly basis. There were very few cases of communities organising together for joint food purchase.

Settlement patterns on occupied farms tended to follow the major road networks, since occupiers relied on public transport. In general, occupiers were not allowed by the base commander to be absent from the farm for more than a few days, even to replenish food stocks. On the other hand, in some locations occupiers were not staying permanently on site and some commuted daily from their original homes to the occupied lands, as in Gonarezhou National Park (beside Chitsa Communal Lands), Pangara Range, (Nyanga Nyarumvurwe Resettlement) and Janee Farm in Gwanda District. In many cases, occupiers organised themselves into groups and developed duty rosters where groups of about 10-12 members rotated to maintaining a presence at the farms.

However, evidence from fieldwork indicated that the systems for sustaining resources, especially food, varied from place to place. For example, there are numerous incidents where farmers whose land had been occupied assisted, either voluntarily or forcibly, in providing the occupiers with food, water, and shelter. In Matebeleland, for example, most farmers supplied the occupiers with game meat from their wildlife ranges while others provided maize-meal. This may well have been a way of limiting poaching and hunting of valuable game on these farms. In most observed cases, occupiers relied on untreated water from rivers and shallow wells since there was mistrust and suspicion between the farmers and the occupying communities. In Makoni District, villagers reported that they refused to use the water that had been supplied by the farmer in water bowsers for fear of being poisoned.

In other cases, such as in Gwanda, the Gwanda War Veterans District Office supplied food to war veterans occupying farms. War veterans in the area who had not occupied farms were required to make contributions of about Z$100 a month towards sustaining those on the farms. In other cases, communities who were registering for resettlement through the War Veterans Office were charged Z$1-200, for the same purpose. In some cases, food supplies to war veterans were reported to have ceased soon after the June 2000 parliamentary elections, together with a weekly allowance they received for occupying the farms.

The number of occupants at any given base varied on a daily basis. The mobility at the bases was high in the initial stages of the occupations. The numbers went down as the rainy season deepened, and later as the cold weather set in. For example, in the case of Gonarezhou National Park, the popular Seveni Jeki base had about 800 people at its peak but the figures dwindled to less than 80 a day (ZERO Field Survey, 2000). Further, the patience of some of the occupiers quickly degenerated as they felt they could no longer sustain their staying in the temporary structures, while receiving only erratic food supplies. The absence of social services in the form of shops and clinics served as a major disincentive for some members to continue participating in the farm occupations.

Some effects of farm occupations

There was no particular discretion in deciding on the quality of the land that was occupied, which may explain why even marginal land in natural regions IV and V was affected. Nor did land use seem to be an important factor. The type of land occupied, and its form of land use, varied from place to place. Data from districts including Nyanga, Mutasa, Makoni, Chiredzi, Bulilimamangwe, Gwanda and Seke, revealed that the occupations – and subsequent gazetting of farms and 'fast track' resettlement programme – negatively affected productivity in reaction to almost all land uses. This included both agricultural production such as maize, wheat, tobacco, horticulture, cattle ranching and dairy production, and non-agricultural sectors such as wildlife, forestry and tourism more generally. It was not possible, however, to establish a full national picture of the extent to which specific land uses were affected

Paradoxically, discussions with occupiers revealed that they had received instructions not to occupy any land that was being productively used and not to disturb farm operations. Yet the 'rules' were broken in certain situations, particularly in circumstances where there were 'skirmishes' between occupiers and the farm owners and their workers. In such scenarios, farming operations were disrupted, whilst in the worst cases, farm operations were brought to a halt. A ZERO study of fast track resettlement (Marongwe, 2001) confirmed this situation.

Field visits showed a great deal of variation in terms of what was happening on the ground. There have been cases like that in the Mazowe area where agricultural production came to a standstill. Tension between large-scale commercial farmers and resettled farmers saw the two sides fighting battles over the land. A meeting of the District Resettlement Committee for Mazowe revealed several examples. At Virginia farm, the farmer was reported to be locking his gates and electrifying the fence to ensure that resettled farmers would not have access to the fields. A police report from Mvurwi showed that a farmer at Msonendi farm ploughed the fields of resettled people who had already planted their crops. There were also numerous reports of war veterans forcing complete or partial work stoppages at some of the farms. Chirobi farm in Mazowe District is an example of a contested area which had seen a lot of skirmishes between the war veterans and resettled farmers on the one hand and the large-scale commercial farmer and his farm workers on the other.

Other unconfirmed reports have painted a negative picture of farm production, with crop losses significantly threatening food security in the country. Seed sales for most crops were reported to have dropped, and some large-scale farmers have been forced to de-stock. Livestock thefts increased in general in most parts of Zimbabwe exacerbated by the increased mobility of people associated with land occupations.

Tourism is a highly sensitive sector that thrives on politically stable environments. The scale and violence of the 2000 farm occupations was widely publicised around the world, and tourist arrivals were very badly affected. Press reports and discussions with some of the affected farmers have confirmed that tourism was one of the sectors hardest hit by the land occupations. Malilangwe

Conservancy Trust and Gonarezhou National Park in Masvingo as well as some farms in the Matabeleland provinces, give an indication of the extent of negative affects of the occupations on tourism in general, and on tourist-based wildlife farms in particular.

Farm workers and their families were especially hard-hit by the farm occupations. The disruption of farm operations led to loss of jobs and income, many farm workers had their homes and properties destroyed and were physically displaced, and provision of services by NGOs such as the Farm Community Trust of Zimbabwe were interfered with. Altercations often broke out between farm workers and the occupying communities and war veteran leadership. Access to farm workers on occupied farms for interviewing purposes proved to be difficult. (See Rutherford, this volume, for an extensive discussion of the relationship between farm workers, farmers, and farm occupations.)

Selecting farms for occupation

Many reasons were given for why certain farms were occupied whilst others were not: proximity to resettlement and communal areas; social relations between farmers and bordering resettlement/communal areas; historical land claims by communities in relation to colonial land appropriations; multiple farm ownership and under-utilisation of land; political affiliation with the ruling party or the opposition; and urban demand for residential land.

Proximity to resettlement and communal farmers

Perhaps one of the most important factors that determined which farm was occupied or not was its proximity to communal or resettlement areas. Farms close to such areas were more likely to be occupied than those that were far away. It was evident that occupiers preferred to remain close to their original homes so as to maintain their line of food supplies. This was found to be the case for many farms that were visited during the course of this study, including Charter Estate Farm in Seke District, Gonarezhou National Park, Malilangwe Conservancy Trust, and farms bordering Chief Gora's area in Mhondoro Communal Lands.

Despite the loco-centric nature of invasions, there were many instances of communities being bussed to occupy distant farms. At a meeting organised by ZERO and Friedrich Ebert Stiftung (a German NGO) to discuss farm occupations in Harare and Bulawayo in May and June 2000, it was reported that people were being bussed from major urban centres such as Harare and Chitungwiza to surrounding farms, particularly those in Seke District. Such movements were noted to be more intense at weekends.

Another explanation as to why occupations tended to concentrate on farms close to communal and resettlement areas was that pressure for land is felt especially acutely in these areas. This conforms to the 'babies' part of Hildyard's 'blood and babies' theory. At the same time, communities had first-hand knowledge of how land on surrounding farms was under-utilised. Such communities could, therefore, be easily mobilised to participate in the land occupations.

Social relations between the farmer and neighbouring communities

Important social concerns that led to the occupation of particular farms included the under-paying of farm workers, impounding of stray cattle that belonged to surrounding communities (and demanding fines before releasing the livestock), and the history of the farmer's association with the colonial government. Bad social relations between a farmer and surrounding communities invariably led to the targeting of farms for occupation by communities and war veterans. Even the land occupations of 1998 tended to target 'un-neighbourly' white farmers. A good example is that of a Marondera farmer in Mashonaland East, who made public allegations that 'her sheep had died because some Africans from surrounding villages and compounds were relieving themselves on the farm.' Consequently, about 70 community members from Svosve communal lands demonstrated against the farmer and camped on her land (*The Herald*, 19 September 1998).

Other examples of poor relations included the impounding of cattle that strayed from surrounding villages onto large-scale commercial farms, the punishing of community residents who were caught collecting firewood illegally from large farms, and the shooting of poachers. In another case, a farmer bordering Taga Resettlement Scheme in Seke District shot several stray dogs; the farm was subsequently occupied. The farmer, popularly known as *MuGreek*, had run away by the time the study team visited the farm.

Historical factors also played an important role in shaping relations between large-scale farmers and surrounding communities. A farm in Nyanga District, Barron Down Estate, was occupied because communities alleged that the farmer was a former staunch supporter of the colonial Rhodesia Front government which used to harass the community. In this case, communities saw it fit to settle their score with the farmer by occupying his farm. Similar cases were noted in the two Matebeleland provinces. For example, Wilfred Hope Farm in Bulilimamangwe District was occupied mainly because the farm was used during the colonial era as a shooting range for training the Rhodesian Army. The local community had also been harassed. Occupiers claimed that military attacks on freedom fighters during the national liberation struggle were carried out from that farm. The social tension between the farmer and the community was high even before the farm occupations started. He was accused of impounding stray cattle and demanding large sums of money or labour from communities, and was alleged to have been aggressive towards his workers.

This is not to suggest that these were the only factors that led to the occupation of farms. For instance, it would seem highly likely that certain communities could not wait any longer to get a piece of land to sustain their livelihood. The slow pace of the resettlement programme over the past 20 years had already provoked some communities to lose faith in the resettlement programme. This being the case, one can argue that some communities participated in the land occupations simply because they wanted to get access to productive land.

Land claims by communities

This study has suggested that continued failure by the country's land reform process to restore historical land rights was socially unsustainable and would always remain a recipe for conflict. Data from discussions with local communities and their leaders, and occupying communities, has confirmed that certain communities would never consider the land reform programme as complete until the question of restitution is addressed. There were numerous cases where occupiers said they occupied a specific farm because they had long-standing historical claims over the land. The claims dated back to the colonial period when communities were forcibly removed from their original homelands to reserves for the creation of commercial farms or state lands.

For example, occupying communities on E.C Meikles Estate in Nyanga District claim to have been evicted during the colonial era and forced to settle in the Murewa area, while some crossed the border to settle in Mozambique. Others occupying the Eastern Highlands Plantation in Nyanga claimed it to be the original home of the Tangwena, Zindi and Chavhanga people. Those occupying Gonarezhou National Park came from communities displaced by the creation of the park in the 1960s, who had been promised restitution at independence that had never materialised. In Gwanda South in Matabeleland, occupying communities were countering their eviction in the 1950s to make way for the demarcation of Dwala Ranch. In Zvimba in Mashonaland West, the occupation of Machiori Farm among others was legitimised through narratives of recovering ancestral graves and honouring the spirits of the ancestors (ZERO field data, 2000).

Despite the fact that displacement of communities took place several decades ago, there was still an expectation that the government would facilitate their return to their original home areas under the current land reform programmes. The passage of time had not diminished the strength of claims by communities. The persistent non-recognition of their claims by decision-makers has only served to defer the finding of lasting solutions to the land problem. In areas where such land claims existed, it became fairly easy for communities to be mobilised to participate in the land occupations.

Multiple farm ownership and under-utilisation of land

Multiple ownership of farms and perceived under-utilisation of land were considered important factors when occupiers decided on which farms to occupy (see Table 1 below). Several farmers whose farms had been occupied were believed to have several farms. As most occupying communities came from areas surrounding the occupied farms, they claimed inside knowledge on the extent of farm ownership patterns in their area. The study could not, however, confirm which of the occupied farmers had multiple ownership of land.

Other farms were occupied because they were considered either too big, under-utilised or a combination of both. These factors were predominant in the case studies for Matebeleland (North and South) and Masvingo provinces. An analysis of the sizes of occupied farms in Chiredzi, Gwanda and Bulilimamangwe districts revealed that most of them were quite extensive in size and mainly used for tourism and cattle ranching.

Malilangwe Conservancy Trust and Gonarezhou National Park (505,300 hectares) seemed to be the largest single blocks of land affected by the occupations in the study area. In Matebeleland, three of the largest occupied farms measured 15,247 hectares, 9,984 hectares and 5,622 hectares. In Chiredzi District, other than Gonarezhou and Malilangwe mentioned above, occupied farms included Eaglemont Range (16,975 hectares) and Fair Range Naude (12,965 hectares). In the case of Nyanga District in Manicaland province, where farming is generally more intensive, the size of farms occupied ranged from 707 to 10,000 hectares, the largest belonging to to the Forestry Commission, a parastatal. These figures seem to confirm the perception that certain farms were deemed too large for individual farm owners and, therefore, deserved to be occupied. By contrast, the size of available household plots in communal and resettlement areas average 1-3 hectares and 5 hectares respectively.

Political affiliation

It has already been observed that the 2000 farm occupations seemed to have been a politically motivated process in terms of party politics. The occupations were championed by war veterans, most, if not all, of whom belonged to the ruling party. Further, the occupations could hardly be divorced from Zanu (PF)'s 2000 parliamentary election campaign. In this respect, it is reasonable to conclude that the farms targeted for occupation were suspected to be owned by members or supporters of the main opposition party, the MDC. The chanting of pro-Zanu (PF) and anti-MDC slogans by the occupiers of farms is a further indication that the occupation of farms followed a political agenda.

There are also examples that land demarcation and allocation was done along party lines. For example, discussions with leaders of the occupations at various farms revealed that one was required to produce a Zanu (PF) party card and a 'data form' if one wanted to be allocated land. However, as discussed here and elsewhere in this volume, the politics of land occupations is more complex and the debate necessarily needs to be much broader.

In the view of the Zimbabwe National Liberation War Veterans Association (ZNLWVA), hostility by farmers to their workers and surrounding communities was a strong factor in the occupation of some farms. In this respect, a combination of social and political factors became important in determining the occupation of particular farms.

Table 1 Major reasons for the occupation of specific farms by war veterans

Name of farm	Province	No. of war vets occupying the farm	Reasons for occupying the farm
Makay	Mashonaland Central	46	Perceived under-utilisation. Owner allegedly contributed to the military training of MDC supporters at Penrose Farm. Owner allegedly found in possession of MDC T-shirts & cards.
Ballineety	Mashonaland West	43	Owner believed to have more than one farm, and one of the farms believed to be under-utilised.
Penrose	Mashonaland West	18	Alleged MDC supporter, who allegedly used his farm for military training of MDC supporters under the guise of training farm guards.
Landscape	Mashonaland West	35	MDC T-shirts and cards recovered from farm.
Pama & Pama	Mashonaland West	65	Farmer alleged to own up to five farms.
Killiamore	Mashonaland West	28	Perceived under-utilisation of farm.
Little England	Mashonaland	40	Farm considered too large for one person.
Bitton	Mashonaland West	30	Farm already designated for resettlement.
Sandringham	Mashonaland West	34	Perceived under-utilisation of farm.
Black	Mashonaland Central	37	Perceived under-utilisation of farm.
Barria	Mashonaland Central	42	Alleged supporter of MDC who urged his workers to attend MDC rallies. Owner allegedly found with MDC T-shirts & cards

Source: Zimbabwe National Liberation War Veterans Association (ZNLWVA), various documents, 2000.

Demand for residential land in urban areas

Zimbabwe's land reform programme has never provided for the land needs of urban populations, particularly for residential development. In fact, the general perception that land reform was meant to benefit the rural populations and was, therefore, a 'non-urban' issue, has wrongly interpreted contemporary conditions (Mbiba, 2000). Although urban development has been completely liberalised, most city dwellers remain without decent accommodation – are in effect landless and homeless – as a result of the high cost of land and building materials.

The 2000 land occupations raised the expectations of some urban dwellers that they would gain access to land for residential development. Some of them, particularly those from high-density suburbs, were easily mobilised to occupy farms and other vacant land in the environs of major cities. In Harare, for example, several farms, which included Stockade Farm, Mt Hampden Farm, Dunhace Farm, York Farm, Kildonesa Farm and Lilfordia Estate were occupied by urbanites.

Some undeveloped land in Kambuzuma, outside Harare, has already seen the permanent (but illegal) development of housing units by residents of Harare. Press reports have confirmed the participation of urban dwellers in the occupation of farms around Harare: 'Yesterday 25 residents from parts of Dzivaresekwa and Kuwadzana descended on Lilfordia Estates in Mt Hampden ... Another group of Harare residents travelled to Parklands Farm in Norton...' (*The Daily News*, 24 March 2000). 'Hundreds of Harare residents have occupied three farms near Harare International Airport and partitioned them into thousands of residential stands' (*The Daily News*, 13 April 2000). The demand for urban residential land was clearly a strong factor influencing the occupation of farms near major urban centres.

Further to the political intent of the farm occupations, the bad performance of the economy could have played an important role in inciting people to participate. Economic hardships, resulting from the poor performance of the housing sector and high rates of unemployment and retrenchment, made the task of persuading urbanites to participate in farm occupations easier. In many cases, the promise of residential land provided people with their only insurance for survival.

Mobilisation and the role of war veterans in 2000

The success of the farm occupations largely depended on the role played by war veterans, who acted as catalysts to the process. This differed from the 1998-99 occupations which were spearheaded by landless communities. The immediate cause of the 2000 farm occupations was the rejection of the Draft Constitution in the February referendum. Among other things, this meant a rejection of the clause which would have allowed the compulsory acquisition of farms by government without payment of compensation for the land itself. This frustrated the hopes of many groups, most notably war veterans.

The Zimbabwe National Liberation War Veterans' Association (ZNLWVA) had battled with the government in pursuit of better welfare provision for its members. During the tenure of the Constitutional Commission and the process that led to the development of the Draft Constitution, about ten war veterans were recruited to participate in the drafting process. The war veterans had two pressing issues that related to the promotion of their interests. The first was that their pensions had to be provided for in the Constitution. The second related to improved access to land. These would entrench and protect the interests of war veterans against any future government that might be unsympathetic towards them. In the war veterans' perspective, the Constitutional Commission did not interpret accurately concerns by the public on the issue of compulsory acquisition of land without paying compensation for the soil.

War veterans demonstrated against two Zanu (PF) members of the Co-ordinating Committee of the Constitutional Commission, for allowing the initial draft to be adopted without ensuring that it reflected the true wishes of the people on the land question. Section 57 was later (undemocratically) amended to include a clause that exempted the government from compensating farmers for acquired land, except for improvements on it. However, the draft went on to be defeated by a 'No' vote in the national referendum. Clearly the rejection of the Draft Constitution was an unacceptable embarrassment to both Zanu (PF) and the war veterans. This appears to have incited the war veterans to lead farm occupations and play a key role in mobilising communities to join them. However, it does not appear from available information that there was a final word 'from above' instructing war veterans to occupy the farms.

The general trend that emerged from research was that the war veterans were involved in an extensive outreach programme in their local areas, recruiting people to go and occupy farms. These included both youths and middle-aged people who, in most cases, claimed to be landless. In all the farms visited, the number of war veterans was substantially less than occupiers from communities. For example, at Pambili farm in Makoni District, the base had about 200 people but only three were war veterans. However, what was interesting was that war veterans assumed 'positions of authority' in all situations where farms were occupied. For example, every base was under a war veteran base commander who would, among other duties, take a lead role in the registering of occupiers, as well as the demarcation and allocation of land.

Organisational structures were developed at most of the occupied farms to facilitate specific activities. They typically included the base commander, base chairman, secretary and vice-secretary, treasurer, political commissar and committee members. These made up a committee that was responsible for the mobilisation of people, in liaison with the local Zanu (PF) party structures. Not surprisingly, there were strong parallels with the military and party command structures of the national liberation struggle.

The main incentive used to lure people into the process of land occupation was the promise of land. The mobilisation committee would visit local communities and call for meetings where those who attended were promised land. The war veterans and the communities would agree on which farms to occupy, set the day and decide on the gathering point. Where it was necessary, arrangements were made to ferry people to the farm (ZERO Field Survey 2000).

In some cases, youths were used to recruit occupiers. In Chiredzi, for example, they frequently surrounded villages, targeting social gatherings such as traditional beer drinking ceremonies to mobilise communities to occupy farms. Some amount of coercion was also used in recruitment, especially of youth. In Chiredzi, the practice was later abandoned after it was discovered that some youths fled from the occupied farms as soon as they were brought in. Some kind of weekly timetable was developed and specific days were devoted to recruitment activities. At the same time, a register was kept at most of the occupation sites, used mainly as a way of checking the movement of people into and out of the occupied farms. Once people were allocated land, they or their representatives were registered and expected to man their 'stands' at all times. Meetings were regularly held to facilitate the flow of 'important information' among the occupiers.

Who were the occupiers?

There is no simple or conclusive answer to this question. One would have to unravel the composition of civil society actors along political, social or even economic lines to begin to gain the necessary insights. However, the following scenarios provide possible starting points:

'They were ZANU (PF) supporters'

Some people perceive the farm occupations as being a completely Zanu (PF)-orchestrated process. However, this makes simplistic assumptions, for example, that there are no opportunists and that people are completely faithful to political parties and only belong to one political party. What would prevent an MDC supporter from posing as a Zanu (PF) supporter in order to be promised free land?

On the other hand, the strain of staying in the open for extended periods may have weeded out those who were not among the Zanu (PF) faithful. At the same time, the overt championing of farm occupations by Zanu (PF) and militant war veterans, the stated opposition to occupations by the MDC, and the chanting of slogans denouncing the MDC, lead to the conclusion that those who occupied farms were predominantly from Zanu (PF).

'It was the landless'

The crux of the matter is how one defines the landless. In the strict sense of the word, it includes squatters and destitutes from both rural and urban areas. To the extent that the majority of the people occupying farms were coming from communal and resettlement areas, it was not 'the landless' who were occupying farms.

There were many cases where the majority of the occupiers came from resettlement areas. Typical examples from the study included the occupiers of Charter Estate in Seke District who came from Masasa Resettlement Scheme, and those on Longfield Farm who came from Chinyika Resettlement Scheme. The common characteristic of people who claimed they originated from the resettlement areas was that they were all youths. They claimed that the existing resettlement schemes did not allow parents to allocate land to their offspring. Thus, all children who had become adults since their parents were resettled could not get access to land in the resettlement areas, unlike most of their counterparts in the communal areas.

Farms that bordered urban areas were occupied mainly by people from towns and cities who were pressing for land for residential plots. This was the case on most occupied farms in the vicinity of Harare. High-density areas such as Kuwadzana, Dzivaresekwa, Chitungwiza and Mabvuku provided the bulk of the people who occupied farms. Farms surrounding the cities were normally occupied by day, while at night most people left for their urban homes. This is an indication that it was not the homeless groups, such as squatters and destitutes, that dominated the group of urban occupiers, but rather the ordinary urban dweller who got excited by the idea of getting a free piece of land. In urban areas, some war veterans led the process of registering people, demarcating and allocating plots and collecting fees. Press reports have indicated that thousands of people were swindled out of their cash under the guise that they would get land for residential development.

The participation of urban people was not confined to Harare, but also occurred in other cities and towns. In Mashonaland West, urban dwellers from different backgrounds organised and occupied farms as far as 30 kilometres from the towns of Chinhoyi and Banket and the mining settlements in the Mutorashanga area. War veterans from the urban areas organised the occupation of farms surrounding such cities. In Chinhoyi and Banket, urbanites who had never had a rural home in Zimbabwe, particularly those of Malawian, Mozambican and Zambian origin, took part in the farm occupations. An important characteristic of these occupations was the flexibility in the choice of farms to be occupied, which had little to do with ethnic identity or ancestral land claims.

Communal and resettlement areas were cited more frequently as providing the bulk of farm occupiers, who tended to settle on the nearest commercial farms, regardless of whether they fell in the same administrative area or not. This went against the normal resettlement procedure of communities being resettled in their own administrative district, except in cases where the district in question did not have commercial farms.

This scenario was also observed in the Mashonaland provinces where communities and war veterans from Mhondoro Communal Lands in Mashonaland West settled on farms in Mashonaland East. Movement across districts was also very common in Matebeleland. In Manicaland, about ten war veterans crossed from Mutasa District to occupy a farm in Nyanga District.

'It was the war veterans'

The study indicates quite clearly that the farm occupations were led and orchestrated by war veterans, who mobilised communities to participate in them. Although it was difficult to count the exact number of war veterans on each of the farms visited, the study managed to do so on some farms, as illustrated in Table 2. In exceptional cases, war veterans occupied farms on their own; in general they comprised only about 20 per cent of the occupying population. In Mashonaland East Province, the percentage ranged from 8 per cent to 100 per cent.

Table 2: Numbers of war veterans on selected occupied farms

Farm name	District	Estimated population	No. of war veterans	% War veterans
Pangara range, Southfield farm	Nyanga	200	40	20%
Pangara range, Burnaby farm	Nyanga	10	10	100%
Barwon Down Estate	Nyanga	50	50	100%
Pambili farm	Makoni	206	3	1.5%
Janee Ranch	Gwanda	12	12	100%
Matetsi River Ranch	Hwange	150	20	13%
Karwa Block	Gwayi	250	50	20%

Source: ZERO Field Study, 2000

Gender dimensions

The gender balance at the occupied farms varied. Some farms, particularly those close to communal and resettlement areas, had fairly even numbers of male and female occupiers. In other cases, wives and husbands participated together in the farm occupations. There were very few cases in the study area where there were no women occupiers at all.

The army and Central Intelligence Organisation (CIO)

There is evidence that shows that the army and state intelligence services played a role in orchestrating farm occupations. The army's role was most visible in the provision of transport, particularly for ferrying food to war veterans on occupied farms. Owing to the sensitivity of the matter, however, the study did not investigate or analyse the extent to which the army and the CIO were involved in supporting the farm occupations.

Farm occupations in Zimbabwe: lessons and policy implications.[3]

The 2000 farm occupations and the subsequent 'fast track' resettlement programme have added new dimensions to the land reform process in Zimbabwe. As the existing policy and legal framework have been presented with many dilemmas, the land occupations have provided key lessons to those involved. At a very general level, it is evident that conflict situations present important opportunities for learning and debate. Regardless of whether the 1998 and 2000 farm occupations were justified or not, the mere fact that they took place, coupled with the irreversibility of the whole process, points to the need to re-think the policies and practices related to such a process. Furthermore, the farm occupations in Zimbabwe could have a ripple effect in other southern African countries facing similar problems.

Opening of dialogue over land between competing actors

Perhaps one of the most important and positive outcomes is that the process opened up a dialogue between large-scale commercial farmers and rural communities. Although many situations were marked by tension, violence and other forms of confrontation, it is remarkable that the antagonists, including farmers, farm workers, communities and war veterans, began to talk directly to one another. Zimbabwe's land reform programme had, until this point, failed to facilitate such dialogue.

In some cases where negotiations took place during occupation, farmers agreed to various land sharing arrangements with the occupiers. Co-existence, forced or otherwise, became a viable option under certain conditions. Such dialogue should have been established as the norm long back, rather than waiting to be initiated through a crisis. At the same time, dialogue was also established between the government and communities, especially after the 1998 occupations when citizens asserted their civic rights with regard to land. This had not happened in quite this way previously. As things now stand, open dialogue needs to be nurtured by all parties, as the nation searches for long-lasting solutions to its land problems.

It is evident that after the 1998 and 2000 farm occupations, governance and land policy issues in Zimbabwe entered a new era.

---

[3] It is acknowledged that a great many additional shifts and challenges have arisen since the initial study underlying this chapter was conducted, especially in terms of the scale, intensity and effects of farm occupations and associated political violence since 2000.

Communities learnt new lessons about engaging the government, as well as private landholders, regarding demands for their rights.

Finding a place for land restitution

The fact that communities were so readily mobilised to participate in and sustain the land occupations, even through the rainy season and into the winter, shows that there was something fundamentally wrong with the existing land reform and redistribution exercise. Fieldwork data show that restitution claims based on ancestral attachments and other historically based dispossessions, were a strong rallying point for participants in the occupations. These were too significant for government to continue ignoring them. As such, policy makers in Zimbabwe need to revisit their position on the restitution of land rights, and begin dialogue with the affected communities.

Non-democratic land reform as a source of discontent

Empirical research has confirmed the frustration felt by communities over the slow pace of the previous land reform programmes. In addition, the non-transparent, non-participatory and often patron-based – and now increasingly partisan – nature of beneficiary selection at the local levels has contributed to the build-up of discontent among communities. The 1998 occupations are particularly illustrative of specific communities' disapproval of previous attempts at land reform by the government.

Jumping the queue for resettlement

The polarisation and politicisation of the land occupations has produced a new set of beneficiaries. The strong role of Zanu (PF) and the ZNLWVA, whose 'parental allegiance' is with the ruling party, has fundamentally shifted the political basis of land allocation under the 'fast track' resettlement programme.

The war veterans have developed their own location-specific resettlement registers at each of the occupied farms, made up of people who participated in the land occupations. Allocation of land has, in the majority of cases, tended to use these registers as a way of rewarding those who participated in the occupations (ZERO Field Survey, 2000). Needless to say, the farm occupiers were predominantly Zanu (PF) supporters. Available evidence has shown a blatant use of political affiliation as a tool for determining the beneficiaries of resettlement. Political statements, including some by government ministers, have publicly ruled out redistribution of land to alleged MDC supporters. The relevance of the old resettlement list that was kept by Rural District Councils is still unclear. Although it was beyond the scope of this study to analyse beneficiary selection, the indications are that many people jumped the queue for resettlement.

Extending resettlement across administrative borders

Farm occupations in 2000 were characterised by the movement of people across the main provincial and district administrative boundaries. This is contrary to the formal conditions of previous resettlement programmes which restricted settlers to their respective 'home' districts and provinces, except in the few cases where districts do not have any large-scale commercial farms for acquisition. The recent farm occupations have shown that there is nothing sacrosanct about such boundaries. In this light, the land reform programme needs to be more flexible in terms of where beneficiaries are to be resettled. Making redistribution conditional on administrative boundaries that have no scientific validity or social basis, needs to be actively challenged.

Attention to urban settlement needs

The demand for land for urban residential development remains high in most areas. At the same time, land prices have skyrocketed. Yet, as already mentioned, land reform continues to be viewed primarily as a rural issue, sidelining the land needs of urban populations. The promise of free land during farm occupations was more than an incentive for urban residents to occupy farms around major cities. Despite the polarisation and politicisation of society induced by the farm occupations, alongside party-political violence, urban people of different social, economic and political backgrounds participated in the farm occupations, and were widely engaged in the subsequent 'fast track' resettlement programme.

The land question must be treated as both a rural and an urban problem. Although demands vary between rural and urban populations, the fundamental question is one of survival, livelihoods and human rights, which cut across the urban-rural divide. In this context, land acquisition and redistribution needs to address demands for urban residential development. More importantly, appropriate land resettlement models should be developed that take advantage of urban infrastructure and services, to give urban residents access to residential and agricultural land in peri-urban areas.

Concluding remarks

The problem of land occupations is not new to this country. Many other studies have confirmed this (Moyo 1995, 1998, 2001; Alexander, this volume). During the early 1980s, the government introduced the accelerated land reform programme as a response to the overwhelming demand for land by communities. This mirrors the experience in countries such as Brazil, where land reforms have mainly been a response to land occupations. But perhaps the main difference between the 2000 farm occupations in Zimbabwe and land occupations elsewhere, is the direct involvement and support of the state. Whilst the 1998 occupations can be seen as spontaneous and independent actions, those in 2000 were strategically-guided political actions (Shanin, 1971). The government clearly supported farm occupations, a move that was in direct contradiction with existing laws that governed acquisition and use of land in the country at that time.

Yet despite the fact that the state encouraged and supported the land occupations, state farms and other state lands were also occupied. This is an indication that mass processes may be easy to start but difficult to control once they have gathered momentum. At the same time, it raises interesting questions as to if or how the government will consent to legitimise occupations in all affected areas, including on state lands, and what this will mean in terms of the overall 'Zimbabwe model' of land reform.

In addition to land hunger and the state's own political project, the memory of colonial displacement and the cultural loss of sacred sites linked to restitution claims, have been as critical to the recent land occupations as they were to more historical struggles. Conspicuous examples include the Tangwena people and their claims over Kaerezi and Nyanga National Park (Manicaland); Sekuru Mushore's claims over Nharira Hills (Mashonaland West); the Ndau people's claims over Chirinda forests (Manicaland), and Chief Manhenga's over Gambuli Farm (Mashonaland West). Our research has demonstrated that one of the underlying causes of land demands and conflicts, both on private and state land, has been the non-recognition by policy makers of such historical land claims. The government's continued refusal to discuss and accommodate this is not only socially unjust but is also a short-sighted refusal to address the underlying causes of many localised land conflicts. At the same time, however, it has to be acknowledged that offering to restore all historical land rights could open a Pandora's Box.

On a broader level, the absence of transparency and good governance in the land reform programme has undoubtedly contributed to the development of tensions and conflicts, and was a major factor in the mobilisation of communities to participate in the land occupations of 1998 and 2000. Since independence in 1980, there has been no democratic participation of communities in public land reform processes, whether in overall decision-making, the choice of farms for acquisition, or the selection of beneficiaries. The Svosve farm occupations of 1998 clearly showed a causal link between the undemocratic nature of land reforms and non-recognition of historical land claims on one hand, and farm occupations on the other. As such, one can argue that Zimbabwe needs to engage in open debate and consider the merits and demerits of restitution as an option in the country's land reform programme. The key issues of such a debate would include the dynamics and legitimacy of land claims; compensating for lost land rights; institutional arrangements for addressing restitution claims; the legal implications of restitution; and methodological issues and procedures for registering, processing and managing land claims.

The land occupations of 2000 gave various (politically privileged) citizens and communities, for the first time, an active role in land redistribution, in terms of deciding which farms to occupy and who the beneficiaries would be. While external mobilisation and support, in the form of war veterans and different state agencies, was a key to their participation, this does not negate the sense of empowerment that some occupiers experienced in the process. The ongoing land occupations have seen an unsteady and unpredictable transfer of power – over land allocation but also other aspects of governance (see Hammar, this volume) – from government departments and Rural District Councils to war veterans. This shift of power has made the overall process of land redistribution and resettlement less transparent and more undemocratic. In addition, the direct involvement of the militarised arms of government in the land occupations and in the subsequent 'fast track' resettlement programme, as well as in post-election retribution, has constituted a reversal of the initial decision-making power which accrued to individual citizens and communities.

References

Appadurai, Arjun, 1996. *Modernity at Large: Cultural Dimensions of Globalization*, Minneapolis: University of Minnesota Press.

Assefa, Hizkias, 1993. *Peace and Reconciliation as a Paradigm: a philosophy of peace and its implications in conflicts, Governance and Economic Growth in Africa*. Nairobi: African Peace Building and Reconciliation Network.

Barraclough, Solon L. 1999a. 'Land reform in Developing countries: the role of the state and other actors', UNRISD Discussion Papers, DP 103, Geneva.

Barraclough, Solon L, 1999b. *An End to Hunger? The Social Origins of Food Strategies*. London: Zed Books.

Coser, L. A., 1956. *The Functions of Social Conflict*. New York: The Free Press.

Deininger, Klaus, n.d. 'Land Policy and Administration: lessons learned and new challenges for the bank's Development Agenda'. World Bank Preliminary Discussion Paper.

Dzingirai, Vupenyu, 2000. 'Land Reform and Campfire'. Conference proceedings of a Thematic Learning Workshop on Natural Resource Management and Sustainable Livelihoods: Compatibility or Conflict? 27 April 2000, Jameson Hotel, Harare. Hosted by ITDG Southern Africa.

Field-Juma, Alison, 1996. 'Governance and Sustainable Development'. In C. Juma and J.B. Ojwang (eds). *In Land we Trust: Environment, Private Property and Constitutional Change*. London: Zed Books.

Hawkes, R. K., 1991. 'Crop and Livestock Losses to Wild Animals in the Bulilimamangwe Natural Resources Management Project Area'. Centre for Applied Social Sciences Working Paper 1-91, University of Zimbabwe, Harare.

Huizer, G., 1999. 'Peasant Mobilisation for Land Reform: historical case studies and theoretical considerations'. UNRISD Discussion Papers, DP 103, Geneva.

Hildyard, Nicholas, 1999. 'Blood, Babies and the Social roots of Conflict'. In M. Suliman (ed.), *Ecology, Politics and Violent Conflict*. London: Zed Books.

Hyden, Goran, 1996. Foreword in C. Juma and J.B. Ojwang (eds). *In Land we Trust: Environment, Private Property and Constitutional Change*. London: Zed Books.

Keane, Fergal, 1996. *Letter to Daniel: Despatches from the Heart*. Harmondsworth: Penguin Books.

Huizer, G., 1999. 'Peasant Mobilisation for Land Reform: historical case studies and theoretical considerations'. Geneva: UNRISD.

Huizer, G., 1991. *Folk Spirituality and Liberation in Southern Africa*. Bordeaux: Centre d'Etude d'Afrique Noire.

Mamimine P. W., N. Nemarundwe and F. Matose, 2001. 'Conflict and Conflict Management of Miombo Woodlands: three case studies of miombo woodlands in Zimbabwe'. Miombo Woodlands Research Project, Centre for International Forestry Studies (CIFOR).

Marongwe, Nelson, 1995. 'Natural Resources Utilisation at Growth Points: A Focus on Murambinda and Gokwe Growth Points'. Unpublished Masters Dissertation, Department of Geography, University of Zimbabwe, Harare.

Marongwe, Nelson, 2001. 'Fast Track Resettlement in Zimbabwe'. Unpublished research report, ZERO, Harare.

Matowanyika, Joseph Z. Z. and Nelson Marongwe, 1998. 'Land and Sustainable Development in Southern Africa: An Exploration of Some Emerging Issues'. Sustainable Land Management Discussion Paper series, No. 1, ZERO, Harare.

Mbiba, Beacon, 2001. 'Contemporary Land Invasions and the Urban Land Question in Southern Africa: With Special Reference to Zimbabwe'. Paper presented at Conference on 'Rethinking Land, State and Citizenship through the Zimbabwe Crisis', Centre for Development Research, Copenhagen.

Moyo, Sam, 1995. *The Land Question in Zimbabwe*. Harare: SAPES.

Moyo, Sam, 1996. 'Land and Democracy'. Paper presented to the International Conference on the Historical Dimensions of Democracy and Human Rights, History Department, University of Zimbabwe, Harare.

Moyo, Sam, 1998. 'The Land Acquisition Process in Zimbabwe (1997/8)'. Harare: UNDP.

Moyo, Sam, 2000a. *Land Reform under Structural Adjustment in Zimbabwe: Land Use Change in the Mashonaland Provinces*. Uppsala: Nordiska Afrikainstitutet.

Moyo, Sam, 2000b. 'The Interaction of Market and Compulsory Land Acquisition Processes with Social Action in Zimbabwe's Land Reforms'. Paper Presented to SARIPS Annual Colloquium on Regional Integration: Past, Present and Future. Harare, 24-27 September.

Moyo, Sam, 2001. 'The land occupations movement and democratisation in Zimbabwe: Contradictions of neoliberalism'. *Millennium: Journal of International Studies*, 30 (2), pp. 311-330.

Moyo, Sam, Proper B. Matondi and Nelson Marongwe, 1998. 'Land Use Change and Communal Land Tenure Under Stress: The Case of Shamva District'. In L. Masuko (ed.), 1998. *Economic Policy Reforms Meso-Scale Rural Market Changes in Zimbabwe, The Case of Shamva District.* Institute of Development Studies, University of Zimbabwe, Harare.

Nkiwane, S. M., 1997. *Zimbabwe's International Borders: A Study in National and Regional Development in Southern Africa, Volume 1: Zimbabwe, Mozambique, Namibia and South Africa.* Harare: University of Zimbabwe Publications.

Ranger, Terence, 1985. *Peasant Consciousness and Guerrilla Warfare in Zimbabwe.* Oxford: James Currey.

Sithole, B. and P.N. Bradley, 1995. 'Institutional Conflicts over the management of communal area resources in Zimbabwe'. Stockholm: Stockholm Environment Institute.

Shanin, Teodor, 1971. *Peasants and Peasant Societies: selected readings.* Harmondsworth: Penguin Books.

Suliman, Mohamed (ed.), 1999. *Ecology, Politics and Violent Conflict.* London: Zed Books.

Swain, Ashok, 1993. 'Environment and Conflict: Analysing the Developing World'. Department of Peace and Conflict Research, Uppsala University, Uppsala.

Tshuma, Lawrence, 1997. *A Matter of (In)justice: Law, State and the Agrarian Question in Zimbabwe.* Harare: SAPES.

Widstrand, C. (ed.), 1980. *Water and Society: Conflicts in Development: Water Conflicts and Research Priorities.* Oxford and New York: Pergamon Press.

Wolf, E., 1969. *Peasant Wars of the Twentieth Century.* New York: Harper and Row.

Chapter 6

Belonging to the Farm(er): Farm Workers, Farmers, and the Shifting Politics of Citizenship[1]

Blair Rutherford

Farm workers and the Zimbabwean crisis: A context for debate

In highly politicised times of stress and urgency, it is easy to rely on readily available narratives, forms of analysis that rely on prototypical explanatory devices from particular discursive traditions. This is not inherently a cause for concern but it does mean that when one tries to introduce other narratives, other explanatory devices, into such politically heated dialogues and arguments one risks the charge of being, at best, indifferent to the plight of one group, and at worst, inhuman and callous.

In this chapter, I run such a risk by providing an account of current events that does not easily fit within the dominant prototypes and tropes used by the two sides of the current crisis in Zimbabwe. This is not because I think it is wrong to strongly adopt a political stance towards the current crisis in Zimbabwe – in fact I think it is imperative. Rather, I think that when it comes to farm workers in Zimbabwe, the ways in which they have been understood and explained are ultimately limited in pointing to ways in which their lives can be improved in whatever future is anticipated. Although there are a wide variety of arguments, asserted ambivalences and stark contradictions within both sides, the polarisation of positions

---

[1] This chapter is based on a paper presented at 'The Zimbabwe Crisis', an international event hosted by the Centre for Development Research, Copenhagen, Denmark 3-5 September 2001. I want to thank Bill Derman for his responses to the paper at the conference and to the other participants for their comments. I especially want to thank the editors for their suggestive comments and, particularly, Amanda Hammar for all the work she has put into this larger project and for her fine editing suggestions.

as the Zimbabwean crisis deepens acts as a strong centripetal force, silencing those heterogeneous voices.

Both the anti-colonial and African nationalist discourses used by the land invaders, Zanu (PF), and their supporters, and the language of human rights and liberal democracy relied upon by the opponents of the invasions and supporters of the Movement for Democratic Change (MDC), are shaped by a historical tradition of imagining farm workers within the nation of colonial and postcolonial Zimbabwe. This tradition can be summarised by the phrase 'belonging to the farm(er)': policy, law, and national attitudes toward farm workers in Zimbabwe have consistently defined their moral consciousness, political predispositions, and civic and legal rights through their location on the farm and presumed relationship with the white farmer. Anti-colonial nationalists tend to understand farm workers as oppressed by white farmers and strive to 'liberate' them from their bondage. Human rights liberal democrats tend to reproduce the assumption that farm workers are benevolently supported by and united with the farmer in the face of invaders and the corrupt state. Be it celebrated or condemned, a narrow understanding of the 'farm' in 'farm workers' has been constitutive of their political and social identification in colonial and postcolonial Zimbabwe. By belonging to the farm(er), the political agency of farm workers has been strongly circumscribed.

By providing an explanation of this historical tradition, how it has shaped understandings of and actions within the current crisis, and how this political tradition enables certain actions of farm workers, obscures others, and disables many more, I hope that I am not perceived to be 'for' colonialism or 'against' democracy. I aim to show the importance of working with and against this tradition to enable a better situation for farm workers on and off commercial farms. I will therefore be suggesting, on the one hand, that the colonial heritage cannot be simply overthrown or nostalgically praised but must be acknowledged as producing certain arrangements of pragmatic action and prototypical discourses which limit the horizon of politics for farm workers. On the other hand, I will suggest how liberal democracy is not only an empowering and inspiring set of rules, processes, and norms but is also deeply entangled with powerful traditions of actions, identities, and discourses that modulate its meanings to the routinised rhythms of the site of commercial farms. Let me be clear that I am not equating both 'sides' of the crisis as being equally harmful to farm workers during this crisis; far from it: the anti-colonial African nationalism in the hands of the land invaders and ruling party is leading to great misery for most farm workers. Although I argue that the democratic language and human rights discourse in the hands of the opposition does not necessarily address some of the main problems and aspirations of many farm workers due to its reliance on this tradition of 'belonging to the farm(er),' my aim is to open up the political dialogues and debates taking place in Zimbabwe and about Zimbabwe to some of these historical entanglements, and not to naively dismiss them.

I begin by noting the resonances of this tradition of 'belonging to the farm(er)' in the current politicised climate. Then I sketch its genealogy. Finally, through some ethnographic examples, I point to the importance of rethinking it in terms of practices of citizenship, access to land, and institutional arrangements for farm workers. In so doing, I seek to add to the important discussion of achieving a better understanding of the 'continuing multi-layered crisis in Zimbabwe' and to suggest how an examination of the dominant stitching of farm workers to the fabric of the nation in Zimbabwe allows a different focus on the 'constantly shifting relationship between land, state and citizenship' from that which is promoted by the two dominant ways of explaining current events.[2]

In the glare of the (inter)national public spotlight

The crisis in Zimbabwe has brought sustained national and international public attention to farm workers for the first time, largely as victims of violence (mainly from the war vet-led land occupiers or historically from white farmers), in terms of economic security (as their source of employment is removed, they are discriminated against in the 'fast-track' land redistribution exercise, or in having no land themselves), and, to a lesser extent, as perpetrators of violence (against 'war vets'[3], against other farm workers and white farmers). As already stated, two dominant discourses are used to explain farm workers. On the one hand, there is much public discussion of the infringement of farm workers' rights of freedom and political choice and public condemnation of the violence that occupiers have brought to bear on farm workers.

---

[2] The quotations come from the overview of the main themes of the conference in Copenhagen in September 2001.

[3] I use 'war vets' as a short-hand to describe the land invaders. Even though most land invaders are neither members of the Zimbabwe National Liberation War Veterans Association (ZNLWVA) nor even fought in the liberation war, in my experience and that of others (Alexander, and Marongwe, this volume) most invasions are led by members of the ZNLWVA.

On the other hand, particularly in the state media, there is criticism of the low pay, hard working conditions, and often poor living conditions of farm workers, and demands that they be allowed to farm for themselves on the land originally taken away by white settlers. These two positions tend to be aligned with and used by the two main political protagonists, the MDC and Zanu (PF). Although the narratives shaping much of this public commentary situate farm workers within large, abstract themes about democracy, African nationalism, the rule of law, and colonialism, they also all tend to situate them vis-a-vis their places of work, the predominantly white-owned commercial farms. The presumed agency of these larger categories of actors – citizens, black Africans – are modulated for farm workers on all sides of the commentary by a particular understanding of their relationship with white farmers.

The difference between the two main perspectives in terms of evaluating the position of farm workers hinges largely on alternative understandings of power relations on white-operated commercial farms.[4] For African nationalists, power is understood to be top-down, replicating colonial if not global patterns of domination which need to be reversed and overthrown, while for liberals, power on the farms is viewed as benign, even non-existent, with oppressive power only associated with the state and with invaders coming from outside the farms.

For example, African nationalists view the political and moral predispositions of farm workers as having been shaped by working for whites. They are presumed to be Africans exploited at the hands of whites who must, by definition, be against their white employers. However, this 'white' power may be so dominant that farm workers are assumed to be living a life of false consciousness, being used by farmers against African nationalists and against what is said to be their own true, underlying class and race interests. Hence, Zanu (PF) spokesmen pointing out that farmers exploit farm workers and thus are inimically against them, as when the late Border Gezi declared at a campaign rally before the June 2000 elections, 'Some of these farmers have failed to provide decent housing for their

---

[4] Although, as of early 2000, perhaps 800 or so of the approximately 4,600 commercial farms have been owned and operated by black Zimbabweans, the weight of history of colonial land expropriation and labour regimes means most commentary presumes that farm workers are working for white farmers. From limited research and media reports, many black commercial farmers seem to draw on idioms and expectations of labour and social relations found within the hierarchical language of kinship and social networks, often resulting in farm workers being paid less and having worse living and working conditions than on white-operated commercial farms.

workers and now they pretend to be drinking from the same cup with the labourers.'⁵

At the same time, many of those decrying the violence against farm workers presume the prevailing situation on the farms prior to the invasions was, if not in the best interests of farm workers, at least benign. For example, in his analysis of the violence of the 2000 parliamentary elections, Carver (2000) brings attention to the fact that farm workers have suffered some of the worst abuses and violence during the land occupations. Wrongly assuming that most farm workers are unionised and therefore, by extension, MDC supporters which made them legitimate targets in the eyes of the perpetrators of Zanu (PF) violence⁶, he also suggests that farm workers are particularly anxious about forced redistribution of their places of employment: 'Education, as well as health and other social provision, is usually provided by the commercial farmers. If the farmers go, all this goes with them unless there is properly planned resettlement' (Carver, 2000:17). In other words, the farm is represented as a place of support and care for farm workers; a place which is being taken away by the war vets and the haphazard 'fast-track' resettlement exercise. As recently declared in an opinion piece by two MDC Members of Parliament, Roy Bennet and David Coltart, the former a commercial farmer himself, farmers must build on what they call the 'obvious union' with their workers. 'The loyalty between these groups,' they propose, 'is an under-developed asset' in this struggle against Zanu (PF).⁷ Here, the farm becomes a place of ultimate solidarity between owner and worker, white and black (see Rutherford (2001b) for further discussion of these two perspectives).

---

5   'Gezi slams whites for funding MDC,' *The Herald*, 3 April 2000. A recent Zanu (PF) press release condemned the Zimbabwe Congress of Trade Unions (ZCTU) two-day national stay-away by declaring: 'The plight of farm workers and their families have been marginalised despite the fact that they are bearing the brunt of the current crisis. Analysts said it was unfortunate that the ZCTU had not taken into account the concerns of the farm workers. Farm workers who on average earn only about US$38 a month have in the past failed to negotiate for salary increases with their employers, most of whom are millionaires because of lack of representation from the labour body, ZCTU. Instead of calling for illegal strikes, the ZCTU should address the concerns of the workers in Zimbabwe and stop being a mouth-piece of opposition parties, championing the destabilisation of the economy. The farm workers deserve to be heard too' ['Hard Facts on Zimbabwe (04 June 2001), Workers defy strike organised by ZCTU' http://www.zanupfpub.co.zw/releases.html (15/06/2001)].

6   Before the violence began, between 20,000 and 60,000 of the 250,000 plus farm workers were members of the General Agricultural and Plantation Workers' Union of Zimbabwe (GAPWUZ), the main trade union for farm workers. Zanu (PF) tacticians said farm workers were affiliated with the MDC because of the presumed strong influence of their employers, white farmers, and not because of their (putative) membership in GAPWUZ.

7   'Opinion,' *Zimbabwe Independent* on-line, 17 August 2001.

Seeping through the rhetoric: Varied responses of farm workers in Mashonaland East

But in practice, many farm workers have not simply been treated by land occupiers and Zanu(PF) activists and leaders as exploited Africans who will benefit from the fast-track resettlement exercise, nor by white farmers purely as fellow citizens to be respected and to join in mutually beneficial solidarity. Power is not simply coercive and emanating solely from white farmers or from outside invaders. Rather it is multifaceted and productive, and is dynamically (re)deployed within various strategies that are not captured by the Manichaean, black and white analyses of either of the dominant narratives (see Foucault, 1991). As an illustration, let me provide some quotations from Mashonaland East farm workers based on interviews that I and research assistants have conducted during 2000-01.[8]

A young, educated foreman who was born in Zimbabwe but whose parents are from Malawi (and have a *musha*, or rural home, in Mutoko), reflected in March 2001, 'I may hate the farm invasions but the truth is that I have no place which I can call my own, while there is a lot of land here in Zimbabwe which is in the hands of the few whites. I would love to have land of my own but at the same time I would want to be employed, so this is rather hard to decide.'

On a neighbouring farm, a middle-aged woman worker recalled, also in March 2001, that during the vote for the Marondera West by-election in November 2000,

> *Zanu(PF) sent a ZUPCO bus to ferry us to the place where we were voting... When we went to vote... it was something else because they [Zanu(PF)] were telling us who to vote for. Those people from Malawi who are here – most of them are not educated. They know how to work only. When there [at the polling station], they were told to put an 'X' where there are Zimbabwe ruins which is a symbol for Zanu (PF). Since they don't know and are afraid of being beaten, they put an 'X' on it. They were afraid of being beaten because in neighbouring farms people were beaten by the war veterans. They were being beaten for being MDC supporters. When they arrived at a farm, they went to the foremen, supervisors, and housemaid demanding to know the people who were given MDC t-shirts. If they say we don't know, then they would be beaten.*

---

[8] I want to thank the Social Sciences and Humanities Research Council of Canada for its financial support for this research.

She later recalled what the war vets had to say about land redistribution: 'The war veterans told us [farm workers] that "we are not going to give you land," but they never told us the reason why. They said "we are going to bring our own people." They said "we don't care about you since you like to work for your *murungu* [white farmer]."'

Another woman worker, a housemaid, on the same farm observed that she was leaving work because she was pregnant and her employer did not give the legally mandated maternity leave. When asked why she does not go to GAPWUZ, she dryly noted that 'the *murungu* here does not like to hear about GAPWUZ. If they hear that you are a member they will fire you. There were others here who were fired when the *murungu* heard that they are members... Since those were fired, I have not heard of any GAPWUZ members here.'

A senior foreman on that same farm observed in October 2000: 'Now what farmers are doing when the war vets come to a farm, they just say "it is okay, take the farm." The farmer then tells the farm workers that "I have nothing to lose, if you let the farm be taken by the war vets it is you who will suffer, so you have to protect the farm for your survival." This is why you hear these days war vets being chased away by the workers or being beaten by hoes and other farming tools [by workers].'

Zanu (PF) activists tell farm workers that they do not qualify for land, implying that they are not as deserving, not as African, as non-farm worker black Zimbabweans. They emphasise farm workers' foreign-ness, their Malawian roots, using their lack of legal belonging, and their murky citizenship status, as a form of coercion at the voting booth. White farmers make farm workers defend the farms while flouting labour laws.

Power is neither simply black versus white, oppressor versus oppressed. Nor is it benign, or absent in the relations between farmers and workers. Although the respective claims of African nationalism and liberal democracy have definitely shaped actions towards farm workers during this crisis, the above examples indicate their limited understanding of the varied responses of farm workers, of how power works on the farms, or of the power of the 'farm' itself in locating farm workers within these two dominant narratives. Such limitations and actions do not bode well for farm workers in whatever future emerges. In fact, neither Zanu (PF)'s intimidation and threats towards farm workers nor farmer coercion and wilful neglect of labour laws are merely creatures of the crisis for farm workers;

they have a much longer history. As such one need not simply dismiss 'democracy' or 'nationalism.' Rather, I argue that it is imperative first to recognise how this dominant tradition of 'belonging to the farm(er)' continues to shape different discourses, practices and policies concerning farm workers, and, then, to struggle to go beyond it.

Boundaries of belonging

Social scientists now understand that a moral imagined community, a sense of belonging to a place amongst strangers, is a crucial component of political membership in the nation. But not everyone fits in, and there is no single sense of belonging. If nationalism is an imagined community – a cultural logic that conceives of the nation as a deep, horizontal comradeship, a belonging to a territorially delimited, sovereign state, in Benedict Anderson's (1991:7) powerful words – others have shown us that this cultural project of political enjoining is not as inclusive as the liberal category of citizenship implies. State-making, as Eric Worby (1998:563) has astutely suggested, often 'evokes a world of abstract values and qualities that are held to distinguish genuine national character, and that calls upon an audience of would-be citizens to identify with those same values and qualities. Such an evocation marks boundaries as it marks bodies; it excludes some identities and subjectivities just as it nominates others for inclusion.' (See also Comaroff and Comaroff, 1999). Belonging to the nation is a particular, albeit powerful, scale-making project that has specific cultural content identifying who belongs and who does not, which itself intersects, overlaps, and co-mingles with other projects of scale-making, memory, and political inclusion and exclusion. I am following Anna Tsing (2000) in using 'scale-making projects' to refer to socio-cultural practices that enable the imagination of particular scales for action, be they local, regional, national or global. The key focus is on how political communities are shaped and defined in intersecting scale-making practices in particular locations; on how, that is, a certain scope of actions and arrangements are enabled, brought into being, by imaginings of certain spatial dimensionalities and hierarchies. Whereas some groups and social identities learn to have the nation or the globe as their field of action in certain practices, others are confined to more circumscribed localities (see also Gupta and Ferguson, 1997 and Ferguson, forthcoming). For farm workers, the farm and farmer have strongly defined their political location in

Zimbabwe. Due to a combination of legal, administrative and social practices initiated during the colonial period by the government and white farmers, moral evaluations by many African small-holder farmers, and strategies of farm workers, the 'farm' and the white farmer have become the horizon of politics and the anchor of identification for farm workers in the dominant imaginings of the postcolonial nation. Let me briefly elaborate.

Colonial officials, missionaries, and settlers in interaction with various African leaders and groups created and recreated the political boundaries and locations of the colony in relation to the nation (and world) at large. This was premised predominantly on spatial divisions between European and African, tribal and modern, rural and urban, men and women, and different tribal/ethnic groups. In terms of 'native policy', the key spaces were the native reserves and urban native locations, the sites for various colonial projects and dangers concerning tribalism, traditionality, modernisation, proletarianisation, detribalisation, and so forth. Although produced and policed through administrative structures, welfare practices, development programmes, academic studies, pass laws, the British South African Police, Native Affairs Department, etc., such sites interacted with competing, overlapping, converging projects of various African men and women as well as the various European administrators and interested parties. Inevitably such interactions altered the consequences of these colonial projects and fears in actual native reserves and urban locations. Yet, given both the constitutive emphasis placed on these locales for colonial and anti-colonial projects and the capacities of narratives of tribal tradition, modernisation, development and liberation to morally frame the current or future nation of (Southern) Rhodesia, these sites became crucial components in the imagination of the colonial, anti-colonial and African nationalist nation for many Europeans and Africans within and outside the country.

For example, the site of native reserves (later known as Tribal Trust Lands and, since independence, as Communal Areas/Lands) was viewed as the natural home for indigenous Africans in much of the colonial period. It was a place which colonial officials commonly viewed with nostalgia or contempt as the roots of tradition in the civilising/westernising/modernising nation. Administrative structures were set up to authorise leaders (chiefs, headmen, kraal-heads) as both civil servants and representatives of their defined communities in relation to the administration, along what officials assumed to be traditional or proto-democratic lines (e.g. in the form of African

Councils). These leaders and this site itself were also viewed by African nationalist leaders and guerrillas as either the source of nationalist culture or evidence of colonial land expropriation and betrayal (see, e.g. Lan, 1985; Ranger, 1985). Such contested ways to imagine the native reserves and the people in them – chiefs, headmen, tribesmen, peasants, smallholder farmers – continued into postcolonial Zimbabwe. In other words, native reserves or Communal Lands have been easily and frequently associated with the nation, both colonial and independent, in one way or the other. Even when they have been imagined as parochially local, it has tended to be in relationship to the presumed cosmopolitan and modern outlook of the cities and the nation at large.[9]

Take, for example, the iterative modernisation programmes promoted in these sites, involving projects which seek to transform practices identified as traditional (and often marked as backward, regressive, undeveloped), such as 'shifting cultivation,' 'subsistence-orientation,' 'witchcraft,' 'indigenous music.' Here the scale of being local and traditional is constituted through the contrast with an imagined national if not cosmopolitan scale, which for the initiators of such projects acts as the desired end-point for those targeted (Worby, 1998, 2000; Rutherford, 1999; Moore, 1999; Turino, 2000). This is not to say that this particular scale-making arrangement – of viewing reserves/Communal Lands and the people in them as local vis-a-vis the nation or even as the backbone of the nation itself – has exhausted the ways and scales in which these areas are imagined. It is rather to say this has become a naturalised association, routinised in administrative practices, journalistic, literary, political, and social science discourses, and in the strategies of seeking economic security or advancement through acquiring a *musha* (rural home) pursued by many Zimbabweans of whatever class, occupation, gender or age.

Belonging to the farm(er)

Whereas native reserves became a key site for the operation of state rule in colonial and postcolonial Zimbabwe – a site to home Africans and to ground modernising and African nationalist projects – European farms became an important location in which to anchor European nationalism in Africa. Shortly after the British South Africa Company realised that its ambitions of finding a 'second rand' in

---

[9] See Ferguson (1999) for a good discussion of cosmopolitan and localist styles of comportment in the Zambian Copperbelt.

the new colony of Rhodesia were not to be fulfilled in the early 1900s, the promotion of European agriculture became the preferred route to increase returns to shareholders and, more enduringly, the crucial means of creating a viable, productive modern colony and white nation in Africa (Palmer, 1977; Phimister, 1988). Accordingly, white farmers became the prototypical 'settlers' in the settler nation, the men and women (or, I should say, 'wives' given the dominant representation of white farming women) who frequently became the metonymical carriers of the white nation itself in a variety of discursive and social practices. This enabled them to have access to not only the best agricultural land in the colony, thanks to the expulsion of any Africans living on designated European farm-land, but also heavily subsidised agricultural support from the colonial governments. They also were treated – and treated themselves – as key citizens of the white nation (Leys 1959; see Mamdani, 1996 for a regional argument).

Moreover, and more importantly here, the workers on these European farms were largely viewed merely as tools for the larger project of aggrandising individual white farmers and the settler nation at large. Farm workers were unlike Africans living in other locations – such as native reserves or, after the 1950s, in most other formal sector occupations where they were legally classified as workers – who became subjects/objects of national projects, whether colonial or anti-colonial in origin. Farm workers became, instead, principally the objects of the national and individual projects of European farmers (Rutherford, 2001a). Whereas looking after farm workers became a constituent part of the identification of being a white farmer in the nation of Rhodesia (Rutherford, 2001d), the site of white farmers did not automatically enable farm workers to be part of national scale-making projects, of projects that imagined the nation as their arena of action. Those representing white farmers, politically and figuratively, as well as white farmers themselves, ensured that farm workers were kept out of most institutional arrangements that were part and parcel of nation-building or state formation.

There are many examples of this subsidiary position of farm workers in national projects. Unlike every other category of worker except domestic servants they were legally under the Masters and Servants Act until the eve of independence in 1979. There were no state or industry regulated minimum standards of pay or living conditions for farm workers. They were not subjects of any government modernising projects, though they often fell under various ad hoc attempts of edification by individual farmers and their spouses. Moreover, they were often not even legally subjects of Rhodesia since many came on their own or were recruited from colonial Malawi, Zambia or Mozambique. Legally, they were in (Southern) Rhodesia solely to work, at times exclusively for white farmers (see Clarke, 1977; Loewenson, 1992; Amanor-Wilks, 1995; Rubert, 1998; Rutherford, 1997, 2001a). They were not permitted to acquire land rights in the native reserves, although some managed to do so surreptitiously.

The demand for foreign workers owed much to the lack of interest and willingness of many Africans within colonial Zimbabwe to work for white farmers for any long period of time. They were dissuaded by the often hard working conditions, the threat of violence from the farmer and his managers and 'boss-boys,' and the low pay (Rubert, 1998). Moreover, it was common for Africans to view those who became permanent farm workers as being unable to become peasant farmers in their own right. A male farm worker – particularly a married adult – who did not also have his own farm land, could be viewed by other Africans as lazy, as needing to work for someone else and unable to be a peasant, a true man, in and of himself. This sentiment draws from both peasantist understandings of masculinity and Christian teachings on becoming independent yeomen farmers (see Rutherford, 2001b). I speculate that such discourses likely intermingled with African nationalist discourses to help further marginalise farm workers from the emergent anti-colonial national projects.

In turn, many farm workers who came from outside of the country did not see themselves as part of colonial Zimbabwe. They were rather members of their own home communities, perhaps colonies, and saw their time on white farms as a way to earn some income and gain experience for their own individual and family purposes. While in colonial Zimbabwe, their political horizons seldom extended beyond the farm itself, though of course many were involved in overlapping and spatially extended networks of kin, friends, and religion (Rubert, 1998). African nationalists occasionally made inroads onto the farms but they were hard to enter given the typically intense forms of surveillance used by white farmers and their state-backed ability to evict and have charged (under the Masters and Servants Act) anyone they thought to be trouble-makers (Rutherford, 2001c).

In short, the farm became the main arena of politics for the majority of farm workers. Farmers had unprecedented control over their working and non-working lives and sought to ensure that they were kept out of any state-wide and nation-building programmes and had limited interactions with overtly political outsiders, be they African political organisations or trade unionists. To keep one's job, to access resources from the farmer for sustenance and perhaps for off-farm economic activities, one had to follow what farm workers call *mitemo yemurungu*, the laws of the farmer. There were forms of resistance, various strategies to adopt, challenge, and benefit from, but the site of politics was predominantly the farm (Rubert, 1998).

In turn, the site of European farms became so firmly tied to the colonial nationalist project that African nationalists viewed it as a white space, and viewed farm workers either as oppressively subjected to it or naively upholding it. Thus, for example, during the liberation war it was common for guerrillas to order farm workers to leave the farms, not only to deny farmers labour-power but also so that the workers could become farmers in their own right (e.g. Kriger, 1992). This call has continued to be made in political rhetoric, academic studies, and even some policy documents in post-colonial Zimbabwe. It competes with the assumption that farm workers, as (lazy) foreigners, should remain labourers for others – in this case new indigenous commercial farmers – and have no rights to land in Zimbabwe (see Moyo, Rutherford, Amanor-Wilks, 2000 for a discussion of this). As Christine Sylvester (2000:150) has put it (deploying the words of Dipesh Chakrabarty), farm workers in postcolonial Zimbabwe are typically placed in the category of the '"not yet" – you are not yet a true class with a history and a mission', not legitimately within the national imaginations of the various social groups of Zimbabwe.

And thus at independence, despite significant legal changes and initial efforts by the ruling party to both improve the situation of farm workers and to recruit them, farm workers did not easily fit within the postcolonial nation in terms of its development policies and institutional arrangements. Rural development focused primarily on the Communal Areas and, intermittently, in the resettlement schemes. Despite the legal merger of local government bodies for the Communal Areas and commercial farming areas in 1988 and its implementation in 1993, farm workers remained disenfranchised from local government elections until 1997 (see Hammar, this volume). Access to health, education, and social services have generally been more limited for farm workers than for people living in the Communal Areas. Their only interactions with politicians have tended to occur during parliamentary elections, typically when Zanu (PF) cadres create unfulfilled promises and threaten them on the basis of their alleged foreign status.[10] One significant difference that independence has brought for many farm workers of foreign descent is that more of them have been able to secure access to land to live on or to farm in the Communal Areas or resettlement schemes.[11] Although there are many farm workers who have no access to land, it is important to emphasise that many do have access to a *musha* – albeit not necessarily the best land, due to the land-giving authorities taking advantage of their desperation and vulnerability (Hughes, 1999).

Since the 1990s, there has been a growing number of people and groups advocating on behalf of farm workers. A common theme of the advocacy of GAPWUZ, national and international NGOs, and academics like myself has been the emphasis on how farm workers are the 'forgotten people' of Zimbabwe, how they have been neglected by the larger state (e.g. Mugwetsi and Balleis, 1994; Amanor-Wilks, 1995, 2001; GAPWUZ, 1997). Indeed it is common for individual white farmers and officials of their organisations to make the same claim, stressing how the responsibility for their welfare rests largely, if not solely, with the individual farmer himself. For some advocates, this leads to calls to remove farm workers from the paternalism of white farmers and let them become farmers in their own right. For others, it leads to calls for state services to farm workers, greater assistance to farmers to augment their pre-existing support, and an increase in what had recently been the growing number of NGO-supported projects aiming to create stronger ties between farm workers and the farm as a way to make them participants in their own development. Although such forms of advocacy and projects have made links to the nation for farm workers, they have tended to do so through existing scale-making mechanisms which over-privilege a particular understanding of the importance of the farm

---

[10] An infamous example was the granting of '$1 citizenship' cards to foreigners predominantly on commercial farms just prior to the 1985 national elections. (Foreignness was defined largely by the citizenship designation on national registration cards – *chitupa* – that for many Zimbabwean-born individuals, whose parents or grandparents are of non-Zimbabwean origins, state 'NCR' – Non-Citizen Resident). Although the Registrar General, Mr. Mudede, stressed to me in a 1998 interview that this legally gave citizenship status to holders of the cards, other senior officials within the Ministry of Local Government have scoffed at such a presumption. Moreover, many holders of such cards are still identified as non-citizens on their chitupa.

[11] A survey by the Agricultural Labour Bureau, Farm Community Trust of Zimbabwe, and USAID, for example, found that 40.5 per cent of male permanent workers on farms maintained a *musha* (Vhurumuku et al., 1999).

for farm workers: the farm either as a source of exploitation from which they should be removed or as a relatively benign place to which their ties should be strengthened (e.g. Auret, 2000). This downplays or neglects other existing or potential forms of scale-making practices.

A brief ethnography of crisis

Judging from the research I carried out in some Mashonaland East and West commercial farming areas from June to August 2000, from my research assistants' interviews since then, and from analyses by NGOs, it seems that farm workers – in these areas at least – are carrying out a variety of strategies to survive the continuing and deepening economic and political crisis, if not to mitigate risks to their security. Some strategies fit within the two dominant positions of this conflict, others go beyond them. Some farm workers are actively defending the farms, while others are coerced into doing so. Some are actively joining the war vets in invading farms, while others are forced into helping them. The majority, however, seem to be calling for land rights for themselves and calling for the right to earn income on farms as well (e.g. FCTZ, 2001a).

Whereas many farmers and their supporters have stressed to me that relationships with 'their labour' and what they call 'race relations' have dramatically improved because of the invasions, most workers have been more ambiguous in their evaluation of their relationships with farmers and the war vets. Many tend to view the claims of both farmers and war vets as partially legitimate: farmers have a right to farm productively and to employ us; we *vanhu vatema* (black people) have a right to some of the excess land that farmers have; farmers, white and black, tend to oppress us; and war vets will probably not give us land. While many try to perform being a farm worker to farmers – the bodily postures, language strategies, and interactions that communicate their obedience and subservience – they also try to perform being an oppressed African to war vets, with talk of their harsh working conditions, often poor living conditions, and need for land. Both performances tend to occur through heightened power and fear; both also pivot around the scale of the farm. The former emphasises belonging to the farm as a subservient dependent; the latter stresses the need to escape that dependence to become farmers in their own right. But these performances are not only directed towards meeting the needs of the farmer and the war vets. They are also used for different ends by men and women farm workers.

Alexander and McGregor (2001) have pointed out that smallholder farmers and residents of Matabeleland North province drew on ZAPU[12] political traditions to forge their widespread rejection of Zanu (PF) and to ignite their support for the MDC in the 2000 parliamentary elections. Analogously, how has the farm workers' marginalisation from national scale-making projects and their corresponding confinement to the level of the farm affected their political memory and responses to the crisis? Although responses differ dramatically from region to region, if not from farm to farm, my research suggests some common points.

First, there is a political memory of anti-politics and class, a politics that either avoids signalling political support or superficially adopts the politics of those in power, be they *makomaradi* – Zanu (PF) comrades – or *murungu*, while using power to try to improve their situation in relation to the farmer whenever and wherever they can. I know of few farm workers – lacking, as they do, a deep tradition of being tied to the nation – who feel committed to any national political party. However, they will tend to support any party that can help them bargain better with management. For example, there are a number of workers and their leaders on some horticultural farms in Goromonzi District whom I know to have been supportive of the MDC during the 2000 parliamentary elections, mainly because Zanu (PF) had failed to help them with their own work grievances and struggles. By the middle of 2001, however, some of their leaders are returning to Zanu (PF) because its officials and youth, the war vets, and the Horticultural Crocodile Union (affiliated with the Zimbabwe Federation of Trade Unions, a Zanu (PF) supported rival to the ZCTU), have been able to promise and win concessions from farmers in the area. As one farm worker leader claimed in June 2001, 'I strongly support the approach taken by war vets in farm labour disputes because I think farmers will only understand negotiations if there is an element of militancy involved to settle farm labour issues. I think that this approach should continue to give the farmers an awareness of the existence and power of the farm workers.' With the backing of the war vets and Zanu (PF), members of the unregistered Horticultural Crocodile Union have the ability to travel on these farms more than GAPWUZ, which as a ZCTU union has largely been seen to be affiliated to the MDC and thus, in the present crisis, its officials are effectively banned from traveling in many commercial farming areas. Moreover, the

---

[12] The Zimbabwean African People's Union.

support of the war vets has enabled the Horticultural Crocodile Union to be quite militant in its demands.[13]

In the Goromonzi area, farm workers have called on this union, the war veterans and Zanu (PF) officials to assist them with legitimate work grievances, such as unfair firing or lack of dismissal pay (as well as for more personal grievances). As a farm worker declared in May 2001,

> *When the Crocodile Union came to Farm X [all farm names are pseudonyms, B.R.] it told workers that the minimum wage should be $5,500 per month. You know workers are happy with the new minimum wages which this union is calling for as it is much more than the existing $1,900 per month salary. The Crocodile Union threatens the farmers who do not pay these minimum wages, saying their farms will be taken if they do not pay their workers this minimum wage.*

The focus on the scale of the farm in these projects means improved working conditions and remuneration and not either a celebration of the presumed convergence of interests between farmers and workers or a wish to escape the farm itself. Class consciousness is strong for many workers, especially younger ones. They know the range of conditions on farms in the area and the vast differences in wealth between farmers and workers. As one worker pithily put it in April 2001, 'The farmer says I can't afford to give you electricity but he then always goes on vacation at Kariba!' Yet this does not necessarily mean that they want the farms to be redistributed. As the same farm worker who was talking about the Crocodile Union observed, 'We may enjoy the taking over of farms but there are situations like what is happening at Farm Z which tells us that we have no use of the farm. The people now on Farm Z are happy that they took the farm but when you look at what is happening at the farm, there is totally nothing. No production at all.'

Recent events on this Farm Z also provide insight into the second theme, related to another aspect of political traditions for farm

---

[13] The Horticultural Crocodile Union is reminiscent of GAPWUZ and its rivals in the early 1980s when they had the support of the Party and when farmers were uncertain of their standing in the new black-ruled Zimbabwe (see Rutherford, 2001c). The focus on workers, particularly in urban areas, has been a recent campaign strategy of Zanu (PF) and the Zimbabwe National Liberation War Veterans' Association (see, e.g., 'Govt pours money into Chinotimba's union,' *Financial Gazette* on-line, 19 July 2001; 'Workers retrieve extorted cheque,' *Daily News* on-line, 2 August 2001; 'ZFTU has no right to stand for workers,' *Financial Gazette* on-line, 2 August 2001; 'Union condemns violence on commercial farms,' *Zimbabwe Independent* on-line, 12 October 2001; 'Plantation workers on rampage over wages,' *The Farmer* on-line, 19 November 2001).

workers: claims to the farm resources deriving from labouring on it. There has been a dispute between different groups of farm workers over rights to fields of onions left on Farm Z when its owners abandoned it. When the owners announced in February 2001 that they were leaving the farm and refused to pay sufficient severance to its workers, the latter called in the local Zanu (PF) councillor and war veterans who negotiated with (and undoubtedly threatened) the owners to get some compensation. They also told the workers to remain on the farm. A month later a few war veterans and supporters arrived with the councillor and 'officially' redistributed the farm to the workers. Although the councillor noted that the original owners may come back in the future to resume farming it, he formed a co-operative amongst the remaining former workers to organise the harvesting and selling of the onions. Unlike many farms that have been completely occupied by people from the urban areas and Communal Lands, this one is predominantly occupied by its former workers – one of these workers even noted that the District Administrator of Goromonzi said it was a unique situation.

However, another group of former workers of Farm Z who had waged a long strike against the owners during 1998-2000 and were living nearby, also claimed rights to the onions. As one declared to a war vet security committee who came upon a group of them digging up onions in May 2001, 'There is not just one group which has to benefit from the onions which were left by the farm owners. After all it is us who started this struggle [against the owners]... Why then should other people who did not start the struggle stop us from getting the onions?'

Although the few war veterans living on Farm Z were upset with this claim, they did not challenge it. Moreover, some of the former workers currently living on Farm Z saw nothing wrong with the others collecting the onions. As one woman said, 'I do not see anything bad in their taking the onions from the fields because they are also farm workers and may want to enjoy the sweat of their pain. Those people have been involved in the farm activities of this farm, planting the onions and working in the irrigation, so they feel entitled to the onions and I personally do not begrudge them for doing so.' Moreover, this woman observed that 'if the whites come back saying they are ready to use this farm again, I think we will all abandon the co-operative and start joining the new farm owners [as workers].' Here, these workers have made claims to resources on the land based on their past labour, while not foreclosing the wish to resume being farm workers in the future.

Belonging to the Farm(er)

Another example of farm workers using their labour ties to the farm to make claims on the land vis-a-vis land occupiers comes from another farm in Goromonzi, partially occupied by war vets and their followers. These occupiers claim, as do those on other farms, that they now rule over all the land, its resources, and the people living on it. On this farm, however, some farm workers have successfully contested those claims. For example, one worker, who said that unlike many other co-workers he still supported the occupiers, complained in April 2001 that the occupiers should only stick to the land issue and not politics. This not only meant that he was against their persecution of alleged MDC supporters but also against their claims of control over the farm. As he recounted, the occupiers 'want to control everything here. For example, we have women who go to cut grass in the bush and then sell it to those who need thatching grass. The war vets told these women to stop this for "the bush now belongs to us." But the women ignored them and continued with their cutting of the grass and,' he added approvingly, 'nothing was done to them.' In short, the claims farm workers have to the farm does not simply include their employment relationship with the farmer, but also the fact that they have put labour into it and thus they have legitimate rights to the resources on the farm, somewhat independently of the farm owner.[14]

Finally, the third theme I want to mention is the importance of also being a peasant. Having a *musha* has become extremely important for many farm workers during the present crisis due to the growing uncertainty of the availability of work. A *musha* can act as both a quasi-sanctuary from the violence and intimidation on the farms and a potential source of economic security. For instance, many workers have recounted that it is important for white farmers to continue to farm and to employ them while, at the same time, demanding that they get land, especially if they do not already have any. They observe the desperation of those who do not have a *musha* in the face of the war vets and their demands; how they do not have any immediate place to go if they are evicted by the war vets or by the *murungu*. Thus many farm workers argue that they should get

---

[14] The claim over land-based resources by the war vets and its contestation by different farm workers is not surprising. Such dynamics are part of a deep tradition of indigenous politics in the region and are common in the Communal Areas and resettlement schemes today (e.g. Lan, 1985; Kopytoff, 1987; Hughes, 1999; Hammar, 2001; Nyambara, 2001; Matondi, 2001). Recent research suggests that many displaced farm workers are fitting themselves into existing informal settlements rather than creating new settlements, although their economic insecurity and that of others in such settlements remains generally high (SC and FCTZ, 2001).

land – particularly that on which they work.¹⁵ Others discussed the importance of having a place to retreat to or to send family members to during times of violence. 'It's as if you enter a new country, where peace prevails,' one farm worker observed in August 2000 of the differences in levels of stress and fear between the Karoi commercial farms where he worked and the area of his *musha* in Mukwichi Communal Land.¹⁶ All emphasised how having a *musha* provides resources to augment one's low wages. Some commented on how the economic threat to white farmers is having negative ramifications not only in terms of living conditions and job opportunities on the farms but also in their own *musha*, since many farmers are no longer lending or giving agricultural inputs to their (favoured) workers.

Having a *musha*, or access to one, is not only important for security, but it can also enable farm workers to be part of other scale-making projects outside the farms. These include converging and diverging projects channelled through nationalism, development, localised land-based political authority, ethnicity or religion. Whereas these tend to be more beneficial to men than to women, to those with clan connections to the land-giving authority than to those without, to those from the district where the *musha* is located than those without, even those farm workers who do not fit into those categories are still better able to increase their possibilities for action and enhanced livelihood by becoming linked to a *musha* than those who are confined to the commercial farms (Rutherford, 2001a:201- 230). It is thus not a surprise that many farm workers are trying desperately to secure some rights to land somewhere.

To summarise, belonging to the farm(er) during this crisis does not only mean either being a loyal worker who wants white farmers to continue farming or being an exploited worker who wants land to farm him- or herself. Many want to improve their working conditions through the power of the war vets, Zanu (PF) and their allies, many make a claim to the farm resources independently of the farmer and in defiance of the wishes of the occupiers, and many want both to be a worker for (white) commercial farmers and to have a *musha*, possibly with support for their own farming endeavours from their employer. Many thus do not easily fit within the wider national claims

---

¹⁵ The media have also carried some of these accounts, especially from farm workers displaced by land invaders. See, e.g., 'Farm workers left with no hope, no homes,' Reuter, 7 August 2001; 'Zimbabwe's black farm workers fear death,' *Daily Telegraph* (U.K.) on-line. 17 August 2001.

¹⁶ However, some Communal Lands have witnessed great political violence, particularly during elections (e.g. ZHRNGO Forum, 2001).

made by the two political parties and their supporters, but they will use those parties and their supporters when and where they can.

Concluding thoughts

Although farm workers have adopted a variety of tactics during this crisis, the foundations of rethinking farm workers' citizenship status, land rights, and institutional arrangements need to be built on. For this to occur, I agree with many others that the land invasions need to stop. In addition to the growing macro-economic instability they are causing, and the accompanying violence and terror, it is clear that few farm workers are actually benefiting from land redistribution[17], while many have lost their jobs, and many, many more face that prospect, with limited alternatives available to them. Nor, however, can the previous status quo be resurrected. To improve the situation of farm workers it is necessary to break that automatic confinement, real and imagined, of farm workers to the scale of the farm in national scale-making projects and arrangements. This requires sustained support by NGOs, trade unions, farmers, civil servants, politicians, and others to work with those farm workers pushing for such changes.

A better future for farm workers requires that they be recognised as potential settlers and as workers with legal rights. It would require challenging notions of foreignness at the national level. In terms of their class rights, it would build on pockets of union activity, as well as that of Zanu (PF) activists. It would require improved working conditions for women farm workers, including the ability to become permanent workers. It would require better social services for farm workers and opportunities for their children to become educated and escape a life of farm work if they so wish. It would require as much effort by farmers as by workers, and efforts by black farmers, especially the newer ones who are undercapitalised and typically draw on idioms of labour relations more commonly found in smallholder farming areas, ignoring the legal labour rights of their workers.

For all of this to occur, one should not expect the powerful – those who have produced the enduring locations and relations of farm workers within the nation – to facilitate the changes. Political

---

[17] The government estimates that fewer than 1,900 of the 122,000 families it claims to have resettled are farm workers; the Commercial Farmers' Union estimates that roughly 10 per cent of the 6 million acres seized have gone to former farm workers; and GAPWUZ states that only three of every 500 people resettled are displaced farm workers ('Storm over land in Zimbabwe,' *Washington Post*, 20 August 2001).

parties, white farmers, black farmers, and the war veterans, generally rely on the historical imagination of farm workers in the nation, stressing one of two particular understandings of the role of the commercial farm(er) in Zimbabwe. There are definitely alternatives produced by individual farmers, NGOs, politicians, government officials and war veterans that need to be supported and linked to the actions of some farm workers. This involves going beyond the historical traditions of confining farm workers to the scale of the farm, to recognising other farm worker claims that are not as publicly known or promoted: claims based on their class interests as workers, and not solely as peasants-in-waiting or allies of the farmer; claims to farm resources independent of the farmer, and existing claims to having or receiving a *musha*. Farm workers have grounded their politics in the farm, but they have also gone beyond it. They need to be supported with new institutional arrangements to link them to local and central government bodies and to (potentially) representative structures like GAPWUZ.[18] Given the great misery befalling so many farm workers, and the limitations of most public approaches towards them, it is imperative not to understand their situation and future only through their relationship to white farmers, but to build on the strategies and practices through which so many of them struggle for improved living and working conditions, and for survival.

---

[18] A number of NGOs had been promoting such efforts, but these have been put into abeyance by the land occupations. New regional arrangements are however emerging (see FCTZ, 2001b). For some approaches to alternative institutional arrangements for farm workers, see Moyo et al. (2000) and Amanor-Wilks (2001).

References

Alexander, Jocelyn, JoAnn McGregor, and Terence Ranger, 2000. *Violence & Memory: One Hundred Years in the 'Dark Forests' of Matabeleland*. Oxford: James Currey.

Alexander, Jocelyn and JoAnn McGregor, 2001. 'Elections, Land and the Politics of Opposition in Matabeleland', *Journal of Agrarian Change*, Vol. 1. No. 4, pp. 510-33.

Amanor-Wilks, Dede Esi, 1995. *In Search of Hope for Zimbabwe's Farm Workers*. Harare: Panos Institute.

Amanor-Wilks, Dede (ed.), 2001. *Zimbabwe's Farm Workers: Policy Dimensions*. Lusaka: Panos Southern Africa and Farmworkers Action Group.

Anderson, Benedict, 1991. *Imagined Communities*, Revised edition. London: Verso.

Auret, Diana, 2000. *From Bus Stop to Farm Village: The Farm Worker Programme in Zimbabwe*. Harare: Save the Children (UK).

Carver, Richard, 2000. 'Zimbabwe: A Strategy of Tension', UNHCR Centre for Documentation and Research, WRITENET Paper No. 04/2000. Geneva: United Nations High Commission for Refugees.

Clarke, Duncan, 1977. *Agricultural and Plantation Workers in Rhodesia: A Report on Conditions of Labour and Subsistence*. Gwelo: Mambo Press.

Comaroff, John and Jean Comaroff (eds), 1999. *Civil Society and the Political Imagination in Africa: Critical Perspectives*. Chicago: University of Chicago Press.

FCTZ, 2001a. *The Impact of Land Reform on Commercial Farm Workers' Livelihoods*. Harare: Farm Community Trust of Zimbabwe.

FCTZ, 2001b. *Southern Africa Regional Conference on Farm Workers' Human Rights & Security*. Harare: Farm Community Trust of Zimbabwe.

Ferguson, James, 1999. *Expectations of Modernity: Myths and Meanings of Urban Life on the Zambian Copperbelt*. Berkeley: University of California Press.

Ferguson, James, Forthcoming. 'Transnational Topographies of Power: Beyond "the State" and "Civil Society" in the Study of African Politics', in Gabrielle Schwab (ed.), *The Forces of Globalization*. New York: Columbia University Press.

Foucault, Michel, 1991. 'Governmentality'. In Graham Burchell, Colin Gordon, and Peter Miller (eds), *The Foucault Effect*. Chicago: University of Chicago Press.

GAPWUZ, 1997. Report on the Workshop on Living Conditions of Farm Workers in Zimbabwe, February, Darwendale. Harare: General Agricultural Workers' Union of Zimbabwe.

Gupta, Akhil, and James Ferguson, 1997. 'Discipline and Practice: "The Field" as Site, Method and Location in Anthropology'. In A. Gupta and J. Ferguson (eds), *Anthropological Locations: Boundaries and Grounds of a Field Science*. Berkeley: University of California.

Hammar, Amanda. 2001, '"The Day of Burning": Eviction and Reinvention in the Margins of Northwest Zimbabwe'. *Journal of Agrarian Change*, Vol. 4, No. 1, pp. 550-74.

Hughes, David, 1999. 'Refugees and Squatters: Immigration and the Politics of Territory on the Zimbabwe-Mozambique Border'. *Journal of Southern African Studies*, Vol. 25 No. 4, pp. 533-52.

Kopytoff, Igor, 1987. 'The Internal African Frontier: The Making of African Political Culture'. In Igor Kopytoff (ed.) *The African Frontier: The Reproduction of Traditional African Societies*. Bloomington: Indiana University Press.

Kriger, Norma, 1992. *Zimbabwe's Guerrilla War: Peasant Voices*. Cambridge: Cambridge University Press.

Lan, David, 1985. *Guns & Rain: Guerrillas & Spirit Mediums in Zimbabwe*. London: James Currey.

Leys, Colin, 1959. *European Politics in Southern Rhodesia*. Oxford: Clarendon Press.

Loewenson, Rene, 1992. *Modern Plantation Agriculture*. London: Zed Books.

Mamdani, Mahmood, 1996. *Citizen and Subject: Contemporary Africa and the Legacy of Late Colonialism*. Princeton: Princeton University Press.

Matondi, Prosper, 2001. 'The Struggle for Access to Land and Water Resources in Zimbabwe: The case of Shamva District'. PhD dissertation, Swedish University of Agricultural Sciences, Uppsala.

McCartney, Irene, 2000. *Children in our Midst: Voices of Farmworkers' Children*. Harare: Weaver Press and Save the Children [UK].

Moore, Donald, 1999. 'The Crucible of Cultural Politics: Reworking 'Development' in Zimbabwe's Eastern Highlands'. *American Ethnologist*, Vol. 26, No. 3, pp. 654-89.

Moyo, Sam, Blair Rutherford and Dede Amanor-Wilks, 2000. 'Land Reform and Changing Social Relations for Farm Workers in Zimbabwe'. *Review of African Political Economy*, Vol. 84, pp.181-202.

Mugwetsi, Thokozani, and Peter Balleis, 1994. *The Forgotten People: The Living and Health Conditions of Farm Workers and their Families*. Gweru: Mambo Press, with Silveira House.

Nyambara, Pius, 2001. 'The Closing Frontier: Agrarian Change, Immigrants and the "Squatter Menace" in Gokwe, 1980-1990s'. *Journal of Agrarian Change*. Vol. 4, No. 1, pp. 534-49.

Palmer, Robin, 1977. *Land and Racial Domination in Rhodesia*. London: Heinemann.

Phimister, Ian, 1988. *An Economic and Social History of Zimbabwe, 1890-1948: Capital Accumulation and Class Struggle*. London: Longman.

Ranger, Terence, 1985. *Peasant Consciousness and Guerrilla War in Zimbabwe*. London: James Currey.

Rubert, Steven, 1998. *A Most Promising Weed: A History of Tobacco Farming and Labor in Colonial Zimbabwe, 1890-1945*. Athens, OH: Ohio University Center for International Studies.

Rutherford, Blair, 1997. 'Another Side to Rural Zimbabwe: Social Constructs and the Administration of Farm Workers in Urungwe District, 1940s'. *Journal of Southern African Studies*, Vol. 23, No. 1, pp. 107-26.

Rutherford, Blair, 1999. 'To Find an African Witch: Anthropology, Modernity, and Witch-Finding in North-West Zimbabwe'. *Critique of Anthropology*, Vol. 19, No. 1, pp. 105-25.

Rutherford, Blair, 2001a. *Working on the Margins: Black Workers, White Farmers in Postcolonial Zimbabwe*. London: Zed Books, and Harare: Weaver Press.

Rutherford, Blair, 2001b. 'Commercial Farm Workers and the Politics of (Dis)Placement in Zimbabwe: Liberation, Colonialism, and Democracy'. *Journal of Agrarian Change*, Vol. 1, No. 4, pp. 626-51.

Rutherford, Blair, 2001c. 'Farm Workers and Trade Unions in Hurungwe District in post-colonial Zimbabwe'. In Brian Raftopoulos and Lloyd Sachikonye (eds), *Striking Back: The Labour Movement and the Post-Colonial State in Zimbabwe, 1980-2000*. Harare: Weaver Press.

Rutherford, Blair, 2001d. 'To be or not to be a settler, or, on becoming Zimbabwean: Politics, Memory, and the Anthropology of Commercial Farms in Zimbabwe'. Unpublished ms.

SC, 2000. *We Learn with Hope: Issues in Education on Commercial Farms in Zimbabwe*. Harare: Save the Children [UK].

SC and FCTZ, 2001. 'Rapid Household Economy Assessment. Chihwiti and Gambuli Informal Settlements. Makonde District, Mashonaland West Zimbabwe. September 25th - 28th, 2001'. Harare: Save the Children [UK] and Farm Community Trust of Zimbabwe.

Sylvester, Christine, 2000. *Producing Women and Progress in Zimbabwe: Narratives of Identity and Work from the 1980s*. Portsmouth, NH: Heinemann.

Tsing, Anna, 2000. 'Inside the Economy of Appearances'. *Public Culture*, Vol. 12, No. 1, pp. 115-44.

Turino, Thomas, 2000. *Nationalists, Cosmopolitans, and Popular Music in Zimbabwe*. Chicago: University of Chicago Press.

Vhurumuku, Elliot, Mark McGuire and Vicki Hill, 1999. 'Survey of Commercial Farmworker Characteristics and Living Conditions in Zimbabwe: Verification Report'. Harare: Agricultural Labour Bureau, Farm Community Trust of Zimbabwe, USAID Famine Early Warning Project.

Worby, Eric, 1998. 'Tyranny, Parody, and Ethnic Polarity: Ritual Engagements with the State in Northwestern Zimbabwe'. *Journal of Southern African Studies*, Vol. 24, No. 3. pp. 561-78.

Worby, Eric, 2000. '"Discipline Without Oppression": Sequence, Timing and Marginality in Southern Rhodesia's Post-War Development Regime'. *Journal of African History*, Vol. 41, No. 1, pp. 101-25.

ZHRNGO Forum, 2001. *Who Was Responsible? Alleged Perpetrators and their Crimes during the 2000 Parliamentary Election Period*. Harare: Zimbabwe Human Rights NGO Forum.

Chapter 7

The State in Crisis
Authoritarian Nationalism, Selective Citizenship and Distortions of Democracy in Zimbabwe

Brian Raftopoulos

As the general crisis in Zimbabwe has deepened, the authoritarian project of the state has become more transparent. The ruling party, Zanu (PF), has articulated this crisis on the terrain of the land question, but has done so through a selective rendition of the legacy of this problem, and in a manner that has produced a series of rhetorical evasions and a growing politics of repression. This has become manifest in several ways. Firstly, the 2000 general election slogan of Zanu (PF), 'The Land is the Economy, the Economy is the Land', sought to narrow the framework of legitimate national interventions, by focusing on the land question as the sole legacy of the demands of the liberation struggle. Moreover the articulation of this problem entailed a flattening of the issues through an essentialised racial discourse which, it soon became apparent, included a series of other exclusions, such as farm workers, urban workers 'without totems', women, and members of the political opposition. This totalising political slogan thus sought to consolidate a core rural electorate, considered the timeless political prerogative of the ruling party, through a violent project of marginalising dissenting groups. However as historians have reminded us, while the land issue was a central factor in the liberation struggle, and remains a major concern for the majority, Zimbabwean nationalism was also a 'human rights movement and a movement for the restoration of dignity' (Bhebe and Ranger, 2001). Wilfred Mhanda, leader of the Zimbabwe Liberators Platform, and former commander of the Zimbabwe People's Army during the liberation struggle, made a similar point at a conference on the 'Crisis in Zimbabwe' held in

Harare in early September, 2001. He stated that the 'liberation struggle was driven by political, economic, social and cultural demands,' and that 'land redistribution was just one of the key economic demands.' A programme of violent land occupations, sanctioned by the ruling party, that abrogates other issues around political and civic rights, is at odds with an important part of the nationalist legacy. Even during the difficulties of the liberation war itself, when violence and coercion formed a central part of nationalist mobilisation, rural communities attempted to impose a moral economy of controls over the activities of the liberation forces, through traditional leaders and long existing party structures (Alexander et al., 2000).

Secondly, as a result of this particular articulation of 'the land question', a devastating rupture has developed in Zimbabwean political discourse, between redistribution and rights issues. As the ruling party has pushed its particular version of redistribution through a section of the war veterans' movement, it has demonised human rights issues as a minority concern, driven by Western-backed opposition forces. As Jonathan Moyo, Zanu (PF)'s leading ideologue, has written:

> The human rights NGOs supporting the MDC under the guise of the NCA, such as David Coltart's Legal Resources Foundation, and Mike Auret's Catholic Commission for Justice and Peace, are well known for using equal political and civil rights to justify unequal economic rights. And that is what the British want to see in Zimbabwe: a spectacle of getting the black majority to use political rights to defend unequal rights between blacks and whites under the guise of democracy.[1]

Through such rhetoric the ruling party has regularly damaged the potentially fruitful dialogue that should ensue between rights and redistribution concerns, insisting on a facile association of the former with a roster of 'others' perceived as outside the authentic national community. Through this same manoeuvre this discourse has driven

---

[1] Jonathan Moyo, 'Observers' impartiality in doubt.' *Sunday Mail*, 11 June 2000. In the *Zimbabwe Mirror*, a paper close to the ruling party, The Scrutator column made a similar assertion; '... one of the tragedies of post-independent Zimbabwe is that we have almost de-politicised a whole new generation away from the reality of imperialism and neo-colonialism, to the abstract notions of "democracy" and "human rights."' ('Towards Election Forecast', 16-22 June 2000.) This rupture can be seen in the opposition Movement for Democratic Change as well. Munyaradzi Gwisai, the Trotskyite MP for Highfield, in his support of the war veterans' factory invasions in May 2001 declared: 'Rule of Law haiuisi sadza. (People do not eat the rule of law.)' *Sunday Mail*, 6 May 2001.

a wedge between the civic movements and the official legacy of the liberation struggle. Mamdani (1998, 1990) has warned of the ways in which rights-talk can indeed sound like 'a defence of settler privilege' in the face of a continued denial of justice for a 'native majority', leading to conditions of 'unaddressed social grievance that could be harvested by a demagogue' like Idi Amin. Similarly Kanyongolo (2001) argues that the 'rhetoric of human rights ... incorporates individualisation and judicialisation as integral aspects of the promotion, protection and enforcement of human rights uncritically, without addressing the fundamental problems that affect these aspects.' While keeping in mind such concerns, a substantive and lasting redistributive programme cannot be achieved without a broad-based democratisation of existing post-colonial polities. As Channock (2000) has written, 'the most important lesson to learn is to doubt radically the often repeated mantra that economic and social rights must be achieved before civil and political ones.' It is with such scepticism that analysts need to approach the anti-imperialist rhetoric that has served as Mugabe's master narrative in confronting the growing criticisms of his regime. For behind the calls for an indigenisation project and cultural authenticity, the anti-imperialist invocations have served to essentialise foreign enemies, and police domestic discontent. The very real need to confront global foes has, in Mugabe's terms, become inextricably bound to the violent marginalisation of internal dissent.

Thirdly, the authoritarianism of the ruling party has been expressed in the assault on central and local government structures, as a precondition for the re-assertion of Zanu (PF) political dominance.[2] The deployment of war veterans against all forms of opposition to state structures, has resulted in the creation of political disorder which serves to reposition a state facing a deepening crisis of legitimacy.[3] Such a mobilisation, in particular at local government level, has plugged into long-standing grievances over the lack of transparency of state structures (McGregor, 2002).

The major objective of this chapter is to trace the emergence of these trends over the first two decades of Zimbabwean independence, by focusing on the economic, political and ideological developments over this period. It will analyse the ways in which a formerly strong nationalist party, with a broad political mandate derived from a liberation struggle, had to confront a growing loss of legitimacy and face the possibility of electoral defeat in parliamentary (2000),

---

[2] See Hammar, this volume.
[3] For a discussion of this process, see Chabal and Daloz (1999).

presidential (2002) and local government (2002) elections. Significantly the contestations of this period have not only produced debates about the present and future trends of Zimbabwean politics, but have generated a flourishing debate about the past against an historical orthodoxy that became, in Terence Ranger's (2001) words, 'dominant and at the same time....stifling.' As we will see in this chapter, Zanu (PF)'s renewed interest in teaching party history to the youth is an attempt to capture and contain more plural visions.

The 1980s: Years of hope, intimations of disaster

At Independence in 1980 the new Zimbabwean Government embarked on the vision of 'national reconciliation'. In economic terms this policy sought to combine a continuity of production structures with policies to improve the conditions of the majority of the population neglected during the colonial period.[4] Confronted with the dilemma of a large support base seeking immediate redress of long-established inequalities, the state aimed for a policy of high economic growth rates, increased incomes and social expenditures, and the promotion of rural development. The first Minister of Economic Planning and Development stated that 'our policy strategy goes beyond the mere increase in the material wealth of society. Equity in the distribution of wealth and income is one of the cornerstones of our economic policy' (Chidzero, 1981). The broad objectives of the initial 'Growth with Equity Strategy' were defined as:
- The establishment of a socialist society.
- Rapid economic growth.
- Balanced development and equitable distribution of income and productive resources.
- Economic restructuring.
- Development of human resources.
- Rural development.
- Worker participation.
- Development of economic infrastructure and social services.
- Fiscal and monetary reform.

Following the 'Growth with Equity' strategy, the government launched the 'Transitional National Development Plan', which set out to bring substantive form to the objectives set out in the former document. What followed for much of the 1980s was an impressive expansion in social services, as the state stretched its resources to achieve a

---

[4] This economic discussion draws heavily on Raftopoulos (2001).

rapid delivery of benefits to a highly expectant constituency. This emphasis in policy underlined the state's concerns with equity in the social sectors, and the use of aid funds to facilitate this process.

The approach to the land question during this period, and indeed until 1997, was based on a slow and cautious market-based strategy. As Sam Moyo (2001:13) has described the policy:

> Land was purchased by the state for redistribution following willing-buyer-willing-seller procedures. This framework was agreed to at Lancaster House. The private sector led the identification and supply of land available for resettlement, while central government was a reactive buyer choosing land on offer. The Government provided land to beneficiaries selected mainly by its district officials under the direct supervision of central government officials.

In addition to this legal process of land acquisition, the 1980s also witnessed low-intensity land occupations, carried out by various communities, sometimes unofficially supported by party officials. However, for the most part the ruling party officially opposed such processes of self-provisioning, preferring to follow the legal, market-driven process (Moyo, 1995; Mtisi, 2001; Nyambaya, 2001). Indeed Prime Minister Robert Mugabe told 'squatters' in 1985:

> If we were to ask your forefathers whether they lived in the same area as their ancestors' graves, the answer would be in the negative. Now that we are buying farms to resettle people, who will stay there if you want to protect ancestors graves? Of course we must protect our ancestors' graves but we must stay on arable land where we can be productive. [5]

Using the willing-buyer, willing-seller process, some 3m hectares of land was acquired by the end of the 1980s for redistribution. Recent research on resettlement programmes begun during this period (Kinsey,1999) indicates that many positive developments resulted in the areas concerned, with settlers being provided with facilities such as potable water supplies, dip tanks, clinics, schools, improved toilets, housing loans, roads and marketing depots. In addition communities in these schemes benefited from reduced cases of alcoholism, decreased domestic violence, and reduced rates of suicide. Thus while the process was certainly slower than many expected, and experienced problems of implementation and funding, it produced many positive and sustainable results. In the post-2000

---

[5] *The Herald*, 28 August 1985, quoted in Mtisi (2001).

environment of a highly politicised fast-track programme, these developments need to be remembered.

In the field of labour relations the state took several policy measures to protect workers, as in the form of legislation such as the Minimum Wages Legislation Act 1980, and the Employment Act of the same year. In 1985 the Government also passed the Labour Relations Act, which gave greater recognition to workers' rights to trade unions. Nevertheless the Act also concentrated a great deal of control in the hands of the Minister of Labour, similar to the controls that characterised the Minister's role under the colonial Industrial Conciliation Act which preceded the new legislation. The persistence of such controls indicated the new government's concern with consolidating the power of the state in these early years.[6] While such policies provided some protection for workers in the 1980s, the longer term effects on income and employment levels were largely negative. Thus although real wages increased in mining, industry and commerce from 1980-82, thereafter they either declined or remained static for much of the 1980s. In the lowest wage sectors of agriculture and domestic workers, wages increased for much of the 1980s. With regard to employment, growth levels averaged a low 1.7 per cent between 1980 and 1989 (Shadur, 1994; Sibanda, 1997).

In economic terms the 1980s could therefore be characterised by a mixture of welfarist social expenditure, slow land reform, attempts at minimum wage regulation, and limited economic growth. The hope that growth would provide a trickle down effect for redistribution to the poorest proved forlorn by the end of the decade, sowing doubts about the development strategy being pursued. Given the dramatic collapse of existing socialist regimes at the end of the 1980s, and the expansive orthodoxy of economic neo-liberalism, there was growing global systemic pressure for the Zimbabwean government to move towards a structural adjustment programme. However, domestic business and state elite interests, in pursuit of more avenues of accumulation, also drove this shift in the development model.[7]

In the political field 1980 witnessed the victory of an uneasy alliance of the two major nationalist parties in the country. Their popular support, as a result of their respective roles in the liberation struggle, ensured them a strong legitimacy in the immediate post-colonial years. However the ruling party still had to establish control

---

[6] For a discussion of these issues see Sachikonye (1986) and Schiphorst (2001).
[7] For a discussion of both these trends, see Bond (1998) and Dashwood (2000).

over the state, and over those sections of the population where its support base was weak. Within the first five years of independence the new government Africanised the state (Raftopoulos, 1986:275-317), and began the process of creating a national army. This was a considerable achievement, taking place as it did in the shadow of a hostile apartheid state. At local government level the 1985 legislation in this area, which established provincial governors, was geared towards expanding the political embrace of the new state, and 'ensuring the perpetuation and dominance' of Zanu (PF) as the monopoly political force in the country (Makumbe, 1996, 1998). Part of this process of extending the presence of the state, included at this stage the marginalisation of traditional authorities, as the assertive new regime sought to forge its vision of modernity on the young nation. This process in turn led to an increasing 'mobilsation of tradition' by traditional leaders, as a reaction to 'the authoritarian implementation of policies which were felt to undermine their authority under the guise of a "modernising" agenda' (Alexander,1993:131-161). In carrying out this task there was a strong element of commandism in the governing style of Zanu (PF), which reflected the often militarist style of politics of the liberation movement (Kriger,1992). This legacy emerged in the context of the struggles against a colonial regime, embedded in repressive politics, and offering few opportunities for democratic participation. Moreover the emphasis on carrying out the transfer of power was effected with little concern with the ways in which such power was exercised with regard to individual and civic rights. This style of state politics soon became apparent in many spheres of Zimbabwean life.

In the sphere of labour, the countrywide wildcat strikes of 1980-82 led to strong state intervention in the creation of a labour movement that would be subject to party control. The history of a weak and divided labour movement allowed the state to create the Zimbabwe Congress of Trade Unions, in 1981, as an arm of the ruling party (Raftopoulos and Phimister,1997; Raftopoulos and Yoshikuni,1999; Raftopoulos and Sachikonye, 2001). For much of the 1980s, workers were regularly reminded about their subordinate role to the party, and, when on strike, chastised for their ingratitude towards the liberation movement. This sentiment was encapsulated in a 1985 Ministerial statement, that combined the threat of reminding the labour movement that it was marginal in the central narrative of the liberation struggle, with the condescension of a nationalist state willing to allow labour into its post-colonial development project. At the ZCTU

Congress in July 1985, the Minister of Labour, Manpower and Social Welfare located the unions as follows:

> *Historically, the trade unions in this country, particularly in the 1960's and 1970's, have operated outside the mainstream of our political life. For example, the labour movement was not directly involved in the liberation movement. Naturally, this important situation resulted in tendencies like opportunism, economism and divisiveness as evidenced by events of the last five years in the ZCTU... Granted that the labour movement operated under extremely difficult conditions under colonialism where they were suppressed and not allowed to associate themselves with political parties; granted too, that after the 1950's there was no labour movement to talk of in the country. For that reason the party and government have strenuously worked to promote the formation, growth and development of the ZCTU.*[8]

Additionally the war veterans were active in mobilising support for the ruling party at the workplace in the early 1980s, pressuring employers to recruit war veterans, and getting involved in workers committees. During this period of fragile relations between employers and the state, businesses often adopted the strategy of employing 'politically-connected lobbyists to walk the corridors of power, to network with new authority figures, and to represent the interests of their employers. Business leaders built on the work of these lobbyists to forge their own links with the new civil servants and politicians' (Dean, 2001:2-3). This approach was apparent until the mid-1980s when the reformed structures of industrial relations began to assert their force, and the government settled into a slower economic reconstruction programme.

The dominance of Zanu (PF) could also be seen in its influence over women's organisations, the student movement, and other civic groups. NGOs adopted a low-profile complementary approach to the state, seeking to assist the social welfare policies of the government. The authority of the ruling party went largely unquestioned, as the majority of organisations in the country fell in line behind the developmentalist discourse of the state (Moyo et al., 2000; Raftopoulos, 2000). If there were criticisms they were, for the most part muted, and few sought to challenge the message of national unity that was evoked at every stage. The emphasis on nation-building, across racial and ethnic boundaries, found few overt adversaries in the fragile

---

[8] Speech by the Minister of Labour, Manpower Planning and Social Welfare at the ZCTU Congress, 27-28 July 1985.

early years of independence. At this juncture Zanu (PF) had an immense reserve of ideological capital at its disposal, a luxury that would begin to dissipate by the end of the 1980s.

However, the veneer of national unity was soon torn asunder in the crisis that developed in Matabeleland in the mid-1980s. The unity between the two major liberation movements, ZANU and ZAPU, forged in the late 1970s under the Patriotic Front, had been based largely on the strategic requirements of negotiations for a political settlement. The tensions that existed between the two movements remained under the united front, and were heightened after the Zanu (PF) election victory in 1980. The immediate causes of the outbreak of violence between the 'dissidents' and government forces was a 'distrust within, and then repression by, the newly formed Zimbabwe National Army' (Alexander, 2000:181). The horrendous response of the state to the crisis has marked the post-colonial history of Zimbabwe in ways that have yet to be confronted, resulting in a lasting cleavage around selective citizenship. Moreover the immunity given to the perpetrators of this violence resembled the actions, in particular during the Internal Settlement period 1978-79, which saw the intensified militarisation of violence and politics in Zimbabwe (CCJP/LRF, 1997; Ndlovu-Gatsheni, 2001).

The Unity Agreement brokered between Zanu (PF) and PF Zapu in 1997 stopped the violence, but ushered in a significant increase in the powers of the executive in the form of the Constitution of Zimbabwe Amendment Act Number 7. The latter effectively weakened and marginalised the legislature, and placed an increasing emphasis on the role of the judiciary in constraining executive intolerance. Added to this were the uneven conditions provided by the state provisions on electoral arrangements. These included the lack of an independent Electoral Supervisory Commission, the monopoly of the electronic media by the ruling party, the abuse of state funding and resources by the ruling party for electoral purposes, state led violence against opposition forces, and irregularities in voter registration and the voters roll. The disparity between the *de jure* rights and freedoms enshrined in the constitution, and the *de facto* political rules developed by the state, have provided opposition parties and civic groups opposing the ruling party, with important openings for contesting Zanu (PF) domination (Makumbe and Compagnon, 2000; Nordlund, 1996). Hence the battles in the courts over the abuse of executive power, and the uneven playing field provided by the electoral laws, became an important battleground for civil society groups, especially in the 1990s.

By the late 1980s the growing intolerance of the state became manifest also in the move towards a one-party state, and the growing corruption of a ruling elite that displayed little regard for deepening structures of accountability. The Willowgate Scandal in 1988 and the executive pardoning of its perpetrators was indicative of these trends, and of the use of the state for a process of 'class formation behind closed doors' (Raftopoulos, 1997; Raftopoulos and Compagnon, 2003). In opposition to these developments dissenting voices began to emerge in the country in the form of student protests and a restructured labour movement with a strong leadership. In addition an opposition party, the Zimbabwe Unity Movement (ZUM), was formed as a result of challenges within the leadership of Zanu (PF). Despite its short history the ZUM performed well in the 1990 election capturing 17 per cent of the total vote and 26 per cent of the urban vote. Moreover in the presidential election Tekere won 16 percent of the votes cast (Makumbe and Compagnon, 2000). However, the most significant of these developments was the emergence of a revitalised labour movement, which from the mid-1980s, developed a more critical and autonomous position towards the state and began to expand its critique of the latter from strictly economic concern to broader issues of political accountability. Additionally the trade unions set out to nurture political alliances with other social groups, such as students, in a process of building a larger consensus around the need for greater state accountability. Thus the first decade of independence ended with growing economic problems, an embryonic opposition movement, and signs of serious fractures in the notion of national unity imposed by Zanu (PF).

The 1990s: Economic liberalisation and political challenge

It was clear by the late 1980s that the government's impressive policies on the expansion of social expenditures were being implemented on the basis of a shrinking economic base. Employment levels were low, growing at only 2.5 per cent from 1985-90, and the prospects for new investment were not encouraging. In a global context in which economic liberalisation was the established orthodoxy, and the international institutions the determining agencies for financial support, the state adopted the Economic Structural Adjustment Programme (ESAP). Over the decade of the 1990s, the effects of this programme on the majority of the population were largely negative, adding to the further marginalisation of a large number of the citizenry. Employment growth decreased from 2.5 per cent during 1985-90 to

1.5 per cent in the years 1996-99. Different sources on wage levels indicate sharp declines. The ZCTU point to a drop in real wages from an index of 122 in 1982 to 80.7 in 1999, while a leading annual earnings survey indicates that the average income in 2000 was 19 per cent lower than in 1980 (Kanyenze, 2001; Price Waterhouse Coopers, 2000). Estimates of the levels of those considered poor have increased from 62 per cent in 1995 to 75 per cent in 2000. Looking at the distribution of the Gross Domestic Income, while the proportion going to wages decreased from 54 per cent in 1987 to 39 per cent in 1999, the percentage share of profits increased from 47 to 61 during the same period (ibid). When one adds to these indicators the deteriorating social services in the country, it is clear that the deregulation of the economy has shown few positive benefits for the majority of Zimbabweans.[9]

The escalating economic crisis during this period predictably provided conditions for dramatic development in the political sphere. Within the ruling party, internal fissures became more apparent as a number of party cadres, frustrated by the lack of accountability of party structures, pursued their political fortunes as 'Independents'. In the election process the courts became a central arena for settling irregular procedures, casting a growing shadow over the fairness of the existing election regulations. The case of Margaret Dongo in Harare South in 1995 was a significant development in this struggle. Dongo, an ex-combatant from the ruling party, challenged Zanu (PF) in an urban constituency, and after a legal battle over irregular election procedures won the seat as an Independent. This victory was an important signal of the growing urban disenchantment with the ruling party. Nevertheless, Dongo's victory also underlined the limitations of various small opposition parties that had a limited membership, and provided little sense of a general political alternative to Zanu (PF).

Under the ESAP labour regime, the decline of workers' incomes resulted in intensified strike actions that were characterised by several features: the involvement of increasing numbers of workers; more nationwide actions; the inclusion of more sectors; more regular recourse to strike action as a tool in the collective bargaining process; recurring actions over unresolved grievances; and the growing militancy of public sector workers (Saunders, 2001). The national public sector strike in 1996, in particular, strengthened the links between the ZCTU and the public sector unions, and shook the

---

[9] At the same time, this process has facilitated increased accumulation among a narrow sector consisting of political, bureaucratic and business elites, thus deepening differentiation.

confidence of the state. The general strike and the mass stay-aways of 1998 established the potential effectiveness of labour as a social movement for change, signalling the escalating momentum for change in the country.

However, it was the skill of the labour movement in developing a broad social front against the government, which showed the effective changes that had taken place in the leadership of the ZCTU. A central figure in these changes was Morgan Tsvangirai, a former clerk in the mining industry and one-time political commissar of Zanu (PF), who epitomised the new challenging voice of labour. Tsvangirai led a group of unionists who spearheaded the deepening of shop-floor structures, the extended training of union members, and the strengthening of the policy content of ZCTU interventions. As the economic crisis in the country spread, the labour movement skilfully articulated the linkages between this crisis and the problems of governance. Taking this linkage further, the ZCTU played a central role in the formation of the National Constitutional Assembly (NCA) in 1997, which has as its major objective the reform of the national constitution. Through this process the ZCTU developed a strong alliance with a wide range of civic groups around issues of democratisation and human rights, a terrain increasingly abandoned by Zanu (PF). The campaign around constitutional reform became a dominant feature of Zimbabwean politics in the late 1990s. The NCA developed a successful mass campaign, and triggered a process of discussion on reform within the ruling party itself, forcing the government to establish a Constitutional Commission in 1999.

The cumulative effect of this alliance between the ZCTU and other civic groups was the build-up of pressure for the creation of an opposition party. In addition to its role in the NCA, the ZCTU organised the National Working People's Convention in February 1999, which was attended by some 1,000 delegates from both rural and urban organisations, to discuss the emerging Zimbabwean crisis and chart a way forward. One of the recommendations from the Convention was that the labour movement should facilitate the formation of a new party. The result of this process was the birth of the Movement for Democratic Change (MDC) in September 1999. In the space of two decades the labour movement had moved from a weak and divided organisation, under the shadow of a dominant nationalist party, to the facilitator of a broad opposition alliance that was challenging for state power.[10]

---

[10] For a more detailed discussion of these issues see Raftopoulos (2001); Raftopoulos and Mazarire (2002).

Parallel to these developments the ruling party faced an even more convulsive challenge from within its own ranks. The war veterans, who had formed a lobbying association in 1992, challenged the authority of the ruling party and President in 1997, by demanding gratuities for their role in the liberation struggle. The veterans have been a key factor in Zanu (PF) politics, having since 1980 played a significant role in mobilising support for the ruling party, often through coercive means. A recent analysis of the role of the veterans summarises their interventions as follows:

> Since Independence the dynamics between war veterans and the ruling party have been remarkably consistent. Their relationship has been characterised by collaboration, conflict and accommodation. Veterans and the party have used each other to pursue their different, though often overlapping, objectives. The party has used veterans to build its power and legitimacy. It has sanctioned and encouraged veterans' violence against its opponents and rewarded them for work well done. It has invoked its role in the liberation struggle to justify its use of veterans and its objectives. Veterans have used their allegedly superior contribution to the liberation struggle to justify their claims for preferential access to state resources – jobs, promotions, pensions, land. In trying to enforce their demands, they have often used violence and intimidation against competitors for resources, as well as party leaders and bureaucrats whom they believed were blocking their progress. (Kriger, 2001:81)

Their challenge to President Mugabe in 1997, in the midst of the growing crisis of legitimacy of Zanu (PF), presented a crucial moment for his survival. The President's decision to give in to the demands of the veterans for a Z$50,000 payment each, saved the President's position but created a host of other problems for Zimbabwe. In political terms the President's decision confirmed the centrality of commandist politics in the policy-making process, effectively marginalising more democratic participation by a broader range of civic groups. The decision also made it clear that as the party's support base eroded, the President would become increasingly reliant on violent means of mobilisation.

In addition to the demands of the veterans, the ruling party also faced increasing pressures from indigenisation groups, such as the Indigenous Business Development Centre (IBDC) and the Affirmative Action Group (AAG) formed in the 1990s, that lobbied for more direct state intervention to assist black entrepreneurs. Confronted by the war veterans, impatient black business groups, and the long-standing pressures for land reform, the government clearly faced a broad range of demands for economic redress. The move towards more direct state acquisition of land in 1997, and part of the rationale for entry into the DRC conflict in 1998 in search of new sources of income, was directly related to the deepening accumulation crisis in the Zimbabwean economy. As the 1990s drew to a close, the political scene was marked both by signs of a strong emergent opposition, and the menacing presence of a coercive ruling party structure being used to re-establish the position of a weakening executive.

2000 and beyond

In many respects the year 2000 constituted an important juncture of political events. The government presented its draft constitution, opposed by the NCA, in the hope of pushing through its preferred reforms. The draft was rejected in a referendum in February 2000, and with it the government's hope of taming a process that had escaped its controls. At one level the government's defeat was a result of the manner in which it ignored important views from its outreach programme, and which were also voiced by the NCA. In particular this related to the excessive powers of the executive. More generally the rejection was a vote of disillusion with the government. Notwithstanding the government's attempt to use the constitution to push its particular land agenda, the No vote represented the first major political defeat for the ruling party since 1980. More ominously for Zanu (PF), the defeat threatened to be translated into a general election victory for the MDC in anticipation of the parliamentary elections in June 2000.

The response of the ruling party was to launch a new offensive on the land issue, led by the war veterans. The President and other party leaders blamed the referendum defeat on the white minority and the West, and promised political retaliation in a volatile, racially cast political discourse. Mugabe urged his party to 'continue to strike fear in the heart of the white man, they must tremble.'[11] 'The white man,' he continued, 'is not indigenous to Africa. Africa is for Africans.'[12] Other groups singled out for their 'betrayal' were civil servants, sections of the black middle class, and urban residents of

---

[11] 'Mugabe attacks whites – again.' *Daily News*, 15 December 2000.
[12] Ibid.

foreign ancestry.[13] The thrust of the attacks was delivered in an anti-imperialist trope that identified internal opposition forces as unpatriotic 'enemies of the state', and therefore beyond the pale of the rule of law. Furthermore the attacks sought to justify the denigration of civic and political rights as minority concerns, in the name of a selective articulation of redistributive issues around the land question. In a further rhetorical move, Mugabe claimed the authority of his message by projecting his constituency as a unified black subject at regional, Pan African and trans-continental levels. In the latter context Andrew Young, drawing on his historical ties with the liberation movement and in his present role as hired gun for the Mugabe regime in Washington, has played a strategic role in attempting to connect the politics of the land struggle in Zimbabwe with a particular interpretation of African-American struggles in the US. The connections of the 'Black Atlantic'[14] have been drawn upon at a time when the policies of a reactionary Republican president make such linkages a credible and important part of the critique of globalisation. However, amidst the dull repetition of the political requirements of a fixed black identity, that proliferates in the government-controlled media in Zimbabwe, it is important to assert the diversity of the experiences which constitute the category 'black'. Moreover these 'cannot be grounded in a set of fixed transcultural or transcendental racial categories' (Hall, 1996:443).

The political agency that formed the modality for Mugabe's ideological attacks was the series of land seizures, led by the war veterans, that were launched soon after the 2000 constitutional referendum. As various studies have pointed out, such occupations have occurred at various intervals over the last twenty years, and have revolved around different issues in particular land zones. However the combination of intensified marginalisation of the landless under neo-liberal land policies, and the prospect of electoral defeat of Zanu (PF), set the stage for the latest display of land occupations since 2000 (Moyo, 2000; Marongwe, 2000). The feature that has most characterised the recent occupations has been the use of widespread violence. Moreover the complicity of the ruling party, state officials, and organs of the state such as the police, army and the CIO, has been an important component of this process, as Zanu (PF) has reinserted itself into rural structures (Zimbabwe Human Rights Forum, 2000, 2001).

---

[13] 'Civil servants accused of betrayal.' *Financial Gazette*, 4-10 May 2000; 'Mugabe attacks suburban blacks for selling out.' *Daily News*, 4 May 2000; 'War Vets halt learning at 250 schools.' *Financial Gazette*, 25-31 May 2000.

[14] Gilroy (1993) provides a subtle analysis of the ambiguities of this tradition.

The effect of the occupations was to connect at certain points with popular grievances around land reform, but in ways that removed the process from the arena of broader public accountability, and consolidated Zanu (PF)'s waning support through violence. This lack of a transparent process of redistribution has resulted in the denial of community involvement in decision-making processes, and the neglect of key groups in the population such as large sections of women and farm workers (Women and Land Lobby Group, 2001; FCTZ, 2001; Rutherford, 2001). The occupations and the violence continued up to the general elections in June 2000, intensifying around the presidential and council elections in 2002, and remain a central feature of the political terrain in Zimbabwe, serving to either weaken or destroy opposition party structures in the rural areas. In addition to the worst election violence in Zimbabwe's history, opposition politicians and their supporters have faced death, violence, harassment and prosecution under the Law and Order Maintenance Act, a key instrument of oppression during the colonial period. Despite these levels of intimidation, the opposition MDC won a significant 57 against the 62 seats of Zanu (PF) seats in the 2000 parliamentary election, the legitimacy of which continues to be questioned in the courts.

The weakness of state legitimacy has become manifest also in Zanu (PF)'s attacks on its own state structures, state officials and laws. A sustained campaign against the judiciary led, in 2001, to the resignation of the Chief Justice and two High Court judges. Pursuant to this were the factory invasions led by the Zanu (PF)-sponsored Zimbabwe Federation of Trade Unions (ZFTU), and supported by a 'Labour Committee' of senior party officials and war veterans. These occupations contravened the Labour Relations Act and abandoned the established industrial relations machinery in order to secure perceived quick victories amongst urban workers, and in so doing undermine the trade union base of the MDC. In rural districts, teachers, health workers and local government officials have been unceremoniously relieved of their duties. This attack on the local state has plugged into long-standing grievances around the lack of financial capacity, maladministration and corruption of local authorities, thus giving the actions 'the appearance of a broader appeal' (McGregor, 2002). The result has been that the ruling party has gained greater control at district and provincial levels, with the Provincial Governor becoming increasingly involved in everyday administration and the Provincial Administrators and District Administrators more subject to party structures (ibid).

However, the process has threatened to undermine the institutional structures at local levels, thus weakening the capacity for public sector professionalism, and expanding the possibilities of decentralised violence. Indeed this strategy has caused consternation amongst certain party leaders who fear loss of control to more anarchic elements. Thus the national party chairman, John Nkomo, warned in January 2001 of 'an element of insolence and indiscipline by some war veterans,' reminding the latter that 'first and foremost the party comes first.'[15]

In the area of the media, the new Broadcasting Services Act (No.3 of 2001), fast-tracked through parliament in April 2001, is geared towards the control of alternative opinions in the electronic media, particularly through the radio which is the dominant source of information for the rural population. The banning of the National Development Association's sponsored programme, 'Talk to the Nation', emphasised the Government's intolerance even towards a sympathetic organisation. The words of the ZBC official justifying the withdrawal of the programme exemplify the lack of a sense of irony of authoritarian regimes:

> *It is not all about money. Live productions can be tricky and dangerous. The setting on the NDA productions was professionally done but maybe the production should not have been broadcast live. You do not know what someone will come and say and there is no way of controlling it.*[16]

The government has also introduced legislation to control foreign funding of political parties and is considering further controls on NGOs by stopping their involvement in civic education. Both these measures are designed to proscribe the viability of opposition forces. Combined with these measures, Zanu (PF) has established alternative civic bodies to rival those organisations that have been critical of the state. Examples of this strategy can be seen in the following sectors: In the student movement, the Zimbabwe Progressive Students Union (ZPSU) and the Zimbabwe Congress of Students (ZICOSU) have been established to counter the Zimbabwe National Students Union (ZINASU), while amongst trade unions the ZCTU has been confronted by the ZFTU. Similar developments have taken place with organisations dealing with constitutional reform, and with residents' organisations. The defining feature of these measures is that they were designed to push centres of dissent to the margins

---

[15] *Zimbabwe Independent*, 19 January 2001.
[16] 'ZBC switches off NDA-sponsored live TV programme.' *The Herald*, 6 June 2001.

of political debate, and create more conducive conditions for a party victory in the 2002 Presidential elections. For most of the independence years, Zanu (PF) was prepared to tolerate a minimum of electoral competition, and the existence of civic bodies that complemented the delivery service of the state, so long as its single party dominance was not threatened. When this situation no longer prevailed and the possibility of political defeat became more apparent, the governing elite lost its façade of tolerance and unleashed its repressive party and state machinery.

These developments have left Zanu (PF) in dire need of complementing its strategy of violence with a more long-term capacity to sustain enlarged constituencies of support. Aside from consolidating its support amongst the war veterans, and the coercive arms of the state, the ruling party has continued its ties of patronage with indigenisation leaders, and has more recently tried to cultivate a base in the sporting and music fraternities around issues of 'cultural authenticity' and increased black representation. Amongst the youth the idea of the national youth service has been revived, to serve as a conduit for the teaching of 'patriotic values' and party discipline. In line with such initiatives, new emphasis is being given to the compulsory teaching of history up to Form Four level, in order to ensure that the history of the country is rewritten and 'accurately told' to reflect the events leading to 'the country's nationhood and sovereignty.'[17] In a preview of such history lessons a ZBC crew was reported, in July 2001, to have criss-crossed the Chimanimani district, an MDC stronghold, giving lessons about the liberation struggle to school students, with the latter being taught the 'history of the liberation war and where they were coming from.'[18] What is being offered in such 'lessons' is not just a particular narrative of liberation, but a closing down of other perspectives on the struggle, and 'other ways of imagining collectivities' (Cooper, 1999:22) not only in the past, but more importantly in the present. In this representation the 'Third Chimurenga' becomes part of an unbroken thread of resistance, in a discredited nationalist historiography.[19] History and politics are presented as coterminous, in a ratifying process that severs alternate linkages and different forms of politics.

[17] 'Compulsory history lessons.' *Daily News*, 26 July 2001.
[18] 'Zanu PF fights for turf.' *Zimbabwe Independent*, 27 July 2001
[19] Raftopoulos (1999); Campbell (2001). Campbell says about the feminist critiques of national liberation movements: 'The critiques of the liberation discourse force a richer concept of African liberation and decolonisation than the simple narrative of settler and native, citizen and subject. This discussion is seeking to break the conceptual crisis of those who seek to defend the ruling party on nationalistic grounds. This nationalism draws from the androcentric approach to militarism and questions of national liberation.'

The links between an authoritarian nationalist politics and a disciplining discourse of liberation have become clear.

Conclusion

Three points can be stressed about the political crisis in Zimbabwe. The first concerns the pervasive violence of the state. In the early 1980s the Mugabe regime used war veterans to consolidate its control of the state, and then proceeded to demobilise this force when its power base was more secure. Similarly, the state attempted to marginalise the influence of traditional authorities as it extended its power to local government level. After two decades of independence, and in the context of a massive loss of state legitimacy, there have been certain reversals in this process. The embattled regime has once again turned to the war veterans to enforce party dominance. The regime has also breached its own laws in order to maintain power. In so doing, this coercive strategy has set out to destroy those civic organisations and processes that have been critical of Zanu (PF) politics.

Secondly, it is clear that a severe break has developed between the discourse and politics of the liberation struggle – as channelled through party ideologues – and that of the civic struggles for democratisation in the post-colonial period. In part this problem can be traced back to long-standing tensions from the period of the emergence of mass nationalism in the 1950s and 1960s. However, the differences have deepened over the last decade. This friction has developed, on the one hand, in the context of a declining liberation movement that has drawn a lethal distinction between a violently driven, 'anti-imperialist' project centred on 'the land question', and the politics of human rights which it has characterised as an imposition of global imperatives. Any sense of national ownership of such rights issues is lost in this characterisation. On the other hand the civic opposition has espoused its agenda largely through the language of citizenship rights, articulated most clearly in the campaign for constitutional reform. This politics of democratisation has not, however, sufficiently negotiated its connections with, or its differences from, the legacies of the liberation struggle. The intervention of the Zimbabwe Liberators Platform has been an important attempt to make such connections.[20] The debate in Zimbabwe clearly has a broader resonance in the post-settler state politics of Southern Africa.

---

[20] For a discussion of the experiences of the Vashandi Group during the liberation war, see Moore (1990).

The third point relates to the ways in which the role of politics had been articulated in Zimbabwean politics. For a dominant faction of the ruling party, violence in the post-colonial period has been viewed as an extension of its use during the liberation struggle: a necessary means to achieve a political end. The dehumanising effects of this strategy on the citizenry have been considered part of the modality for maintaining state power. The forces of opposition have, in response, used their critique of this violence as a pivotal part of their demand for an alternative politics.[21] This critique, however, has not confronted the systemic violence that post-colonial states like Zimbabwe continue to be subjected to by the forces of global finance. This lack of a critical scope on globalisation remains a weakness of the opposition perspective. As a result, opposition groups are not sufficiently preparing for the difficult confrontations and choices that any government in a globally marginalised state will have to make in a project of economic and political reconstruction. These ambiguities in Zimbabwean politics are the terrain on which any attempts at a post-nationalist politics must be conducted.

---

[21] See Resolutions from the 'NCA All Stakeholders Conference', held on 31 March 2001; Resolutions of the conference 'Crisis in Zimbabwe: A Time to Act', held in Harare on 4 August 2001.

References

Alexander, Jocelyn, 1993. 'Things Fall Apart, The Centre Can Hold: Processes of Post-War Political Change'. In Laurid S. Lauridsen (ed.), *Bringing Institutions Back in – the Role of Institutions in Civil Society, State and Economy*. IDS, Roskilde University.

Alexander, Jocelyn, JoAnn McGregor and Terence Ranger, 2000. *Violence and Memory: One Hundred Years in the 'Dark Forests' of Matabeleland*. Oxford: James Currey.

Bhebe, Ngwabi and Terence Ranger (eds), 2001. *Historical Dimensions of Democracy in Southern Africa*, Volume 1. Harare: University of Zimbabwe Publications.

Bond, Patrick, 2000. *Uneven Zimbabwe: A Study of Finance, Development, and Underdevelopment*. Trenton, NJ: Africa World Press.

Campbell, Horace, 2001. 'The exhaustion of the patriarchal model of liberation: Lessons from Zimbabwe'. Mimeo.

CCJP/LRF, 1997. Breaking the Silence Building the Peace: A Report on the Disturbances in Matabeleland and the Midlands 1980 to 1988. Harare: Catholic Commission for Justice and Peace.

Chabal, Patrick and Jean-Pascal Daloz, 1999. *Africa Works: Disorder as Political Instrument*. Oxford: James Currey.

Channock, Martin, 2000. '"Culture" and Human rights: orientalising, occidentalising and authenticity'. In Mahmood Mamdani, 2000.

Chidzero, Bernard, 1981. 'Development Overview'. In Report on Conference Proceedings, Zimbabwe Conference on Reconstruction and Development. Harare: Government Printer.

Cooper, Frederick, 1999. 'Africa's Pasts and Africa's Historians'. *African Sociological Review* 3(2), p. 22.

Dashwood, Hevina S., 2000. *Zimbabwe: The Political Economy of Transformation*. Toronto: University of Toronto Press.

Dean, Howard, 2001. 'The Labour Wars: Invasions of Firms and Businesses – Hostage Taking as the new face of labour negotiations'. IPMZ, Labour Relations Information Service, April.

Farm Community Trust of Zimbabwe, 2001. 'The Impact of Land Reform on Commercial Farm Workers' Livelihoods'. Mimeo.

Gilroy, Paul, 1993. *The Black Atlantic: Modernity and Double Consciousness*. London: Verso.

Hall, Stuart, 1996. 'New Ethnicities'. In David Morley and Kuan-Sing Chen (eds), *Stuart Hall: Critical Dialogues in Cultural Studies*. London: Routledge.

Kanyangolo, Fidelis Edge, 2001. 'A Critique of the Rhetoric of Human Rights in Malawi'. Paper presented at the Nordic Africa Institute/SARIPS Conference on Interrogating the New Political Culture in Southern Africa, Harare, 2001.

Kanyenze, Godfrey, 2001. 'The Labour Market under Economic Reform: The Case of Zimbabwe'. Paper prepared for SAPRIN/Poverty Forum.

Kinsey, Bill H., 1999. 'Land Reform, Growth and Equity: Emerging Evidence from Zimbabwe's Resettlement Programme'. *Journal of Southern Africa Studies*, Volume 25, Number 2.

Kriger, Norma, 1992. *Zimbabwe's Guerrilla War: Peasant Voices*. Cambridge: Cambridge University Press.

Kriger, Norma, 2001. 'Zimbabwe's War Veterans and the Ruling Party: Continuities in Political Dynamics'. *Politique Africaine*, No. 81, March.

Makumbe, John Mw., 1996. *Participatory Development: The Case of Zimbabwe*. Harare: University of Zimbabwe Publications.

Makumbe, John Mw., 1998. *Democracy and Development in Zimbabwe*. Harare: SAPES.

Makumbe, John and Daniel Compagnon, 2000. *Behind the Smokescreen: The Politics of Zimbabwe's 1995 General Election*. Harare: University of Zimbabwe Publications.

Mamdani, Mahmood, 1996. *Citizen and Subject. Contemporary Africa and the Legacy of Late Colonialism*. Princeton, NJ: Princeton University Press.

Mamdani, Mahmood, 1998. 'When does a Settler Become a Native? Reflections on the Colonial Roots of Citizenship in Equatorial and South Africa'. Inaugural Lecture as A.C. Jordan Professor of African Studies, University of Cape Town, 13 May.

Mamdani, Mahmood, 2000. *Beyond Rights Talk and Culture Talk*. Cape Town: David Philip.

Mandaza, Ibbo (ed.), 1986. *Zimbabwe: The Political Economy of Transition*. Dakar: CODESRIA.

Marongwe, Nelson, 2000. *Conflicts over Land and other Natural Resources in Zimbabwe*. Harare: ZERO.

McGregor, JoAnn, 2002. 'The Politics of Disruption: War Veterans and the Local State in Zimbabwe'. *African Affairs*, 101, pp. 9-37.

Moore, David, 1990. 'The Contradictory Construction of Hegemony in Zimbabwe: Politics, Ideology and Class in the Formation of a New African State'. D.Phil. York University.

Moyo, Sam, 1995. *The Land Question in Zimbabwe*. Harare: SAPES.

Moyo, Sam, 2000. *Land Reform under Structural Adjustment in Zimbabwe*. Uppsala: Nordiska Afrikainstitutet.

Moyo, Sam, 2001, 'The Interaction of Market and Compulsory Land Acquisition Processes with Social Action in Zimbabwe's Land Reform'. Paper presented at the SARIPS Colloquium on Regional Integration: Past, Present and Future. Harare, September.

Moyo, Sam, John Makumbe and Brian Raftopoulos, 2000. *NGOs, the State and Politics in Zimbabwe*. Harare: SAPES.

Mtisi, J.P., 2001. 'Caught Between the Devil and the Deep Blue Sea: Post-Colonial State's Response to the Squatter Problem in Forest areas In Manicaland in Zimbabwe'. Paper presented at the seminar: 'History Matters: Valedictory Workshop in honour of Terence Ranger.' University of Zimbabwe, 28-29 June.

Ndlovu-Gatsheni, Sabelo J., 2001. 'Political Confusion, Militarism, Violence and the Internal Settlement, 1978-1980'. Paper presented at the seminar 'History Matters: Valedictory Conference in honour of Terence Ranger.' University of Zimbabwe, 28-29 June.

Nordlund, Per, 1996. 'Organising the Political Agora: Domination and Democratisation in Zambia and Zimbabwe'. D.Phil. thesis, Uppsala.

Nyambaya, Pius S., 2001. 'The Closing Frontier: Agrarian Change, Immigrants and the "Squatter Menace" in Gokwe villages, 1980s and 1990s'. Paper presented at the seminar: 'History Matters: Valedictory Workshop in honour of Terence Ranger.' University of Zimbabwe, 28-29 June.

Price Waterhouse Coopers, 2000. 'Earnings Survey-Zimbabwe 1980-2000'. Draft Report, December.

Raftopoulos, Brian, 1986. 'Human Resource Development and the Problem of Labour Utilisation'. In Mandaza (ed.), op cit.

Raftopoulos, Brian, 1997. 'The State, Politics and the Indigenisation Process in Zimbabwe: Class Formation Behind Closed Doors'. Paper presented at a SARIPS Seminar, Harare, September.

Raftopoulos, Brian, 1999. 'Problematising Nationalism in Zimbabwe: A Historiographical Review'. *Zambezia*, 26, (ii).

Raftopoulos, Brian, 2000. 'Civil Society, Governance and Human Development in Zimbabwe'. Background paper prepared for the Zimbabwe Human Development Report.

Raftopoulos, Brian, 2001. 'The State and Poverty Reduction Policies in Zimbabwe: 1980-1997'. In Wilson, et al., op cit.

Raftopoulos, Brian and Ian Phimister (eds), 1997. *Keep on Knocking: A History of the Labour Movement in Zimbabwe 1900-1997*. Harare: Baobab Books.

Raftopoulos, Brian and Tsumeo Yoshikuni (eds), 1999. *Sites of Struggle: Essays in Zimbabwe's Urban History*. Harare: Weaver Press.

Raftopoulos, Brian and Lloyd Sachikonye (eds), 2001. *Striking Back: The Labour Movement and the Post-Colonial State in Zimbabwe 1980-2000*. Harare: Weaver Press.

Raftopoulos, Brian and Gerald Mazarire, 2002. 'Civil Society and the Constitution-Making Process in Zimbabwe'. Mimeo.

Raftopoulos, Brian and Daniel Compagnon, 2003. 'Indigenisation, the state bourgeoisie and neo-authoritarian politics'. In Staffan Darnolf and Liisa Laakso, *Twenty Years of Independence in Zimbabwe*. London: Palgrave.

Ranger, Terence, 2001 'History Matters'. Valedictory Lecture, University of Zimbabwe, Harare, 31 May.

Rutherford, Blair, 2001.'Farm Workers and Trade Unions in Hurungwe District in Post-Colonial Zimbabwe'. In Raftopoulos and Sachikonye, op cit.

Sachikonye, Lloyd, 1986. 'State, Capital and Trade Unions'. In Ibbo Mandaza (ed.), op cit.

Saunders, Richard, 2001. 'Striking Ahead: Industrial Actions and Labour Development in Zimbabwe'. In Raftopoulos and Sachikonye, op cit.

Schiphorst, Freek B., 2001. 'Strength and Weakness: The Rise of the Zimbabwe Congress of Trade Unions (ZCTU) and the Development of Labour Relations 1980-1995'. PhD thesis, The Hague, Institute of Social Studies.

Shadur, Mark, 1994. *Labour Relations in a Developing Country: A Case Study on Zimbabwe*. Aldershot: Ashgate.

Sibanda, Godfrey and Arnold, 1997. 'The Labour Sector'. Background Paper for the Zimbabwe Human Development Report.

Wilson, Francis, Nazneen Kanji and Einar Braathen (eds), 2001. *Poverty Reduction: What Role for the State in Today's Globalised Economy?* London: Zed Books.

Women and Land Lobby Group, 2001. 'Report on the Gender Analysis of Land Reform Documents'. Mimeo.

Zimbabwe Human Rights Forum, 2000. 'Who was Responsible? Alleged Perpetrators and their Crimes during the 2000 Parliamentary Election Period'. Harare. Mimeo.

Zimbabwe Human Rights Forum, 2001. 'Politically motivated violence in Zimbabwe 2000-2001: A Report on the campaign of political repression conducted by the Zimbabwean Government under the guise of carrying out land reform'. Harare. Mimeo.

Chapter 8

Land, Growth and Governance: Tenure Reform and Visions of Progress in Zimbabwe

Mandivamba Rukuni and Stig Jensen

Zimbabwe is experiencing a combination of crises that is affecting all its own citizens as well as millions of others in the region. Initially, when Zimbabwe's sharp political and economic decline began in early 2000, it was suggested that the country was facing a land crisis. However, developments since early 2000 have made it increasingly clear that there is a serious governance crisis, which in turn has precipitated a major food crisis. Hardly anyone present at the independence celebrations in 1980, or in the subsequent years of abundant agricultural production, would have imagined a Zimbabwe that today teeters on the brink of a catastrophic famine. This chapter examines some of the institutional causes underlying the precipitation of food insecurity and hunger in Zimbabwe, and proposes various changes that might reverse such a trend.

The chapter argues first and foremost that fundamental changes in land tenure institutions are needed to guide the process of state acquisition and land redistribution, and to align these processes with economic and other democratic institutions. The efficient management of natural resources, critical for food security as well as sustainable growth, is dependent on the political, legal, and administrative capabilities of both the government and the rural communities. The lack of power of rural land owners (or lack of democracy) is translated into insecure tenure rights. Tenure security, in terms of exclusive land rights for groups and individuals, is the very basis of political and social power and status. When such rights are overly subordinated to the state, it follows that the political and economic rights of rural people are diminished, and that democratic processes and institutions are undermined. Corrective measures for Zimbabwe's land reform programme should include three strategic objectives: to achieve political stability, to establish a broader base for economic growth, and to satisfy the need for social integration.

It is important to remember that land reform in general, and tenure reform in particular, cannot be isolated from other social and political processes but must rather interact with them. Therefore, various related aspects are discussed here such as the political power-plays around the land question, and agriculture's broader significance for Zimbabwe. These are vital elements for an understanding of the transformative potential of land tenure reform, alongside the modernisation of Zimbabwe's agriculture.

If wishes were horses...

If wishes were horses, Zimbabwe's land reforms over the last 20 years would have created an African paradise: a country of growing economic prosperity with high levels of employment and ever reducing levels of poverty, hunger and malnutrition; a country of peace and stability where political systems are pregnant with tolerance, wisdom and the internal ability to transform it peacefully in ways that uphold continued prosperity of a young, vibrant and diverse nation of peoples; a country whose social strengths are to be found in the diversity of its people's ethnic, racially rich cultural tapestry. Most Zimbabweans have a deep love for their country; they have dreamed of a land of prosperity, emerging from the colonial bondage of the twentieth century into a twenty-first century of physical and spiritual liberation for its peoples of all races and ethnicity.

For many Zimbabweans, independence in 1980 brought the promise of progress and freedom, whereby land reform was a prerequisite for achieving three major goals: economic growth, political stability, and social integration. Given the painful realities of today's Zimbabwe, it is ironic that the land reform programme should lie at the centre of a national crisis characterised by massive erosion of these three major goals so that, instead, the young nation is experiencing significant political instability, economic collapse, and strained racial and ethnic relations. One reason why the situation has moved in this direction is due to an intensification of conflicts associated with the politics of land.

The political landscape and the 'fast track' programme

Since the Constitutional Referendum of February 2000, widespread farm occupations, mainly in commercial farming areas and led to a large extent by militant war veterans from the national liberation struggle, have taken on a political and violent tone (see Marongwe, this volume). Events following in the wake of the Constitutional Referendum marked the start of the so-called Zimbabwe Crisis.

It is important to note that this period is not the first (or last) in which the nation has experienced major internal political differences among its people around land policy, resulting in political rivalry and conflicts. During white settler rule in the 1960s, Ian Smith's Rhodesian Front fought minority-based white elections on the back of a burning land issue, while more liberal whites sought to de-racialize land ownership and access. More significantly, the national liberation struggle itself, begun in the late 1960s and concluding with independence in 1980, was fought to a large extent over the question of land. Prior to this there was continuous resistance to colonial land policies such as the Land Apportionment Act of 1930 and Land Husbandry Act of 1952, that caused widespread dispossession of black Africans' land.

Today, the emergence of a major political opposition party in the form of the Movement for Democratic Change (MDC) proffers a challenge to Zanu (PF)'s long held monopoly in determining land policy. In a thriving nation, this situation would have offered the opportunity for rich policy dialogue and a political process that may have led to greater effectiveness and efficiency in the delivery of development. This has not been the case in Zimbabwe. Instead of healthy political debate and democratic evolution, developments have gone from bad to worse with extensive political violence and a crude polarisation of society. The ruling party has attempted to control the judicial system, the media, and other vital parts of society through political appointments and legislation that are aimed at eliminating criticism and preventing the opposition from influencing the Zimbabwean society.

One of the most contentious political issues that emerged in the constitutional review process leading up to the referendum, had to do with the responsibility of compensating (mainly white) commercial farmers for the land that would be forcibly acquired by the government as part of their proposed land reform and resettlement programme. Zanu (PF) has argued that this is the responsibility of the British government, as the former colonial power. The MDC and the independent umbrella constitutional reform group, the National Constituional Assembly (NCA), which initiated the debate about a new constitution, argue on the other hand that Zanu (PF) is simply using the land issue to forestall major constitutional reforms that will offer greater scope for democracy and political reform. Since the referendum, the political environment has continued to be explosive. Council and parliamentary by-elections have been attended by localised conflicts, and at the national level, political violence increased in connection with the national parliamentary elections in June 2000, and the presidential election in March 2002.

These developments have all had devastating consequences for the land reform process. The violence directed towards white farmers and black farm workers as part of the political campaign for the June 2000 parliamentary elections led to the freezing of donor support for a proposed new Land Reform and Resettlement Programme that had been widely welcomed at a large donor conference in Harare in September 1998. In a situation where the government itself has limited financial and institutional capacity to support the programme, this lack of resources necessarily created further problems, not least a threat to the legitimacy of the government in terms of fulfilling its political promises. This led the government to adopt a 'fast track' land resettlement programme in June 2000, based around the compulsory acquisition of farms and the fact of actual occupations by thousands of settlers. Compensation was only to be paid for the value of improvements to the land. Plans to acquire land for redistribution had been announced several years earlier by the President.[1] Originally, 1,471 farms were listed for acquisition, but many were subsequently de-listed as a result of successful legal appeals made by farmers through the courts. This served to delay further the intended land reform process that was so critical to Zanu (PF)'s political project.

The most important instruments used to support the 'fast track' programme were Constitutional Amendment No. 16 and amendments to the Land Acquisition Act that included legal provisions allowing the government to acquire land with no compensation (except for improvements). Occupation of land could thus occur before any compensation was paid. The procedures include using government ministries, security institutions, and political party structures to identify suitable land. This leads to a government notice and immediate acquisition. Settlers who are identified through a parallel (and highly partisan) selection process

---

[1] *The Herald*, 27 November 1997.

immediately occupy 'allocated' portions of land. There is no lease, permit or legal documentation or formal process for fast-track settlers.

After launching the 'fast track' programme, negotiations continued between government officials, leaders of the war veterans, and the Commercial Farmers Union (CFU), and in the beginning with some major donors. However, these negotiations do not appear to have kept pace with 'quick and dirty' practices on the ground. The so-called war veterans and thousands of other land seekers quickly understood the political signals and carried out many land occupations.[2] Western donors' interest in supporting the government's land reform process and in continuing development co-operation with Zimbabwe waned as the situation became increasingly undemocratic. Co-operation between Zimbabwe and the large bilateral and multilateral funding institutions was replaced with political sanctions, targeted boycotts, and Zimbabwe's overall isolation by the West. By contrast, most African states continued to recognise the legitimacy of the Zimbabwe government, and financial assistance (particularly in the form of much needed fuel supplies) was provided by allies such as Libya.

The 'fast track' process has not only been critical for Zimbabwe's relationship with foreign countries; it has also had widespread domestic consequences. Agricultural productivity has fallen dramatically, causing shortages of some of the most important crops and the danger of widespread starvation. It has also caused extensive loss of jobs within both the agricultural and downstream industrial sectors. Farm workers have been especially hard hit, losing both jobs and housing.[3] A further indication that the government means business in its redistribution of land is the directive that those farms listed for expropriation had to be evacuated by 10 August 2002 at the latest, the penalty for not doing so being heavy fines or jail sentences. At the same time, the government has taken the initiative to remove some occupiers from certain farms, often where such properties have been earmarked for occupation by high-ranking politicians or those in the bureaucratic and business elite.

---

[2] For more about farm invasions and war veterans, see Nelson Marongwe (this volume).
[3] For more about farm workers in the Zimbabwean crisis, see Blair Rutherford (this volume).

Key roles of land, agriculture and natural resources in national development

In Zimbabwe, the traditional roles of land, agriculture, and natural resource development have been essential for the country's overall economic growth, in terms of the following:
- Providing adequate and affordable food for the growing population. The process of industrialisation and urbanisation is more efficient when food is cheaper for the growing industrial labour force. Today, however, food has become relatively difficult to obtain and very expensive and consumes a greater proportion of urban incomes and time. Consequently, levels of urban poverty are greater than in the past.
- Supplying raw materials to the growing and diversifying domestic industrial sector.
- Releasing labour for the industrial sector. Today, however, there is increasing unemployment as businesses close or slow down due to economic hardship.
- Enlarging the size of the effective market for the products of the domestic industrial sector; hence, when Zimbabwe has a good agricultural season, almost all categories of businesses thrive.
- Providing employment and livelihood opportunities as well as alleviating poverty for a large percentage of the rural population.
- Earning and saving foreign exchange through exports, with agriculture contributing 40% of total export earnings.
- Accumulating domestic savings for investment and capital formation.

The effects of the ongoing crisis in Zimbabwe have undermined most of these positive results. However, it is important not to see the present crisis as isolated from the extremely unequal distribution of land in the past, since this is the root of many problems in the present. Historically, most of these benefits were produced by large white-owned commercial farms that thrived with substantial subsidies from the then Rhodesian Government. After independence in 1980, with significant support provided by the Government of Zimbabwe especially in terms of credit, infrastructure, markets and more favourable pricing policies, smallholder farmers proved that they could be equally vibrant contributors to economic growth. The success of the small-scale cotton sector was emblematic in this regard. All this means that it is possible to spearhead a national land reform programme that can transform the face of commercial agriculture, by offering expanding opportunities for smaller farms and more intensively farmed land.

A brief history of post-independence land reform

Initially, land reforms in Zimbabwe were relatively successful, with evidence of increases in productivity and incomes. Subsequently, reforms slowed down as costs escalated and political priorities shifted. Moyo (2000) has divided the history of Zimbabwe's land reforms into three major periods. The early period, from independence until the mid-1980s, was characterised by comprehensive planning, purchase of land on a 'willing seller, willing buyer' basis, and fairly intensive resettlement. The second period, from the mid-1980s to the mid-1990s, saw reduced activity and reduced financial commitment from both donors and government. The third period, from the mid-1990s onwards, has seen a growing politicisation of the question of land and resettlement, with a move towards compulsory acquisition of prime land and 'fast track' resettlement. These three periods are outlined in greater detail below.

1980-86: Substantial market-based land acquisition and resettlement

In the early 1980s, resettlement constituted a significant cornerstone in fulfilling the promises of land made during the liberation struggle. Originally, some economic resources were earmarked for resettlement and there were initial plans for an Accelerated Redistribution Programme. The land reform programme was founded on market-based land purchases (voluntary seller/buyer). However, in practice this meant that mainly marginal lands were transferred for redistribution in the resettlement programme.

The period was also characterised by other broad investments in social development, especially for health and education through the establishment of schools and clinics, and with the goal of achieving free and open access to the education and health systems. Investments were also made in the development of physical infrastructure, in the form of road systems, safe drinking water and sanitation facilities, and the establishment of rural business centres.

There was great international interest in the newly independent Zimbabwe, contributing to international economic support in the form of grants and loans. One of the most important donors was Britain, Zimbabwe's former colonial power. During this period, the

British government co-financed land acquisition in co-operation with the Zimbabwean government through a system of matching grants. In practice, this meant that the government only partially paid for land in the resettlement programme.

1987-96: Reduced progress in reforms and re-thinking of resettlement policy

During this period, land acquisition and settlement slowed down considerably. The limited availability of good quality land, especially in the more high-quality agro-ecological regions, was a contributing factor. Most land available for purchase was in the drier Natural Regions IV and V, which also had poor access to water. Difficulties in sourcing finance to purchase the land that was available added to the decline in progress with the reform process. Doubts were also mounting about the sustainability and productivity of some of the resettlement models. This was not only due to the poor quality of the land and other biophysical conditions, but also the high cost of providing social and physical infrastructure (schools, clinics, etc.) for newly resettled communities. In addition, the government scaled back the institutional capacity for resettlement, scrapping the Ministry of Lands in 1986 so that responsibility for reforms was scattered across several government ministries and departments.

In the same period, there was also a new orientation in policy that shifted away from a primary emphasis on addressing landlessness to a focus on support for capable small farmers, as well as for 'indigenous' black commercial farmers. This was consistent with the introduction in the early 1990s of an IMF-sponsored economic structural adjustment programme (ESAP), but also catered politically to an emergent black elite. During this period, various initiatives were taken by the land hungry, in the form of spontaneous occupations, to demonstrate their need for land. Even though these occupations were low intensity, scattered, and low profile, and were mostly met with evictions by government, they were a symptom of local dissatisfaction with the government-led process of reform. Yet the government still showed interest in resettlement, as evidenced by legislation passed to allow compulsory acquisition (subsequently amended in the Constitution and through the Land Acquisition Act, 2000).

Disagreements between Britain and Zimbabwe about the land reform process led to renegotiation of British support for the resettlement programme. More generally, however, interest in Zimbabwe among the international donors was waning, with fewer externally funded large-scale development activities, possibly linked to the new focus on reducing public sector spending under ESAP.

1997-present: Compulsory land acquisition and the targeting of prime land

Since the late1990s, the politicisation of land has intensified considerably. When war veterans collectively pressured the government in 1997 for compensation, access to land was also a key issue. Similarly, a spate of spontaneous land invasions across the country in 1998 gave strong signals of growing popular discontent with the government's record on land reform. Combined with the emergence of a viable political opposition in late 1999, land has since become a key party political issue. It has played a central role in the constitutional reform campaigns, the parliamentary elections in 2000, and the presidential election in 2002. While all sides agree on the need for substantial land redistribution, there are strong disagreements between opposing parties on the extent and method of such redistribution. This has led to widespread tensions and ultimately a breakdown in the land policy process, with the government embarking on a 'fast track' resettlement process characterised by limited planning, compulsory acquisition, partisan selection, immediate occupation, and uncertain compensation. War veterans and other militant ruling party supporters have played a key role in facilitating this process.

Developments since February 2000, in particular the widespread disruption of commercial agriculture, forced displacement of thousands of farm workers, loss of jobs in both the agricultural and industrial sectors, and loss of foreign currency earnings and investment, compounded by a serious drought in the 2001/02 growing season, have created serious economic problems, both within the public sector and with regard to increasing poverty and hunger.

The international community has been consistently involved in the land reform process, for example, through the international donor conference on land reform held in Harare in 1998. This resulted in agreement about both the premises for and the initial financing of a new land reform and resettlement programme, but was conditional on, among other things, the Government of Zimbabwe demonstrating 'transparency' and 'accountability' in the programme. Support for an inception phase of the programme was guaranteed, but implementation faltered and trust was broken on both sides. Finally, support for the programme was entirely suspended.

As the political and economic crisis deepened after February 2000, President Obasanjo of Nigeria hosted a Commonwealth meeting at which the government of Zimbabwe signed the Abuja Agreement.[4] The introduction to this agreement states:

> Land is at the core of the crisis in Zimbabwe... A programme of land reform is, therefore, crucial to the resolution of the problem. Such a programme of land reform must be implemented in a fair, just and sustainable manner, in the interest of all the people of Zimbabwe, within the law and constitution of Zimbabwe.

Although guidelines for the land reform process were agreed to, with the help of international arbitration, this did not alter the fact that the land question was characterised by serious – and violent – conflict and sustained lawlessness. These conditions have caused the international donor community to withdraw from further negotiations, while nationally, the negotiations between the government and Commercial Farmers Union seem to be stalemated. As a result, agricultural production is almost paralysed, contributing substantially to the looming threat of starvation of millions of Zimbabweans.

Why land tenure is the key to land and agrarian reform

Recent developments in Zimbabwe demonstrate the extreme complexity of questions of land, for which there are no simple or single solutions. Yet one essential dimension of any meaningful land and agrarian reform is land tenure. The issue of people's land tenure rights is assuming greater and greater significance in every African country, including Zimbabwe, and this issue will be a crucial one in the twenty-first century. African governments in general, and the Zimbabwe government in particular, have to appreciate that the modernisation and transformation of their agrarian systems into urban-industrial economies invariably requires fundamental changes in many institutions, including those of land tenure.

The distribution of land ownership is a major factor in this transition from one form of social and political order to another. Barrington Moore (1966, quoted in Dorner 1992) sums up the experience of all industrialising countries as being linked to the separation of a substantial segment of the ruling classes from direct

---

[4] For the full text of the Abuja agreement, see http://www.mdczimbabwe.com/archivemat/other/regional/starsa010907txt.htm

ties to the land.[5] Zimbabwe faces the danger of succumbing to the African legacy. This can be summed up as the lack of political wisdom or vision in terms of public policies, particularly within the areas of agriculture and natural resource management, which thereby undermines the scope for broad-based social and economic progress. Erratic rural economic growth is translated into pervasive poverty, hunger, unemployment and environmental decline. It is widely accepted that rural economic development is ultimately dependent on building strong and effective national and rural institutions that can empower communities.

In the case of Zimbabwe, it is now clear that in order to achieve economic development and social progress, agriculture and natural resource management and the land reform issues associated with them, can no longer be divorced from issues of politics, democracy and good governance. In this regard, Zimbabwe has to learn to engage with questions of democracy and good governance in a manner that goes beyond the current rhetoric of multiparty politics, taking the high road to long-term nation building. Agricultural growth and efficient management of natural resources are dependent on the political, legal, and administrative capabilities of rural communities to determine their own future and to protect their natural resources and other economic and social interests. The lack of this power (or lack of democracy) is translated into insecure tenure rights, abuse of common property and resources, disenfranchisement of the rural population – particularly women and youth – and the breakdown or weakening of rural economic and social institutions.

Land tenure reform, land reform, and tenure security

For clarity, let us differentiate between land reform and land tenure reform. Land reform encompasses any change that redistributes land. Because land is a finite resource and its ownership generally symbolic of wealth, social status and political power, all forms of land reform are political in nature. Land reform, therefore, often involves restructuring patterns of wealth, income flows, social status, prestige etc., which are the very basic elements or ingredients of

---

[5] Peter Dorner (1992) refers to the Asian experience in relation to Latin America. He cites the land reforms in Taiwan and South Korea as having occurred early in their growth and industrialisation process, and argues that the industrial sector was never as closely tied to the non-egalitarian rural structures as is often the case in Latin America.

politics. Land reform is a revolutionary process and passes power, property and status from one societal group to another. Land tenure reform, on the other hand, involves changes in the rules that govern land and related property rights. This explains then the close association between land reform and land tenure reform and why these two often go together. The scholarly literature on tenure places emphasis on the need for tenure security, and that the various types of tenure (including the 'registered title') can be secure or insecure depending on social, legal and administrative institutions in a given society. Security of tenure is associated with four sets of rights:

- *use rights:* rights to grow crops, trees, make permanent improvements, harvest trees and fruits, and so on;
- *transfer rights:* rights to transfer land or use rights, i.e. rights to sell, give, mortgage, lease, rent or bequeath;
- *exclusion and inclusion rights:* rights of an individual, group or community to exclude others from the rights named above; and
- *enforcement rights:* the legal, institutional and administrative provisions to guarantee rights.

The four major categories of property rights define uses that are legitimately viewed as exclusive and also define who has these exclusive rights (Feder and Feeny, 1991). Institutional arrangements include instruments for defining and enforcing property rights, be they formal procedures or social customs, beliefs, attitudes, and so on, determining legitimacy and recognition of these rights (Taylor, 1988). Enforcement often requires a buttress of instruments such as courts, police, financial institutions, the legal profession, land surveys, cadastral and record keeping systems, and land titling agencies.

Tenure systems fall into four broad categories: open access, communal, private, and state (see Table 1 below). In most countries, for all practical purposes, there are few areas that are truly open access. As a general observation, some land may appear or behave as open access but such land is usually state-owned or communal. When the state or community lack adequate legal and enforcement capacity, or such capacity comes under pressure, the resultant insecurity of tenure is evidenced through land use patterns that mimic open access systems. Exclusivity (to an individual or group) therefore defines the degree of tenure security. Under communal tenure, exclusive rights are assigned to a group. Individual or family rights are also assigned under most traditional tenure systems.

Table 1: Categories of land tenure systems

Category	Exclusive Rights
Open access	None
Communal	Defined group
Private	Individual legal entity
State	Public sector

Migot-Adholla et al. (1991) have argued that most foreign anthropologists, colonial administrators, as well as some nationalistic ideologues who view these systems as static polar contrasts to Western property rights systems, have incorrectly represented indigenous African land rights systems. It is critical to recognise that both traditional African and Western tenure systems have a strong component of private ownership and rights. What distinguishes the two is simply the broader institutional context and capacity. Even in Western industrialised countries, private land rights are not treated as God-given or sacred; private property is rather a creative innovation of the state. After all, private property is not and cannot be an absolute right (Dorner, 1992). Dorner provides a powerful argument for why private land rights in Western countries have proved to be a highly innovative state intervention:

> *It is not very helpful, nor is it accurate, to say that private property and enterprise made the United States great and that this is what the United States has to offer in the struggle for economic development around the world. In fact, it is our open and flexible political system that has allowed us to make private enterprises within the United States consistent with the general public interest, as Marx thought it would never be. However, there is no reason to expect that private enterprise will automatically function in the public interest in a system lacking political institutions and the middle-class society in which they rest. (Dorner, 1992:10)*

The absence of such an open and flexible political system in Zimbabwe has inevitably led to the highly controversial 'fast track' land resettlement approach. There are other examples of such institutional failure of political systems that have led to land conflicts. A recent and relevant case is Kenya as it moved into multiparty politics in the late 1980s. Once again, land conflicts were primarily an outcome of party-political contestations as well as related political-ethnic rivalry. Where the tradition of multiparty politics is young and inflexible, land will continue to be a political football. In this situation, political groupings will choose at their own convenience when and where private property rights are to be viewed as legitimate or not. When the state does not enforce the four tenure rights adequately, then *de jure* private property becomes *de facto* open access. This in fact is the situation unfolding in Zimbabwe under the 'fast track' resettlement programme.

Insecurity of tenure in the resettlement programme in Zimbabwe is worsened by the fact that all land resettled since 1980 remains state-owned. Resettled farmers have recognised this weakness and wish to have other forms of more secure tenure, including leases with options for title. While the Phase 1 resettlements of the 1980s were planned sufficiently to offer scope for conversion of tenure, it appears extremely difficult to rationalise the tenure system – or lack of it – that is unfolding under the 'fast track' programme.

Governance issues and implications

The Government of Zimbabwe, like most African governments, designates resettlement land and traditional (communal area) land as state-owned. Most governments accept the *de facto* prevalence of customary tenure, while at the same time maintaining *de jure* state ownership. This allows bureaucrats, politicians and influential people to exercise privilege and authority over traditional land and rural communities. There is a great need to decentralise government and strengthen traditional institutions (including the capability for just conflict resolution) in resettlement areas. Highly centralised systems of government are judged as the most serious threat to tenure security for land users under all types of tenure in Zimbabwe.[6] The Land Tenure Commission recognised the need for major institutional reform in relation to strengthening both democratic redistribution processes and tenure security, and recommended that '...the proposed agricultural policy be formulated with strong participation of the farming sectors. In the process, the current institutions for research, extension, credit, marketing and land settlement have to be thoroughly reviewed, reformed and decentralised.'[7]

The problem of over-centralisation is particularly serious for communally held land, state-owned land occupied by communities

---

[6] Land Tenure Commission, 1994.
[7] Ibid. Vol 1, p.142.

under customary rights, and resettled land. Communities occupying such land have limited exclusivity of rights because state bureaucrats and politicians also claim institutional authority over the land, and in the worst cases these state functionaries may be the *de facto* landlords.

Ministries of local government in most African countries have responsibility for enforcing the state-controlled system and often subordinate traditional institutions to the state bureaucracy. A growing body of research on tenure demonstrates that the most important characteristic of tenure security under indigenous systems is the ability to bequeath land to offspring. The tenure system needs to have clearly defined land transfer rights so as to minimise future conflicts. At the community level, the community development processes are dependent on the tenure system to the extent that individual and family rights are clear and enforceable by law. Moreover, common property is best managed when, in aggregate, the local community can democratically establish rules and regulations and enforce them with backing from state institutions.

From crisis to a prosperous future

Most Zimbabweans are still looking forward to a stable and prosperous future. However, this requires taking stock of issues and developments and creating common ground. We have argued here that modern land reforms in themselves can lead to national prosperity, both economically and socially. In this regard, Zimbabwe has a lot to learn from land reforms that took place in Asia during the middle of the last century. The national prosperity we see in Asia today was rooted in long-term investments in agriculture and particularly in smallholder agriculture. Land reforms in Asia based on modernisation and surplus production not only allowed greater access to land for the landless; they were also backed up with massive investments in rural development that led to dramatic 'green revolution' increases in production and yields, as well as incomes and food security for previously poor households. Today, land is hardly a political issue in the prosperous nations; instead, mainstream economic and other social issues are at the heart of the politics of the day.

By contrast, Zimbabwe falls into a category similar to Latin American countries where land reforms are fraught with violent political conflict and contribute to the perpetual inability of these countries to enjoy stable economic and social progress.

The question is: How can Zimbabwe move toward the Asian modernisation type of solution?

The initial aspect of this key question entails the political will to build bridges and craft a future that lives up to the dream of a nation that most of its citizens envisaged at its birth. Having established such a national political platform, the rest is relatively straightforward. Below we discuss some of the key elements towards a successful reform programme.

The planning process

There is no substitute for long-range planning. A combination of high ideals like economic and rural development and social and political stability can hardly be achieved by accident. In fact, failing to plan is planning to fail. Experience and history have taught us this hard lesson, and Zimbabwe is no exception to it. Planning and budgeting for such major investments also means that the programme is less likely to be erratic in its implementation – that is, starting and stopping or slowing down to such a degree as to create political problems. A thoughtfully paced programme is more desirable than an accelerated one or a slow erratic one. In other words, the programme has to keep moving at a reasonable and manageable speed. After the first period of resettlement in the 1980s, there was a lot to learn from successes and failures, but there is no evidence of rigorous self-reflection and self-criticism that was able to draw out lessons and plough them back into the new programme.

Land tenure

One of Zimbabwe's major failures in its land reform process has been the persistence of land tenure insecurity. All resettlement continues to be on a government permit with no rights for land users to ultimate ownership or leasing. The 'fast track' approach is even more questionable in this regard. Combined with the dubious status of land tenure rights in communal areas, this means that more and more land in the country is settled on the basis of considerable legal and institutional vagueness. This in turn means that the whole foundation for social and economic progress is weak. Democracy and human rights are better protected when the relationship between people and the resources around them is clear. Such clarity includes provisions in the law and judiciary institutions that lead to minimal conflict and offer workable systems for conflict resolution. Economic investments and growth also flourish when national systems offer such clarity and thus provide fertile ground for building *trust* in the nation, mostly in the national and social systems and institutions. Trust is the currency on which great nations are built. Nations prosper quicker where trust is at high levels; not necessarily trust in individuals but rather trust in the entire social and governmental system. Land tenure is at the centre of all this, since such institutions and systems have to build from the ground up, from the household, village and community level to the national level. At village and community level, legal and administrative systems must deliver trust, security and competence.

In connection with tenure security, the significance of trust in social systems depends very much on the context. Characteristic of well-functioning communities within communal lands, for example, is that individuals feel a sense of belonging and security in their community, which may mean a preference for the traditional system of communal rights. When the focus is on resettlement areas, however, the situation is different. In this case, the majority preference is for private property rights to the land, because there is seldom an organic history of trust in the community, which has generally been quite recently established, or in an often imposed traditional system. This is also the pattern most frequently seen in an urban context.

Institutional capacity for land reform

Building sufficient capacity, including the capacity of the private sector and civil society, is essential for effective government. In 1986, Zimbabwe's government abolished the central lands ministry and scattered the responsibilities to various other ministries. This slowed down progress and reduced capacity. Government needs to build and maintain sufficient capacity for comprehensive programmes to succeed. This capacity includes policy development, land acquisition and planning, settlement, and back-up production support by service institutions. These must be factored into the assessment and building of institutional capacity. In the case of Zimbabwe, such capacity has been consistently absent in most of the developments around land reform. Given the urgent need to address land reform in such a way that it results in immediate economic and social gains, it is important to enable the participation of the private sector and civil society in the various processes and steps of the reform.

Conclusion

In times of crisis, visions for the future are difficult; the focus is on survival. Experience from the recent years of crisis in Zimbabwe shows that revitalising economic growth and social development, and opening a way out of hunger, requires basic change. An important component in this process is re-establishing trust, not only trust in the political system but also trust between fellow citizens. The violent polarisation of society (along party lines) that has characterised the years of crisis has been destructive in relation to political stability, economic growth and social integration.

Reversing this trend may be difficult in the present situation; it is necessary, however, not only for Zimbabwe's future, but also for the success of Africa's own development plan, the New Partnership for Africa's Development (NEPAD), which received the full support of African leaders at the inaugural meeting to found the African Union in Durban in July 2002.

If the conditions of democracy and good governance are fulfilled, the possibility is again open for agriculture to play the role of economic generator in society, as food producer, workplace, and source of domestic and export incomes. The need for modernising and democratising the agricultural sector is clear, but political initiatives require not only land reform but also land tenure reform. While other countries, especially in Asia, can undoubtedly provide inspiration for the process of land tenure reform, it is of central importance to draw on Zimbabwe's own knowledge, experience and traditions. Another important dimension is to include all stakeholders in the process of developing both land reform and land tenure reform. A third dimension is to take into consideration the institutional structures that already exist in rural areas. A fourth is to establish trusting and co-operative relations between national and local level institutions, ensuring a meaningful devolution of power.

Taking land tenure security seriously within the land reform process is a necessary step towards alleviating poverty and avoiding hunger.

Bibliography

Boserup, Ester, 1981. *Population and Technological Change*. Chicago: University of Chicago Press.

Bowyer-Bower, Tanya and Colin Stoneman (eds), 2000. *Land Reform in Zimbabwe: Constraints and Prospects*. Aldershot, UK: Ashgate.

Bruce, John W., Shem E. Migot-Adholla and J. Atherton, 1993. 'The Findings and their Policy Implications: Institutional Adaptation on Replacement'. In John W. Bruce and Shem E. Migot-Adholla, 1993.

Bruce, John W. and Shem E. Migot-Adholla, 1993. *Searching for Land Tenure Security in Africa*. Dubuque, IA: Kendall/Hunt Publishing.

Central Statistical Office, 1998. Annual Statistical Digest. Government of Zimbabwe: Central Statistical Office.

Dorner, Peter, 1992. *Latin American Land Reforms in Theory and Practice*. Madison: The University of Wisconsin Press.

Feder, Gershon and David Feeny, 1991. 'Land Tenure and Property Rights: Theory and Applications for Development Policy'. *The World Bank Economic Review* 5.1, pp. 135-154.

Land Tenure Commission, 1994. 'Report of the Commission of Inquiry into Appropriate Land Tenure Systems'. 3 Volumes. Harare: Government Printer.

Matowanyika, Joseph Z., 1997. 'The History of Land Use in Zimbabwe from 1900'. Paper to Leadership for Environment and Development (LEAD) conference, Zimbabwe.

Migot-Adholla, Shem, Peter Hazell, Benoit Blorel and Frank Place, 1991. 'Indigenous Land Rights Systems in Sub-Saharan Africa: A Constraint on Productivity'. *The World Bank Economic Review* 5.1, pp. 155-175.

Moore, Barrington, 1966. *The Social Origins of Dictatorship and Democracy*. Boston: Beacon Press.

Moyo, Sam, 1999. *Land and Democracy in Zimbabwe*. Monograph Series. Harare: SAPES.

Moyo, Sam, 2000. 'The Political Economy of Land Acquisition and Redistribution in Zimbabwe, 1990-1999'. *Journal of Southern African Studies* 26:1.

Palmer, Robin, 1977. *Land and Racial Discrimination in Rhodesia*. Berkeley and Los Angeles: University of California Press.

Place, Frank, Michael Roth and Peter Hazell, 1993. 'Land Tenure Security and Agricultural Performance in Africa: Overview of Research Methodology'. In John W. Bruce and Shem E. Migot-Adholla, 1993.

Roth, Michael, Richard Barrows, Michael Carter and Don Kanel, 1989. 'Land Ownership Security and Farm Investment: Comment'. *American Journal of Agricultural Economics*, Vol. 71, pp. 211-14.

Rukuni, Mandivamba (Chairman), 1994. *Report of the Commission of Inquiry into Appropriate Agricultural Land Tenure Systems*. Harare: Government Printer.

Rukuni, Mandivamba and Karl Eicher (eds), 1994. *Zimbabwe's Agricultural Revolution*. Harare: University of Zimbabwe Publications.

Sukume, Chrispen, Ephias Makaudze, Ruvimbo Mabeza-Chimedza and Nancy Zitsanza, 2000. 'Comparative Economic Advantage of Crop Production in Zimbabwe'. Technical Paper No. 99. Office of Sustainable Development, Bureau for Africa, USAID.

Taylor, J.F.A., 1988. 'The Ethical Foundations of the Market'. In Vincent Ostrom, David Feeny and Hartmut Picht (eds). *Rethinking Institutional Analysis and Development: Issues, Alternatives and Choices*. San Francisco: Institute for Contemporary Studies Press.

Tshuma, L., 1997. *A Matter of (In)Justice: Law, State and the Agrarian Question in Zimbabwe*. Harare: SAPES.

Chapter 9

The Zimbabwe Crisis in its Wider Context: The Politics of Land, Democracy and Development in Southern Africa

Ben Cousins

> *Due to the political past of most of the southern Africa countries, land restitution and land redistribution are imperatives for political, social and economic stability... Unfortunately, the result of failure with land reform cannot be ring-fenced to the country concerned, but its effects will be felt in the region.*[1]
>
> *It is thus absolutely imperative that the post-election discourse immediately turns to the greater challenge of building a democratic political culture in Zimbabwe, and in our region more broadly.*[2]
>
> *SA will avoid the Zimbabwean trap if we succeed in strengthening our democracy so that citizens play an active role in public life. Those who look for a 'strong' government which will implement the 'right' economic policies and provide 'firm management' instead of strengthening democracy are unwittingly paving the way for that which they deplore.*[3]

It is clear that the 'Zimbabwe crisis' has a profoundly regional, if not continental, dimension. Negative responses to the crisis include concerns that coercive and authoritarian political practices will prove contagious, fears that nervousness about respect for the rule of law

---
[1] Joint statement by commercial farmer unions from Zimbabwe, Namibia and South Africa. *Farmer's Weekly*, 16 June 2000, 'Unions unite to condemn Zim action'.
[2] Xolela Mangcu, 'Zimbabweans will prove that elections do not equal democracy', *Sunday Independent*, 3 March 2002.
[3] Steven Friedman, 'Africa's democrats can still have the last laugh', *Business Day*, 11 September 2002.

(and of property rights in particular) is deterring foreign investment, anxiety about massive and illegal migrations by Zimbabweans into neighbouring countries, and worries over the knock-on effects of the continuing meltdown of the Zimbabwean economy.[4] Commercial farmers in South Africa and Namibia fear that they might be next in line for 'copycat' land invasions. Zimbabwe is widely seen as a crucial first test for NEPAD (New Economic Partnership for Africa's Development), which attempts to link support for economic renewal with the promotion of democracy and 'good governance', but regional and international commentators have not been encouraged by how 'the crisis' has been handled thus far.

A recent study estimates that in the three years between 2000 and the end of 2002, Zimbabwe's crisis cut the growth of South Africa's gross domestic product by 1.3 per cent and led to between 20,000 and 30,000 actual and potential job losses.[5] It resulted in the weakening of the rand, higher inflation and higher interest rates. These effects came through reduced exports of goods and services, a drop in tourism, failure by Zimbabwe to service its debt, and reduced foreign direct investment. Over the past three years fears of just such effects have fuelled widespread criticism of the South African government's response to the crisis.[6]

More positive responses have also been in evidence. Heads of state of some regional governments, and some sectors of civil society (for example, the Landless People's Movement in South Africa), have expressed support for land occupations and confiscation of commercial farms by the Zimbabwean state. Some analysts (such as Moyo, 2002) see 'fast track' land reform in Zimbabwe as spearheading a more radical approach to land questions in the region, which combines social mobilisation 'from below' with state expropriation, and demonstrates that there are viable alternatives to market-based land reform. Mugabe's anti-imperialist rhetoric has received praise in some quarters, and his vigorous defence of fast track resettlement earned him a standing ovation at the World Summit on Sustainable Development in Johannesburg in September 2002. Responses to the crisis from within the region are thus deeply divided.

At another level, the crisis suggests that a reconsideration of the politics and economics of development in Southern Africa in the

---

[4] 'Africa needs to bring Mugabe to his senses', *Sunday Independent*, 13 January 2002.
[5] Jonathan Katzenellenbogen, 'SA is paying dearly for the crisis in Zimbabwe', *Business Day*, 21 March 2003.
[6] 'A heavy responsibility', *Mail and Guardian*, 15 to 21 March 2002.

post-liberation/post-independence era is now due. The 1990s saw transitions from one-party regimes to multi-party systems in a number of countries (Mozambique, Lesotho, Zambia, Malawi), and racially exclusive oligarchies in Namibia and South Africa gave way to majority rule and representative democracy. Liberal democracy was thus established as the dominant form of the state in the region, if only in the minimalist sense of regular, competitive elections. But as Zimbabwe so vividly illustrates, the formal institutions of liberal democracy can co-exist with blatant corruption and patronage, violent intimidation of opposition parties and civil society groups, and elections whose freeness and fairness are highly questionable.

The deeper problem revealed by the crisis is the failure of 'developmental democracies' in Southern Africa to significantly reduce the high levels of poverty and inequality bequeathed by colonialism or apartheid. These problems have persisted, or deepened in some cases, despite the abandonment in the early 1990s of socialist policies or at least rhetoric (for example by Mozambique, Zimbabwe, and leading components of the South African liberation movement), and the acceptance of either imposed or 'home-grown' structural adjustment programmes by most countries in the region. Strongly promoted by the World Bank and other international donor agencies, these were supposed to promote high rates of foreign direct investment, steady economic growth, rising employment and improved incomes. But these outcomes have failed to materialise.

Instead, poverty remains the single biggest problem throughout the region, both exacerbated by and exacerbating a raging HIV/AIDS pandemic to which few governments seem able to develop an adequate response. The scale of the problem was highlighted in dramatic fashion in 2002-03 when a major famine, caused in part by severe drought and in part by maladministration, saw millions of people threatened with starvation, with aid agencies warning of a massive humanitarian crisis that 'is getting out of control'.[7]

Urbanisation of the population of the region is increasing, but most people still live in rural areas, the greatest concentrations being in those portions previously designated as native reserves (now 'communal areas'). Contemporary rural poverty is thus rooted in part in an unresolved 'land question', in which the unequal distribution of land contributes to an inherited dualistic and highly discriminatory agrarian structure. This is dominated by a commercial farm sector at the expense of small-scale, peasant

---

[7] 'Southern Africa heading for a 'perpetual crisis', *Cape Times*, 20 March 2003.

producers and a poorly paid and insecure population of farm workers. Given the fact that in South Africa, Namibia, and (until recently) Zimbabwe[8] the great majority of commercial farmers are still white, the failure of land reform to date to transform racial patterns of ownership and production makes land a powerful symbol of incomplete transformation of the colonial/apartheid inheritance.

As the history of the continent and the Southern African region reveals, economic malaise has political effects (as well as, of course, causes), and is deeply implicated in the complex politics of the post-independent African state. Continuing poverty and under-development pose fundamental challenges to the new democracies of Southern Africa, and the Zimbabwe crisis resonates so deeply because it dramatically highlights basic questions facing all the countries in the region. In relation to politics, what are the prospects for democracy and the institutions that underpin it? More fundamentally, how appropriate is the liberal representative version of democracy for developmental states in the region? If it is not, what are the alternatives? In relation to economic policy and development strategies, how likely is it that standard 'neo-liberal' policies, and associated initiatives such as NEPAD, will succeed in reducing high levels of poverty and inequality, and if not, are there feasible alternatives?

In relation to questions of land, how can land be redistributed on a large scale in the ex-settler economies of Southern Africa in a manner that reduces rural poverty but at the same time does not undermine commercial agricultural production of both food and export products? Is expropriation in some form or other the only effective mechanism, or are there market-friendly (but pro-poor) alternatives? What form should rural property rights take: is individual title required for security of land tenure, or are there alternatives, based on 'communal' forms of tenure? These issues are in turn linked to the agrarian question, which asks: what wider transformations of the structure of the agrarian political economy are required to reduce structural poverty and inequality, and what policies can promote such transformations?

In terms of both politics and land questions, how important is the 'politics of identity' likely to be in the coming decades? Social identity underpins and frames claims to citizenship, land, and developmental resources, and often provides greater potential for

---

[8] Fast track resettlement since 2001 means that this is no longer true for Zimbabwe. Just how sustainable this will prove is still an open question – it is not inconceivable that a sizeable proportion of farms could be returned to their former owners, depending on the trajectory of political change.

political mobilisation (for example in terms of ethnicity, race and nationality) than does class – despite the centrality of class relations in explaining persistent poverty decades after liberation has been achieved.[9]

Finally, a key question relates to the political feasibility of alternative forms of democracy, economic policy frameworks, and approaches to land reform. It is one thing to propose alternatives, another to build sufficient political momentum to put them in place. Thus despite the bankruptcy (in every sense of the term) of the Mugabe regime, there is little clarity as yet on how it can be removed from power, either through internal political processes or through a combination of these with external pressure. Consideration of political feasibility requires analysis of the balance of political forces, in both the short-term and over a longer time period, and identification of the likely agents of change.

This chapter does not attempt to address all these dimensions. Instead, it focuses on the issue of *liberal versus alternative forms of democracy*, and links this to analyses of *land and agrarian questions* in Southern Africa which suggest that *alternative approaches to development* are required if the current impasse in land reform in the region is to be resolved. While the chapter focuses on the region as a whole, for several reasons particular emphasis is given to the politics of land, democracy and development in South Africa. Despite some obvious differences between South Africa and its neighbours, they face broadly similar developmental challenges, not least in relation to land reform. They equally share a common political challenge: how to consolidate and deepen democracy. In addition, as a result of longstanding economic ties, and a range of political relationships between both state and non-state actors (such as trade union movements), policies and processes in South Africa clearly have significant impacts on the political economies of its neighbours. This influence is now being extended beyond the region as a result of the NEPAD initiative, as well as growing levels of investment by South African companies in East, Central and West Africa. If South Africa were to embark on a radically different developmental path, with land and agrarian reform as an important component, and spurred by a revitalisation of struggles to deepen democracy, then the broader impacts would be potentially profound.

---

[9] Seekings and Nattrass, 2002.

The politics and economics of development in Southern Africa

Debates on the meaning of democratisation must be located in their 'developmental' context. After decades of conflict driven by armed struggles for national liberation, the 1990s were a decade of peace for Southern Africa, with Angola as the exception that highlights the rule. After negotiated transitions to democratic rule in Namibia, Mozambique and then South Africa in 1994, it seemed to many that serious attention could turn at last to the huge task of 'reconstruction and development'. Development, now virtuously linked to democracy, became the focus of what ruling parties such as South Africa's ANC have somewhat rhetorically identified as a 'second liberation struggle' against the twin legacies of poverty and inequality.[10]

These transitions took place at the same time that major shifts were taking place within the global political economy. In the late 1980s and early 1990s 'actually existing socialism' in the Eastern bloc collapsed under the weight of its own contradictions, and as the dust of the Berlin Wall settled it became clear that only one model of development was now on offer. A 'new world order' was emerging, dominated by the United States, international financial institutions and globalising multinational corporations. Capitalism was seen as having triumphed over the socialist alternative, and a precondition for development assistance from anywhere in the wealthy North was now the acceptance of neo-liberal models of economic management. This new orthodoxy, the so-called 'Washington Consensus', centred on structural adjustment policies and programmes, with its core components including market liberalisation, privatisation, deregulation and reductions in public sector spending. This approach to macro-economic management now dominates global policies on trade, tariffs and services, as well as development aid, although there has been some rethinking of the role of the state in recent years, and a greater focus on the social consequences of structural adjustment.[11]

The demise of Soviet Union and East European communism had a direct impact on political and economic choices made in post-liberation Namibia and South Africa, and hastened the abandonment

---

[10] The metaphor of continued 'liberation struggle' is a familiar trope in the region, frequently drawn upon by nationalist parties to sustain their political ideology and legitimise certain forms of nation-building. In Zimbabwe, the state-supported land invasions since 2000 have been represented as the 'Third Chimurenga', part of a continuum of nationalist, anti-colonial struggle. (See Hammar and Raftopoulos, this volume.)

[11] See the *World Development Report 1997: The State in a Changing World* (World Bank, 1997).

of 'socialist' policies in Mozambique and Zimbabwe. International Monetary Fund (IMF) loans were made conditional on adoption of structural adjustment policies. Unequivocal messages were transmitted, via the World Trade Organisation and other global forums, that only market-friendly policies would be acceptable to international capital. Governments in the region were quick to comply. Even in South Africa, where loans from the IMF were not required or requested, the 1994 Reconstruction and Development Programme (RDP), in which the state is envisaged as driving development, gave way very quickly to the Growth, Employment and Redistribution (GEAR) plan of 1996,[12] in which primacy was accorded to slashing state expenditure, reducing corporate taxes, phasing out exchange controls, encouraging wage restraint, reducing inflation, and privatisation (Marais, 1998:161-2). Unfortunately, these policies have not been very successful in promoting economic growth, and strikingly unsuccessful in relation to poverty reduction.

Poverty and inequality

Southern Africa is the wealthiest sub-region on the African continent, accounting for around 35 per cent of continental GDP, with its 1998 per capita GDP of $1,502 the highest in Africa (ADB, 2000). This masks considerable disparities between some relatively high income countries (Botswana, South Africa, Namibia and Swaziland) and others that are some of the poorest in the world (Mozambique, Malawi, Zambia, Angola, and now Zimbabwe). Within all these countries there is a highly skewed distribution of wealth, so that per capita GDP and GNP statistics do not accurately represent the true extent of poverty.

Selected development indicators for nine countries in the region are shown in Table 1. Six countries are classified by the World Bank as 'low income', two (Namibia and Swaziland) as 'middle lower income', and two (Botswana and South Africa) as 'middle upper income'. Gini coefficient scores, indicating the degree of income inequality, are extremely high in four of the five countries for which data are available, including South Africa. High proportions of the population in most countries of the region live below the international poverty line of $1 per day, and even higher proportions live on below $2 per day. Indices of social development (such as infant mortality) also show severe levels of poverty in most of the region.

---

[12] On release by the government this plan was immediately declared 'non-negotiable' in its broad outlines. It was also characterised by government as not only consistent with the RDP, but in fact as the practical means to achieve the goals of the RDP (Marais, 1998:161).

Table 1. Development indicators in selected Southern African countries

	GNP/capita in US$ (2000)	World ranking (1999)	Pop. below national poverty line (%)	Pop. below international poverty line (%)		Gini index	Under 5 mortality rate per 1000
				< $1/day	< $2/day		
Angola	240	194	-	-	-	-	208
Botswana	3300	84	-	33.3	61.4	-	95
Lesotho	540	152	49.2	43.1	65.7	56.0	141
Malawi	170	199	54.0	-	-	-	227
Mozambique	210	193	-	37.9	78.4	39.6	193
Namibia	2050	105	-	34.9	55.8	-	105
South Africa	3020	86	-	11.5	35.8	59.3	86
Zambia	300	176	86.0	63.7	87.4	52.6	176
Zimbabwe[1]	480	154	25.5	36.0	64.2	56.8	154

Source: World Development Report 2000/2001

[1] Poverty rates in Zimbabwe have increased dramatically since 2000 as a result of unemployment, drought, rampaging inflation, and contraction of the formal economy in general (ICG, 2001:13).

A recent survey in seven Southern African countries (Bratton and Mattes, 2002) confirms this pattern of pervasive poverty. High levels of unemployment and underemployment are found, and even those in work are often employed in part-time or temporary jobs. Women are more likely to be unemployed than men, and rural people more so than urban. An average of two-thirds of the surveyed households experience shortages of cash, and significant proportions often go without food. In relation to shortages of clean water, some countries (Botswana, South Africa) score relatively well, but in four countries over 40 per cent of surveyed households experience such shortages, and the regional average is 36 per cent.

Poverty and inequality are rooted in structural features of the region's political economy and the pathways taken in the course of capitalist development in periods of colonial or apartheid rule. Key features of the region's economies thus exhibit a high degree of continuity with the past, and transitions to majority rule and multiparty democracy have not been accompanied by fundamental transformations of the colonial legacy. Common features include a high degree of dependence on minerals and agricultural products for export earnings, imports consisting largely of manufactured goods from the developed industrial economies, and large trade balance deficits. Only South Africa and Zimbabwe have diversified economies and reasonably well developed manufacturing and service sectors, although these are currently in rapid decline in Zimbabwe.[13] The region is also highly vulnerable to the negative consequences of contemporary 'globalisation' (Bond, 2000). These include volatile exchange rates as a result of currency speculation; low levels of foreign direct investment due to poor profitability, with what foreign investment there is occuring on terms highly favourable to transnational capital; declining terms of trade with industrial economies; and aid conditionalities that insist on liberalisation of southern economies despite the persistence of trade barriers and massive agricultural subsidies in the north.

The region's economy is dominated by South Africa, which in 1995 accounted for 62 per cent of total SADC exports and 59 per cent of its imports. South Africa is also the main supplier of both consumer and capital goods to the rest of the region, and acts as an important market for some of the primary products exported from its neighbours. The region is thus 'integrated' in a highly skewed fashion (Bond, 2000:232-37).

---

[13] The manufacturing sector's contribution to GDP in Zimbabwe plunged from 25 to 15 per cent between 1998 and 2002 (*Cape Times*, 9 October 2002).

In the densely settled rural areas of the region where the largest proportion of the population lives, there is continued dependence on wage incomes and remittances, and peasant agriculture remains underdeveloped. The former 'native reserves', now known as 'communal areas', were historically created as a source of cheap wage labour, and bear the imprint of a long history of circular migration (Arrighi, 1970). Some significant successes in increasing peasant production have occurred, but the benefits are unevenly spread as a result of social differentiation within rural communities (Cousins et al., 1993).

Commercial agriculture is still dominated by large commercial farms or plantations, many still white-owned, and the agrarian economy remains highly dualistic in character. 'Emergent' black commercial farmers have increasingly acquired large farms in Zimbabwe,[14] Namibia and South Africa since the advent of democracy in these countries (Lyne and Darroch, 1997; Moyo, 2000; Pohamba, 2002), but they are still in the minority.

Poverty, inequality and class in post-apartheid South Africa

More evidence that structural poverty continues to exist despite the efforts of 'democratic developmental states' is provided in recent analyses from South Africa. Since 1994 inflation has stabilised and moderate economic growth (1 to 3 per cent per year) has occurred. There have been substantial improvements in the provision of infrastructure and social services, such as clean water for 8 million people, electricity for 1.5 million households, and free medical services to all pregnant women and children under the age of seven (de Swardt, 2003).

Despite these achievements, there is compelling evidence that structural poverty is worsening. Unemployment has risen rapidly over the past decade, from 16 per cent in 1995, escalating to 29 per cent in 2002, but if those who are too discouraged to continue to actively seek work are included, the figure rises to 40 per cent. Employers have increasingly chosen capital- rather than labour-intensive techniques to improve competitiveness and there has been a dramatic decrease of employment in the semi-skilled mining and commercial farming sectors.[15] Between 45 and 55 per cent of all South Africans presently live in poverty.[16] Rural poverty is a major

---

[14] Most recently this has been speeded up through the A2 model of fast track resettlement, but the trend had already begun in the 1990s.
[15] Simbi & Aliber, 2000.
[16] Aliber, 2003.

problem, as over 70 per cent of all poor people reside in rural areas and nearly half of these are chronically poor (Aliber, 2003).[17] Expansion of the 'social wage' (basic services, housing and social grants) offsets this decline in the income of the poor to some extent, but the chronically poor find it difficult to pay even minimal amounts for electricity and water, and often end up selling their government-built houses for small amounts of cash.

As in the rest of the region, HIV/AIDS is contributing to impoverishment. Currently around 4.2 million people (and 20 per cent of all adults) are infected with the HIV virus. Without effective measures to prevent AIDS, the number of cumulative deaths is expected to grow to about 6 million in South Africa by 2010, which will result in more than one million AIDS orphans by that year (de Swardt, 2003:45).

Seekings and Nattrass (2002) echo de Swardt's emphasis on the growing divide within South African society and suggest that class divisions are now more important than race.[18] The emerging class structure consists of an increasingly multi-racial upper class (corporate elites plus professional and managerial groups); a 'middle' group of mostly urban, employed workers; and a marginalised group of farm and domestic workers plus the unemployed with little income from assets or entrepreneurial activities (the 'underclass'). The upper class comprise 12 per cent of the population but earn 45 per cent of all income; the middle group comprise 48 per cent of the population and earn 45 per cent of income, and the marginalised comprise 40 per cent of the total but earn only 10 per cent of income. The 'underclass' makes up 28 per cent of the total population.

For Seekings and Natrass contemporary inequality is no longer primarily inter-racial, but intra-racial, 'driven by two income gaps: between an increasingly multi-racial middle class and the rest, and between the African urban industrial working class and the African unemployed and marginalised poor' (ibid:25). To reduce inequality while ensuring growth in income, they recommend a 'social democratic policy agenda', aimed at sustained job creation (including low-wage, labour-intensive employment), improvements in education, 'democracy deepening asset redistribution' (worker ownership of firms plus land reform),[19] and welfare reform. Other authors also argue for a large-scale redistribution of productive assets, in concert with a range of other policies such as skills

---

[17] Aliber 2003.
[18] This is also the major thrust of Terreblanche's (2002) recent book on inequality in South Africa.
[19] These proposals will be discussed in more detail below.

development and infrastructure development (de Swardt, 2003:18; Terreblanche, 2002:466; Makgetla and van Meelis, 2003:103).

A key issue is the political feasibility of such proposals. Seekings and Natrass 'hope that the democratic process will lead to heightened pressure on the government to respond'. For them the prospects for appropriate 'development' are integrally linked to the strength and effectiveness of democratic processes. But are 'democratic processes' to be understood only in terms of elections, parliamentary opposition, and civil society lobbying, or are new forms of politics required that involve higher levels of active participation than those that normally occur within the framework of liberal democracy?

The politics of land reform in the region

Against the backdrop of large rural populations suffering high levels of poverty, the persistence of racially unequal land ownership is politically highly charged. It is not surprising, therefore, that land reform loomed large in the rhetoric of liberation movements, and has continued to feature in the policies of post-independence governments. In practice, however, these governments have given much lower priority to land reform than their manifestoes would suggest (as evidenced by national budgets). The Zimbabwean pattern – of land issues temporarily gaining a high profile at election time only to drop back into relative neglect in between elections – is common throughout the region. In no country has land reform, together with restructuring of the agricultural sector, been the central thrust of post-independence rural development. Consistently, there has been 'a general failure by governments to integrate land policy into either a rural development strategy or a wider social and economic development vision' (FAO, 2003:2).

There are several reasons for this, varying in their importance and specific configuration in different countries. They include: the dominance of neo-liberal economic policies with their strong emphasis on attracting foreign capital; donor wariness because land is such a 'politicised' issue; the widespread scepticism of policy makers about prospects for small-holder agriculture; elite accumulation strategies that include the acquisition of private land for investment or speculation; the strength of commercial agricultural lobbying groups; the weakness of progressive civil society groupings; and the fact that 'the rural poor' are not an organised political constituency.[20] The balance of political forces around land and

---

[20] For recent overviews of land policies in the region see Lahiff (2002) and FAO (2003).

agriculture in Southern Africa has tended to generate somewhat timid and/or conservative land policies, despite occasional inflammatory speeches by political leaders.

The same disjunction between ideology and practice is evident in the responses of politicians in the region to the land component of the Zimbabwe crisis. Thus support by SADC for Mugabe has emphasised the centrality of 'the land question' (with a primary emphasis on the injustice of racially skewed land distribution) and the legitimacy of confiscatory land reform, but this has not been accompanied by any substantial increase in support for their own land reform efforts. Two examples spring to mind: Namibia and South Africa. In both countries redistribution is a key component of land policy.

Land policy in Namibia

Namibian President Sam Nujoma, like Mugabe, used the platform of the World Summit for Sustainable Development to attack critics of fast track resettlement in Zimbabwe. He has made several speeches calling for 'arrogant white farmers' to stop demanding high prices for land offered for resettlement, and referred explicitly to the possibility of Zimbabwean-style land invasions.[21] A ruling party (SWAPO) congress in 2002 called for government to set aside R100 million to buy more farms for the landless, but observers are of the view that this is unlikely to materialise given the high budget deficit. Between 1990 and 2002 only R105 million had been spent on acquiring 118 farms for resettlement. In contrast, over 300 farms have been acquired by wealthier black Namibians using the Affirmative Action Loan Scheme (Pohamba, 2002).

Political dynamics help to explain the continued discrepancy between ideology and practice. In the colonial era only a minority of Namibians (Herero, Damara and Nama pastoralists in the former 'Police Zone' in the central and southern regions) suffered direct dispossession of their lands by the settler state (Melber, 2001; Werner, 2002). The majority of rural people, who are sedentary agro-pastoralists in northern regions such as Ovamboland, were not dispossessed, and they constitute the political base of the ruling party. As a result, 'the land question has never occupied as important a place in the public imagination of SWAPO's main constituency and their expectations about the future as among the dispossessed

---

[21] Johan Grobler, 'Reform for the landless?', *Mail and Guardian*, 20 to 26 September 2002.

proper....who are a small minority. Politically they wield no power as they are poorly organized, if organized at all' (Werner, 2002:2-3).

Tenure reform policies for Namibia's communal areas are of direct relevance to SWAPO's constituency in the densely settled lands of the northern regions. Here a process of individual enclosure of communal grazing land, through fencing of grazing camps by relatively wealthy local and non-local elites, has been under way for some time. In terms of the recently promulgated Communal Land Reform Act, all communal land continues to vest in the state, but customary rights to residential and arable plots, which will continue to be allocated by traditional authorities, can be registered with Regional Land Boards. Leasehold rights can also be issued. No provisions are made for community property rights over resources such as grazing. The institutional framework has been designed 'for the primary purpose of serving a new form of land tenure on communal land: long term leasehold and possibly title' (Werner, 2002:7).

Werner (2002:6-7) comments that 'traditional authorities are likely to be strengthened at the expense of communities', and that the Land Boards will be concerned primarily with the legalisation and formalisation of enclosed land. The new law 'does very little to strengthen access of small-scale and marginal farmers to communal land'.[22] Politicians and chiefs (elites who stand to benefit from formalising private enclosures of communal land) control local politics. Ordinary members of SWAPO in the northern areas are tied into the dominant 'ethnic' form of politics in which patronage plays an important role, and are currently not able to mount effective challenges to the elite or to elite-friendly policies. On the rare occasions that they have attempted to do so, the ruling party has easily out-manouevred them.[23] A significant factor is the weakness of the non-governmental organisations in Namibia, especially in the land sector.[24]

A recent overview of land in the region comments that in Namibia:

> ... the lack of practical policy and a real commitment to equitable implementation in practice is being exploited by national elites who have enclosed large areas where customary land rights prevail but are not surveyed and lack effective

---

[22] But see Twyman et al. (2002) for another view.
[23] In 1999 a march of 1,000 communal farmers demanded a halt to the Communal Land Reform Bill because it entrenched the power of chiefs. The leader of the march was subsequently elevated to the cabinet and no more was heard of these demands (Johan Grobler 'Reform for the landless?', *Mail and Guardian*, 20 to 26 September 2002).
[24] NGOs are stronger in the natural resources sector in Namibia, where they have successfully promoted legislation and policies that confer rights to the proceeds of wildlife tourism (Werner, 2002:8-11).

legal protection. A class of emerging black commercial farmers might redress (slightly) the skewed racial access to land, but will do little to address underlying issues of poverty and a real redistribution not just of land but also of wealth in other forms (FAO, 2003).

Land politics in South Africa

In South Africa, by contrast, land NGOs are relatively strong, and the potential for progressive civil society organisations to influence land policy would appear to be much greater. Most emerged in the course of the struggle against forced removals during the apartheid era, and many have decades of experience of promoting a 'pro-poor' perspective on land. They are provincially based, have long experience of rural fieldwork, and assist client communities to access rights and resources within land reform programmes, as well as engaging in policy critique and advocacy. Most land NGOs are linked to each other through a national co-ordinating office, the National Land Committee (NLC), which gives them a high profile in national policy debates. The NLC has organised important events such as the Community Land Conference of 1994, which brought together hundreds of delegates from rural communities and helped give emerging land policy a broadly pro-poor thrust. In recent years the NLC has provided significant support to emerging social movements such as the Landless People's Movement (LPM) and the Land Access Movement of South Africa (LAMOSA).

Despite their apparent strength, however, NGOs' influence over government land policy has waned since the halcyon early days of the transition to democracy between 1994 and 1996, when their members (and ex-members, now working in government) did indeed play a key role in drafting land reform laws and policies.

This decline in influence became clearly evident after the second democratic election in 1999 when Thabo Mbeki took over the presidency, and a new Minister of Agriculture and Land Affairs was appointed. Although there were important continuities in the problematic market-based approach to land acquisition,[25] a major shift in the targeting of land redistribution policy occurred: emergent black commercial farmers were to be the major beneficiaries, and the goal of de-racialising commercial agriculture now took clear precedence over that of reducing poverty and promoting sustainable livelihoods.

---

[25] See Lahiff (2001) for an analysis of these continuities and the limitations they impose on land redistribution policies in South Africa.

Since then the powerful white commercial farming union, Agri-SA, together with the still rather weak National African Farmer's Union (NAFU), have become much more important partners of government than any other civil society grouping. Alarmed by both the possible ripple effect of the Zimbabwean farm invasions and by the continuing onslaught on white farmers in the form of farm murders and attacks (and of possible links between the two[26]), they have realised that 'for their own survival, South African farmers have no choice but to help the government with land reform'.[27] Agri-SA and NAFU worked closely with the Department of Agriculture to produce the 2001 Strategic Plan for South African Agriculture (NDA, 2001), in which land reform constitutes one of its 'core strategies'.

In addition to efficient lobbying by the representatives of (existing and aspirant) landed capital, there are a number of other influences on South African land reform policies. According to Lahiff (2002:38), the most important are economic policy considerations, whereby the government has clearly demonstrated its commitment 'to preserving the present structure of large-scale commercial agriculture, along with the upstream and downstream agro-businesses on which it depends.' At the same time, small scale subsistence agriculture 'is not seen as having any potential for economic growth, particularly for what are, for government, the key areas of export earnings, taxable revenue and formal job creation.' It is thus no surprise that the land reform budget from 1994 to 2002 was never more than 0.4 per cent of the total.

The South African media have accorded a high profile to farm invasions and fast track resettlement in Zimbabwe, and in response to widely expressed fears that 'this could happen here too' there has been an increase in government rhetoric around speeding up land reform. In June 2000 the Minister of Land Affairs raised the possibility of land expropriation or paying for land at less than market value, in order to meet land redistribution targets (Lahiff and Cousins, 2001:657). However, there has been no move in this direction since then, and these were clearly remarks aimed at defusing mounting criticism of land reform policies rather than indicating a fundamental shift in policy. Since then government officials have often made comparisons between Zimbabwean and South African land reform, mostly in a self-congratulatory manner that stresses the 'orderly' nature of land reform in South Africa,

---

[26] 'Rising terror of farm killings: slow pace of land reform fuelling attacks?' *Farmer's Weekly*, 14 April 2000.

[27] 'SA land invasion threats', *Farmer's Weekly*, 26 May 2000.

and firm action against land invaders is always promised. This was seen to be no idle threat when thousands of homeless people invaded empty state land in Bredell, a peri-urban area near Johannesburg, in mid-2001, and the state had them removed within days. The sanctity of private property rights in the eyes of government was clearly demonstrated to the wider world.

On that occasion the Pan African Congress (PAC), much weakened since its heyday in the 1960s as a rival liberation movement to the ANC and ineffective as an opposition party since 1994, attempted to make political capital out of the land invasion. Party leaders referred explicitly to the unresolved land question and called on government to follow the Zimbabwean route. However, the PAC was roundly denounced as 'opportunist' by other political parties and many commentators, and since then has made no concerted attempt to use land as a rallying cry.

It has been left to extra-parliamentary groups to attempt to forge a radical politics of land and agrarian reform. The Landless People's Movement (LPM) first emerged in 2001 in Mpumalanga Province in response to farm worker and tenant labour evictions from commercial farms. Since then, with the support of NGOs, it has been launched in several other provinces, drawing in diverse interest groups (Greenberg, 2002). These include residents of sprawling informal settlements around towns and cities, dissatisfied land restitution claimants, land-hungry people from overcrowded former 'homelands', and even some chiefs.[28] The LPM has called for an end to farm evictions and a strengthening of the rights of workers and tenants, faster progress in land restitution, and a large-scale redistribution of land aimed at ending landlessness, poverty and hunger. It has attacked market-based approaches and the principle of 'willing-seller, willing-buyer'.

High-profile marches have been organised in support of local struggles against evictions, as well as in the context of international conferences, such as the World Conference on Racism, and the World Summit for Sustainable Development (WSSD). The WSSD march, calling for 'land, food and jobs', saw the LPM link up with a range of other radical civil society groups, such as the Anti-Privatisation Forum, and many speakers denounced the ANC government for its neo-liberal policies. The march was at least four times as large as one sponsored and led by the ANC – a severe embarrassment for the ruling party. The LPM invited Mugabe to address them, suggesting

---

[28] For a comparative example of diverse interests represented in the 2000 land occupations in Zimbabwe, see Marongwe, this volume.

that there is strong gut-level support for forcible redistribution, Zimbabwe style. LPM members have been arrested for holding 'illegal gatherings', and the movement's growing profile has seen it attract the attentions of the National Intelligence Agency, indicating that government might be worried about the prospect of organised farm invasions.

However, the significance of the LPM should not be overestimated. At present it is clearly a 'nascent popular movement' rather than a well-organised grouping with a coherent ideological framework and clear strategies, ready to lead an emerging politics of land (Greenberg, 2002:5). According to Greenberg, weaknesses include naïve expectations that the threat of land invasions will force government 'to deliver', simplistic ideas about influencing land policy through being elected to local government or parliament, and uncritical support for Zanu (PF) and fast track resettlement. Organisational weaknesses were in evidence at a 'Week of the Landless' event during the WSSD attended by over 5,000 people.

Rural social movements in South Africa are clearly at an embryonic stage, but deepening rural poverty means that social and economic conditions are conducive to their further growth. As Moyo (2002:1) comments for the continent as a whole: 'peasant organisations are re-emerging...as a potential force in a possible endogenous movement for alternative forms of development.' In South Africa the key issues are how effective organisation 'on the ground' will prove to be, and whether or not alliances can be forged with other social movements that have emerged in recent years (Hart, 2002:29). In either sense, the diversity of social and class identities within the category 'the landless' will have to be confronted and given political expression. Anger over unequal land ownership and continuing insecurity of the land rights of the rural poor could see more occupations of both state and privately owned land in the next few years. To date these have been sporadic, small-scale and mostly in urban and peri-urban areas, but some have involved dissatisfied land restitution claimants in rural areas (Lahiff and Cousins, 2001:662). If current weaknesses can be overcome, the LPM could well become the catalyst for an organised land occupations movement in future, and emerge as a significant political force.

The failings of South African land policy

Government's current land reform policies – for restitution, redistribution or tenure reform – are unlikely to satisfy the varied demands of rural people, partly because land reform is so underfunded (Turner, 2002). It is true that the 2003 budget saw a doubling of funds for the land restitution programme, to help it meet its December 2004 deadline for the resolution of around 70,000 land claims. This is clearly the high priority land reform sub-programme for government at present, perhaps because of the powerful symbolism of state redress for land dispossession.

However, critical questions continue to be raised as to the impact of restitution on the overall distribution of land holdings and poverty, given the fact that the majority of claims resolved to date have been in urban areas, and settled through cash payments (Hall, 2003a). Rural claims are in general larger (involving hundreds or thousands of households per claim), more complex, and much more expensive than the urban claims. The Land Claims Commission acknowledges that a major weakness of the restitution programme is the inadequacy of post-settlement support for rural claimants returning to land.[29]

Yet even were South Africa's land reform programme to be better funded, it would not prevent rising dissatisfaction over land, since the underlying assumptions and their programmatic expression are inappropriate and ill-suited to the goal of poverty reduction. As Lahiff (2002:50) comments:

> ...*market-based redistribution becomes piecemeal redistribution, securing benefits for a lucky few but leaving the fundamental structures of the agrarian economy, and the problems of mass rural poverty and landlessness, largely intact.*

The alternative to market-based land reform is clearly an approach that gives the state, as well as popular organisations, a central role in both acquiring land and planning for its productive use. Proponents emphasise that land questions must be located firmly within the framework of a broader agrarian reform that restructures agrarian social, economic and political relations in fundamental ways (Kepe and Cousins, 2002; Wildschut and Hulbert, 1998). In addition to infrastructure and service provision for the beneficiaries of land reform, agrarian reform would need to include a focus on the redistribution of political and economic power, to prevent elite capture and the reproduction of power relations on commercial farms and within agro-food commodity chains (Kepe and Cousins,

---

[29] Wallace Mgoqi, Chief Land Claims Commissioner, presentation on land restitution to a seminar at the Centre for Conflict Resolution, University of Cape Town, November 2002.

2002:2). Agrarian reform thus connects strongly the agendas of pro-poor land reform, bottom-up development and deep democratisation (Levin and Weiner, 1997).

Communal land rights, chiefs and democracy

In South Africa, as in Namibia, the legal status of land rights in communal areas is a key focus of the tenure reform component of land reform. Other aspects include the tenure security of commercial farm workers and tenants, for whom legislation passed since 1994 provides a measure of protection from arbitrary eviction.[30] In communal areas, however, progress has been slower, and controversy has surrounded attempts to legislate a new regime of rights and their administration (Cousins and Claassens, 2003). The politics of tenure reform, centred mainly around competing notions of property rights, resonates with similar dynamics elsewhere in the region (FAO, 2003). At issue is the poor recognition and definition of communal land rights in law, the low status of women's rights within these regimes, the breakdown of land administration (which means that rights are increasingly insecure in practice as well as in law), negative impacts on development planning and investment, and the contested role of chiefs in relation to land.

Across Africa one of the key legacies of colonialism was a dualistic land tenure system that differentiated sharply between 'customary land rights' and western systems of private property. Mamdani (1996:18) suggests that this is only one aspect of a more general dualism arising from policies of indirect rule. These created a 'bifurcated' state, with two forms of power under a single authority. Power in urban areas was framed by discourses of civil society, civil rights and the separation of powers, in rural areas by community, custom and a unitary 'traditional' authority. The latter constituted a 'decentralised despotism' of subjects ruled by chiefs and a regime of extra-economic coercion, largely reproduced in post-colonial states. This fracture between urban and rural regimes contributes to truncated forms of democracy, and the continuing struggle for a deeper democratisation of state and society has to confront a divide between citizen and subject, between rights and culture (ibid:3).

However, it does not follow that the conversion or 'upgrading' of communal tenure to individual freehold tenure (private property) is

---

[30] Civil society organisations argue that these provisions are too weak, and often ineffective in practice (Hall, 2003b). A review of the relevant legislation is currently under way. Interestingly, recent years have seen a great deal of contact between South African NGOs concerned with farm dwellers and their counterparts in Zimbabwe.

a necessary requirement of democratisation. Privatisation and individualisation have a poor record in Africa. In Kenya, for example, where titling has been attempted on a large scale since the 1950s, customary patterns of land allocation and inheritance have persisted and the anticipated free market in land has not emerged. Title deed registers have rapidly become outdated and agricultural credit has not significantly increased. Heightened inequalities of land ownership have resulted from manipulation of the registration process by the politically well-connected, resulting in increased levels of landlessness and rural-urban migration (Quan, 2000).

It is now widely accepted, even by the World Bank, that freehold title is not a 'magic bullet' for increasing security of tenure in Africa. This has resulted in wider acceptance of core features of communal tenure: rights to land and natural resources are shared and relative, flexible boundaries exist between a variety of social units, and rights are nested within a hierarchy of social and administrative units or levels (Okoth-Ogendo, 2002). Emerging policy recommendations call for greater recognition in law of such rights, the strengthening of local institutions for land administration and land management, and support for institutions and procedures for mediation and negotiation, particularly at the local level (IIED, 1999).

Translating these general prescriptions into law and policy is far from straightforward. There is continuing debate on how best to provide legal recognition of customary rights. Some suggest codification, others registration either centrally or at the local level, but these can backfire and as an unintended consequence produce increased unpredictability and institutional incoherence (Lund, 1998). Local institutions are vulnerable to the power plays of elites, as well as to a 'politics of exclusion' (Lavigne Delville, 1999; Peters, 2002) and measures to promote transparency and accountability (that is, democratisation) are required (Ribot, 2002). This means that the powers of unelected traditional authorities have to be circumscribed, even in cases where their presence and legitimacy in the eyes of rural people means that they cannot be simply discounted or ignored (Cousins, 1997).

It also means that central government has a key role to play in ensuring accountability, through oversight of local bodies and the application of sanctions (ibid: 18). Some analysts emphasise the key role of negotiation and conflict resolution for securing land rights, and stress the importance of state support for local institutions to mediate conflicting interests (Berry, 1993; Cousins, 2002; Moore, 1998). This resonates strongly with the view that democratisation in Africa requires a strong and capable central state, both willing and able to empower citizens through locally accountable, representative institutions.

South African debates on communal land rights

In Southern Africa it is clear that meaningful tenure reform in communal areas depends crucially on wider processes of democratic decentralisation (Ntsebeza, 2002), but can also contribute to such processes by clearly specifying people's land and resource rights, setting out practical procedures for their realisation, and creating institutional frameworks that are accountable to rights holders (Alden Wily and Mbaya, 2001). These issues were clearly identified as core concerns in the Rukuni Commission's findings on land tenure reform in Zimbabwe (Rukuni, 1994), and are at the centre of current debates in South Africa on the Communal Land Rights Bill (CLRB).

A draft of the CLRB published in 2002 provides for 'transfer of title' of communal land from the state to its current occupants. Complex procedures for transfer include a rights inquiry, community meetings, and adoption of community rules on tenure. Registration of these rules converts the community into a 'juristic person' capable of owning land, yet crucially, there must be agreement about the size, nature and boundaries of what and who will constitute the 'community' that will hold the land title. Once the rules are registered a land administration committee can be elected, made up of community members. Traditional leaders must be on the committee in an ex-officio capacity, but cannot comprise more than 25 per cent of members. A key issue is that of the role and powers of chiefs. Groups such as the Congress of Traditional Leaders of South Africa argue for the transfer of title to traditional authorities, on the grounds that they have always held land rights in trust for their communities, and that they are not inherently undemocratic and unaccountable.[31] This lobby objects vehemently to the '25 per cent' rule.

Civil society organisations have expressed highly critical views of the CLRB (Cousins and Claassens, 2003). The key flaw identified in the bill is the underlying paradigm of a transfer of freehold title, requiring clear boundaries to be drawn between communities. This could open up and exacerbate boundary disputes and ethnic differences. In addition, transferring title will effectively privatise communal land. Since government refuses to provide services and infrastructure on privately owned land, the effect will be to insulate

---

[31] Patekile Holomisa, 'Resolving communal land rights a vital link in reform process', *Business Day*, 21 May 2003.

poor rural areas from local government development programmes. This would force rural people to choose between ownership rights and development. The procedure for transfer of title is long-winded and intricate, and until transfer occurs the status of people's existing rights to occupation and use remains unclear. In addition, women's land rights are not adequately provided for.

Dominant forces within the ruling party seem set on pushing through the CLRB in 2003, and may secure support from some quarters on the basis that the bill limits the powers of traditional leaders. Alternatively, fierce controversy over the potentially negative impacts of the CLRB may see it being shelved until after the 2004 general election, or the parliamentary process may result in significant amendments.

Informing the politics of tenure reform in South Africa are competing understandings of livelihoods, rights and institutions. The dominant view within the state appears to be that communal areas and the livelihoods they support are marginal to the mainstream economy and hardly worth investing in.[32] This could explain why the CLRB does not provide for ongoing state support for local land administration bodies. In relation to land rights, the view from within government is clearly that only land titling (meaning private ownership) provides adequate tenure security – although forms of group title must be made available, given the strong demand for a community-based form of tenure.

In contrast, NGOs and community members see land-based livelihoods in rural South Africa as a key focus for local economic development aimed at poverty reduction, in which local government, backed by a strong developmental state, has a key role to play. Securing rights to home sites, fields and common property is urgently needed, and this need not take the form of titling. The alternative is rights defined clearly in law (that is, 'statutory rights'), as in Mozambique or Tanzania, where the state retains nominal ownership of community land (Alden Wily and Mbaya, 2001). Community calls for support by government for accountable local institutions, as well as for greater clarity on the relationship between land administration committees and local government, stand in stark contrast to the minimalist provisions of the CLRB.

The South African debate underlines the centrality of the two issues that have dominated wider debates on tenure reform in the region (appropriate definitions of land rights, and democratic land

---

[32] This contrasts markedly with the Zimbabwean context, and accounts in part for the different shape of land politics in each setting.

administration). But it also illustrates the importance of adequate resource allocations for implementation and institutional support. This is one of the lessons from Uganda, where a process of consultation and vigorous debate preceded the comprehensive Land Act of 1998, but little thought was given to implementation and its costs (Palmer, 2000:277).

It is also a key lesson from Mozambique, where a progressive 1997 Land Law emerged from an extensive 'Land Campaign' driven by a range of NGOs in a process hailed as one of the most participatory and democratic in recent Mozambican history (Negrao, 1998; Palmer, 2000; Tanner, 2002). Consensus was achieved on three core issues: continued state ownership of land, recognition and protection of existing rights including customary rights, and the opening up of land and other resources for private sector development. However, implementation has been much slower than expected because of institutional problems arising from the distribution of responsibilities across several state bodies, and for political reasons: 'key interest groups within Mozambican society and beyond... see community consultation [on land rights] as an impediment to investment' (Tanner, 2002:48). The NGOs that led the Land Campaign have become 'over-stretched' or 'lost touch with their local constituency' (ibid), and this lack of enthusiasm for implementation has 'undermined the ongoing struggle for recognition and protection of customary rights, and encouraged those calling for changes to the law, including privatisation of land' (Lahiff, 2002: 18).

Pressure for privatisation has little to do with questions of security of tenure, and everything to do with easing acquisition for purposes of speculation. Much of it comes from state officials and their allies, 'members of the elite who have organised land concessions but do not have the money to develop the land or carry out the plans on which their provisional title was based' (Hanlon, 2002:18). Competing notions of land rights, as in South Africa, are integrally linked to very different conceptions of 'development' and the role of the state in promoting it.

Democratisation in the region

As noted above, the 1990s saw liberal democracy established in most countries in the region, but a critical interrogation of the significance of these 'democratic transitions' is required. This section explores the meaning of these transitions in a comparative perspective, with a particular focus on South Africa, before turning to a discussion of alternative forms of democracy.

Definitions of democracy

If we accept a minimalist and procedural definition of democracy, then democratisation has undoubtedly occurred. Bratton and van de Walle (1997:13) propose the following definition:

> ... *a form of political regime in which citizens choose, in competitive elections, the occupants of the top political offices of the state... a transition to democracy occurs with the installation of a government chosen on the basis of one competitive election, as long as that election is freely and fairly conducted within a matrix of civil liberties, and that all the contestants accept the validity of the election results.*

They contrast this with a comprehensive definition of democracy, requiring the existence of a number of interlocking institutions (such as independent legislatures and courts, a free press, and viable opposition parties) and widely shared political values. Bratton and van de Walle argue that for their purpose (a comparative analysis of political reform is Sub-Saharan Africa in the 1990s), this is not a useful approach, since one risks not finding any evidence at all of democratic transitions (ibid: 12). In addition, a substantive definition of democracy, they argue, would involve evaluating regimes on how well they perform in terms of goals such as economic growth, the distribution of income and public service provision. They assert that there is no firm evidence that political democracy promotes or inhibits economic growth or income equality, and so they prefer to focus on the criterion of competitive elections.

Democratic transitions in Southern Africa

This narrowing of the analytic frame for assessing democracy is far too restrictive; nevertheless, a minimalist and procedural approach does have its uses. Table 2 shows that significant changes in political regime occurred in the region between 1989 and 1995, and that multiparty systems have now become the norm rather than the exception.[33] This pattern mirrors that for Sub-Saharan Africa as a whole: the number of countries with multiparty systems increased

---

[33] The exceptions are Angola, which continued to be wracked by civil war between the contested election of 1992 and the cease-fire of 2002, and Swaziland, where the ruling elite, centred on the monarchy, resists any move towards a democratic constitution and political competition.

from 9 to 38 in this period. Of the elections that took place in the region in 1990-94, six can be considered 'founding elections' that ended the monopoly politics of authoritarian regimes (ibid:7-8).

Table 2. Political transitions in Southern Africa 1989-1995

Country	Regime* in 1989	Democratic transition?	Regime in 1995
Angola	One-party plebiscitary system	No: founding election 1992, not accepted by loser	One-party plebiscitary system
Botswana	Multiparty system	Continuity in system	Multiparty system
Lesotho	Military oligarchy	Yes: founding election 1993	Multiparty system
Malawi	Competitive one-party system	Yes: founding election 1994	Multiparty system
Mozambique	One-party plebiscitary system	Yes: founding election 1994	Multiparty system
Namibia	Settler oligarchy	Yes: founding election 1994	Multiparty system
South Africa	Settler oligarchy	Yes: founding election 1994	Multiparty system
Swaziland	One-party plebiscitary system	No: blocked transition	One-party plebiscitary system
Zambia	Competitive one-party system	Yes: founding election 1991	Multiparty system
Zimbabwe	Multiparty system	Continuity in system	Multiparty system

Source: Bratton and van de Walle, 1997

* Definitions:
1. One-party plebiscitary system: voters mobilized and controlled through one-party 'plebiscites' (one-party elections, rallies etc)
2. Multiparty system: voters enjoy universal franchise and equality before law; plurality of parties free to contest open elections.
3. Military oligarchy: Power concentrated in narrow elite; elections few or suspended, limited opportunities for political participation.
4. Competitive one-party system: limited political competition; party primaries or parliamentary elections involve two or more candidates from a single official party on an established policy platform.
5. Settler oligarchy: bureaucratic-authoritarian regimes in which racial minorities deny political rights to majority through restrictive franchise and coercion.

Political change towards at least a minimal form of liberal representative democracy thus took place on a significant scale, but was qualified by the continuation of 'neo-patrimonial' forms of politics within the new institutional arrangements. These are regimes in which 'the right to rule is ascribed to a person rather than to an office' (ibid:62). The ruler and his inner circle use government administration for purposes of patronage, and relationships of loyalty and dependence pervade the formal system.

In Southern Africa, as well as more widely across the continent, there has been much less alternation of political leadership through competitive elections than one might expect, and old guard elites often continue to dominate political life; legislative and judicial institutions remain weak, as do opposition parties, the independent media and civic associations; practices such as clientelism and corruption continue; and the widespread adoption of democratic values and practices has only just begun (ibid:8-9; 235). While a minimum of civil liberties may need to be present for a transition to qualify as democratic, these liberties are often under threat in neo-patrimonial regimes; for example, harassment of opposition supporters, with the police turning a blind eye, is common around election time. By contrast, in a consolidated democracy there will be viable opposition parties, a lively civil society, civilian control over the military, independent legislatures and judiciaries, and a free press (ibid:13). Bratton and van de Walle's 'comprehensive' definition of democracy then becomes relevant.

A brief tour of the region reveals how faltering the move towards consolidated democracy has been. In Lesotho there was a complete breakdown of public order after the 1998 election, when the losing opposition refused to accept the result, despite the election being declared free and fair. Opposition supporters engaged in widespread looting and arson in the capital and other towns, and the security forces declined to intervene. This resulted in the South African army being called in to restore order. Part of the problem was the inappropriate character of the British-style, first-past-the-post electoral system, which meant that the opposition was hardly represented in parliament despite winning 40 per cent of the overall vote.[34] After long negotiations, mediated by donors, a mixed system allowing proportional representation was agreed before the May 2002 election. This was declared free and fair, and despite some opposition protests, widely accepted by the populace. Whether Lesotho can now

---

[34] Roger Southall, 'Five reasons the region can't ignore Lesotho poll', *Business Day*, 21 May 2002.

move beyond its post-independence history of 'dictatorship, military rule and political violence'[35] remains to be seen.

Southall[36] notes the relevance of proportional representation systems within the region, given blatant manipulation of constituency systems by ruling parties, and the way that incumbents have 'rigged the rules to ensure re-election' in recent elections in Zambia, Malawi and Zimbabwe. In Malawi, Bakili Muluzi also attempted to secure support for amendments to the constitution to allow him to run for a third term, a move that was eventually defeated. His government is widely perceived to be authoritarian and corrupt,[37] and the legislature has been co-opted by the president using clientelist strategies such as appointing MPs to government positions (Bratton and van de Walle, 1997:247).

Similar clientelist strategies have been pursued by the Movement for Multiparty Democracy in Zambia. Here too an attempt by the incumbent president, Chiluba, to amend the constitution and run for a third term, was strongly opposed and then dropped in 2001. His successor, Mwanawasa, was elected after widespread accusations of electoral fraud, and ethnic politics are still deeply entrenched.[38]

Politics in Mozambique is characterised by elite corruption, a judiciary whose independence is in question, attacks on the independent press, and a weak civil society. Braathen and Orre (2001) suggest that the institutionalisation of democratic values, norms and rules has not occurred in Mozambique, and 'the country endures a permanent political crisis'.

In Namibia the dominance of the ruling SWAPO party was consolidated in the second post-independence election in 1999, with weak showings by the opposition parties despite the unpopularity of President Nujoma's 1998 decision to send troops to the Democratic Republic of Congo, and the perception that SWAPO's politics are in general highly autocratic and unaccountable (Simon, 2000). Melber (2002:165) notes 'an erosion of democratic values and norms despite the existence of institutions and a canon of virtues as enshrined in the Constitution'.

Botswana is the region's outstanding example of free elections and multiparty competition, sustained over thirty years. Even here, however, 'there are still many obstacles in the political system that undermine the quality and meaningfulness of electoral choice'

---

[35] Ibid
[36] Ibid
[37] In 2001 three cabinet ministers were dismissed after a major corruption scandal in the education sector.
[38] 'Ethnic politics a persistent theme', *Business Day*, 25 February 2002.

(Selolwane, 2002). Chief amongst these is the unbroken dominance of the party that won the first post-independence elections in 1964, the Botswana Democratic Party. Given persistent poverty and deep inequality, why have opposition parties not performed better? One reason is the 'first-past-the–post' electoral system. Another, is the weakness of alternative economic management strategies proposed by the opposition, compared with the ruling party's track record of four decades of sustained economic growth (ibid). In relation to human rights, the current forced resettlement of San villagers from the Central Kalahari is a major cause for concern.

As Bratton and van de Walle (1997:233-60) spell out clearly, the consolidation of democracy in Africa is confronted by a number of problems. Neo-patrimonialism lives on within the context of 'nominally democratic politics', and the deepening of democracy depends on the strength of the state apparatus relative to the countervailing powers of actors outside of government. One-party dominance is a major problem, since if this prevents alternation in leadership, 'democratic rule will not even reach the minimal threshold for consolidation' (ibid:253). Melber's (2002:165) characterisation of current political regimes in the region is even harsher:

> The post-colonial politics of the ruling parties often displays ...tendencies to autocratic rule and the subordination of the state under the party, as well as politically motivated social and material favours as a reward system for loyalty or disadvantages as a form of coercion in cases of dissent...'

Post-apartheid democracy in South Africa

How does South Africa rate in terms of the consolidation of democracy? This question has been vigorously debated in recent years, and although the comparative strength of South African democracy within the region is clear, analysts identify a number of weaknesses. These call into question the 'quality' and strength of democracy in South Africa (Southall, 2001; Lodge, 2002; Graham, 2002). Left critics are more forthright, pointing to neo-liberal economic policies that benefit both old and emerging elites which are bolstered by a 'truncated' democracy, and within which 'the boundaries of opposition and debate... are progressively narrowed' (McKinley, 2001:185).

On the positive side of the balance sheet, South Africa has a widely praised constitution with a strong Bill of Rights that enshrines the underlying principle of equality and includes a number of socio-economic rights (such as access to land, health care, housing, water, and food), as well as rights of free expression and association, and freedom from arbitrary treatment and discrimination by the state (Albertyn, 2002). The constitution underpins an institutional order that includes a range of legislatures (at national, provincial and local levels), a multiplicity of political parties, an independent judiciary and autonomous Constitutional Court, a number of commissions to protect specific rights (for example, a Human Rights Commission and a Gender Commission), and other watchdog bodies such as a Public Protector and an Independent Broadcasting Authority (Southall, 2001:16).

Political parties are well institutionalised, and are competitive in free and fair elections supervised by an Independent Electoral Commission. Levels of intimidation of voters have declined since the founding election of 1994 (Maseko, 2002). A proportional representation system ensures that many small minority parties have seats in parliament, which is at times the site of robust debates on government policy. According to Lodge (2002), the state apparatus demonstrates an increasing capacity to convert socio-economic rights (such as housing) into realities, through implementing development policies.

Civil society, despite a discernible weakening since 1994, remains vigorous and diverse, comprising a range of civics and community-based organisations, NGOs and a large, independent and powerful trade union movement, as well as middle-class professional associations. Emergent social movements such as the Treatment Action Campaign and the Landless People's Movement allow for the expression of highly critical views of the state and in certain instances their campaigns (as in relation to treatment of HIV/AIDS) have influenced government policies. Legal activists have won important Constitutional Court rulings in support of socio-economic rights (for instance the Grootboom judgement on the right to adequate housing). The press and broadcasting media are independent and assertive, creating space for public debate.

On the negative side, one party, the ruling ANC, dominates political life in South Africa. In 1999 the ANC secured just under the two-thirds of national parliamentary seats needed to unilaterally change the Constitution. It now rules in eight of the nine provinces,[39]

---

[39] In the Western Cape this has occurred not through a victory at the polls but through an alliance with the New National Party agreed in 2002, and as a result of recent legislation allowing floor-crossing.

and won by far the majority of seats (60 per cent) in local government elections in 2000. The opposition is highly fragmented and at present does not pose a threat to the ANC's electoral dominance (Lodge, 2002:157). One reason is that in elections to date, voter affiliations have continued to coincide with race to a large extent, and an interest-based (and, in particular, class-based) politics has yet to emerge despite the increasing salience of class in determining socio-economic status (Habib and Taylor, 2001; Maylam, 2001). At the same time, the party list system that accompanies proportional representation has allowed the ruling party to exercise increasingly strict control over its MPs, and led to a weakening of parliament's role of overseeing the executive arm of government.[40] It has reduced the accountability of elected representatives to the electorate, and limited the space for free debate within political parties. The ANC has also blurred the distinction between the party and the state through political appointments to key positions in the civil service, parastatals and regulatory bodies.

A key question in a representative democracy is how accountable government is to its citizens. One-party dominance, where rulers do not in practice run the danger of being replaced by voters, brings this into question (Southall, 2001:17). Graham (2002:90) comments that popular control over elected decision makers in South Africa is weaker than it should be, because the citizenry has been demobilised since 1990, 'oversight through technical means is limited and largely available to particular civic elites', and 'the legislatures appear to be in the hands of party caucuses which consider the interests of the party, and in the case of the ruling party, the executive over the interests of citizens and individual elected representatives'. All this makes effective opposition to the ruling party, not only from political parties but also from civil society groupings as well as from dissidents within the liberation alliance, critically important.

For some liberal critics (Giliomee and Simkins, 1999) the problem of one-party dominance in a racially divided society like South Africa derives from the fact that the mass base of the ruling party has assumed a primarily racial identity. Compelled by economic realities to maintain friendly relations with the business classes, the new rulers have shed their radical populism, abandoned the unemployed and non-unionised workers, granted concessions

---

[40] The clearest example is the ANC's moves in 2001 to undermine the independence of the standing committee on public accounts during an investigation of possible corruption in the R60 billion arms deal (Lodge, 2002:166).

to organized labour, and sought to build an alliance with the black middle class and the labour aristocracy. In seeking to manage the contradictions between these divergent interests, the ruling party mixes coercive with democratic procedures, non-racialism with Africanism, the free market with labour market regulation, and state patronage of African contractors with monopolies for white-controlled corporations. It also seeks to concentrate power over the party and state machinery, justifying this by reference to the goal of 'transformation', and criticism and opposition is labelled as 'racist'. Democratic institutions would therefore need to be much stronger than they are at present if the power of the executive is to be kept in check. This 'strong' view of ANC political dominance, achieved in part through an appeal to race rather than class, is echoed in the analyses of some left critics (McKinley, 2001; Habib and Taylor, 2001).[41]

In terms of the ANC's internal politics, the party amended its constitution in 1997 to strengthen the control of the national executive over all structures, and re-asserted the principle of 'democratic centralism'. An increasingly authoritarian approach to internal political life has been evident in recent years (Lodge, 2002; McKinley, 2001). Within the Tripartite Alliance (comprising the ANC, the Congress of South African Trade Unions (COSATU) and the South African Communist Party (SACP)), a number of tensions and strains have been evident since 1994, particularly in relation to economic policy. Habib and Taylor (2001:221-22) feel that the centralisation of power in the ANC is inimical to democracy, and effective parliamentary opposition can come only from a party based on the organised African working class but able to articulate the interests of the unemployed, the lower middle class and the rural poor. Formation of such a party would require COSATU and the SACP to break with the Tripartite Alliance.

Webster (2001) argues that COSATU is unlikely to undertake such a break, since union leaders continue to have hopes of influencing government through the Alliance, 'rather than opting for the political wilderness' (ibid:267). An alternative is that COSATU emerges as a left pressure group within the Alliance, perhaps within the framework of a social pact, where the unions agree to co-operate with government in opening the economy to international competition

---

[41] Racial categories are equally invoked by opposition parties in a continuation of 'race populism' (Mare, 2001), while traditional leaders invoke both customary powers and ethnic identities. Such trends are likely to continue at the expense of social identities such as class (Maylam, 2001).

in return for concessions for workers. Webster goes on to suggest strong parallels with the Zimbabwean case, where conflict between unions and government over time led to the formation of a powerful opposition party, open and violent confrontation, and an organised challenge to the ruling party.[42] In South Africa, however, this could undermine nation-building and economic reconstruction, and the labour movement finds itself in a fundamental dilemma.

For van Lieres (forthcoming) South African democracy comprises a complex and explosive configuration of liberal and non-liberal elements, juxtaposing divergent politics and discourses: juridical, liberal individualism, on the one hand, and collectively-based cultural and customary identities on the other. Underlying these is a situation of extreme marginalisation, so that 'while the majority of people's legal status is assured, their experience of citizenship remains ambiguous. They remain excluded from economic equality and empowerment and effective democratic participation in the public sphere' (ibid:2). Liberal constitutionalism has not resulted in consensus on the meaning of 'justice', and this has produced disjunctures between rights and justice, and democracy and justice (ibid:27). Some groups (such as the Khoe-San) have relied on substantive land claims to advance their collective interests rather than a rights-based politics.[43] The danger is that authoritarian forms of politics, based on appeals to race, ethnicity or cultural identity, could entrench themselves within the liberal democratic order, with the state willing to tolerate them for the sake of 'order' (ibid:1).

Many commentators agree that the most fundamental challenge to democracy in South Africa is the depth and intractability of social and economic inequality. This effectively 'excludes people as individual citizens and as groups of citizens' (Graham, 2002:92). Tsele (2002:81) comments that the real test of equality is not in the content of a constitution or Bill of Rights 'but rather in their actual realisation for ordinary citizens'. Apartheid's inheritance of massive poverty and inequality raises doubts about definitions of democracy that do not attempt to integrate the substantive dimension, that is, that do not address the question of whether or not democracy is effective in resolving problems of highly skewed relations of production and distribution and the social ills that follow.

---

[42] These parallels might help explain the South African government's lack of support for the opposition in Zimbabwe.
[43] This resonates strongly with Raftopolous's critique (this volume) of the 'rupture' between discourses of rights and redistribution that have occurred in the Zimbabwean context.

Contested discourses of democracy

So what, then, is democracy? According to Luckham et al. (2000:7), the idea of democracy arose in the context of struggles against despotic rule and injustice. The Athenian model of direct or participatory democracy gave sovereign power to free and equal citizens constituted in an assembly. In contrast, the liberal representative model places emphasis on institutional arrangements that pre-empt tyranny: governments elected through free and fair elections in which every citizen's vote counts equally, universal suffrage, and freedom of conscience, information and expression. Adults have the right to stand for office and to oppose their government, and to form independent associations including political parties. Tyranny is avoided through the separation of powers, constitutionalism, the rule of law and the protection of individual rights, including private property rights.

From liberal democracy to democratic politics

The modern version of liberal democracy fuses two historical developments: (a) the bourgeois revolution, which gave rise to the idea of a limited or *liberal state* with elected representatives, a separation of powers, and the division between the public and private spheres; and (b) political mobilisation of the masses to press for the extension of the franchise, the expansion of citizenship to include social and economic entitlements, and *democratic* government which is accountable to citizens via free and fair elections (Held, 1997:8). Mass political parties are supposed to help restrain the abuse of power of elites by providing a mechanism for active participation in politics and access to policy makers, but have often become instruments of direct control or vehicles for patronage and elite dominance (ibid:8).

This points to an important distinction: between *democratic institutions* and *democratic politics*. The former are emphasised in dominant strains of political science, which stress the formal or procedural aspects of democracy. Democratic politics, in contrast, refers to 'the struggle for power or for access to rulers and collective goods' (Luckham et al., 2000:10). Democratic politics aims to keep the institutions of democracy to their promise, and to give citizens the ability to hold to account powerful interests in both the public and the private sphere. Democracy is thus not to be equated simply with current versions of Western liberal democracy: it is 'simultaneously a (contested) set of values; an (inherently contradictory) system of rule; and a (necessarily unfinished) emancipatory process' (Luckham, 1998:308). In terms of the latter, a key focus is the 'deep politics' of society, which is concerned with the lived conditions of socio-economic existence.

'Deep politics' have always been the main focus of the left. For Marx the inherent limits of what he termed 'bourgeois democracy' are rooted in the false claim that the state represents the interests of the public as a whole, as opposed to the private interests of individuals. But this view of the public order assumes that social and economic life, and indeed political life, is not circumscribed and defined by class relations built on exploitation. A seemingly 'neutral' state that in formal terms treats citizens as equals and defends their rights (for example, to hold property), in practice sustains the privileges of the class that owns most property. Thus the liberal notion of a 'minimalist' state masks a coercive state that protects the minority that benefits most from the 'free market' economy. Rather than being detached from them, the liberal state is deeply embedded in social and economic relations and reinforces, codifies and administers the structure and operation of these relations (Held, 1997:130).

This critique appears anachronistic at first sight. After all, as the new millennium begins there are few surviving states founded on the Marxist vision of 'people's democracies' as an alternative to capitalist liberal democracy, and their record is one scarred by repression. Yet liberal democracy is falling into disrepair at the very moment of its triumph:

> A democracy deficit has opened, manifest in public apathy about politics, an erosion of standards in public life, and widening socio-economic inequality. Globalisation has eroded the capacity of elected governments to take decisions concerning their own citizens.... A double disempowerment has apparently occurred, both of democratic institutions and of the citizens they serve (Luckham, 1998:307).

The quality of real world democracies, even in the societies in which they first originated, thus falls far short of the democratic ideal. In Africa, as noted above, the distance between promise and reality is even greater.

Democracy debates in Africa

More than a decade ago Issa Shivji (1991a) suggested that a sharp divide exists between views of democracy that equate it with the liberal representative form of state, and those in which it denotes emancipatory struggles for freedom and equality, and against oppression and exploitation. Both meanings are socially and historically grounded, and thus contingent. In Africa, where economies were dominated by foreign capital, liberal democracy was part of the ideology of domination, and a justification for rule by a local comprador class. However, this does not mean that questions of institutional form, electoral rules, constitutional frameworks, the content of rights, and limitations on the exercise of power are unimportant. These can be critically important sites of engagement with the core issues of *popular* (as well as liberal) democracy.

In similar fashion, Mamdani (1990) emphasises the importance of social and political context, and thus of the nature of the social forces pushing for democratisation. This makes the human rights movement 'contested terrain', without a pre-determined meaning. As in the 1980s in Africa, an emphasis on human rights can assist conservatives seeking to displace the revolutionary focus of emerging popular movements. On the other hand, reform movements can also contribute to emerging struggles against repressive regimes. No such struggle can ever denounce the agenda of human rights and the rule of law. Rather, the goal must be to define these concepts and their political implications in an expanded fashion, so that they lead to, rather than displace, a discourse of power and popular sovereignty. The key question is the character of the social forces promoting the agenda.

Both Mamdani and Shivji write from a perspective that recognises the necessity of connecting politics and economics in arguments about democracy, but are at pains to emphasise the equivocal experience of 'popular democracy' in Africa to date. Echoing Fanon's earlier critique of the 'limits of national consciousness', they discuss the tendency for post-colonial regimes in Africa to monopolise power, often using the language of socialism or radical politics to justify their aims. Examples include Tanzania, Ethiopia, Egypt, Libya, Mozambique and Uganda. In some cases political rule has been underpinned by a militarisation of the state. Here 'liberators have turned tyrants and continue to tyrannise through the barrel of a gun' (Shivji 1991a:79). The Party becomes part of the state rather than of civil society, and begins to depend upon the use of coercion rather than persuasion. Over time the Party ceases even to be a ruling party, but a 'supreme political existence which holds the last word on the social good and the political truth' (ibid:85).

The effects of this monopolisation of power are fourfold. The autonomous organisation of different interest groups in civil society is suppressed; the autonomous articulation of these interests in the media is severely circumscribed, if not suppressed; the cumulative result of these two processes is the development of a 'closed society', both institutionally and ideologically; and a political culture of intolerance is generated, leading to a 'politics of unanimity' rather than a 'politics of consensus'. These describe precisely the thrust of political culture in Zimbabwe since 2000, and as shown above, are beginning to be evident within South Africa too.

John Saul (1997a) links the narrowing of the debate in Africa (with its primary focus on multiparty systems and electoral politics) to the current dominance of neo-liberal doctrines. Advocates of conceptions of democracy in terms of 'competing elites', such as Diamond (1993), are explicit about the need to deflate the state and invigorate the private economy, but this represents for Saul a 'dramatic abandonment of the politics of public purpose and a fetishisation of the market'. In Przeworski's (1991:37) formulation, a 'stable democracy requires that governments be strong enough to govern effectively but weak enough not to be able to govern against important interests...democratic institutions must remain within narrow limits to be successful'.

The narrow view of democratisation is termed by Saul the 'political science' view, and is contrasted with a 'political economy' approach. The former tends to 'bracket off' the latter's concerns about structural inequality. Nevertheless, for Saul, as for Shivji and Mamdani, some of the concerns of the political science theorists are valid, and debates around constitutions, electoral systems, human rights and the rule of law are far from irrelevant. For the political economy school, 'procedural' definitions of democracy are important, but insufficient.

Alternative forms of democracy

What are the (desirable) alternatives to liberal democracy, in Africa and more widely? Many on the left answer 'popular democracy', but acknowledge, unapologetically, the difficulty of specifying this alternative more concretely. According to Shivji (1991b:255) 'its exact contours and forms of existence can only be determined in actual social struggles in given, concrete social conditions'. For Saul (1997b:231) the answer cannot be separated from resistance and struggles within the 'economic' side of the political economy terrain, that is, struggles against the global hegemony of contemporary capitalism; struggles to 'bring capital under social control'. There are severe limitations on how much institutional reform can achieve without such grounding, which means that genuine popular empowerment 'must continue to be built painstakingly – conceived, renewed, struggled for, given institutional form – from the bottom up' (ibid). In Southern Africa this means looking to social movements (particularly organised labour but other forms of progressive popular organisation as well), to contest deal-making between the state and capital while simultaneously seeking to explore and extend more direct and participatory forms of democracy.

Robin Luckham (1998:311) notes the difference between 'people's democracy' (now clearly an outmoded form of state) and popular democracy as 'goal and process', where the focus is on the opening of democratic spaces from below rather than on whole system alternatives to liberal democracy. He distinguishes four traditions of analysis, all of them relevant in Southern Africa today. One approach advocates participatory, deliberative or radical forms of democracy. These extend the notion of democracy beyond the public sphere into the workplace and the home, and emphasise a reinvigoration of civil society (through social movements in particular) that can also begin to transform power relations within the state. In the South African context this accords with calls by analysts such as Marais (2001:287-89) for the left to pursue transformative visions of self-management (worker ownership, co-operative enterprises, reinvigorated neighbourhood structures), for COSATU to extend its links with other progressive sections of civil society and build a popular social alliance around campaigns with broad appeal, and for civil society groups to seek entry points for engagement (or even alliances) within the state and the ruling party.

A second approach emphasises the reform of liberal democratic institutions. This takes the form of either attempts to hold them to their promise of accountable government, or the introduction of more consensual modes of decision-making such as plebiscitary voting using new technologies, 'consociational' power-sharing arrangements, or decentralising powers to local communities in one or other version of municipal democracy. In Southern Africa the latter has been the subject of much debate and some policy reform (Conyers, 1990; de Valk and Wekwete, 1990; Manor, 2000; IDS, 2003), yet often local democracies are created but given no powers, or powers are devolved to non-representative or upwardly accountable local authorities (Ribot, 2002). This remains a crucial area of engagement, because 'an egalitarian, democratic state must...

find a way of combining strong central direction with forms of institutional decentralisation that strengthen the voices of the poor' (Nattrass and Seekings, 1998:216).

A third perspective derives from the proliferation of participatory approaches to development in recent years, which stress empowerment of the rural and urban poor in development projects. Although the links with participatory democracy have remained somewhat undeveloped, for some analysts and practitioners the political implications of participation and the potential challenge it poses to local power holders are clear – as are the pitfalls of 'depoliticised' participatory development (Nelson and Wright, 1997). In Southern Africa these approaches have been enthusiastically promoted for some years and continue to form part of the standard rhetoric of both government agencies and NGOs, but in practice the record in terms of meaningful participation is mixed. This is partly because of the severe limitations of engaging in 'empowerment' only at the micro-level, when many of the constraints on development are located at wider (national or international) levels.

A fourth approach attempts to 'democratise democracy' through ensuring that 'democratic structures at all levels address the concerns of the great mass of citizens and not merely those of political elites' (Luckham, 1998:315). Both democracy and socialism have to be reconstructed 'from the bottom up', and gender and minority rights have to be affirmed. This approach has an affinity for social democracy, with its broader concept of citizenship, focus on socio-economic rights, and notions of deepening political participation. These emphases are common in critical policy advocacy within Southern Africa at the current time, with many on the left acknowledging that social democratic policies are more feasible in the short to medium term than a transition to socialism – which is, in any case, difficult to define with any precision these days.

Activism that focuses on socio-economic rights and policies to give them practical expression is widespread in the region, with NGOs and social movements (drawing on the skills of public interest lawyers) in the forefront of mobilisation from below in the name of citizenship rights (Liebenberg, 2002). These can take the form of campaigns to keep governments to the promise of their constitutions, as in the Treatment Action Campaign in South Africa, or campaigns to amend national constitutions and extend the bounds of democracy (as in Zimbabwe and Swaziland). This approach might be termed 'radical constitutionalism'.

These different approaches are not mutually exclusive and have much in common. They all stress democratisation as active political engagement, invigorating and giving content to the institutional frameworks of liberal democracy. They tend to function as 'visions of the good society' rather than as alternative institutional designs; 'as ways of confronting power, extending choice, and creating spaces for participation in the framework of modern states' (Luckham, 1998:309). Being grounded in particular contexts and emancipatory struggles, they express themselves in diverse forms and through a wide range of agencies. Their relevance in contemporary Southern Africa is highlighted by the collapse of liberal democracy in Zimbabwe and the bankruptcy of authoritarian forms of rule by Zanu (PF). Even in South Africa, where liberal democracy receives its strongest expression in the region, the inadequacy of formal and narrowly institutional approaches in the face of continuing poverty and deepening inequality, means that a 'democracy of content' is increasingly the focus of political debate.

The crisis of developmental democracy in Southern Africa

One common response to the Zimbabwe crisis within the region is to re-assert the values of 'good governance' (implicitly within the framework of liberal representative democracy, thus including protection of private property rights), and to call for more effective neo-liberal economic management, so that 'democracy can deliver development'.[44] Another (usually less explicit) response is to call into question the institutions of liberal democracy, and to invoke instead various forms of identity politics, including authoritarian nationalism of the Zanu (PF) type, or perhaps a return to 'African traditional democracy'. Land redistribution is potentially a rallying call for this form of politics – but as Zimbabwe demonstrates, it can easily be accompanied by corrupt, abusive and exclusionary practices. A hybrid of these, perhaps descriptive of current realities in many Southern African countries, is the (selective) retention of liberal democratic institutional forms by one-party dominated regimes, which then govern in an authoritarian manner.

None of these responses are adequate to the crisis of developmental democracy in the region. As in Zimbabwe, the discontents and tensions produced by underlying socio-economic realities must sooner or later find expression in political processes

---

[44] 'A heavy responsibility', *Mail and Guardian*, March 15 to 21, 2002.

of one kind or another, that are likely to challenge the current framework of liberal democracy, neo-liberal economic policies and the reproduction of unequal property relations. Authoritarian responses are feasible but hardly desirable. We are therefore left with little alternative but to seek to create a political and economic order that deepens democracy, reduces poverty, and attacks the foundations of structural inequality. Recognition of the ineffectiveness of market-based approaches means that the centrality of the state must be re-asserted, but in reconfigured relationships with other forces in society. Issues of state capacity then become crucial, but also of accountability. This requires a continuation of the struggle for democratisation as an 'unfinished emancipatory process'.

Land and agrarian reform in the new politics of democracy and development

A new politics of development and democracy could well emerge in Southern Africa in the decade to come, but it will have to include a clear and central focus on land and agrarian reform, or risk losing purchase on the roots of structural inequality. This is one of the signal lessons from Zimbabwe, and one that many analysts are now beginning to understand[45] – including those linked to the labour movement, who have tended in the past to focus mainly on job creation, service delivery, and the social wage in the context of industrial and urban development. Nevertheless, the linkages between alternative development policies, democratic politics and radical approaches to agrarian reform are not as clear and explicit in contemporary debates as they could be. These connections are suggested clearly by the logic of an argument for agrarian reform that begins with the structure of the political economy, outlines why current approaches to land reform are inadequate, suggests an alternative conception of land reform which requires specific roles and capacities for the democratic state, and considers the political feasibility of such a reform. It is only possible to present the bones of this argument here, but some of the flesh is contained in previous sections of this chapter.

The structure of the political economy: Southern African societies are scarred by poverty and inequality, not least in the agrarian economy. They are highly dualistic, with a 'core' that is well connected to the international economy, and a large 'periphery' (informal urban settlements and rural areas) characterised by weak local economies,

---

[45] For South Africa, see Vavi, 2001; Hart, 2002; Makgetla and van Meelis, 2003.

casual and seasonal work, low-income forms of self-employment, prostitution and crime. The population of this periphery is socially and economically differentiated, as reflected in diverse livelihood strategies. The articulation of rural and non-rural activities and income streams is weakened by the 'redundancy' of the rural poor within struggling capitalist economies, leading to a crisis of social reproduction. HIV/AIDS exacerbates this crisis, undermining the viability of the household as a unit and placing gender relations under great stress. Land-based livelihoods (in which women play a central role) remain important and their value is often underestimated, but they are constrained by inadequate access to high quality land (as a result of historical dispossession) and insufficient support in the form of research, extension, micro-finance, input supply and marketing (Shackleton et al., 2001).

Current approaches to land reform: Market-based programmes of land redistribution fail to deliver sufficient land of appropriate quality, and are biased towards an emerging black capitalist class ('accumulation from above'). Neo-liberal fiscal policies hamstring the capacity of the state to implement land reform on a large scale, and land reform is not an integral component of coherent programmes of rural development. Support services to beneficiaries are weak or absent. Tenure reform to create strong land rights has not yet occurred in practice, is hampered by orthodoxies around private property, and has yet to confront the central issue of women's rights. Equivocal stances by governments towards traditional leaders and patriarchy undermine the democratisation of communal tenure and land administration. Rights-based approaches are artificially separated from asset redistribution and livelihood enhancement.

Alternative approaches and agrarian reform: Land reform is urgently required across Southern Africa, to create equitable access to high quality land, to secure people's rights to land and resources within a range of tenure systems (including both group and individualised systems as options and with gender equality as a critical goal), and to increase the tenure security of farm-workers and labour tenants and provide them with access to land in their own right. A pro-active state can make use of market mechanisms (and expropriation where necessary) to target land reform in regions of emerging opportunity where need (and thus demand) are also found. This would then allow planning for area-based land reform, in which infrastructure and support services could be provided to land reform projects in a cost-effective manner, and redistribution and tenure reform could be integrated. However, land reform will only be effective if embedded within a broader agrarian reform that creates the conditions for processes of 'accumulation from below', through improved access to inputs, equipment, draught power, marketing outlets, infrastructure, and support services such as extension, training and marketing advice. Agrarian reform aims to fundamentally transform the social and political relations that underpin systems of production, and to change the balance of economic power (Levin and Weiner, 1997).

Rethinking the role of the state: Radical agrarian reform requires the state to play a central and leading role, and to devote sufficient resources to redistribution, tenure reform and rural livelihoods support, but also to work in close collaboration with NGOs and other service providers. Concerted efforts to strengthen the relevant capacity of both state and non-state agencies are needed. Supporting institutional development at local community level is vital, and facilitates active participation by rural people in agrarian reform. Decentralising implementation to district or local levels can assist co-ordination of government and non-government programmes, but will only be effective if mechanisms for strong downward accountability accompany the transfer of resources. Democratising land administration is crucial if rights to land and resources (particularly among the most marginalised, including women) are to be realised in practice, and local institutions will require ongoing support from the state.

Political feasibility: The prospects for radical agrarian reform in the region have improved over the past three years, partly because events in Zimbabwe have prompted a reconsideration of the land issue. There is now widespread agreement that unresolved land questions are a political time-bomb, and that progress in land reform in most countries in the region needs to be speeded up. Emerging social movements such as the Landless People's Movement in South Africa have given a new edge to civil society critiques of government policies. There is the beginning of a real interest in agrarian reform by the labour movement. It is clear that renewed pressure for fundamental changes in current economic policies is now being exerted by a number of diverse interest groups, organisations and campaigns, and that the central importance of land and agrarian reform to poverty reduction is being recognised more widely than before. These trends help to create the conditions for rural social movements to begin to mobilise on a large scale, and to build alliances with popular organisations active in other sectors.

The logic of this argument can be extended to the broader terrain of alternative development policies and struggles to deepen democracy. The starting point must be the recognition of 'structural dynamics that sunder society into pockets of privilege and vast hinterlands of deprivation' (Marais, 2001:306). In former settler colonies in the region, as in South Africa, transitions to majority rule democracies have ushered in 'a lopsided structure – two nations disguised as one, a hybrid social formation consisting of increasingly deracialised insiders and persistently black outsiders' (Bundy, 1999:11). This structure is being reproduced rather than transformed in even the relatively strong economies of the region (Botswana, South Africa), and despite significant economic growth in others (Mozambique). As with mainstream land reform, market-based development policies in line with neo-liberal prescriptions are proving utterly inadequate to the task of poverty reduction and social transformation.

Alternative policy frameworks are urgently required, and have been proposed. For example, in South Africa COSATU has called for a set of integrated policies to boost economic growth, job creation and redistribution, linking macro-economic, labour market and industrial policies with a comprehensive social security system (including a basic income grant) and asset redistribution (for example, via land reform). Makgetla and van Meelis (2003) emphasise that the central thrust of this progamme is a radical restructuring – of the production structure (towards labour intensivity), of markets (focusing on the expansion of domestic demand rather than only on exports), of spatial structure (addressing the lack of infrastructure in rural areas), and of class relations (making large capital accountable, promoting co-operatives and supporting substantial growth in small and micro-enterprises). Alternative policies along broadly these lines have been proposed elsewhere in the region too, for example by the Zimbabwe Congress of Trade Unions (ZCTU).

As with agrarian reform, these alternative policy frameworks assume a central role for the state, partly to overcome the resistance of vested interests (in combination with popular pressure), but also in 'directing the growth path, by defining property and power relations, and by how it directs services spatially and sectorally' (Makgetla and van Meelis, 2003:97). Generating an alternative to neo-liberalism will involve building alliances beyond the nation-state so that the global economic power of the northern 'triad' (the United States, Europe and Japan) can be challenged (Amin, 2003).

However, the need for a strong central state must be balanced by an ongoing politics of democratisation of the state, at all levels. As in the case of land administration bodies, downwardly accountable local government is a necessary prerequisite of appropriate development planning and service provision, but local officials must also be horizontally accountable to elected representatives, and upwardly accountable to policy makers who are responsible for developing coherent national programmes. And yet the state is not the only game in town. A democracy of real substance requires politicised popular organisations and social movements that engage with the state, help keep it accountable, and focus on ongoing efforts to open up democratic spaces 'from below'.

'A festering wound that won't go away'

What then are the prospects for a new politics of land, development and democracy in Southern Africa today? As events in Zimbabwe so clearly demonstrate, changes in the balance of political forces can dramatically alter the terrain of state policy, and a crucial variable is the degree of mobilisation and organisation of ordinary citizens – always recognising that this population is highly diverse and internally differentiated, and that collective interests are not simply givens but constituted by 'political leadership and political choice' (Bernstein, 1997). The possibility that mobilisation will follow appeals to race or ethnicity, or reactionary forms of populism, cannot be discounted. There are no guarantees that a truly democratic politics will generate wide appeal throughout the region as the promise of liberal democracy begins to look increasingly threadbare.

A key factor in coming years will be the direction taken by the labour movement, which retains the potential to anchor a progressive popular movement against neo-liberal capitalism. One of its strengths is the strong regional linkages it maintains, which helps to sustain its focus on the politics as well as the economics of democratic transformation. The building of effective alliances between organised labour and other elements of civil society, and especially emerging social movements, is the central challenge in the period to come, albeit on terms that differ markedly from those of the largely urban social movement unionism that characterised South African civic politics in the 1980s (Hart, 2002). As Hart notes,

> ...full-scale commitment to broader livelihood issues would mean moving away from a rearguard defence of rapidly diminishing formal sector jobs, and incorporation within corporatist arrangements...At the same time, a movement to

> secure livelihoods is unlikely to succeed without the active contribution of organized labour, and a revival of the democratic practices forged in the labour struggles of the 1970s and 1980s.

With regard to the structure of the agrarian economy of the region, it is founded on a highly skewed distribution of land and natural resources, as well as on the weak and insecure property rights of the majority of rural people. This is a festering wound on the body politic of post-liberation Southern Africa that will be healed neither through neglect nor the palliative of de-racialising commercial agriculture. Radical surgery is required, but, as Zimbabwe demonstrates so clearly, this must not itself threaten the life of the patient. A vital condition of recovery is the extension of the struggle for democracy, as well as the adoption of development policies that bring real reductions in poverty and inequality.

References

ADB (African Development Bank), 2000. *African Development Report*. Abidjan: African Development Bank.

Albertyn, Cathi, 2002.'Protecting Citizen's Equality and their Ability to Control Decision-makers'. In Graham, Paul and Coetzee, Alice, (eds), 2002. *In the Balance? Debating the State of Democracy in South Africa*. Cape Town: Institute for Democracy in South Africa.

Alden Wily, Liz and Sue Mbaya, 2001. *Land, People and Forests in Eastern and Southern Africa at the Beginning of the 21st Century*. Nairobi: Natural Resources International and The World Conservation Union.

Aliber, Michael, 2003. 'Chronic Poverty in South Africa: Incidence, Causes and Policies'. *World Development*, Vol. 31, No. 3.

Amin, Samir, 2003 'The Alternative to the Neoliberal System of Globalisation'. *New Agenda* 10: 87-107.

Arrighi, Giovanni, 1970, 'Labour supplies in Historical Perspective: A Study of the Proletarianisation of the African Peasantry in Rhodesia'. *Journal of Development Studies*, Vol. 6, No. 3: 197-234.

Berry, Sara, 1993. *No Condition is Permanent. The Social Dynamics of Agrarian Change in Sub-Saharan Africa*. Madison: The University of Wisconsin Press.

Bernstein, Henry, 1997. 'Social change in the Southern African countryside? Land, and production, poverty and power'. Occasional Paper 4, Cape Town: Programme for Land and Agrarian Studies, School of Government, University of the Western Cape.

Bond, Patrick, 2000. *Elite Transition. From Apartheid to Neoliberlaism in South Africa*. London and Pietermaritzburg: Pluto Press and University of Natal Press.

Braathen, Einar and Aslak Orre, 2001. 'Can a Patrimonial Democracy Survive? The Case of Mozambique'. *Forum for Development Studies*, No. 2: 199-239.

Bratton, Michael and Nicolas van de Walle, 1997. *Democratic Experiments in Africa. Regime Transitions in Comparative Perpsective*. Cambridge: Cambridge University Press.

Bratton, Michael and Robert Mattes, 2002. 'Popular Economic Values and Economic Reform in Southern Africa'. Afrobarometer Paper No. 10, Cape Town, Accra, and East Lansing: Institute for Democracy in South Africa, Ghana Centre for Democratic Development and Michigan State University.

Bundy, Colin, 1999. 'Truth or Reconciliation'. *Southern African Report* (August), Toronto.

Conyers, D., 1990. 'Centralization and Development Planning: A Comprehensive Perspective'. In Peter de Welk and Kadmiel Wekwete (eds), 1990, pp. 15-34.

Cousins, Ben, Dan Weiner and Nick Amin, 1992. 'Social Differentiation in the Communal Lands of Zimbabwe'. *Review of African Political Economy*, No. 53: 5-24.

Cousins, Ben, 1997. 'How Do Rights become Real? Formal and Informal Institutions in South Africa's Land Reform'. *IDS Bulletin* 28(4): pp. 59-68.

Cousins, Ben, 2002. 'Legislating Negotiability: Tenure Reform in Post-Apartheid South Africa'. In Kristine Juul and Christian Lund (eds): *Negotiating Property in Africa*. Portsmouth, NH: Heinemann.

Cousins, Ben and Aninka Claassens, 2003. 'Communal land tenure in South Africa: livelihoods, rights, institutions'. *Development Update*, Vol. 4, No. 3.

de Swardt, Cobus, 2003. 'Unravelling chronic poverty in South Africa: Some food for thought'. Unpublished paper. Cape Town: Programme for Land and Agrarian Studies, School of Government, University of the Western Cape.

de Valk, Peter and Kadmiel Wekwete (eds), 1990. *Decentralising for Participatory Planning: Comparing the Experiences of Zimbabwe and Other Anglophone Countries in Eastern and Southern Africa*. Aldershot: Avebury Press.

Diamond, Larry, 1993. 'Three Paradoxes of Democracy'. In Larry Diamond and Marc F. Plattner (eds), *The Global Resurgence of Democracy*. Baltimore: Johns Hopkins Press.

FAO (Food and Agriculture Organisation), 2003. 'Seeking Ways Out of the Impasse on Land Reform in Southern Africa: Notes from an informal 'think tank' meeting'. Unpublished paper. Rome: FAO.

Giliomee, Hermann and Charles Simkins (eds), *The Awkward Embrace: One-Party Domination and Democracy*. Cape Town: Tafelberg.

Graham, Paul, 2002. 'In the Balance?' In Paul Graham and Alice Coetzee (eds), 2002. *In the Balance? Debating the State of Democracy in South Africa*. Cape Town: Institute for Democracy in South Africa.

Greenberg, Stephen, 2002. 'Making Rights Real: Where to for the South African Landless Movement after the WSSD?' Paper presented to the third workshop of the Pan-African Programme for Land and Resource Rights', Nairobi, November 2002.

Habib, Adam and Rupert Taylor, 2001. 'Political Alliances and Parliamentary Opposition in Post-Aparthied South Africa'. In Roger Southall (ed.), *Opposition and Democracy in South Africa*. London and Portland: Frank Cass.

Hall, Ruth, 2003a. *Rural Land Restitution*. Cape Town: Programme for Land and Agrarian Studies, School of Government, University of the Western Cape. (Evaluating Land and Agrarian Reform in South Africa series; No. 2.)

Hall, Ruth, 2003b. *Tenure Reform on South African Farms*. Cape Town: Programme for Land and Agrarian Studies, School of Government, University of the Western Cape. (Evaluating Land and Agrarian Reform in South Africa series; No. 3.)

Hanlon, Joe, 2002, 'The land debate in Mozambique: will foreign investors, the urban elite, advanced peasants or family farmers drive rural development?' Research paper commissioned by Oxfam GB - Regional Management Centre for Southern Africa.

Hart, Gillian, 2002. 'Linking land, labour and livelihood struggles'. *South African Labour Bulletin*, Vol. 26, No. 6: 26-29.

Held, David, 1997. *Models of Democracy*. Cambridge: Polity Press.

ICG (International Crisis Group), 2001. 'Zimbabwe in Crisis: Finding a Way Forward'. ICG Africa Report No. 32, July 2001, Brussels: International Crisis Group.

IIED (International Institute for Environment and Development), 1999. 'Land Tenure and Resource Access in West Africa: Issues and Opportunities for the Next Twenty Five Years'. London: International Institute for Environment and Development.

Kepe, Thembela and Ben Cousins, 2002. *Radical land reform is key to sustainable rural development in South Africa*. Policy Brief No 3, Cape Town: Programme for Land and Agrarian Studies, School of Government, University of the Western Cape.

Lodge, Tom, 2002. *Politics in South Africa. From Mandela to Mbeki*. Cape Town and Oxford: David Philip and James Currey.

Lahiff, Edward, 2001. *Land Reform in South Africa: is it meeting the challenge*. Policy Brief No.1. Cape Town: Programme for Land and Agrarian Studies, School of Government, University of the Western Cape.

Lahiff, Edward, 2002. 'The politics of land reform in Southern Africa'. Theme paper for a project on Sustainable Livelihoods in Southern Africa, (www. ids.ac.uk/ids/env/igpp).

Lahiff, Edward and Ben Cousins, 2001. 'The land crisis in Zimbabwe viewed from south of the Limpopo'. *Journal of Agrarian Change*, Vol. 1 (4): 652-666.

Lavigne Delville, Phillipe, 1999. 'Harmonising formal law and customary land rights in French-speaking West Africa'. IIED Issue Paper No. 86, June 1999. London: International Institute for Environment and development.

Levin, Richard and Daniel Weiner (eds). 1997. *"No more tears..." Struggles for land in Mpumulanga, South Africa.* Trenton NJ: Africa World Press.

Liebenberg, Sandra, 2002. 'South Africa's Evolving Jurisprudence on Socio-Economic Rights: An Effective Tool in Challenging Poverty?' *Law, Democracy and Development*, Vol. 6, No. 2: 159-192.

Luckham, Robin, 1998. 'Are There Alternatives to Liberal Democracy?' In Mark Robinson and Gordon White (eds), *The Democratic Developmental State. Politics and Institutional Design.* Oxford: Oxford University Press.

Luckham, Robin, Anne Marie Goetz, Mary Kaldor, with: Alison Ayers, Sunil Bastian, Emmanual Gyimah-Boadi, Shireen Hassim and Zarko Puhovski , 2000. 'Democratic Institutions and Politics in Contexts of Inequality, Poverty and Conflict. A Conceptual Framework'. IDS Working Paper 104. Brighton: Institute of Development Studies.

Lund, Christian, 1998. *Law, Power and Politics in Niger. Land Struggles and the Rural Code.* Hamburg: LIT Verlag.

Lyne, M.C. and M.A.G. Darroch, 1997. 'Broadening access to land markets: Financing emerging farmers in South Africa'. *Development Southern Africa*, Vol. 14, No. 4: 561-68.

Makgetla, Neva and Tanya van Meelis, 2003. 'Unpacking Unemployment'. *New Agenda* 10: 87-107.

Mamdani, Mahmood, 1990. 'The Social Basis of Constitutionalism in Africa'. *Journal of Modern African Studies*, Vol. 28, No. 2: 359-74.

Mamdani, Mahmood, 1996. *Citizen and Subject: Contemporary Africa and the Legacy of Late Colonialism.* Princeton N.J: Princeton University Press.

Manor, James, 2000. 'Local Government in South Africa: Potential Disaster Despite Genuine Promise'. Paper prepared for the Department of International Development. Brighton: Institute of Development Studies.

Marais, Hein, 2001. *South Africa, Limits to Change. The Political Economy of Transition* (second edition). London, New York and Cape Town: Zed Books and University of Cape Town Press.

Mare, Gerhard, 2001. 'Race, Democracy and Opposition in South African politics: As Other a Way as Possible'. In Roger Southall (ed.), *Opposition and Democracy in South Africa*. London and Portland: Frank Cass.

Maseko, Sipho, 2002. 'Popular Selection of Decision-makers'. In Paul Graham and Alice Coetzee (eds), 2002. *In the Balance? Debating the State of Democracy in South Africa*. Cape Town: Institute for Democracy in South Africa.

Maylam, Paul, 2001. 'The Politics of Adaptation and Equivocation: Race, Class and Opposition in Twentieth-Century South Africa'. In Roger Southall (ed.), *Opposition and Democracy in South Africa*. London and Portland: Frank Cass.

McKinley, Dale T., 2001. 'Democracy, Power and Patronage: Debate and Opposition within the African National Congress and the Tripartite Alliance since 1994'. In Roger Southall (ed.), *Opposition and Democracy in South Africa*. London and Portland: Frank Cass.

Melber, Henning, 2002. 'From Libersation Movements to Governments: On Poilitical Culture in Southern Africa'. *African Sociological Review*, No. 6 (1): 161-72.

Moore, Sally Falk, 1998. 'Changing African land tenure: reflections on the incapacities of the state'. *European Journal of Development Research*, 10(2): 33-49.

Moyo, Sam, 2000. 'The Political Economy of Land Acquisition and Redistribution in Zimbabwe, 1990-1999'. *Journal of Southern African Studies*, Vol. 26, No. 1: 5-28.

Moyo, Sam, 2002. 'Peasant Organisations and Rural Civil Society in Africa: An Introduction'. In Mahmoud Ben Ramdhane and Sam Moyo (eds), *Peasant Organisations and the Democratisation Process in Africa*. Dakar: Council for the Development of Social Science Research in Africa.

NDA (National Department of Agriculture), 2001. *The Strategic Plan for South African Agriculture*. Pretoria: National Department of Agriculture.

Nattrass, Nicoli, and Jeremy Seekings, 1998. 'Democratic Institutions and Development in Post-apartheid South Africa'. In M. Robinson, and G. White (eds), *The Democratic Developmental State. Politics and Institutional Design*. Oxford: Oxford University Press.

Negrao, Jose, 1999. 'The Mozambican Land Campaign, 1997-99'. Paper presented to the Workshop of the Associative Movement, Maputo, December 1999.

Nelson, Nici and Susan Wright, 1997. *Power and Participatory Development*. London: Intermediate Technology Development Group Books.

Ntsebeza, Lungisile, 2002. 'Decentralisation and natural resource management in rural South Africa: problems and prospects', Occasional Paper 22, Cape Town: Programme for Land and Agrarian Studies, School of Government, University of the Western Cape.

Okoth-Ogendo, H.W.O., 2002. 'The tragic African commons: A century of expropriation, suppression and subversion'. Occasional Paper No. 24. Cape Town: Programme for Land and Agrarian Studies, University of the Western Cape.

Palmer, Robin, 2000. 'Land Policy in Africa: Lessons From Recent Policy and Implementation Processes'. In Camilla Toulmin and Julian Quan (eds), *Evolving land rights, policy and tenure in Africa*. London: International Institute for Environment and Development and Natural Resources Institute.

Peters, Pauline, 2002. 'The Limits of Negotiability: Security, Equity and Class Formation in Africa's Land Systems'. In Kristine Juul and Christian Lund (eds), *Negotiating Property in Africa*. Portsmouth, NH: Heinemann.

Pohamba, Hifikeunye, 2002. 'Namibia Country Paper'. Paper presented to World Bank workshop on land policy, Kampala, April 2002.

Przeworski, Adam, 1991. *Democracy and the Market*. Cambridge: Cambridge University Press.

Quan, Julian, 2000. 'Land tenure, economic growth and poverty in Sub-Saharan Africa'. In Camilla Toulmin and Julian Quan (eds), *Evolving land rights, policy and tenure in Africa*. London: International Institute for Environment and Development and Natural Resources Institute.

Ribot, Jesse C., 2002. *African Decentralisation. Local Actors, Powers and Accountability*. Geneva: United Nations Research Institute for Social Development.

Rukuni, Mandivamba, 1994. *Report of the Commission of Inquiry into Appropriate Agricultural Land Tenure Systems*. Harare: Government Printers.

Saul, John, 1997a. 'For Fear of Being Condemned as Old Fashioned: Liberal Democracy vs Popular Democracy in Sub-Saharan Africa'. *Review of African Political Economy*, No. 73: 339-53.

Saul, John, 1997b. 'Liberal Democracy vs Popular Democracy in Southern Africa'. *Review of African Political Economy*, No. 72: 219-36.

Seekings, Jeremy and Nicoli Nattrass, 2002. 'Class, Distribution and Redistribution in Post-Apartheid South Africa'. *Transformation*, No. 50: 1-30.

Selolwane, O.D., 2002. 'Monoploy politics: How Botswana's Opposition Parties Have Helped Sustain One-Party Dominance'. *African Sociological Review*, No. 6 (1): 68-90.

Shackleton, Charlie, Sheona Shackleton and Ben Cousins, 2001. 'The Role of Land-Based Strategies in Rural Livelihoods: The Contribution of Arable Production, Animal Husbandry and Natural Resource Harvesting in Communal Areas of South Africa'. *Development Southern Africa*, Vol. 18, No. 5.

Shivji, Issa G., 1991a. 'The Democracy Debate in Africa: Tanzania'. *Review of African Political Economy*, No. 50: 79-91.

Shivji, Issa G. (ed.), 1991b. *State and Constitutionalism: An African Debate on Democracy*. Harare: Southern African Political Economy Series Trust.

Simon, David, 2000. 'Namibian Elections: SWAPO Consolidates its Hold on Power'. *Review of African Political Economy*, No. 83: 113-115.

Southall, Roger, 2002. 'Opposition in South Africa: Issues and Problems'. In Roger Southall (ed.), *Opposition and Democracy in South Africa*. London and Portland: Frank Cass.

Tanner, Christopher, 2002. 'Law Making in an African Context: the 1997 Mozambican Land Law'. FAO Legal Papers Online No. 26.

Terreblanche, Sampie, 2002. *A history of inequality in South Africa, 1652-2002*. Pietermaritzburg and Sandton: University of Natal Press and KMM Review Publishing.

Tsele, Molefe, 2002. 'A Response to the Democracy Index'. In Paul Graham and Alice Coetzee (eds), 2002. *In the Balance? Debating the State of Democracy in South Africa.* Cape Town: Institute for Democracy in South Africa.

Turner, Stephen (ed.), 2002. *Land and agrarian reform in South Africa: A status report.* Research Report No. 12, Cape Town: Programme for Land and Agrarian Studies, School of Government, University of the Western Cape.

van Lieres, Bettina, forthcoming. 'Marginalisation and Citizenship in Post-Apartheid South Africa'. In Steven Robins (ed.), *Limits to Liberation. Culture, Citizenship and Governance after Apartheid.* Oxford and Cape Town: James Currey and David Philip.

Vavi, Zwelinzima., 2001. 'Zimbabwe: Lessons for South Africa and Southern Africa'. *New Agenda* 2: 153-58.

Webster, Eddie, 2001. 'The Alliance under Stress: Governing in a Globalising World'. In Roger Southall (ed.), *Opposition and Democracy in South Africa.* London and Portland: Frank Cass.

Werner, Wolfgang, 2002. 'Land and Resource Rights: Namibia Case Study'. Paper presented at inaugural workshop of the Pan-African Programme for Land and Resource Rights. Cairo, March 2002.

Wildschut, Adele and Stephen Hulbert, 1998. *A Seed Not Sown: prospects for agrarian reform in South Africa.* Johannesburg: Interfund.

World Bank, 2000. *World Development Report 2000/2001: Attacking Poverty.* New York: Oxford University Press.

Printed in the United States
18703LVS00004B/139-165